Transformative Innovation in Times of Change
Lessons for Africa from the 2020 Global Pandemic

Edited by

*Erika Kraemer-Mbula, Rebecca Hanlin, Rob Byrne,
Chux Daniels and Ann Kingiri*

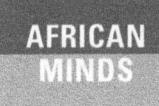

Published in 2023 by African Minds
4 Eccleston Place, Somerset West, 7130, Cape Town, South Africa
info@africanminds.org.za
www.africanminds.org.za

© 2023 African Minds

All contents of this document, unless specified otherwise, are licensed under a
Creative Commons Attribution 4.0 International Licence.

The views expressed in this publication are those of the authors.
When quoting from any of the chapters, readers are requested to acknowledge all of the authors.

ISBN (paper): 978-1-928502-76-0
eBook edition: 978-1-928502-77-7
ePub edition: 978-1-928502-78-4

Copies of this book are available for free download at:
www.africanminds.org.za

ORDERS:
African Minds
Email: info@africanminds.org.za

To order printed books from outside Africa, please contact:
African Books Collective
PO Box 721, Oxford OX1 9EN, UK
Email: orders@africanbookscollective.com

This work is based on research supported entirely by the
National Research Foundation of South Africa (Grant Number: 118873)

Table of Contents

Foreword   v
Preface   vii

1   Introduction   *Erika Kraemer-Mbula, Rob Byrne, Rebecca Hanlin, Chux Daniels and Ann Kingiri*   1

SECTION I: RETHINKING POLICY FRAMEWORKS

2   Pairing social innovation and resilience to achieve transformative change: From innovative solutions to innovative ways of understanding problems   *Dieunedort Wandji and Jeremy Allouche*   18

3   Strengthening innovation ecosystems in Africa: Seeking out systemic changes in the wake of the 2020 pandemic   *Olugbenga Adesida, Geci Karuri-Sebina and Krishnie Thaver*   45

4   Unlocking systemic barriers to health innovations in Africa   *Albert Edgar Manyuchi and John Ouma-Mugabe*   83

5   Revisiting resource-based development strategies in the post-pandemic era   *Keun Lee*   112

SECTION II: PROBLEM-SPECIFIC POLICY RESPONSES

6   Harnessing innovation in the informal food services sector: Insights for public policy   *Il-haam Petersen, Nazeem Mustapha, Nicole Dunn-van Rheede and Glenda Kruss*   138

7   Enabling inclusive technological change through transformative policies: Frugal innovations from medical device manufacturing firms in South Africa   *Sanghamitra Chakravarty and Peter Knorringa*   169

8   Endogenous pharmaceutical innovation: Epistemological perspectives from Benin and South Africa   *Ogundiran Soumonni and Aimé Sègla*   207

9   A pro-poor science–policy interface in Africa *Joanes Atela,
    Nora Ndege and Mark Pelling*   244

SECTION III: CROSS-CUTTING ISSUES

10 Different strokes of the fourth industrial revolution: Lessons
    from the pandemic on technological change and
    prospects for Africa *Julius Gatune, Geci Karuri-Sebina,
    Ann Kingiri, Edward Lorenz and Diederik de Boer*   280

11 Sustainable development finance and investments: Theoretical
    and policy implications for Africa *Jacob Park*   302

12 Industrial recovery in post-pandemic sub-Saharan Africa
    Massoud Hedeshi   324

SECTION IV: REFLECTIONS AND CONCLUSIONS

13 Sectoral reflections: Energy transitions and mobile money   352
    Reflection 1: The energy sector in sub-Saharan Africa in light
    of pandemic responses *Rob Byrne*
    Reflection 2: Mobile money, the pandemic and policy *Ann Numi,
    Josephat Okemwa and Ann Kingiri*

14 Conclusion *Rebecca Hanlin, Erika Kraemer-Mbula, Rob Byrne,
    Chux Daniels and Ann Kingiri*   375

About the authors   396

Foreword

In the context of pressing planetary, peace and socio-economic challenges, sustainable and innovative solutions require an efficient, transparent, inclusive and vibrant scientific community not only stemming from scientists but from the whole of society. A global understanding of the importance of science, technology and innovation (STI) systems and their associated policies is essential and central to modern life and sustainable development. The COVID-19 global pandemic brought into focus the importance of science and technology in shaping our world today and in the future and how open science practices such as access to scientific data, the sharing of scientific information and collaboration beyond the scientific community can speed up research and strengthen links between science policy and society. Countries that have long-term investment in robust and dynamic STI ecosystems and governance are building back better economically, socially and digitally post-pandemic. Transforming the present and securing the future through international cooperation for future skills development, biodiversity conservation, climate change actions, ICT, AI, digital and data science, ocean science and engineering at all levels require robust STI policies with supported infrastructures to enhance resilience of people, planet and peace.

The role of African governments in ensuring that their STI systems and policies are robust enough has therefore become even more important. Africa governments need to democratise science and the entire scientific process in fostering openness, transparency and inclusiveness. Unesco's global standard setting instrument on Open Science acknowledges the importance of STI to respond to global threats and challenges by providing solutions to improve human well-being and environmental sustainability and respect for cultural diversity, foster social and economic development and promote democracy and peace.

The time is now for African countries to harness the opportunities and potentials provided by the expansion of information and communication technologies and global interconnectedness to accelerate *The Africa We Want 2063* agenda and foster knowledge societies and highlighting the importance of STI and the digital gap existing between and within countries in Africa. Strengthening STI ecosystems for sustainable development is imperative. The transformative potential of open science for reducing the existing inequalities in STI and accelerating progress toward the implementation of the of SDG 2030 in Africa and the achievement of Africa *Agenda 2063* and beyond cannot be overemphasised. As a result, this book is an important addition to work that endeavours to help the African continent move on from the devastating impacts of the pandemic, biodiversity loss and climate change. It provides examples of how governments can mitigate against such crises in the future by learning lessons from this pandemic. Importantly, the case studies explored in this book illustrate how many of the examples of resilience provided by many African countries predate the pandemic.

These examples of resilience are important for other STI stakeholders too. As we move into the implementation of the *Unesco Recommendation on Open Science*, the vast diversity of the laws, regulations and customs in different African countries determines the pattern and organisation of STI. Leaving no one behind in building back better requires multi-stakeholder actors as well as action in several different areas. The focus of this book on issues such as the financing of innovation, the skills and capabilities for STI as well as the importance of the often-voiceless actors in the STI ecosystem all resonate.

A key message from this book is the importance of new combinations of STI policy expertise. The book makes an important point about the need to acknowledge that STI is necessary to address developmental issues beyond the economic – to address the sustainable development goals. Related to this it makes an important call for more transformative STI policy and a need for policy discussions on STI to not be siloed only within and between the traditional STI actors. It highlights the need for more policy mix; for recognition of policy dialogue across traditional policy boundaries.

Finally, I am extremely pleased that this book is being made freely available. The importance of promoting open science to improve access to scientific information and enhance the opportunity for scientific knowledge to be beneficial for all. This is a must read for all.

Peggy Oti-Boateng (PhD)
Senior Science Advisor for Natural Sciences, Former Director:
Division of Science Policy and Capacity Building, Natural Sciences Sector,
Unesco Headquarters, Paris

Preface

With every crisis come profound challenges and opportunities for transformation. The years 2020 to 2022 had catastrophic effects on the lives and livelihoods of people around the world. Although it began as a health crisis, the effects of the COVID-19 global pandemic (henceforth referred to in this book as 'the pandemic' while earlier pandemics will be named, for example, the Ebola pandemic) have had far-reaching ramifications, which were especially severe for Africa. The human toll, the widespread damage to livelihoods and businesses, as well as the pressures on African governments' already thin budgets, have exposed the region's vulnerability and put its resilience under severe test.

The idea for this volume emerged in mid-2020 at a time when we started perceiving the effects that the new virus and associated mobility restrictions were bringing to Africa. The volume was conceptualised within the DSI/NRF/Newton Fund Trilateral Chair in Transformative Innovation, the 4IR and Sustainable Development, an international research programme based on a collaboration between three organisations: the University of Johannesburg; the African Centre for Technology Studies (ACTS) in Kenya; and the Science Policy Research Unit (SPRU), at the University of Sussex in the UK. The programme builds on the expertise of these three partners to strengthen African scholarship for examining transformative innovation and its policy dimensions, in the context of rapid technological change (especially in digital technologies) and the efforts to achieve inclusive and sustainable development.

The work of the Chair has become more relevant than ever before in light of the pandemic, given the exacerbation of social inequalities and the acceleration of digitalisation. This programme contributes to the need for transformation in the broad sense, understood as the simultaneous change in various systems. In the African context, transformation is deeply connected to societal change, specifically through the reduction of social inequalities and exclusion. This book raises questions such as: what are the triggers and models for innovation that have emerged in response to the crises? What types of innovation are needed to build systemic resilience in Africa? What is the role of public policy in managing transformation, especially innovation policy? What are the key lessons from these 'times of change' that can inform the field of innovation and development?

To answer these questions, the Chair's partners launched a call for papers in August 2020. About 50 proposals were received and 12 were selected to be developed as full papers. Workshops with over 30 authors of the papers were held in 2020 and 2021, which helped refine and align the diverse contributions. The call was deliberate in welcoming contributions from both academic experts and practitioners to provide a broader range of insights and create a platform for transdisciplinarity.

It is worth mentioning that the book was produced in an environment of uncertainty and constantly changing narratives about the pandemic and its effects. From a narrative of survival in 2020 to contain the spread of the virus which centralised the roles of government leadership, evidence-informed decisions, solidarity and a scientific race to develop a vaccine taking centre stage; to a later narrative in 2021 focused on socio-economic recovery, building back better, managing vaccine inequalities and visions and proposals for post-pandemic societies. In 2022, we saw a move to a narrative of post-pandemic (rather than post-COVID-19) and 'learning to live with the virus' with societies in the Global South learning to navigate the harsh economic realities by looking at opportunities emerging in the digital and regional spaces. The production of this book embeds some of these dominant narratives in different chapters, as they were developed over such unstable ground.

This experience has put a spotlight on the importance of innovative solutions, and the role of the public sector, raising a new interest in governance systems and structures, and ways to strengthen governance overall. The pandemic has propelled countries across the world to innovate and develop more resilient systems and strategies that will enable us to gain the capacity to tackle the complex challenges we face today and those that are yet to come. We hope this book helps us extract some valuable lessons from the pandemic experience. After all, learning from a crisis may well be our best way to prepare for the future.

The editors
October 2022

CHAPTER 1

Introduction

*Erika Kraemer-Mbula, Rob Byrne, Rebecca Hanlin,
Chux Daniels and Ann Kingiri*

In 2020, the world started to deal with a rapidly unfolding pandemic, a situation it had not seen in two generations. Starting in China, the 'flu-like' virus – now referred to as SARS-CoV-2 and the cause of the disease COVID-19 – spread around the world with amazing speed, leading to high levels of mortality as well as long-lasting morbidity for many. Countries responded by closing their borders and issuing stay-at-home orders, with knock-on effects for education, routine healthcare, security, religious observance, industrial production, environmental targets and more. There was no area of life that was not been affected by the virus and the ensuing pandemic.

The evidence for, knowledge of, and debates about, the virus have evolved since it was first detected, as far as its origins, epidemiology, treatment and prevention are concerned. Its shocks have affected multiple dimensions of human life, with industries struggling with workers suddenly needing to work from home, schooling having to go online, transport systems having to shut down, etc. These matters have required discussion not just by medical or public health experts, but also with multiple stakeholders, communities and citizens.

Politicians, industry and civil society – as groups but also as individuals – had to make decisions rapidly. A key area of knowledge that was sought was that of the scientific and research communities. Decision-makers were urged to seek all sorts of evidence to allow them to make quick decisions related to the spread of the virus, and on ways to mitigate its multiple social and economic effects. Making these decisions required knowledge that many did not have at their fingertips before. It has led to a significant number of discussions (and subsequent journal papers, books and commentaries)[1] on the value of knowledge, whose knowledge counts and what knowledge is the most important. A lot of discussion focused on the prominence given to, and particular forms of, 'scientific' advice (Unesco, 2021).

Science advice or 'science for policy' is focused on 'providing scientific evidence to inform public policy-making' (Gluckman et al., 2022, 1). One of our key concerns, and a rationale for this book, is the need to enhance the quality and type of evidence that is available to policy-makers in Africa to inform decisions on science, technology and innovation (STI) funding, training, development, commercialisation and use. There are two specific foci to this. One, it is important to ensure support for science, technology and the resulting innovation (defined in this book in broad terms as the introduction of new things into new environments) is directional, that is, that there is a purpose to STI activity that is focused on transformative change. In this way innovative activity is focused on solving social and environmental problems affecting the continent and not just the economic issues being faced by African countries. Two, STI policy takes time and effort to change. Like much public policy, it is dominated by incrementalism, punctuated by limited examples of major change but rather significant levels of drift (Wieble and Cairney, 2020). Crises, such as the pandemic, are opportunities for major policy change.

The pandemic as a lens for considering transformative innovation

As we write this, more than two and a half years since the pandemic was first acknowledged, we can begin to see how the successes and failures of the response have affected STI at national and international levels. Among the successes, perhaps the most celebrated was the accelerated development of vaccines against the disease, the first of which were administered through public programmes within a year after starting the research process. It is difficult to quantify precisely how much this vaccination effort has cost.

---

1 For summaries of some scientific papers and books, see https://www.nature.com/articles/d41586-020-00502-w and https://www.springernature.com/gp/researchers/campaigns/coronavirus

One estimate puts it at approximately USD 7.62 billion, around 90% of which was provided by public money, with a further USD 45.4 billion committed to advance purchase agreements.[2] Another estimate puts the public funding at over USD 110 billion.[3] This higher figure included spending on therapeutics for the pandemic, but this spending is estimated to be only 5% of the total. Whatever the exact cost, it has been expensive. Nevertheless, many might argue that given the cost to economies of the lockdown measures, this spending was highly effective. While it is easy to agree with this argument, research by Oxfam for the People's Vaccine Alliance indicates that private profiteering from selling vaccines could mean that countries paid up to five times more than the production costs (Marriott and Maitland, 2021).

This begins to point to some of the failures, or at least problematic features, of the way STI operates, and the role it plays in our social and economic systems. The drive for vaccine development most obviously highlighted the issue of socialising risks versus privatising profits, and how the protection of private profit was being achieved, in part, by the enforcement of intellectual property rights held by private interests, even as the money that created the intellectual property came overwhelmingly from public funds. As a result, the poorer countries of the world struggled to purchase vaccines and were prevented from establishing local production that might have alleviated such constraints. To call this an injustice seems inadequate. But, if overcoming the pandemic required achieving near universal vaccination, the situation furthermore was clearly perverse from a societal perspective, as it most likely prolonged the pandemic for everyone. The global public health emergency declared in 2022 on Monkeypox was another example of the inequalities and inequities of vaccine innovation.[4]

The response to the pandemic in developing vaccines was evidence of an end-of-pipe approach to 'correcting' the 'wrongs' that emerged from the way we currently practise STI, and it is evidence of the way we understand the relationship between STI (and other social and economic) activities and the wider environment. In the case of the SARS-CoV-2 virus, it most likely crossed over from non-human animals as a result of the ways in which we have been treating natural habitats, combined with our industrial forms

---

2   This estimate was given on the Global Health Centre website as of 8 July 2021, and the full dataset can be downloaded at https://www.knowledgeportalia.org/covid19-r-d-funding
3   The KENUP Foundation estimates, as of early January 2021, that governments spent EUR 93 billion. https://www.businesswire.com/news/home/20210110005098/en
4   See https://www.nature.com/articles/d41586-022-02036-9 and https://qz.com/monkeypox-vaccinations-in-africa-would-have-spared-the-1849364894

of livestock farming.[5] In straightforward economics terms, these practices may have been profitable (for some), but they have been central to creating public health crises. The vaccination solution was then a method to deal with the problems these unsustainable practices had caused. As we have seen, dealing with the problems in this way can create highly profitable economic opportunities for some.

It is perhaps not surprising that, in recent years, there is growing concern with innovation policy that focuses first and foremost on economic growth and profit maximisation. It has led to multiple calls for a new generation of innovation policy, which some have referred to as 'Frame 3' thinking (Schot and Steinmueller, 2018), some have related to 'mission-oriented' policies centred around innovations that tackle societal challenges (Kattel and Mazzucato, 2018) and others in terms of the re-orientation of innovation systems to solve macro-level societal problems (Ghazinoory et al., 2020) and address sustainability (Lundvall, 2022). These calls generally emphasise the importance of directionality, participation and coordination of different actors, and the expansion of innovation policy beyond its conventional boundaries of STI into other policy domains. This volume draws from these theoretical lenses and adds to them, in order to better understand the relationship between innovation, inclusion and sustainability outcomes, and the role of public policy grounded in the context of Africa.

Transformative innovation for Africa and in Africa

Putting aside, for now, how we think about STI and its relationship with our environment, and turning to more specific developments within the general dynamics of how the pandemic unfolded, we see a number of issues of particular significance for the African region.

First, the pandemic highlighted the enormous value of research, human resources for research, and research infrastructure. However, as African countries face one of the most serious economic crises of this century, pressure on public funds materialised in reductions in research funding. This puts African countries in more vulnerable positions in the long run, leaving the continent increasingly less prepared for the next emerging crisis. Second, it accelerated the ongoing digital transformation on the continent

---

5   As suggested in the WHO-convened Global Study of Origins of SARS-CoV-2, high-density farming provides the conditions for potential enzootic circulation. https://www.who.int/health-topics/coronavirus/origins-of-the-virus

(Kaplinsky and Kraemer-Mbula, 2021), thereby increasing the dependence on digital technologies; millions of Africans moved to work online, and digital solutions were at the forefront of fighting the health crisis, as well as ensuring continuity in education, business and family matters. However, these millions have also exposed the deeply entrenched inequalities that exist on the continent, where, despite the fast penetration of mobile phones, only 28% of the population uses the internet and has benefitted from these opportunities. The digital divide especially affects women in Africa, where only one out of every seven African women is likely to use the internet, as opposed to one out of every five men. The digital divide and its gender dimension put at risk the security and even physical safety of women during the pandemic. And, third, the pandemic has also opened spaces for collaborative innovation. In the collective efforts to find global solutions to the effects of the virus, the pandemic showed that collaboration and partnerships are critical for African research and innovation systems to lead to useful/usable outputs. Collaboration can be a means to fast track the development of research capabilities in Africa. However, fast tracking raises important questions related to the governance of research and collaboration, and issues around ethics and power imbalances in global research dynamics.

Before we sketch the various chapters in this book, it is useful to reflect briefly on three aspects of innovation in relation to Africa: (1) innovation in times of crisis; (2) innovation benefits for all; and (3) innovation in the future. We do this, not because innovation in Africa is necessarily different from other parts of the world (although there are arguments that Africa has the potential to leapfrog beyond other parts of the world if it embraces technological change).[6] We reflect on these three areas because, relative to other parts of the world, there has been less attention focused on how innovation takes place on the continent and what the ecosystem for innovation does, should and could look like. A recent study (Lema et al., 2021) found that despite a significant increase in academic papers written each year on innovation in developing countries, the majority are written in upper-middle income countries, predominately China, and not in low- or low-middle income countries (which make up most of Africa).

As we progress through this discussion, it is important to note that, in this book, we use a broad definition of innovation. That is, in addition to

---

6 https://www.forbes.com/sites/francoisbotha/2019/04/02/why-africa-has-the-ability-to-leapfrog-the-rest-of-the-world-with-innovation/?sh=323a69e5ece6

the traditional definition of innovation as changes in products, services, organisational processes and/or business models that improve the market performance of formal-sector private firms, we include changes that may be motivated or characterised by imperatives other than or integrated with private profit. Here, we include notions of grassroots, frugal, social and inclusive innovation. Some or all of these may include so-called 'non-traditional' innovation actors, such as community groups, informal-sector businesses, civil society, and so on. But we could further argue that changes in social or cultural practices can also be understood as forms of innovation. Facilitating any form of innovation – indeed, crucial to all innovation processes and outcomes – is the ability to identify, use and develop knowledge. Here, we also embrace a broad view by encompassing the possibility that both formal and informal knowledge can play a role in generating innovations.

Innovation in times of crisis
The pandemic triggered many innovations, and science and technology have been central to addressing the shocks of the pandemic. The innovations we have seen in this particular time of crisis are of two kinds. One, there have been the immediate innovation responses to the pandemic in the way individuals, sectors and communities have responded to emerging challenges. For instance, we saw the acceleration of digital solutions in the education sector, the informal sector devising solutions to 'track-and-trace' needs, the re-purposing of production facilities to accommodate the need to produce personal protective equipment, humanitarian responses to the pandemic, new business models, and so on.

Two, there were innovation efforts to find medium- to long-term solutions to 'living with' the pandemic. Clear examples of this were the vaccination efforts, and the establishment of new institutional arrangements to manage the mobility of people, scientific collaboration, data gathering, analysis and sharing.

Questions of relevance to understanding innovation in times of crisis include: What are the triggers and models for innovation in such times? In what ways are innovation processes in times of crisis inherently organic, or in what kinds of ways can we manage these processes? How do we connect innovation (processes and outcomes) more effectively with achieving resilience?

Innovative solutions for all
The pandemic highlighted the difficulties of ensuring access to innovation, or of focusing on the 'right' forms of innovation, in crises, but also in

stable times. This ignites interest in – and raises questions about – global innovation dynamics and the necessary 'preconditions' in Africa for the pandemic. These global dynamics relate to the growing digitalisation (and the severity of the digital divide in Africa), North–South diffusion of technologies, and the concentration of technological capabilities in high-income countries. These dynamics are related to growing global disparities and inequalities. Such disparities are shaped by relevant contextual and infrastructural factors that affect the functioning of innovation systems in different territories, as well as by political economy dynamics, such as the power of incumbents and regulatory frameworks. These preconditions need to be seriously considered if innovation solutions are going to be inclusive – that is, work for all – in line with the Sustainable Development Goals (SDGs) and the global agenda of 'leaving no one behind'.

Innovation for the future

Innovation is at the heart of development in Africa, but what is development in the African context? In 2013, African Union (AU) member states crafted an African-driven vision, *Agenda 2063: The Africa We Want*, that outlined what the African continent should look like in 50 years based on the pillars of wealth generation, regional integration and the attainment of a peaceful society – all driven by Africans. Adopted by the AU in 2015, it constitutes the strategic framework for the socio-economic transformation of the continent. It has a strong identity component, which emphasises that transformation needs to be endogenous, integrate the continent and raise the profile of African culture, values and heritage. It also fosters domestic resource mobilisation, and has flagship projects focusing on transport, information and communication technology (ICT), and energy infrastructure. Nevertheless, the disruptions from the pandemic have placed new demands on the ability of the continent to realise both *Agenda 2063* and the SDGs. This calls for (new and) renewed emphasis on ensuring innovation-led development that is directed towards transformative change – that is, development that addresses economic prosperity goals alongside social and environmental challenges.

One of the byproducts of the pandemic was the need to underscore this economic prosperity pathway with resilience, systems thinking and sustainability. In this sense, innovation (as well as science and technology) must not only be seen as a way to avoid crises, but also as a means to avoid unsustainable path dependencies and lock-in – in policy as well as products and solutions. Innovation, in this regard, should be steered towards enhancing the resilience of the relevant systems; that is, innovation should enhance the ability of society to understand, recover and re-orient in response to external disruption or internal system failures.

New innovation policy considerations

Having reflected on some of the issues the pandemic exposed globally, and in the African region, as well as having touched upon what these highlighted about STI at several levels, and what innovation-related future scenarios might be, we turn to considerations of what this means for new kinds of innovation policy. Many, if not all, of these considerations are not new in themselves; they pre-date the pandemic, but the pandemic gave them heightened significance and provided renewed justification to examine them more critically and more seriously. In broad terms, we can identify four areas of debate that give rise to several points of relevance to the focus of this book.

1. Local STI capabilities and systems, and how these relate to resilience.
2. Understanding the ways in which power, politics and new technologies serve to reproduce or challenge social injustices and inequalities.
3. The role of indigenous knowledge in informing STI and public policy choices.
4. The ways in which public policy can drive transformative change.

The first point we can make arising from these areas of debate is that multiple forms of innovation are required. The pandemic brought this to the fore, but it has always been true for the functioning of economies, and of societies. Specifically, the result is that other types of knowledge, beyond scientific, have also become essential, both to help us understand how to use scientific and technological innovations, and to help us develop new products, new processes, new business models, new ways of doing things. In other words, innovation is needed more than ever, not only to overcome the ongoing crises, but also to respond effectively to future shocks. The pandemic spurred a number of rapid innovations, many of them technology-enabled. Virtual education, telemedicine and digitally supported modalities of work expanded all over the world. Also, non-technological innovations, often community-based, emerged. These innovations have shown advantages and disadvantages. On the one hand, they have enabled the sustaining of activities that would not otherwise have been possible; on the other hand, they have exposed the deep-rooted inequalities in our societies related to gender, race, ethnicity, income, access to medical treatments and digital technologies, and more.

Second, because different forms of knowledge and innovation are required, expertise needs differ. This book is particularly focused on one type of expertise: the realm of innovation or, more broadly, STI policy. This has traditionally been dominated by a focus on national competitiveness and economic growth. However, current production and consumption systems continue to create instabilities in our natural environment and social structures. As African economies and societies are severely put to the test, we are now urged to re-imagine the future of Africa under post-pandemic, and other social and climate-related crises. Moreover, the pandemic has brought to the fore the importance of resilience, sustainability and inclusion to adequately confront challenges in highly uncertain environments. With a climate crisis already upon us, these are likely to be the norm in the future.

Third, building on the second point and, as we argued above, if we are to make positive progress in resilience, sustainability and inclusion, we need not only to understand how to theorise on the relationships between STI and our social and natural environments, but also to understand how innovation policy can be used as a tool for transformative change. Innovation or STI policy will not be sufficient to achieve transformative change, but it may be possible to develop 'better' policy in conjunction with understanding how power and politics will play out as we seek to transform the currently unjust social structures and damaging STI practices we need to leave behind.

Finally, and as alluded to in the preceding paragraph, this book is focused specifically on theoretical and practical responses to innovation and innovation policy in the context of Africa. It uses the pandemic as a lens to stimulate thinking on ways in which innovation can be harnessed to provide short-term and long-term transformative solutions for Africa. It combines both conceptual/theoretical approaches and practical views that provide concrete policy recommendations.

Summary of contributions from the chapters

The book is organised into four sections: (I) Rethinking policy frameworks, (II) Problem-specific policy responses, (III) Cross-cutting issues and (IV) Reflections and conclusions.

Section I: Rethinking policy frameworks

In Chapter 2, Dieunedort Wandji and Jeremy Allouche explore how conceptual linkages between resilience thinking and social innovation can enable a focus on innovative ways of understanding problems in order to achieve transformative change. They argue that current conceptualisations of innovation are constrained within dominant technological and Western-centric paradigms that exclude vernacular innovation practices. Drawing from the relational dynamics between multiple crises in Côte d'Ivoire, and vernacular responses to them, the authors observe that resilient practices harnessed through the complexity of social problems constitute innovative solutions that are perpetuated across time, scales and space. The authors therefore argue that pairing resilience and innovation uncovers the ways in which social innovation can be both transformative and continuous.

Chapter 3, authored by Olugbenga Adesida, Geci Karuri-Sebina and Krishnie Thaver, explores the continuities and emerging systemic changes that have been taking place within African innovation ecosystems since the onset of the pandemic. The chapter uses comparative insights into innovation dynamics before and during the pandemic to inform targeted policy recommendations, with the goal of strengthening the innovation ecosystems in African countries. The authors generate their insights from a mixed-methods approach, using two primary data sources: (1) a pre-pandemic dataset compiled from a set of existing databases and (2) a new dataset collected through an innovation survey undertaken in late 2020, after the advent of the pandemic. This comparative analysis is then supplemented with secondary data and literature sources found through desktop study. The study finds that global responses to combat the pandemic instigated several changes in the African innovation landscape, shifting some of the obstacles to innovation and innovation practices. However, the nature of the changes varied: some were systemic; others were non-systemic. The authors argue that systemic changes could be leveraged to enhance African innovation ecosystems through targeted policy design and the collaboration of key actors.

Continuing the interest in systems, in Chapter 4, Albert Edgar Manyuchi and John Ouma-Mugabe explore the systemic barriers to health innovations that were employed for addressing the pandemic. They show that barriers to innovations for responses in Africa are systemic and structural. They are systemic in the sense that they were interrelated and interacting in various ways, thereby affecting different aspects of national health systems, and were structural because they were embedded in the social and physical structures of those systems. The authors argue that many of the health inventions and technologies that resulted from the pandemic will remain stunted: they will not evolve into innovations unless various interrelated and interacting social, economic, policy, institutional and technical barriers in the innovation system are unlocked. This, the authors argue, requires the careful choice and deployment of various integrated policy instruments, especially those spurring the further development, deployment, diffusion and adaptation of nascent health technologies.

Chapter 5, by Keun Lee, explores the disruptions and opportunities that the post-pandemic era poses for emerging economies seeking new modes of development and 'catch-up'. The author proposes a stronger reliance on domestic resources for a more resilient pattern of development, to be pursued by specialising in resource-based sectors with low entry barriers for many resource-rich emerging economies. Lee identifies three enabling conditions for resource-based development (RBD). First, upgrading by resource sectors requires an industrial policy of 'getting prices wrong'. Second, the eventual emergence of locally controlled firms plus local ownership of resources may be an important ingredient for long-term success with RBD. The third issue is to overcome the 'double resource curse' by promoting high value-added or processed products by making bold policy moves to promote innovation-based upgrading combined with non-exchange rate-linked asymmetric support for the resource sector, such as preferential loans, entry controls and subsidies.

Section II: Problem-specific policy responses

Chapter 6, by Il-haam Petersen, Nazeem Mustapha, Nicole Dunn-van Rheede and Glenda Kruss, explores the effect of the pandemic on the most vulnerable populations through the lens of informal enterprises. They argue that a better conceptualisation and empirical understanding is needed of the pathways through which informal enterprises evolve to becoming sustainable and profitable businesses. Based on the findings of a study on informal food enterprises in South Africa, the authors investigate how innovation supports the kinds of business evolution required to build and strengthen local food systems serving low-income and impoverished households. The authors analyse the relationship between the crisis events prompting an innovation response for survival or growth and the evolution of informal food enterprises towards manifesting different levels of formality over time. They argue that creating pathways for economic recovery post-pandemic requires public policies that engage with the realities and persistence of the informal sector and policies that recognise the central role of innovation in enterprise resilience and growth.

In Chapter 7, Sanghamitra Chakravarty and Peter Knorringa analyse frugal innovations that emerged during the pandemic to address medical device and diagnostics shortages through local manufacturing. They explore firm-level innovation processes by adapting the heuristics of an 'institutional triad' to highlight the institutions, interactions and tensions between the three stages of innovation – generation, production and diffusion. The chapter discusses the ways in which South Africa can enable its medical device manufacturing sector to reconcile the twin objectives of industrial growth and social development, including lowering its own healthcare costs. The authors use empirical evidence from three case studies to demonstrate that some small and medium-sized enterprises (SMEs) engaged in medical device manufacturing in South Africa have high levels of innovation capabilities, successfully bringing various frugal innovations to the market. Based on their findings, the authors argue that more proactive state support for SMEs would be needed to enable more inclusive technological change in which both economic and social goals can be achieved simultaneously.

Chapter 8, by Ogundiran Soumonni and Aimé Sègla, discusses the need for endogenous innovation. By reflecting on the types of knowledge that have become relevant and valid in tackling novel disease – from both the public health and medicinal points of view – the authors propose a conceptual framework that could help reveal potential pathways for anchoring endogenous innovation in the domain of the pharmaceutical industry. The chapter tests this framework in the cases of Benin and South Africa, and the authors reflect on the implications of the analysis for endogenous pharmaceutical innovation in Africa during the post-pandemic era.

The issue of different types of knowledge is also treated in Chapter 9, authored by Joanes Atela, Nora Ndege and Mark Pelling. In this case, the chapter focuses on the role of science in political processes and how it shapes policies that respond to societal needs. Through questionnaire interviews, case studies and science–policy dialogues convened during the African Research and Impact Network International Conference on COVID-19, the chapter assesses the models of the science–policy interface that were applied to respond to the pandemic in four African countries (Malawi, Ghana, Nigeria and Kenya), and discusses the implications for the poor. The analysis reveals that the pandemic exposed and reinforced the traditional top-down science–policy linkages in which politically aligned expert committees were set up to inform decisions on the pandemic, and that the different science–policy interface models pursued had different outcomes, especially for the poor. Based on these findings, the authors highlight solutions for home-grown innovation and opportunities for bottom-up science–policy models that are pro-poor in the face of crises such as the recently experienced pandemic.

Section III: Cross-cutting issues

In Chapter 10, Julius Gatune, Geci Karuri-Sebina, Ann Kingiri, Edward Lorenz and Diederik de Boer investigate the opportunities and challenges that the unfolding Fourth Industrial Revolution presents in Africa. The chapter balances a discussion of the potential for leapfrogging and catch-up with the view that the emerging digital platform companies may be establishing monopolistic positions, often to the benefit of foreign investors. Drawing on a variety of secondary sources, the chapter argues that the pandemic has accelerated these trends, as actors were forced to rethink their business models in the wake of the imposed shutdowns. The chapter examines the effect of the pandemic on the linkages between the formal and informal sectors in Africa, and the authors argue that there is a need for regulations that strike a balance between support for new business models and ensuring that there is a level of self-determination and equity in the value captured.

Chapter 11 by Jacob Park explores new and emerging models of SDG investment and finance, and examines how these models might be applicable to the African context. The author reviews the academic literature and analyses three mini-case studies (climate change investment and finance, conservation impact investment fund, and development impact bond), in order to examine two SDG-related investment and finance questions: What types of policy and business mechanisms can most effectively catalyse and accelerate the financing, particularly private-sector support, of SDG priorities? Which financial mechanisms have the best potential for Africa in terms of applicability and suitability? To fully understand what role blended finance and other SDG finance mechanisms are likely to have in Africa's post-pandemic future, Park argues that the international community needs to deepen its understanding of three critical issues: (1) the nexus of finance, innovation and sustainable development in a non-WEIRD (Western, educated, industrialised, rich and democratic) context; (2) what constitutes systemic and transformative (versus transient and incremental) innovation; and (3) the context for scalable triple-nexus financing solutions.

Chapter 12 by Massoud Hedeshi analyses sub-Saharan African countries' industrial development challenges and potential in the context of the pandemic. The chapter examines these issues in four parts: (a) the transient nature of pandemics and the unlikelihood of a major exacerbating effect on SSA's chronic economic vulnerability as a result of the pandemic; (b) a long-term deindustrialisation trend that is exacerbated by the activities of many multinational corporations in the region; (c) the misallocation of scarce regional resources toward non-essential imports and debt; and (d) the high opportunity cost of the realisation of SSA's long-term industrial development potential caused by externally imposed, non-productive policies that have been designed to maintain detrimental terms of trade for Africa since the early 1980s. Arising from this analysis, the author argues that the key to sustainable industrialisation by SSA countries is to take full ownership of their means/factors of production and distribution in a collective manner.

Section IV: Reflections and conclusions
Chapter 13 provides two sectoral reflections exploring the implications of the pandemic as seen through its effects in Africa on the energy sector (by Rob Byrne) and on mobile money (by Ann Numi, Josephat Okemwa and Ann Kingiri). Each of these reflections is a much shorter piece than the other main chapters. And both reflections include the observation, as with many of the chapters, that the pandemic revealed important vulnerabilities, especially for those who are poor and/or marginalised.

Chapter 14, authored by the book's editors, attempts to summarise the key themes of the book before offering a synthesis of the findings and insights from across all the chapters. Building on this synthesis, the chapter further offers some thoughts on what lessons we can draw from the pandemic for better theorising (transformative) innovation systems. And the chapter ends with a discussion of what policy lessons we can draw.

Concluding remarks

As can be seen from the above descriptions of the chapters, the book covers a lot of ground, addressing the challenge of learning from the pandemic by engaging a variety of methods and from a range of perspectives. This was the hope when we began the process of developing the book. Our intention was to facilitate the opening up of discussions on transformation, transformative innovation and sustainable development in Africa. We believe the contributions the various authors have made provide a rich basis for this opening up, and we are confident readers will be able to find something – we hope many things – that are of interest and relevance to their own work on promoting transformative change across the African region and perhaps elsewhere.

References

Ghazinoory, S., Nasri, S., Ameri, F., Montazer, G. A., and Shayan, A. (2020). Why do we need 'problem-oriented innovation systems (PIS)' for solving macro-level societal problems? *Technological Forecasting and Social Change,* 150, 119749. DOI: 10.1016/j.techfore.2019.119749.

Gluckman, P., Quirion, R., Denis, M., and Allen, K. (2022). Principles and structures of science advice – an outline. An ISC-INGSA Occasional Paper. https://council.science/current/blog/principles-structures-science-advice/

Kaplinsky, R., and Kraemer-Mbula, E. (2022). Innovation and uneven development: The challenge for low- and middle-income economies. *Research Policy,* 51(2). https://doi.org/10.1016/j.respol.2021.104394

Kattel, R., and Mazzucato, M. (2018). Mission-oriented innovation policy and dynamic capabilities in the public sector. *Industrial and Corporate Change,* 27(5), 787-801.

Lema, R., Kraemer-Mbula, E., and Rakas, M. (2021). Innovation in developing countries: Examining two decades of research. *Innovation and Development,* 11(2-3), 189-210. DOI: 10.1080/2157930X.2021.1989647.

Lundvall, B. Å. (2022). Transformative policies for sustainable innovation systems (No. 239). Lund University, Department of Economic History.

Marriot, A., and Maitland, A. (2021). *The Great Vaccine Robbery: Pharmaceutical corporations charge excessive prices for COVID-19 vaccines while rich countries block faster and cheaper route to global vaccination* (Policy Brief). The People's Vaccine. https://reliefweb.int/sites/reliefweb.int/files/resources/The%20Great%20Vaccine%20Robbery%20Policy%20Brief%20final.pdf

Schot, J., and Steinmueller, W. E. (2018). Three frames for innovation policy: R&D, systems of innovation and transformative change. *Research Policy,* 47(9), 1554-1567.

Unesco. (2021). *Unesco Science Report: The race against time for smarter development.* Unesco.

Wieble, C.M., and Cairney, P. (2020). Policy concepts in 1000 words: Policy change. https://paulcairney.wordpress.com/2020/06/19/policy-concepts-in-1000-words-policy-change/

SECTION I

RETHINKING POLICY FRAMEWORKS

CHAPTER 2

Pairing Social Innovation and Resilience to Achieve Trans-formative Change

From innovative solutions to innovative ways of understanding problems

Dieunedort Wandji and Jeremy Allouche

Introduction

In Côte d'Ivoire, like in most countries, responses to the pandemic have fostered many innovations. This has ranged from making data-driven policy decisions with the RECOVR survey[1] to designing an electronic nano-server, serving as hotspot and storage device, through which midwives – with or without internet access – can access learning materials and training regarding the pandemic.[2] There is, however, a case to argue that these innovations, based mainly on 'hard' science and technology, tend to occlude the part played by innovations resulting from new societal arrangements.

---

1   https://www.poverty-action.org/recovr-study/recovr-c%C3%B4te-divoire-tracking-effects-covid-19-pandemic
2   https://cotedivoire.unfpa.org/

For example, in the case of RECOVR, nothing is said about the background of the midwives accessing this nano-server technology for pandemic-related training. Yet the outcomes of the training and their impact on local public health were shaped in greater part by the prior experiences of these midwives as social products from communities that have used vernacular strategies to address other crises such as war, previous pandemics, or lack of health infrastructures. Arguably, these technology-driven innovations do benefit from the societal context of multiple crises, for example in the case of Côte d'Ivoire where responses to the pandemic built on existing (non-)technological innovations. Nevertheless, the narrative around innovation in the context of the pandemic has predominantly reflected a scientific and technological bias. For example, Dr Matshidiso Moeti, the World Health Organization (WHO) regional director for Africa, stated that:

> *Innovation propels human advancement. In times like these when we are confronted with a major public health emergency such as the COVID-19 pandemic, we know that our hope for a better tomorrow lies in finding creative, ground-breaking or avant-garde solutions.* (WHO, 2020)

Perhaps it would be fair to assume that the solutions Dr Matshidiso Moeti discusses here are of scientific and technological orders. Most innovation discussions in relation to the pandemic were framed in this way. This does not, however, cancel the fact that this 'major public health emergency' unfolded alongside other pressing problems, such as food crises and health emergencies (e.g. malaria) faced by many populations, with little or no support from their national governments, nor the benefits of science and technology-based innovations. Innovations based on vernacular social practices are not usually paid enough attention because they are not considered products of scientific knowledge or technologies that can directly be linked to economic growth (Coad et al., 2018; Griliches, 1960). Leading organisations likely to influence various innovation policies continue to see 'hard' science as the key driver of innovation (Tushman, 2002). The Organisation for Economic Co-operation and Development (OECD), for instance, views 'distance from the technological frontier' as one of the key factors weakening the ability to innovate (2020, 2). Thus, overlooking non-technological innovations not only embeds the dominance of a particular epistemology of innovation; it also limits their ability to contribute to transformative change.

Strictly speaking, technology does not necessarily refer to the sophistication of high-tech combinations or even low-tech artefacts but any sort of cognitive arrangement. Technology can be broadly defined as any type of 'useful knowledge' (Mokyr, 2011, 4), and innovation understood as new methods, ideas, or products derived from an improved codification of existing useful knowledge or, simply, as a 'better vehicle or understanding and creating social change in all of its manifestations' (European Commission, 2010; Phills et al., 2008, 34). However, despite this one-size-fits-all understanding of both technology and innovation, there is a case to argue that its reigning epistemological paradigm imposes a strong bias towards scientific solutions over other forms of innovations, especially those based solely on new societal arrangements – that is, social innovations (SI).[3]

In contradiction to this restrictive scientific and technological bias, imaginations of disasters are limitless. As generally illustrated in popular culture, cinematographic scenarios of disasters or Frankenstein-type epidemics, and graphic representations of other man-made calamities. The paradox is striking between an infinite world of problems on the one hand, and the limited scientific spectrum within which the search of solutions is confined on the other hand. Yet, 'the history of life is a history of innovations' (Wagner, 2011, 1), and indeed 'useful knowledge' seems to be ubiquitous equipment common to all humans in 'our game against nature' (Horn, 2018; Mokyr, 2011, 284). This contrasts with imaginations of solutions to human problems that appear to be constrained within the scientific paradigm of innovation. Technological innovation as synonymous with a useful mobilisation of 'hard' sciences or high-tech has led to a distinction, and indeed, a tension between technology-based innovations and non-technology-based approaches (Schmidt and Rammer, 2007).

Non-technology-based approaches to innovation, as understood in this chapter, simply frame a process of finding solutions, which is not heavily restricted by the scientific parameters defining innovation. This understanding of innovation also subscribes to a perspective that eschews the linkages between technology and its desired impact on the market economy in terms of growth or revenues. Instead, we find an apposite description of social innovation in the understanding that SI remains committed to its definition as 'a large revitali[s]ation of the social aspects involved in any kind of innovation, technological innovation included'

---

3 Even SI, understood as a subfield of innovation that focuses primarily on social transformation goals, tends to prioritise high-tech solutions and artefacts such as ITC (Smith, 2017).

(Van der Have and Rubalcaba, 2016, 1924). This is still framed within the parameters of sustainability science which is driven 'by the problems it addresses rather than by the disciplines it employs' with a focus on 'creating a dynamic bridge between [knowledge and action]' (Clark, 2007, 1737). The type of knowledge that interests us here is embedded in non-technological vernacular practices, and as such, our focus on non-technology-based innovations does not reject the notion that 'hard' technologies and other artefacts such as Information and Communication Technologies (ICTs) can redirect innovation capacity towards goals of social development (Fals-Borda and Rahman, 1991). This simply means that SI does not always have to rely on 'hard' technology and that the impact of innovative social practices cannot be measured only through the lens of revenues or growth in the market economy or significant changes in the dominant Western-centric material culture.

Significant transformations occur as human societies constantly seek innovative solutions to the various crises they face at local levels by simply adjusting their collective habits and conventions or adopting new ones. These innovative practices imply crafting new sets of behaviours that transform the existing social organisation (Godin, 2008). We argue that the dominant understanding of innovation as driven mainly by technology and scientific knowledge[4] is somehow counterintuitive and restrictive of our insights into the potential of transformative change embedded in innovative social arrangements, as we shall argue in later sections of this paper. Innovation emerged initially as a very broad concept, speaking to the development of new ideas in multiple fields (education, aviation, healthcare, etc.) (Meissner et al., 2017). Therefore, the ubiquitous human equipment of innovation contrasts with the narrowness of its 'current tools' (OECD, 2020, 3), despite persistent calls to broaden and diversify understandings of innovation (Radjou, 2009; Vrande et al., 2010; Wieczorek et al., 2015). An analysis of popular responses to the pandemic teaches us that non-technological SIs as framed in this epistemological context are also at least as important as the technology-based innovations and as well as the SIs assessed only through their impact on the dominant Western material culture (Yoka Lye and Ngaki Kosi, 2020). Broadening and diversifying our understanding of innovation for transformative change involves paying more attention to non-technological forms and ideally non-Western contexts.

---

4   See this current framing in our case study on Côte d'Ivoire, https://www.gsma.com/mobilefordevelopment/blog/akwaba-to-the-cote-divoire-tech-ecosystem/

We argue that this broadening of understandings can also be enriched by pairing innovation with resilience thinking on a more conceptual level. Resilience is understood as the capacity for a system (community, group, nation, etc.) to deal with incremental or abrupt change through adaptative, coping, or transformative strategies. Walker et al. define resilience as 'the capacity of a system to absorb disturbance and reorganise while undergoing change so as to still retain essentially the same function, structure, identity and feedbacks' (2004, 4). Beyond its initial notion of 'bouncing back', current thinking on resilience includes its conceptual relation to adaptive capacity and long-term transformation (Carpenter and Folke, 2006; Pelling, 2011). This chapter argues that we can achieve a clearer path for transformative change by pairing up resilience and SI as an emerging proposal in both academic and policy contexts (Moore and Westley, 2011; Westley and Antadze, 2010). In other words, we can explore the ways in which SI, as the capacity to adapt and cope in the face of given problems, articulates with the capability to innovate over and over again. This path is predicated on the ways in which SI actors factor the wider context of multiple crises into their problem-solving strategies. In this chapter, we seek to obtain the lessons that resilience thinking can offer from analysing some examples of SIs. Studying this path is also an answer to the call for unorthodox, interdisciplinary and potentially controversial approaches to studying innovation (Coad et al., 2021).

This chapter seeks to answer the central questions: How do we establish and substantiate the conceptual linkages between SI and resilience? What does a resilience lens teach us about innovation? How do lessons from pairing resilience and innovation illuminate the conditions or impediments for transformative change? Examples in this chapter are drawn from preliminary research undertaken in Côte d'Ivoire under a new Global Challenge Research Fund (GCRF) project called Islands of Innovation in Protracted Crises.

In the second part, we start by providing a brief overview of the current constraints on broadening innovation. The third part of this contribution examines the similarities and connections between SI and resilience within a framework of transformative change. We then use our illustrative case of Côte d'Ivoire in the fourth part to discuss how the context of resilient practices drives the outcome of SI initiatives and how the resilience systemic approach can illuminate the broadening of the SI specific-problem approach. Before concluding this chapter, the fifth part offers a brief analysis of how pairing resilience and innovation illuminates the conditions or impediments for transformative change.

Does innovation stand in the way of transformative change?

A cursory survey of SI frameworks readily available online reveals a suppression of vernacular knowledge and experience, supplanted by top-down processes targeting communities as mere recipients and not producers of innovative knowledge (see framework samples in Figures 2 and 3).

The WHO recently hosted a series of discussions that engaged directly with African innovators, with accordingly a more open-minded approach to 'home-grown creative solutions aimed at addressing critical gaps in response to COVID-19' (WHO, 2020). In fact, according to the WHO, 12.8% of the 1,000 new technologies and new modifications to existing technologies in responses to the pandemic came from Africa (OMS, 2020). However, these leading African innovations were in the scientific and technological domain (Woods, 2020), thus reinforcing the ongoing bias towards technology-based innovative solutions.

At the same time, this points to a problem Drucker (1985) highlighted almost half a century ago, that is, the inability of innovative science and technology to solve all human problems, especially when the infatuation with new technology-based innovation is detrimental to other important SIs. Indeed, based on the prevalence of technology in the type of African innovations celebrated by WHO as per above, one could rightly argue that these innovative responses from Africa are merely the adapting of technology and strict scientific knowledge to the context of Africa.

With the difficulty of formulating a universal response to the pandemic and its effects in the aftermath, it seems everyone is looking to achieve innovation, yet there is a context-dependent hierarchy in the production of innovative knowledge, which tends to minimise ideas from non-Western milieus. Diverging experiences and success stories of innovation out of Africa during this pandemic are underscoring the need for an innovation framework, one that goes beyond just 'including' African innovative contributions to technology. Otherwise, the inclusion of non-Western examples of technological innovation appears to be just ornamental as reflected in much of the way in which examples of African innovation are associated with the narrative of innovation generally, and SI in particular. For instance, explanations of the health innovations/successes/resilience in Africa have tended to dismiss African agency by attributing these to fate or the natural setting (BBC, 2020). This still arguably highlights the dominant Western-centric paradigm in the conceptualisation of innovation.

Similar to the narratives around SARS or H1N1,[5] explanations of African resilience to the pandemic essentially revolved around sheer coincidence, ranging from low connectivity to immunising endemic malaria (Hajizadeh and Behnemoon, 2020). Even though they were acknowledged, patterns of social behaviour that might have contributed to these divergences in outcomes were categorised as debrouillardise (fending for oneself) in informal settlements (see Ijjasz-Vasquez et al., 2020).[6] Scientific hypotheses for the contributing factors to a mild impact of the pandemic and low case fatality observed in Africa included warm climate, the predominantly young demography, the cross reactive-immunity resulting from previous infections, and the universal BCG (tuberculosis) vaccine policy, or malaria treatments. Nevertheless, these hypotheses 'have not yet been confirmed by rigorous evaluations' (Umviligihozo et al., 2020). In other words, strict science is not yet able to explain what could potentially have contributed to the resilience observed in Africa, but the foreground has been given to scientific hypotheses rather than non-scientific vernacular pathways. Not only technological contributions from non-Western contexts are deprived of agency, but non-technological examples of SI from vernacular practices in Africa are also not emerging as central to rethinking the innovation framework. Consequently, the confusion still persists as to whether African experiences and innovators are being showcased in narratives of innovation as central elements or simply as geographical footnotes to complement the mainly Western narrative of innovation. This also begs the question regarding the role played by agency as a key driver in the innovation process (Howells, 2006).

However, just highlighting these contradictions, though a worthwhile effort, is insufficient. It is important to go beyond just showing that the term 'revamp' utilised by Radjou (2009) in his discussion of 'polycentric' innovation leaves the impression that the inclusion of non-scientific models and non-Western forms of innovation cannot be central in the conceptualisation of broadened innovation. The adverse impacts of the technology-driven and the Western-centric paradigm of innovation pose the question of the epistemic significance of highlighting African innovations. At a time when the limits of technology-driven innovation have been evidenced and the

---

5   SARS (severe acute respiratory syndrome). H1N1 (strain of the flu (influenza) virus also known as 'swine flu').

6   See also https://africarenewal.exposure.co/youth-engagement-for-global-action-nbsp-nbsp-nbsp-nbsp-nbsp-nbsp-nbsp-nbsp-nbsp-nbsp-nbspnbsp?source=share-africarenewal

problems facing the world too complex to fit within Western-centric solutions alone, emphasis should be diverted to non-technological and non-Western social practices that could strengthen the ability to manage crises. In the absence of scientific certitude as to differing outcomes of the pandemic, for instance (Umviligihozo et al., 2020), it is the African contextual discrepancy that centralises the continent's experiences and indeed innovative ideas. However, much as this contextual question cannot be presented as a marginal mimicry of technological novelty unfolding in the context of Africa, it can neither be limited to articulating a specifically Afrocentric epistemological alternative to the question of SI, supported by the unmuting of the local transformative agency. In relation to the pandemic, for example, the public health lens for resilient responses to epidemics needs to be widened towards a vernacular non-technological SI perspective to deepen our understanding of the human ability to respond to crises. An entry point to this perspective is the study of the intersections between SI and resilience and how these contribute to broadening innovation.

SI and resilience: Similarities, connections and constraints

Resilience and SI are conceptually related because, as systems approaches, they both deal with the thinking on how human systems (communities, regions, groups, etc.) organise to face major crises or disruptions (Walker et al., 2004, 5). Just like resilience, SI is indeed also particularly needed in contexts of crises (Ganin et al., 2016; Horn, 2018; Ijjasz-Vasquez et al., 2020). Similarly, the exploitation phase in the Systems Dynamics Model (Figure 1) represents the time and/or space where, following a rapid change after a destabilising event (crisis), new systems are created through mobilisation of social and other forms of potential capabilities that the system had produced from past crises, that is, previous resilience cycles. From an SI perspective, new institutions and practices may emerge at this stage (see Figure 2 'idea generation' and Figure 3 'participative and collaborative approaches') in the same way that new political, cultural, and social relationships offer a coherent interpretation of linked human and environmental processes for resilience (Cochrane, 2015).

So, according to these figures, resilience and SI can rightly be said to differ in their respective outlooks on change. While SI focuses on change and transformability from the recent past to a not-too-distant future, resilience posits more on the inextricable links amongst the components within the system that ensure the balance between system change and continuity. Put differently, whereas resilience is interested in the conditions under which

Figure 1: Holling's systems dynamics model

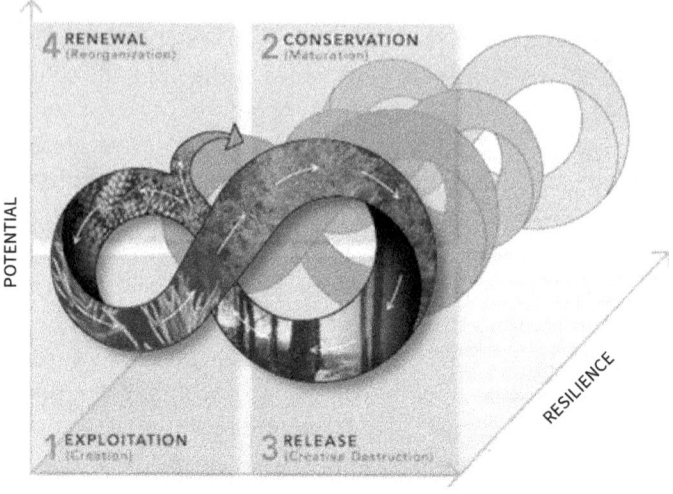

Adapted from Holling et al. (2002) (credit: Mcafee et al., 2010).

Figure 2: Social innovation framework, Gianmarco Marinello

	SENSING	IDEA GENERATION	PROTOTYPING
Mission	Find the root cause!	Play with the insights!	Solve the problem!
Mindset	EMPATHIC	OPEN-MINDED	RAPID
Process	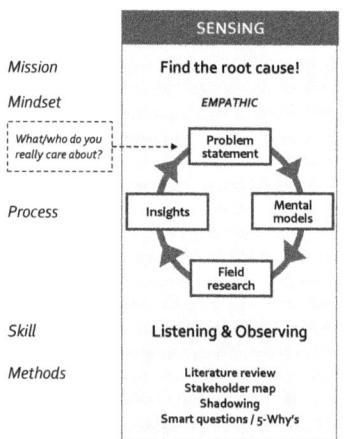	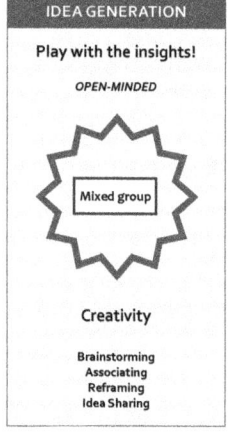	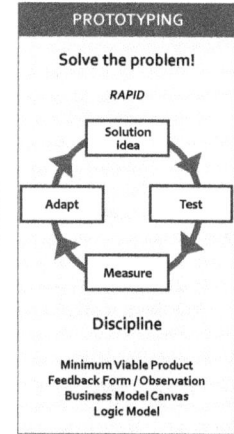
Skill	Listening & Observing	Creativity	Discipline
Methods	Literature review Stakeholder map Shadowing Smart questions / 5-Why's	Brainstorming Associating Reframing Idea Sharing	Minimum Viable Product Feedback Form / Observation Business Model Canvas Logic Model

Source: Gianmarco Marinello (2021). Retrieved from www.gianmarco-marinello.com

Figure 3: The fundamental elements of change

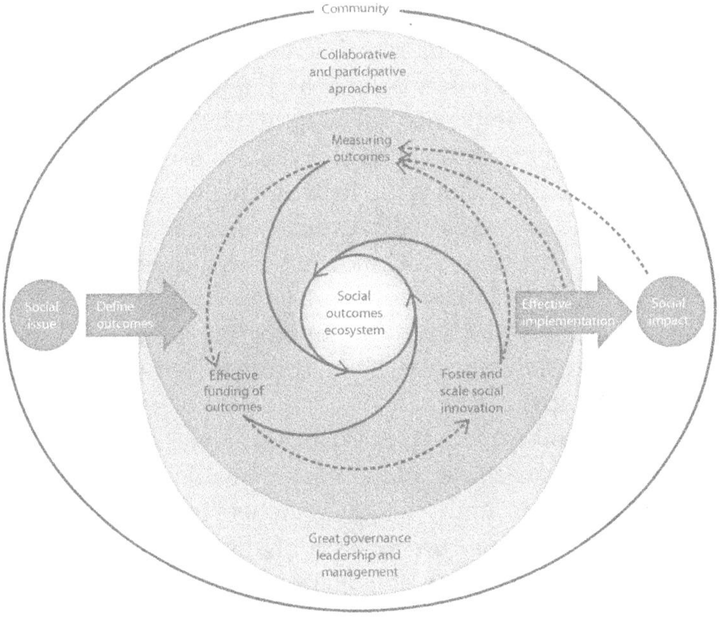

Community
- Collaborative and participative approaches
- Measuring outcomes
- Social outcomes ecosystem
- Effective funding of outcomes
- Foster and scale social innovation
- Great governance leadership and management

Social issue → Define outcomes → Effective implementation → Social impact

Source: Centre for Social Impact (Australia).

a system (e.g. a human community) survives major disruptions within a specific environment, SI is focused on the instrumentalities of novel solutions that address these disruptions at the social level. More specifically, SI is framed differently as aligned better with the process of finding solutions to challenges that impede societal welfare (Schot and Steinmueller, 2018, 1554), whereas resilience is invested in the patterns that enable the system to undergo change without disbanding. Nevertheless, rather than contrasting these two concepts, these subtle divergences can come together to complement one another within a transformative change ethos.

Several scholars have explicitly engaged the relationship between resilience and SI (Fougère and Meriläinen, 2021; Westley, 2013). One of the main connecting points identified between SI and resilience is their ability to embrace solutions for complex problems by juxtaposing elements that do not normally belong together to address intractable problems (Moore and Westley, 2011). Westley further contends that while 'the similarity between the cycle of innovation and the cycle of the release and renewal of resilient ecosystems is striking', the main pillars of resilience theory suggest that for the broader system to innovate effectively, closer attention should be paid to how society builds the 'capacity for repetition – over and over again, forever' (2013, 7). Fougère and Meriläinen (2021), on their part, suggest that pairing up resilience with innovation can help illustrate the 'dark sides' of SI, such as its adverse impacts on marginalised communities. This is indicative of the complementarity between SI and resilience thinking across three main themes: (1) complexity, (2) sustainable change and (3) continuity. So, while resilience thinking enhances the ability of SI to look at problems systematically, SI illuminates the instruments by which social systems become resilient or are eventually transformed for continuity, especially by foregrounding the actors behind these processes (Westley, 2013). In the pandemic and post-pandemic eras, the complex socio-economic ramifications of crises and their overlapping impact on various sections of society mean that SI will need to be more and more tuned to the requirements of a transformative change.

Inasmuch as transformability addresses social problems and refers to change as conceptualised in the sustainability transitions literature (Kivimaa and Kern, 2016; Turnheim and Geels, 2012), many SI transformative pathways also resonate with resilience processes as change management at system level. But, the framing of SI and resilience within a transformative change agenda somehow encompasses a reflection beyond addressing specific social problems or studying how resilience strategies come together to maintain and perpetuate a system. Instead, it requires a different focus on how to add a renewable dimension to innovative solutions, making SI a continuous process rather than a mere temporal device. The transformative change framing of innovation sees experiments 'as temporary spaces for actors working together on a variety of concrete pathways' (Schot and Steinmueller, 2018, 1563). It is the SI's transformative agenda that projects it further into the resilience cycle by suggesting that, in addition to experimentation/exploitation, provision should be made to look at the impact of SI at system level. With a particular focus on how individual examples of SI pull themselves together into cross-context resilient practices, the next section argues that synergising these two lenses (SI and resilience) can help us to better understand transformative change. This is illustrated through examples drawn from the context of Côte d'Ivoire, where communities facing multiple crises come up with sustainable solutions while building the capacity to recreate such solutions over and over again.

Formations and 'trans-formations'

The ways in which crises are formed, related, and constituted from many sources also reverberate on the many facets they develop as social problems.

Hence socially innovative practices produce transversal transformative effects across several sectors. This 'trans-formation' effectively gestures to the transversality of the resilience process over time, along with the notion of continuity in future constructions of such transversal resilience. In a 2018 World Bank report, Côte d'Ivoire came 147th (out of 178) among countries most at risk of climate change-related disasters (Banque Mondiale, 2018, 33). Other disruptions over the past three decades have included two major waves of armed violence (1999–2002; 2010–2011) (Huff et al., 2016, 59–63), natural hazards such as floods and landslides (Ketcha et al., 2017), eco-environmental stresses, especially in the West (most notably the degradation of protected forest areas) and in the North, as well as chronic zoonotic diseases affecting livestock, farming and livelihoods (Bassett and Koné, 2017; Kiewisch, 2015), and regular outbreaks of epidemics (such as cholera and meningitis, and now the pandemic). Furthermore, climate change prediction around rising temperatures could seriously disrupt the region with its reliance on cocoa production (Comoé and Siegrist, 2015). Given the concomitance of these crises, we have sought to look at innovative practices in relation to multiple crises.

The above crises or disruptions affecting the social dimension of life can be illustrated by obvious intersections such as those constituted between climate change, livelihoods and epidemics, or between conflicts and agriculture. Apart from underscoring the multiplicity of crises that the same communities may face and for which they demonstrate various forms of innovation, the literature on resilience in Côte d'Ivoire brings into sharp relief the relationship between conflicts and resilience (Bearth and Baya, 2010), or between eco-environmental stresses and disruptions to the livelihoods of communities that depend on farming or livestock to sustain their living (Kiewisch, 2015).[7] For instance, Chérif explains how climate change and associated consequences on agriculture increase the vulnerability of rural farmers in the mountainous region of Goh (2013, 1–5) – more details below. Another example is how the socio-political crisis in Abidjan prompted farming populations to change the way fresh produce was grown and marketed, and this resulted in the emergence of sustainable peri-urban agriculture as a form of social innovation. In fact, before the year 2000, fresh food production in the city's periphery was low and consisted

---

7   See also subsistence agriculture (Comoé and Siegrist, 2015), or the swollen shoot disease that causes a sharp and rapid decrease in cocoa output, as the disease eventually kills cocoa plants, leaving farmers in very vulnerable economic positions (Kouakou et al., 2012).

mainly of food produced for home consumption rather than market sales. Starting in 2000, and particularly after the beginning of the socio-political crisis in 2002, many additional cultivation sites emerged on the periphery of Abidjan. Farmers were thus able to make up for income loss due to the political situation by innovatively reorienting their capacities and assets in ways that met their essential needs (Babo, 2010). The argument here is that recognising the intersections between the pandemic and climate change, for instance, is not the apanage of high-level policy-makers. In a multiple-crisis context, citizens perceptively factor in all the crises in their design of innovative solutions to one problem. We find that streamlined within these bottom-up social innovation practices, a strong acknowledgement of intersections between these crises is present since they are addressed as such.

Hence, the ability of human communities to find innovative ways to manage economically in the face of multiple crises implies perhaps a more intuitive understanding of how the crises develop, intersect and overlap into multifaceted problems. In other words, bottom-up vernacular SIs in these contexts cannot be dissociated from the formation of the crises. A long-term perspective over these forms of SI with built-in awareness of how crises are constituted offers to move from a strictly problem-specific paradigm of SI to a system's approach with broader impact. When, for example, we consider 'rain rituals' performed by rural farmers in the mountainous region of Goh (2013, 1–5), a transversal reading of this performance reveals that it not only addresses climate change and its associated consequences on agriculture, it is also a spiritual tool to deal with the psychological impact of vulnerability. This practice seeks and certainly achieves transformation across multiple aspects of the same social problem or several social problems. Hence, the notion of 'transformation' is gesturing to the transversality of these dynamics. As these rituals can be renewed every year, the systemic resilience perspective thus also enables a view of a series of SI instances as a vast array of resilient strategies hinging upon a localised matrix of never-ending innovation. Hence, pairing up resilience and SI can contribute to better addressing the intersections between crises and provide a more sustainable framework for contextual solutions.

Knowledge of SI context drives the outcome of system resilience
It is crucial to envisage SI as inscribed within a wider social context and structured by a multitude of other problems. The significant number of studies that have indeed focused on resilience in Côte d'Ivoire (Banque Mondiale, 2018; Bearth and Baya, 2010; Chauveau, 2000; Comoé and Siegrist,

2015) can be revisited from a SI perspective to see how vernacular innovative practices emerge in the face of various crises and produce innovative arrangements to combine and integrate multiple solutions to different (facets of) problems.

There are many examples of how the adverse impact of resource scarcity and climate change is mitigated locally, especially in the agricultural sector. Already in 1996, a paper by Léonard and Oswald (1996) demonstrated how farmers were innovating and putting into place a more sustainable form of agriculture in the context of this resource scarcity crisis, developing what they have termed as forest-agriculture without any forest anymore. This entails diversifying types of crops and different practices for better soil management. Another recent project led by CIRAD[8] on farmer innovations and resilience in the face of climate change on cocoa farms has examined the adoption and impact of the use of chicken droppings in cocoa farms in a context of massive deforestation, loss of soil fertility, more frequent droughts, and the relatively high price of fertilisers.[9] Finally, a study by Golou et al. (2019) focused on farmer innovations in the context of land saturation caused by migratory flows. The study shows how different communities have implemented innovative agricultural strategies based on the introduction of cashew nut cultivation, normally adapted to savannah areas, used by farmers in the southern forest as an alternative crop to restore impoverished land. Here we see that innovative practices brought about at the community level do not only show an awareness of concurrent and related problems (such as the combination of deforestation, soil fertility, the high price of fertilisers), they are also cast as part of much wider transformative efforts against certain structural dynamics, even though they are not explicitly articulated as such.

Other scholars have also investigated how communities have developed their own mechanisms to avoid violence, faced with military crises and violence (see Allouche and Jackson, 2019; Allouche and Zadi Zadi, 2020). As an example of the awareness of how crises are constituted, some rural communities quickly realised the potential ramifications of the 2002 political violence on land-related violence. As soon as the conflict started in 2002, these communities endeavoured to implement clear and consensual mechanisms for land usage (Allouche and Jackson, 2019). This was the

---

8   Centre de Coopération Internationale en Recherche Agronomique pour le Développement (Center for International Cooperation in Agricultural Research for Development)
9   htps://umr-innovation.cirad.fr/en/projects/cedeao

case in the Yacoli Dabouo village, a large 7,000-inhabitant village located in the Soubré department. A village council representing the different communities was put in place to sensitise the illegal nature of selling land. The management committee administered all the land-to-land management and tenure transactions and then sent them to the subprefect office for registration procedures only. This means that discord arising after these transactions at any point can be arbitrated by the subprefect office more transparently and neutrally. Apart from being an example of SI on the part of communities embroiled in multiple crises with various ramifications (war, land dispute, deficient legal framework, state absence, etc.), the timing of the initiative in the case of the Yacoli Dabouo village demonstrates an acute awareness of the problem-formation process as well as a community-led innovative practice. In the specific political context of 2002, where state resources would have been reoriented towards the political crises, this SI preemptively mitigated the negative outcome of the political crisis, based on the knowledge of its potential ramifications and an understanding of participating actors in that context.

Another study that considers the potential of vernacular innovative practices to achieve peace in the Ivorian context was conducted by Koffi et al. (2014). Although the study was more conceptual rather than referring to specific examples, it reflected on the collective capacity to transcend trauma through ethical vernacular values. It specifically looked at the non-institutional aspects of forgiveness, reconciliation and dialogue as tools to progressively recover 'national social cohesion' that had been lost to the multiple economic and socio-political crises. Referring to post-electoral and political violence in the country, Koffi et al. recognise that the effective 'social durability' (2014, 30) of these innovations cannot be dissociated from the process of containing the multidimensional vulnerability of the national community. Put differently, forgiveness as an innovative solution to protracted conflict, for example, must work better alongside measures to tackle economic hardship. Hence, the notion that the passage of time will help address war-related trauma is predicated upon the shared value of forgiveness but steeped in the shared assumption that other aspects of the problem are addressed as per contextual knowledge. Post-conflict periods are also critical moments of SI during which collective introspection can help re-centre certain values that elicit community-based forms of social innovation. Interestingly, the ability of these vernacular SIs to embrace multiple (facets of) problems is an enduring understanding of how these innovations reach beyond a specific problem and are conjugated amongst themselves based on contextual vernacular knowledge.

Thus, looking at these vernacular SIs from a resilience perspective allows us not only to break down the transformation of social systems into their constituting sequences and actors but also examine how the mutual linkages ensure the sustainability of transformative change thereafter. It becomes clearer how the implementation of successful bottom-up SIs articulates with a more resilient social system in the long term. This is because looking at these SIs using a resilience lens also allows us to identify who the social actors are and what roles they play to challenge established conventions and problem causes so as to bring about immediate transformative change and potentially future transformative changes in new contexts. At the same time, the systemic and cyclic perspective of resilience with a long-term view over these actors and sequences of SI allows us to identify amongst these actors those likely to leverage innovative ideas for much greater system impact, maybe extending from community level to regional level. The resilience lens does this by identifying key elements of the SI device, likely to sustain the renewal and diffusion of innovative practices across space, scales and in the future. By combining the problem-focused SI approach with the system-focused resilience perspective, as is going to be the case in the next section, we can study innovative ideas and actors, as well as how certain types of actors operating at system level work to make transformative change a renewable occurrence.

The specific problem approach vs the systemic problem approach

As demonstrated by the interplay between various aspects of many crises in the Ivorian context above, the ways in which problems facing human communities are constituted across space and time cannot accommodate a framing of SI that looks at a problem without its relationship to other concurrent problems. Yet, SI is usually seen as focusing on the specific problem, albeit by bringing together many elements into innovative solutions. Resilience thinking, on the other hand, problematises problems as disruptions that need to be overcome by the combined efforts of elements within the resilient system itself. For instance, there are two complementary ways of looking at SI in the area of micro-economics observed in the village of Assoum (Côte d'Ivoire), a social space heavily impacted by the pandemic. The agricultural sector in this village especially bore the brunt of lockdown measures and travel restrictions promulgated by political authorities without much support to populations thus affected. Our preliminary research in Assoum (whose local economy rests mainly on market gardening) has observed that villagers had to stop crop production because they were unable to sell their crops to the cities for many months. Without government assistance, while their livelihoods were thus compromised, the villagers came up with the idea of borrowing money from microfinance institutions against nothing, if not uncertainty. Of course, like in many countries across the world, these rural microfinance institutions were set up for the sole purpose of lending money to these market gardeners, but with a system of guaranteed repayment whereby the entire crop production was committed against the loan – a social innovation in and of itself. The other SI emerged because the same loan was being henceforth made against nothing and in times of uncertainty when no one could foretell how long the lockdown was going to last. This challenged the traditional relationship between these microfinance institutions and the villagers in a way that redefined the lending procedures even after lockdown ceased. By mobilising their social capital, villagers were able to foreground trust and hope as bankable commodities in rural agriculture.

One way of looking at this novel development would be to focus on the financial problem it thus effectively solved and the transformative change brought about in the social setup. The SI perspective allows us to 'zoom in' on which social ingredients were combined to arrive at this solution, namely the role played by individual and groups of villagers such as association leaders or ordinary farmers on the one hand, and maybe other actors internal to the microfinance institutions who were championing this shift in thinking and lending practice on the other hand. In addition, we may also study how and why the social capital constituted by these actors contributed to this transformative change and the extent to which this can be rolled out in other contexts. However, a resilience perspective studies this rural financial sector and the local market gardening community as constitutive parts of the same ecosystem that pulled various elements together to reorganise and avoid collapsing in the face of a crisis.[10] Furthermore, such an approach, first of all, interrogates the choice of market gardening as opposed to traditional cash crops in Côte d'Ivoire (cocoa and coffee) as a possible track record of how the said ecosystem had faced and survived past disruptions. The advantage of bringing these two perspectives together is that they will now enable the analysis to trace, over time and space, those ingredients evidenced from the SI perspective (problem-specific) that are likely to ensure that the ecosystem (resilience) continues to find ways of successfully facing crises over and over again (sustainable, transformative change).

---

10   See Figure 1 (Holling's systems dynamics model).

The scale of crises and the autonomous capabilities of the communities facing them come together in a complex web of relations that can be used to better understand how those novel ideas challenging conventions come about and the conditions under which similar ideas might emerge again. These sites of innovation provide an opportunity to (a) advance the understanding of innovation as the sine qua non-condition for and an integral part of the resilience process and (b) posit that the framing of SI can be expanded to mirror the complexity and multiplicity of the problems it seeks to address. Hence, in addition to the uses of the resilience-innovation link (Fougère and Meriläinen, 2021; Westley, 2013), the next section develops a framework to see how this link can provide a path to study the conditions of sustainability and continuity for transformative change.

Building a framework to pair SI and resilience approaches

While the focus on African innovations during the pandemic era has helped show that broadening is required even within the scientific and technological paradigms (Hajizadeh and Behnemoon, 2020), the question remains as to why this context was excluded in the first place and how much this exclusion can tell us about SI. The explanations given were are limited. These limited explanations consist mainly in critically acknowledging that: (1) Western-centric assumptions, or indeed any self-absorbed innovation processes, that centralise the producers and geographical loci of innovation, miss out on alternative pathways that could also contribute to transformative change (Fougère and Meriläinen, 2021); (2) innovation policy designs are dominated by strict scientific knowledge even when reality defeats scientific predictions (Umviligihozo et al., 2020); (3) large national and international institutions tend to respond to the need for innovation by promoting technological breakthroughs while relying on the past when searching for solutions to present crises and emergencies (thereby creating restrictive, iterative and linear relationships between existing solutions and innovation) (Ramalingam, 2013). However, in light of the examples of SI in Côte d'Ivoire and how they articulate with resilience, in the long run, addressing the three explanations above would be helpful but not sufficient. Addressing them might help improve the impact of innovative solutions, but looking at social innovations in multiple-crisis contexts from the combined lenses of resilience and innovation allows us to make an important conceptual change. This combined approach points to the possibility of shifting attention away from the dominant focus on innovative solutions to focusing on innovative ways of understanding problems in the first place.

In order to achieve this, we consider the ways in which multiple crises are constituted, related and dealt with transversally in the examples studied above. In the case of Côte d'Ivoire, the focus on both the relationship between parts of the social system facing multiple crises on the one hand (resilience), and the elements brought together from bottom-up in the process of solving social problems (SI) on the other hand, leads to the reimagination of SI as not just finding innovative solutions, but also as probing how the plural vulnerability of social groups is streamlined into the innovative process and, more importantly, how this process is repeated over time. Then, we emphasise the continuity of the innovative process over time, that is, the ability of social groups who find innovative solutions for specific crises to be able to repeat it repeatedly. This second emphasis is the part played by resilience thinking in that it helps foreground such actors and patterns that ensure the adaptability of the whole system across time and space.

The benefit of such a dual approach is that the mutual relationships uncovered between the problems become sites of innovation that bear the seeds of sustainable, transformative change. It is, however, worth noting that our focus on the formation of problems or crises differs slightly from the political line of enquiry that is limited to questioning the structural origins of crises and the ways in which top-down SI policies can lead to further disruption and/or marginalisation as demonstrated by authors such as Fougère and Meriläinen (2021, 7–8). The proposed approach in this chapter, as illustrated in Figure 4, is about four key objectives: (1) challenging the limits imposed unto our own understanding of SI by the thematic silos, top-down approaches adverse to vernacularity, and sectoral restrictions within which crises are often boxed; (2) conceptualising crises as integral elements of an ecosystem inside which complex relationships provide a space for SI to embrace its constituent parts through the agency of ordinary social actors; (3) rethinking the notion of novelty in SI by questioning the jurisdiction of its timeline; and (4) combining a granular examination of SI actors and sequences with a systemic analysis of the conditions under which transformative change repeats itself over time.

The framework conceptualises SI as drawing from a contextual matrix that adds a multidimensional layer to any perceived problem. As seen with the convergence of crises X, Y and Z into a social problem (or the facets thereof), a specific SI process cannot be seen as addressing only one problem or one aspect of a problem. The contextual knowledge and experience (K and E) of innovation actors are intuitively factored in, both in understanding the social problem (its formation) and in the design of the socially innovative solution. Additionally, this intuitive knowledge and experience are carried

Figure 4: Proposed SI-resilience approach pairing framework

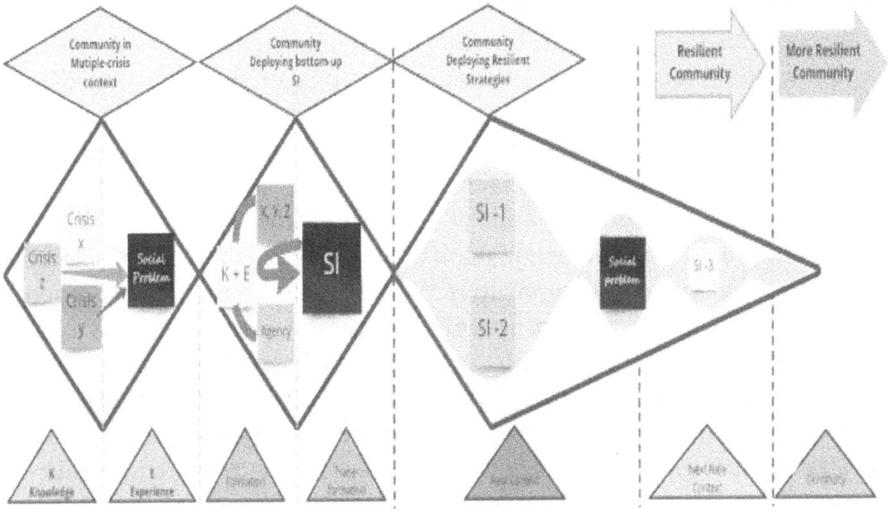

Source: Authors' own.

over into new contexts, thus ensuring the community's ability to recreate new solutions continuously. This framework thus highlights the plurality of facets to a problem to emphasise the agency of innovation actors as ingrained in their knowledge of the problem context. We argue that the outcome of SI processes depends on this intuitive knowledge of the multiple-crisis context. In Figure 4, walking backwards on the transformative change trajectory also lays bare the relationship between innovation and resilience: the former being the device and the latter the process through which this device moves across space and time. As Figure 4 indicates, innovative practices based on single paths miss out on the multidimensional nature of each specific problem and the extent to which the contextual matrix feeds into the overall innovative solution. This is one of the blind spots in innovative frameworks that do not create space for non-scientific or intangible variables. A case in point in the African context was a focus on health innovations during the pandemic, which failed to give as much attention to the social actors and context shaping the so-called 'surprising' resilience of the continent or the vernacular experience of health workers, therefore suppressing from the framework both the agency of innovation actors and their ability to renew or diffuse the innovative process.

In a specific social context, bringing together several facets of problems that feed into the design of specific innovative solutions (see X, Y and Z in

Figure 4, second column) enables the framing of SI to achieve two things: (1) highlight how individual problems are interrelated; and (2) intuitively take into account the 'blind spots' in the interrelation between different crises. In other words, since specific innovation for one crisis might increase vulnerability to another crisis, a framework should consider how various shocks or disruptions interact with one another over time. A resilience outlook on innovative practices enables us to see this more clearly. Hence, instead of locating a site of innovation in the face of the present crisis, the site is moved one scale up in the merging point between two or several problems as prompted by individual innovative devices. Therefore, the proposed framework also highlights awareness of how the effectiveness of innovation can be limited or even thwarted by overlooking the relationship between the crisis being addressed and other crises located in different times or spaces. This framework thus situates resilience as mediating the context through innovation so that the innovative process interlocks with the ability to face multiple crises in varying contexts and repeatedly over time.[11] This is a path to effective and lasting transformability because it can be transposed and transferred significantly. This is appropriate for innovation research, not least because the consequences of the pandemic extended beyond the sphere of public health to generate economic and socio-cultural impacts. In the context of non-scientific knowledge, the remaining difficulty now is how to excavate the patterns of relationships between these various crises that might not be readily observable through the main problem that a given type of innovation is seeking to address.

We propose that the answer to this conundrum can be divided into three steps. The first step would comprise adopting this multidimensional approach which connects the driving (f)actors of SI to resilience outcome. The second step develops from the main argument of this paper and is based on lessons learned from the African experiences and examples of innovation: bringing together various transformative trajectories for a specific social context into a matrix that can serve as a seed of innovation to build on previous successful examples within the same context. The third step involves foregrounding the agency of innovation actors as indissociable from the SI itself. These three steps aim at harnessing innovation and complement the proposed framework with resilience as an entry point into unknown connections and relationships between crises. Like in the case

---

11 See SI-1, SI-2 and SI-3 in Figure 4 above as resilience cycles repeat themselves, carrying innovative capability within.

of the unexplained resilience to the pandemic in Africa, the multiplicity of hypotheses simply indicates that, although no single hypothesis has been rigorously evidenced, this resilience is grounded in the plurality of strategies (both scientific and non-scientific) to overcome other multiple crises. Since SI can be understood as an integral part of the resilience process, an effective SI process should mirror this resilience in its identification of the problems it seeks to address. Put differently, since it can at least be demonstrated that effective resilience pulls from multiple innovation sequences addressing separate problems, the SI framework within which communities promote their resilient vernacular practices is one that thus strives to embrace all the potential problems related to the one it is tackling. This results in a systematic look at how human problems are constituted, interconnected and localised. The proposed framework and the three steps to excavate connections and relationships between crises consequently offers an insight into understanding what forward-thinking transformative change could look like.

Conclusion: Understanding formations to create transformations

This chapter has sought to draw lessons from African experiences of innovation in a multiple-crisis context against the backdrop of the pandemic. It argues that widening the scope of innovation must do more than simply expanding the jurisdiction of certain Western-based geographic poles or acknowledging non-technological/non-scientific forms of innovation. It has made a case for a broader conceptual underpinning to study SI beyond a mere loosening of the social dimension in the concept of innovation. Instead, it has examined how allowing the conceptualisation of innovation to mirror the interplay between crises from a system approach can provide a path to transformative solutions that are renewable, and therefore transferrable. In the post-pandemic era, both the diverging outcomes of data-based predictions and examples of innovation coming out of Africa, especially in the health sector, refocus the debate on expanding SI. Reflecting on how to ground innovation in the context of Africa, this chapter has, first of all, explored known barriers to broadening innovation definitions, such as the dominance of strict scientific knowledge. It finds that other forms of knowledge need to be brought into the SI conceptualisation framework, not just as an addition to existing centralised processes of designing and conceptualising innovation, but rather as a way of decentralising innovation, both geographically and epistemologically. The following empirical analysis supports our recommendation for a framework that harnesses innovation outside the spatial coordinates of a Western-centric world, beyond the data-driven models based exclusively on science and technology, and away from the iterative linearity of innovative improvement by better alternatives.

As laid out in this chapter, the consequence of this is that the conceptual underpinnings of innovation generally can be extended to escape the iterative linearity and the narrow focus on the creative process of finding innovative solutions to specific problems. Instead, it advocates innovative ways of understanding problems by pairing up SI and resilience thinking to examine innovative strategies. As a result, bringing various resilience paths into a single matrix constitutes another starting point (a seed of innovation) for a novel SI framework. In this framework, there is conceptual space for envisaging SI as an integral part or tool of the resilience dynamics or conceiving transformative change itself as an outcome or by-product of the community resilience process. As illustrated by empirical data from SI examples and resilience practices observed in Côte d'Ivoire, when the two lines of thinking (resilience and SI) are brought together, the complex relationship that binds multiple problems emerges as the prime target of a truly innovative process. In other words, the relationship amongst social problems and the ability of communities facing them points to sites of innovation where resilience can also be understood as an expression of trans-formative change (across several sectors), that is, transformative change is related mainly to connectedness in the resilience cycle.

Therefore, the combined approach is not just about applying the most effective approach to learn how survivors organise to successfully recover from major shocks or crises. It is about mapping the complex relationships between these multiple shocks and how these are mediated through the SIs offered so that the potential for transformative change is plotted across a continuum that escapes the current compartmentalisation of challenges faced by individuals and/or communities. This appears as an essential step in alternative efforts to harness innovation. Innovation may therefore be seen as a renewable element of a resilience strategy to overcome problems, especially if the context is allowed to substantiate the agency of actors with intuitive knowledge and experience of how the problems intersect and interrelate. Most importantly, the proposed framework not only breaks down the solution-focused approach when dealing with innovation, but it also centres vernacular experiences as related to multidimensional crises and thus creates the space for shifting the focus, from solutions to problems; from problem formation to resilient trans-formation, and ultimately from present to future.

Acknowledgements

The writing of the paper on which this chapter is based was supported by the DSI/NRF/Newton Fund Trilateral Chair in Transformative Innovation, the Fourth Industrial Revolution and Sustainable Development. The research material used is derived from the preliminary research for the project Islands of Innovation in Protracted Crises: A New Approach to Building Equitable Resilience from Below (see https://www.ids.ac.uk/projects/islands-of-innovation-in-protracted-crises-a-new-approach-to-building-equitable-resilience-from-below/).

References

Allouche, J., and Jackson, P. (2019). Zones of peace and local peace processes in Côte d'Ivoire and Sierra Leone. *Peacebuilding, 7*(1), 71-87.

Allouche, J., and Zadi Zadi, P. (2020). Crise post-électorale en Côte d'Ivoire et logique de la non-violence en milieu urbain: une illustration à partir des villes de Gagnoa, Guiglo et San Pedro en 2010–11. *Canadian Journal of African Studies/Revue canadienne des etudes africaines, 55*(1), 1-19. DOI: 10.1080/00083968.2020.1723657.

Babo, A. (2010). Sociopolitical crisis and the reconstruction of sustainable periurban agriculture in Abidjan, Côte d'Ivoire. *African Studies Review, 53*(3), 101-120. http://www.jstor.org/stable/40930968

Banque Mondiale. (2018). *Pour que demain ne meure jamais: La Cote d'Ivoire face au changement climatique.* World Bank.

Barrett, C. B., and Constas, M. A. (2014). Toward a theory of resilience for international development applications. *Proceedings of the National Academy of Sciences of the United States of America, 111*, 14625-14630.

Bassett, T. J., and Koné, M. (2017). Peanuts for cashews? Agricultural diversification and the limits of adaptability in Côte d'Ivoire. In: S. F. Chari (Ed.), *Other Geographies: The influences of Michael Watts* (79-96). John Wiley.

BBC. (2020). Coronavirus: Ten African innovations to help tackle Covid-19. https://www.bbc.com/news/world-africa-53776027

Bearth, T., and Baya, J. (2010). Guerre civile et résilience écologique: Le cas du Parc national du mont Sangbé à l'ouest de la Côte d'Ivoire. *Cahiers Agricultures, 19*(3), 220-226.

Carpenter, S., and Folke, C. (2006). Ecology for transformation. *Trends in Ecology and Evolution, 21*, 309-315.

Chauveau, J.-P. (2000). Question foncière et construction nationale en Côte d'Ivoire: Les enjeux silencieux d'un coup d'état. *Politique Africaine, 78*, 94-125.

Chérif, S. (2013). La résurgence des anciens rituels de demande de la pluie en contexte de réchauffement. *Climate Change Technology Conference,* 2013, 1-12.

Clark, W. C. (2007). Sustainability science: A room of its own. *Proceedings of the National Academy of Sciences, 104*(6), 1737-1738.

Coad, A., Nightingale, P., Stilgoe, J., and Vezzani, A. (2021). Editorial: The dark side of innovation. *Industry and Innovation*, 28(1), 102-112. DOI: 10.1080/13662716.2020.1818555.

Cochrane, J. (2015). The sphere of tourism resilience. *Tourism Recreation Research*, 35(2), 173-185.

Comoé, H., and Siegrist, M. (2015). Relevant drivers of farmers' decision behavior regarding their adaptation to climate change: A case study of two regions in Côte d'Ivoire. *Mitigation and Adaptation Strategies for Global Change*, 20(2), 179-199.

Drucker, P. F. (1985). *Innovation and Entrepreneurship: Practice and principles*. Harper and Row.

European Commission. (2010). European Commission. http://ec.europa.eu/DocsRoom/documents/19042

Fals-Borda, O., and Rahman, M. A. (1991). *Action and Knowledge: Breaking the monopoly with participatory action research*. Apex.

Fougère, M., and Meriläinen, E. (2021). Exposing three dark sides of social innovation through critical perspectives on resilience. *Industry and Innovation*, 28, 1-18.

Ganin, A., Massaro, E., Gutfraind, A., Steen, N., Keisler, J. M., Kott, A., Mangoubi, R., and Linkov, I. (2016). Operational resilience: Concepts, design and analysis. *Scientific Reports*, 6, 19540(2016).

Godin, B. (2008). *Project on the Intellectual History of Innovation* (Working Paper no. 1). http://www.csiic.ca/PDF/IntellectualNo1.pdf.

Golou Gizèle, Z., Kouassi Bruno, K., Yao Sadaiou Sabas, B., and Jan, B. (2019). Migration and agricultural practices in the peripheral areas of Côte d'Ivoire state-owned forests. *Sustainability*, 11(22), 6378.

Griliches, Z. (1960). Congruence versus profitability: A false dichotomy. *Rural Sociology*, 25, 354-356.

Hajizadeh, R., and Behnemoon, M. (2020). Is the new coronavirus disease (COVID-19) pandemic halted by malaria epidemics? *The Archives of Bones Surgery*, 8(1), 319-320.

Holling, C. S., Gunderson, L., and Ludwig, D. (2002). In quest of a theory of adaptive change. In: *Panarchy: Understanding transformations in human and natural systems* (3-24). Island Press.

Horn, E. (2018). *The Future as Catastrophe: Imagining disaster in the modern age*. Columbia University Press.

Howells, J. (2006). Intermediation and the role of intermediaries in innovation. *Research Policy*, 35(5), 715-728.

Huff, A., Dowd, C., Okech, A., Shahrokh, T., Zadi Zadi, P., Mahama, S., and Allouche, J. (2016). Violence and Violence Reduction Efforts In Kenya, Uganda, Ghana and Ivory Coast: Insights and lessons towards achieving SDG16. Institute of Development Studies.

Ijjasz-Vasquez, E., Baker, J., and Cira, D. (2020). Innovations in the time of COVID-19: Rising to the pandemic's challenges in Africa's informal settlements. *World Bank Blogs*. https://blogs.worldbank.org/nasikiliza/innovations-time-covid-19-rising-pandemics-chal

Kassoum, T., and Memon, F. (2020). Causes and expressions of the rapid spread of the new coronavirus 'Covid-19' in Côte d'Ivoire. *European Journal of Social Sciences Studies*, 5(2), 32-52.

Ketcha, M., Kablan, A., Dongo, K., and Coulibaly, M. (2017). Assessment of social vulnerability to flood in urban Côte d'Ivoire using the MOVE framework. *Water*, 1-19.

Kiewisch, E. (2015). Looking within the household: A study on gender, food security, and resilience in cocoa-growing communities. *Gender and Development*, 23(3), 497-513.

Kivimaa, P., and Kern, F. (2016). Creative destruction or mere niche support? Innovation policy mixes for sustainability transitions. *Research Policy*, 45(1), 205-217.

Kline, S. J. (1985). Innovation is not a linear process. *Research Management*, 28(4), 36-45.

Koffi, K. J. M, Ouattara, M., Ballet, J., and Mahieu, F-R. (2014). Résiliences et équilibres en Côte d'Ivoire post-crise. *Éthique et économique/Ethics and Economics*, 11(1).

Kouakou, K., Kébé, B. I., Kouassi, N., Aké, S., Cilas, C., and Muller, E. (2012). Geographical distribution of cacao swollen shoot virus molecular variability in Côte d'Ivoire. *Plant Disease*, 96(10), 1445-1450.

Léonard, É., and Oswald, M. (1996). Une agriculture forestière sans forêt. Changements agro-écologiques et innovations paysannes en Côte-d'Ivoire. *Natures sciences sociétés*, 4(3), 202-216.

Marinello, G. (2021). Social innovation framework. [Blog post]. https://gianmarco-marinello.com/blog/

Masten, A. S. (2001). Ordinary magic: Resilience processes in development. *American Psychologist*, 56(3), 227-238.

Mcafee, B., de Camino, R. V., Burton, P. J. Eddy, B. G., Fähser, L., Messier, C., Reed, M. G., Spies, T., Vides, R., Baker, C., Barriga, M., Campos, J., Corrales, O., Espinoza, L., Gibson, S., Glatthorn, J., Martineau-Delisle, C., Prins, C., and Rose, N.-A. (2010). Managing forested landscapes for socio-ecological resilience. In: G. Mery, P. Katila, G. Galloway, R.I. Alfaro, M. Kanninen, M. Lobovikov, and J. Varjo (Eds), *Forests and Society: Responding to global drivers of change* (401-439). International Union of Forest Research Organizations (IUFRO).

Meissner, D., Polt, W., and Vonortas, N. S. (2017). Towards a broad understanding of innovation and its importance for innovation policy. *The Journal of Technology Transfer*, 42(5), 1184-1211.

Mokyr, J. (2011). *The Gifts of Athena: Historical origins of the knowledge economy*. Princeton University Press.

Moore, M. L., and Westley, F. (2011). Surmountable chasms: Networks and social innovation for resilient systems. *Ecology and Society*, 16(1), 1-13.

Organisation for Economic Co-operation and Development (OECD). (2020). *Broad-based Innovation Policy for All Regions and Cities*. OECD Publishing.

OMS. (2020). La COVID-19 stimule l'innovation en matière de santé en Afrique. *WHO*. https://www.afro.who.int/fr/news/la-covid-19-stimule-linnovation-en-matiere-de-sante-en-afrique

Pelling, M. (2011). *Adaptation to Climate Change: From resilience to transformation*. Routledge.

Phills, J. A., Deiglmeier, K., and Miller, D. T. (2008). Rediscovering social innovation. *Stanford Social Innovation Review*, 6(4), 34-43.

Radjou, N. (2009). Polycentric innovation: The new global innovation agenda for MNCs. *Harvard Business Review*. https://hbr.org/2009/11/polycentric-innovation-the-new.html

Ramalingam, B. (2013). *Aid on the Edge of Chaos: Rethinking international cooperation in a complex world*. Oxford University Press.

Schmidt, T., and Rammer, C. (2007). Non-technological and technological innovation: Strange bedfellows? *SSRN Electronic Journal*.

Schot, J., and Steinmueller, W. E. (2018). Three frames for innovation policy: R&D, systems of innovation and transformative change. *Research Policy*, 47, 1554-1567.

Smith, A. (2017). Social innovation, democracy and makerspaces. *Science Policy Research Unit Working Paper Series, SWPS 2017-10*. https://ssrn.com/abstract=2986245 or http://dx.doi.org/10.2139/ssrn.2986245

Thompson, N. (2004). Innovativeness and performance: Evidence from the manufacturing sectors. *Journal of Strategic Marketing*, 12(4), 255-266.

Turnheim, B., and Geels, F. (2012). Regime destabilisation as the flipside of energy transitions: Lessons from the history of the British coal industry (1913–1997). *Energy Policy*, 50, 35-49.

Tushman, M. (2002). A structural approach to assessing innovation: Construct development of innovation locus, type and characteristics. *Management Science*, 48(9), 1103-1122.

van der Have, R. P., and Rubalcaba, L. (2016). Social innovation research: An emerging area of innovation studies? *Research Policy*, 45(9), 1923-1935.

Vrande, V. V. d., Vanhaverbeke, W., and Gassmann, W. (2010). Introduction: Broadening the scope of open innovation. *International Journal of Technology Management*, 52(3), 221-235.

Wagner, A. (2011). *The Origins of Evolutionary Innovations: A theory of transformative change in living systems*. Oxford University Press.

Walker, B., Holling, C., Carpenter, S. R., and Kinzig, A. (2004). Resilience, adaptability and transformability in social–ecological systems. *Ecology and Society*, 9(2), 5.

Westley, F. (2013). Social innovation and resilience: How one enhances the other. *Stanford Social Innovation Review*, Summer, 5-8. https://ssir.org/articles/entry/social_innovation_and_resilience_how_one_enhances_the_ other#

Westley, F., and Antadze, N. (2010). Making a difference: Strategies for scaling social innovation for greater impact. *Innovation Journal*, 15(2).

WHO. (2020). WHO showcases leading African innovations in COVID-19 response. https://www.who.int/news-room/feature-stories/detail/who-showcases-leading-african-innovations-in-covid-19-response

Wieczorek, A. J., Hekkert, M. P., Coenen, L., and Harmsen, R. (2015). Broadening the national focus in technological innovation system analysis: The case of offshore wind. *Environmental Innovation and Societal Transitions*, 14(2210-4224), 128-148.

Woods, D. (2018). The strategic agility gap: How organisations are slow and stale to adapt in a turbulent world. In: F. Daniellou and R. Amalberti (Eds), *Human and Organisational Factors in High-Risk Companies*. Foncsi.

Woods, D. D. (2020). What matters when we are in the middle of evolving Covid-19 pandemic? *Zenodo*.

Yoka Lye, A., and Ngaki Kosi, J. M. (2020). La perception culturelle de la maladie en RDC et ses leçons de résilience. https://resiliencecongo.org/2020/11/12/la-perception-culturelle-de-la-maladie-en-rdc-et-ses-lecons-de-resilience/

Zadi, P. A. (2013). The dynamics of restraint in Côte d'Ivoire. *IDS Bulletin*, 44(1), 72-86.

CHAPTER 3

Strengthening Innovation Ecosystems in Africa

Seeking out systemic changes in the wake of the 2020 pandemic

Olugbenga Adesida, Geci Karuri-Sebina and Krishnie Thaver

Introduction

In Africa, the pandemic intersected with socio-economic systems already under heavy strain with pre-existing developmental challenges, disrupting the lives of millions of people and with a disproportionate impact on poor households and small and informal businesses (Jayaram et al., 2020a). The pandemic and its emerging aftermath significantly challenged decision-makers to act quickly (Ashkenas, 2020) to reduce the infection rates whilst finding ways to mitigate the dire local impacts (Beech, 2020). The pandemic was also recognised as having catalysed innovation across the world (CCEF, 2020), including in Africa, stimulating innovation out of necessity and forming opportunities within the new and unexpected circumstances. Given the challenges brought on by the crisis and the need to increase the resilience and sustainability of economies, the future of Africa was reshaped for a post-pandmic age (Davies, 2020).

Based on an ongoing enquiry about the state and development of Africa's innovation ecosystems (Adesida et al., 2016), this chapter examines the African innovation space through an ecosystems lens. It aims to identify and understand the systemic obstacles and responses – particularly from the perspective of innovators – that obstructed the path of effective innovation-driven development pre-pandemic. It further seeks to identify new opportunities or challenges for innovation that have been experienced since the advent of the pandemic, as well as examine whether these shifts or changes were systemic to the innovation ecosystems or just transient responses to the pandemic.

Key concepts used in this chapter are 'systemic changes' and 'innovation ecosystems'. Systemic change can be defined as a transformative change within the instruments and mindsets in a system that leads to actors within the system changing their behaviours (Jenal, 2020). A change can be seen as systemic once it transforms the primary methods that are used in the system for doing things (Jenal, 2020). Lomax developed a framework of three components for systematically identifying systemic changes: (1) changes in system states, (2) change in the resilience or capacity of the system, and (3) connectivity to the change impetus (Lomax, 2019).

Innovation ecosystems are a dynamic set of actors, practices and infrastructures that govern the performance of initiatives and innovations (Granstrand and Holgersson, 2020; Moore, 1996). The innovation ecosystem comprises various actors, including start-ups, hubs, civil society, government, private organisations and academia, which act together to develop and execute innovation.

The innovations triggered by pandemic in Africa provide an opportunity to learn about how some of the challenges Africa had been facing with its innovation ecosystems could be addressed. This research attempts to understand how innovations and lessons from this period can be leveraged towards developing transformative solutions for Africa in a post-pandemic world and to assess whether or not substantial changes are emerging in the innovation ecosystems on the continent.

As such, the questions guiding this enquiry, with a diagram illustrating the research strategy, are listed below:

- What were the systemic issues hindering the African innovation ecosystems prior to the pandemic?
- What were the new challenges facing African innovation ecosystems in the age of the pandemic?
- How do these changes relate to the previous systemic issues identified?

- Are these changes sustainable, or were some simply reactions and non-systemic?
- What were the useful insights and recommendations learnt, and how can these be translated to robust policies?

Figure 1: Research objectives strategy schematic

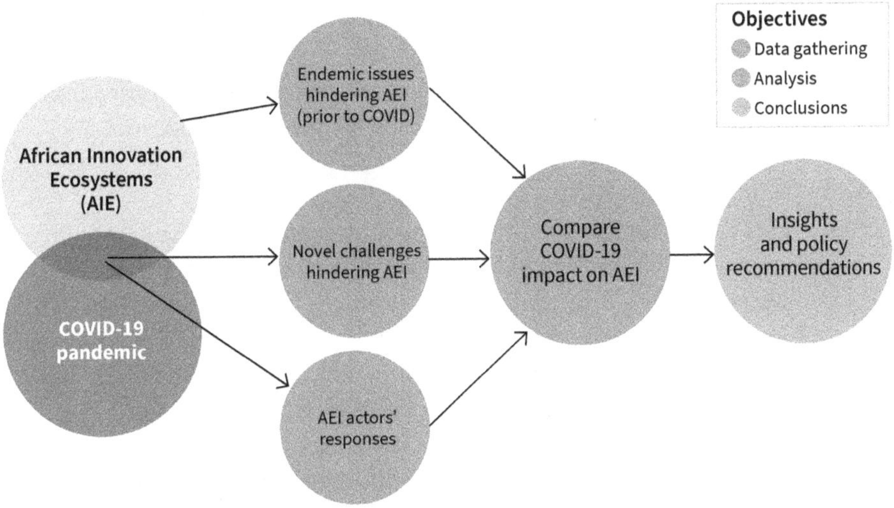

Objectives
- Data gathering
- Analysis
- Conclusions

African Innovation Ecosystems (AIE) → Endemic issues hindering AEI (prior to COVID) → Compare COVID-19 impact on AEI → Insights and policy recommendations

COVID-19 pandemic → Novel challenges hindering AEI → Compare COVID-19 impact on AEI

COVID-19 pandemic → AEI actors' responses → Compare COVID-19 impact on AEI

Source: Authors' own.

The pre-pandemic situation

Africa has a wide range of developmental challenges, which include energy access, water, food insecurity, health epidemics, education, climate change, as well as governance (Adesida et al., 2018). Many of these developmental challenges pre-date the pandemic and inform the core elements of the United Nations Sustainable Developments Goals (SDGs), which the world has subscribed to achieving by 2030. Innovations were also taking place prior to the onset of the pandemic on the continent. However, these were in spite of systemic challenges that continue to stunt and hamper Africa's innovation ecosystems (Adesida and Karuri-Sebina, 2013; Adesida et al., 2018). Addressing these kinds of systemic challenges to the innovation ecosystems would require identifying and breaking the barriers in knowledge, culture, governance, policy, regulations, infrastructure, or resources that prevented the flourishing of innovation (Adesida and Karuri-Sebina, 2013; Adesida et al., 2018).

The unfolding of the Ebola pandemic in West Africa in 2014 provided valuable insights into the types of changes and obstacles that can be observed during a pandemic. The key obstacles identified during the Ebola crisis were that medical resources were scarce, infrastructure was poor, and cultural practices, beliefs and misinformation contributed to the proliferation of the disease (IDS, 2015). The changes in practices such as data analytics and simulation were used to improve health systems, and e-learning was used to empower healthcare personnel (IDS, 2015). From this example we can learn, for instance, that investment programmes are important to rebuilding a less vulnerable society and that education-enabled preventative measures.

Africa's challenged innovation ecosystems

A broad literature identifies and converges around numerous systemic weaknesses that have bedevilled African innovation ecosystems over time, including limited economic infrastructure, weak systems, limited capabilities, and poor policy and governance (Lorenz, 2016). McKinney (2016) identifies systemic obstacles such as access to capital, physical infrastructure, legal systems and human resources. A lack of skills, innovation capacity, entrepreneurial culture and support from policy-makers have also been noted as impediments to innovation on the continent (IBM Communications, 2013). These observations resonate with the evolving findings from the multi-stakeholder dialogues about innovation systems convened under the Africa Innovation Summit (AIS) platform since 2014.[1]

The economic and social infrastructure gap has been identified as a significant challenge to Africa's development (Adesida et al., 2018). In the power generation sector, for example, significant deficits exist. Access and reliability are low, and the cost is quite high. In the meantime, compared to other developing or emerging economies, African countries are not investing as much or as needed (McKinsey, 2016). In light of the outsized importance that digitalisation, automation and artificial intelligence have acquired and are expected to maintain in the future, digital infrastructure is critical for the innovation ecosystems. The good news is that Africa has witnessed significant improvements in its digital infrastructure with increasing access to mobile telephony and the internet (McKinney, 2016). However, significant problems persist with Africa's digital infrastructure, including high costs, low quality and reliability.

Another critical factor hindering the innovation ecosystems on the

---

1   https://www.africainnovationsummit.com/

continent is inadequate institutional infrastructure. African systems are weak while the institutions are inadequate. Innovation ecosystems actors play important roles in cultivating a thriving and sustainable environment (Edquist, 2001). Weak institutions demonstrate broken synergies among actors, which prevent interactive learning and therefore limit the opportunities and potential for innovation (Egbetokun et al., 2007; Iizuka et al., 2015; Muok and Kingiri, 2015; Oyelaran-Oyeyinka et al., 1996). These effects can be translated into weaker policy and control measures enacted and rolled out by the decision-makers (Voeten and Naudé, 2014). According to Mudombi and Muchie (2014), Africa has weak systems that are not ideal for innovation at both the national (and international) levels. Lorenz (2016) has argued that the strength of Africa's systems is negatively impacted by factors like institutional quality, which encompasses the rule of law, corruption and transparency, and lack of accountability.

Ndubuisi Ekekwe, the founder of the African Institute of Technology, argues that although Africa has the ability to attract foreign investment, investors are deterred by the inability of African legal systems to offer robust property rights and IP protection (McKinney, 2016).

Africa is also lagging in educational capabilities (Mwiti, 2015). Many of the educational systems on the continent are underfunded and underperforming. The relevance and quality of education highlight a disturbing fact that most of Africa's educational systems may not be fit for purpose. Although there are numerous colleges and universities in sub-Saharan Africa, there are significant weaknesses in the programmes offered by many of the academic institutions, and many are simply unable to meet global standards (IBM Communications, 2013). Africa requires investment for capability development in various aspects, from research, design and production, to the marketing processes that relate to innovation (Lorenz, 2016). Lorenz (2016) argues that these constraints are further exacerbated in Africa by the low-income settings of many countries in the region.

Other critical constraints within the continent relate to governance and the lack of access to risk capital. Iizuka et al. (2015) argue that Africa has weaknesses embedded in governance systems. The result is that innovation policy-making lacks coherence, consistency and the necessary long-term commitment. Additionally, the lack of coherence in policy across national, regional and continental levels is problematic. This does not allow for the necessary regional cooperation and collaboration. The lack of access to capital is a common and pressing challenge across the innovation ecosystems in Africa. While there is an increasing flow of investment into Africa, it is not enough. The investment flows into the continent are concentrated mainly in Kenya, Nigeria and South Africa. The result is a lack of risk capital for scaling up innovations across the continent (Adesida et al., 2018). The challenge of funding is not only at the enterprise level but also affects the ecosystems. Investment in building the various elements of the innovation ecosystems has been far lower than needed.

A pre-pandemic innovation dataset

Two datasets were analysed to gain direct insights into the pre-pandemic innovation ecosystems with respect to the challenges experienced by start-ups. These datasets came from the African Innovation Summit (AIS) and the World Health Organization (WHO), the source being the data of the application from their open innovation competitions held in 2018 and 2019, respectively.

The call by AIS was part of its programme to select 50 start-ups to showcase their innovations during the 2018 Summit. The call focused on start-ups with a minimum viable product (MVP) or innovation ready to scale that focused on addressing the challenges facing African countries. The AIS used the opportunity to collect data from applicants. Over 500 African start-ups responded to the call, covering 49 countries. Of the applicants, 21% were MVPs, while the ready segment represented 18%. Key sectors represented included: healthcare, food security and agriculture, energy, water and sanitation, governance, education, ICT and financial.

The WHO call followed the same approach but focused on innovations in the health sector. Over 2,000 start-ups participated in the call by WHO, and applications were received from 81 countries. Of the applicants, 18% were MVPs, while the ready to scale segment represented 19%. Key sectors represented included: healthcare, non-profit, technology, academia, manufacturing, research, consulting, service, governance and pharmaceuticals.

Both the WHO and AIS calls were managed by the same team using similar platforms. The overlap of content and fields of the datasets allowed for their combination into a singular database. The merged pre-pandemic dataset totalled 3,052 unique data records, with data covering solutions from 83 different countries in total. The data from this combined source were categorised through a qualitative coding method and further analysed to collate a baseline on the main obstacles faced by start-ups in African innovation ecosystems. Figure 2 indicates the relative representation of the sectors in the pre-pandemic dataset.

Figure 2: Activity of sectors within start-ups in the African innovation ecosystems from pre-pandemic dataset

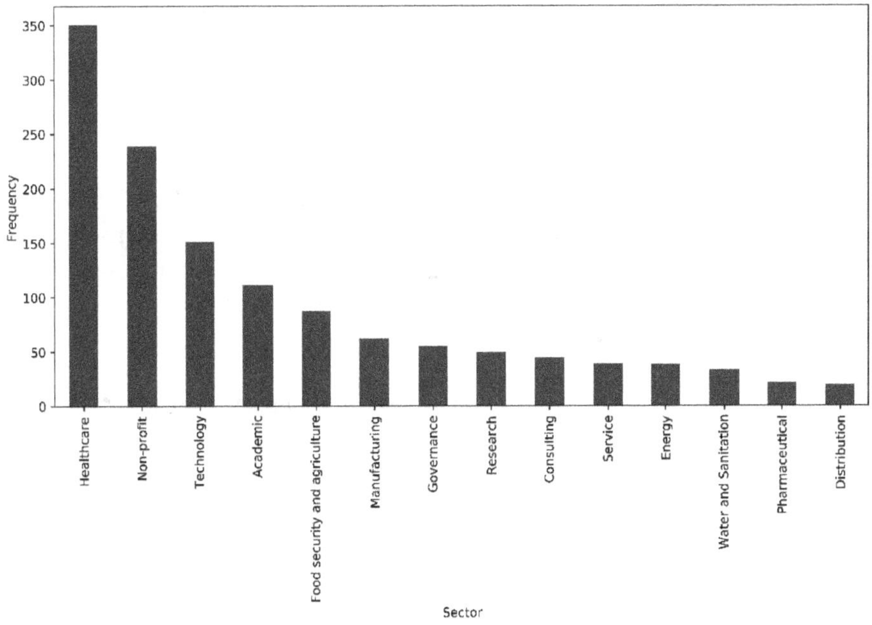

Source: Authors' own.

The data indicated high activity in the healthcare, non-profit and technological[2] sectors. This may be partly attributed to the relatively larger WHO dataset, which focused on health, resulting in a combined dataset in which health emerges as the dominant innovation sector among the start-ups. However, the AIS dataset also highlighted a significant amount of activity in the health sector, as well as within the food security sector

The findings highlighted Nigeria as a major hub of activity in the start-up innovation space in Africa. This is also corroborated by Kazeem (2019), who lists Nigeria as having the most tech hubs in Africa in 2019. While the activity in the ten most active countries correlates well between the two datasets, the only exception is Rwanda which is significantly better represented on the AIS dataset than the WHO dataset. This can partly be explained by the fact that the AIS in 2018 was held in Rwanda. There is also an acknowledgement

---

2   Enterprises that categorised themselves as part of the technology sector typically produce software applications.

of Rwanda's emerging role as a major innovation actor on the continent (Forbes Africa, 2018; Kazeem, 2019). Overall, the AIS and WHO data appear to share the same kind of breakdown in terms of countries and sectors. In terms of which countries were fostering the most innovations, the dataset indicates that Nigeria is leading the way in cultivating a stronger innovation environment, followed by Kenya, Uganda, Tanzania and South Africa. This would be expected given that Nigeria and South Africa are the biggest economies on the continent (AfDB, 2020), and Nigeria is the most populous country in Africa. Kenya, with its famed mobile tech innovations (including M-Pesa), is not a surprise as a leading country in the African innovation scene. Uganda and Tanzania are also witnessing significant growth in their innovation spaces, with fast-growing hubs and start-ups.

Figure 3: Activity of start-ups (by country) within the African innovation ecosystems in the pre-pandemic dataset

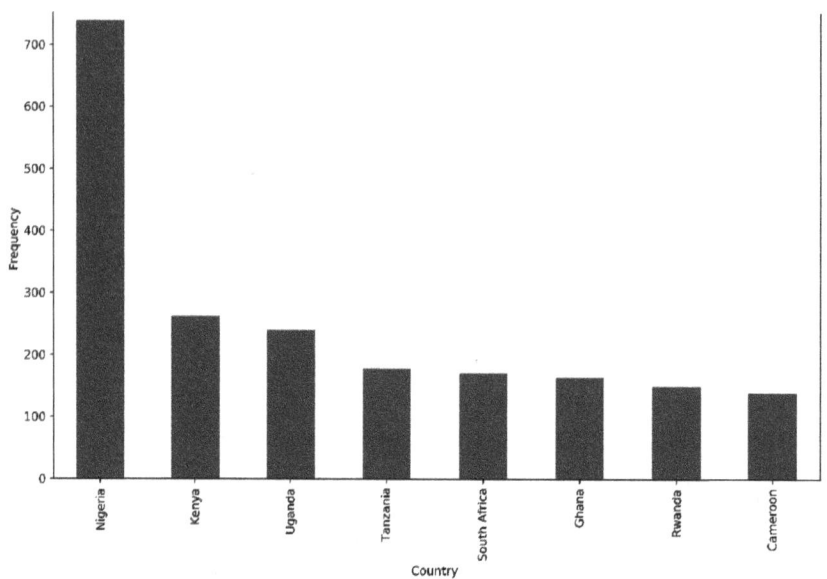

Source: Authors' own.

Figure 4 depicts the obstacles faced by African start-up innovators from the pre-pandemic dataset. Based on the rankings, the main obstacles to innovation in Africa identified were insufficient resources, lack of investors, lack of financial access, technical expertise, poor stakeholder buy-in, requirements for partners, weak governance and poor infrastructure. The

Figure 4: Ranking of the frequency of obstacles that are experienced in initiatives in Africa from the pre-pandemic dataset

[Bar chart showing frequency of obstacles in descending order: Resources (~610), Investors (~525), Finance Access (~510), Technical Expertise (~470), Stakeholder Buy-In (~290), Partnerships (~270), Governance (~245), Infrastructure (~210), Marketing And Publicity (~145), Socio-Political/Ethno-Religious (~115), Data/Analytics (~100), Logistics (~90). X-axis: Obstacle. Y-axis: Frequency.]

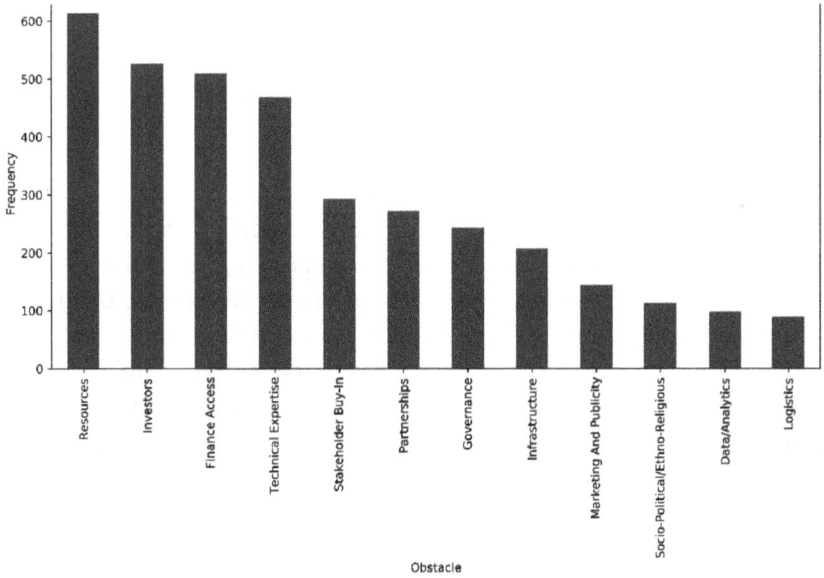

Source: Authors' own.

resources category includes new or additional manufacturing facilities, equipment, materials, manpower and land, whilst the infrastructure category is about the requirement of improving access to basic necessities like water and electricity, better road and transportation systems, as well as improving the technology infrastructure landscape.

Though it ranks lower, the data/analytics or the information sector category requires close attention in the context of an emerging Fourth Industrial Revolution. Improvements in this category are tied to improvements in the other categories. For example, improving financial access, investment, mentorship, resources and digital infrastructure is likely to reduce the obstacles posed by data/analytics. This dependence may explain why it ranks lower than the other main categories.

The socio-political/ethno-religious obstacle identified in the pre-pandemic dataset may also require closer inspection. This issue encompasses how culture and religious beliefs, political instability, linguistic barriers and a lack of trust in technology can impact the innovation ecosystems (Magezi, 2015). Many innovators are looking for methods to help foster trust in innovations by their consumers. Figure 4 is an indicator of the main to medium rankings of the challenges identified in the pre-pandemic dataset. Worth noting is the fact that bureaucracy was identified as an obstacle but was indicated as a lesser challenge than logistics.

Methodology: Studying innovation in Africa amid the response to the pandemic

Innovation catalysed

The advent of the pandemic has stimulated innovation in Africa and has created opportunities to harness emerging technologies. There were innovative solutions in the creation of new products, processes, business models, the adoption of emerging technologies, as well as the leveraging of established technologies. These solutions have emerged to directly tackle the pandemic, as demonstrated in the health sector or are indirect consequences of policy regulations used to mitigate and control the spread of the disease. More than 120 health technology innovations developed in Africa that were used to combat the pandemic (WHO Africa, 2020).

According to the WHO Africa (2020), Africa innovated significantly in the fields of applied disease surveillance, contact tracing, treatment and other healthcare spheres. From all the technology innovations worldwide that were aimed at the pandemic, Africa represents 12.8% (WHO Africa, 2020). Some of the noteworthy innovations were re-purposing drones, face shields, hand sanitiser, semi-automated hand-washing machines, reusable face masks, diagnostic testing kits (AI Chatbots and diagnostics robots), oxygen delivery products (respirators), e-commerce platforms and virus trackers (United Nations Development Programme [UNDP], 2020a, 2020b, 2020c, 2020d, 2020e). It should also be noted, though, that innovations were happening in the fields of technology in telemedicine, information and communication technologies (ICTs), artificial intelligence (AI), robotics, even prior to the start of the pandemic (UNDP, 2020a, 2020b, 2020c, 2020d, 2020e) – so it is an augmented rather than a new phenomenon.

The study informants

The primary data sources were not constrained to any specific actor within the innovation ecosystem. However, the data sources primarily represented innovators, start-ups and technology hubs (self-defined as such). These data enable the identification of some of the challenges and obstacles faced by the African innovation ecosystem. Start-ups and small businesses face particular resource bottlenecks in the ecosystem, which means that they face considerably more problems than other ecosystem actors (Jackson, 2021).

In the largely low- and middle-income African continent of nations, it is argued that the roles of start-ups are even more critical as they count as 'engines' for innovation (Doruk and Söylemezoğlu, 2014). Start-ups play a significant role in innovation ecosystems as they can have the ability to solve several of Africa's endemic challenges due to their way of bringing new thinking and solutions to financial inclusion, e-health, market access, etc. (Moore, 2019). Start-ups can solve critical challenges for various actors in the ecosystem from the private sector, government, civil society, as well as stimulate economic growth (Moore, 2019).

A new pandemic-era innovation survey
The primary dataset regarding changes experienced in African innovation ecosystems due to pandemic was obtained through the use of a rapid online survey that was developed by the authors using Google Forms and deployed under the AIS banner. The target population was innovators and technology and innovation hub actors in Africa identified through AIS, and the survey was distributed both online through email and by mobile phone via WhatsApp. The main database of contacts comprised the contacts from the AIS and WHO databases (approximately 2,500 unique email contacts).

The aim of the survey was to gather data from actors in innovation ecosystems around Africa with respect to new experiences, observed differences in practices, and possible emerging recommendations since the advent of the pandemic. There were five main areas of enquiry in the survey:

1. The effect of the pandemic on the challenges facing African innovation ecosystems.
2. The effect of virtualisation on African innovation ecosystems.
3. Practice changes due to the pandemic (except for virtualisation).
4. Policy changes due to the pandemic.
5. Recommendations and opportunity areas.

The survey was conducted in October 2020 and was shared with the list of email addresses of the responders in the pre-pandemic dataset. It was also extended through networks to relevant innovation communities. There were 96 valid responses to the survey (out of 103 submissions) by actors who were active across 37 countries. The most represented country in the survey was Nigeria, followed closely by Kenya, as indicated in Figure 5.

Figure 5: Countries in which survey respondents operate*

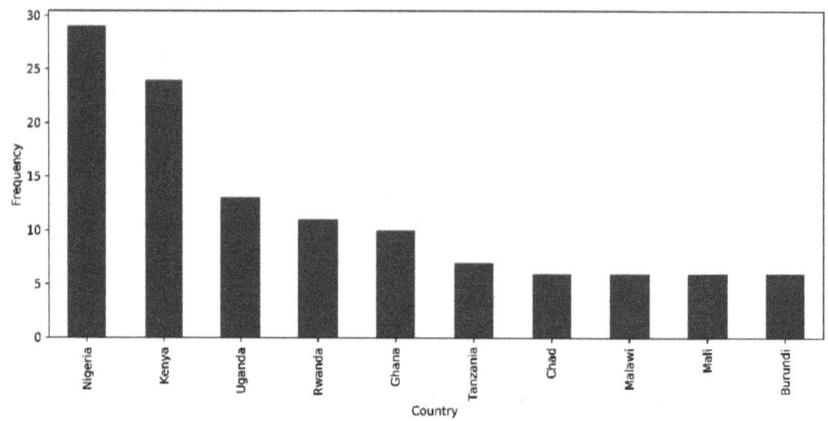

* The data were analysed through coding to develop additional fields of context based on the open questions in the survey.
Source: Authors' own.

The number of unspecified countries, as well as the under-representation of South Africa, were noted.

One of the main biases in the data is self-selection bias as the respondents chose to respond to the survey, which was only available online and in the English language. This implies a probable bias towards English-speaking, more formal innovators. As the survey was distributed to the lists collected through the AIS and WHO processes, this may also introduce a bias into the type and networks of the respondents, in particular and likely skewed towards health and technological innovations.

Findings: Comparative experiences

From the data obtained from the rapid survey and pre-pandemic dataset we aim to explore the differences between the two periods as we sought to understand the effects of the pandemic on African innovation ecosystems. The survey data reflected actor experiences (negative and positive) with existing obstacles, as well as the impact of the adoption of new practices. The survey also gathered information on what policy changes had affected the innovation ecosystems and where there were opportunities for actors to effect positive lasting change in African innovation ecosystems.

The following sections expound on which policies had the greatest impact on the innovation ecosystems and how obstacles and practices changed to adapt to the new conditions. The recommendations and opportunities of actors were analysed to determine where underlying patterns could be used to guide policy recommendations.

Policy changes due to the pandemic identified from the survey

The survey elicited responses on government policy changes or regulations that impacted African innovation ecosystems during the pandemic. These were shown to have been lockdowns, social distancing, travel ban restrictions, mitigation and control measures to prevent infections, relief funds and subsidies, easier access to loans, tax reductions, online education support and reduction in electricity costs. This is confirmed by Ngomsi et al. (2020), who refer to similar interventions by governments throughout Africa. These policy changes were necessary to contain the spread of the pandemic and to limit the economic downfall that ensued. These measures were the drivers that enhanced the use of practices like virtualisation and other digital technologies and drove the local manufacture of medical equipment.

Changing obstacles to innovation and scaling

In order to provide a substantive basis for the analysis of the survey data, a systemic categorisation methodology was applied to categorise the nature of the changes to the African innovations ecosystems caused by the pandemic.

Systemic categorisation methodology: The categorisation of changes as systemic or non-systemic was done according to a three-component model (Lomax, 2019). Effectively the following questions were asked:

1. Was there a change to the operations of the innovation ecosystems?
2. Was the resilience or adaptive capacity of the system improved?
3. Was the change driven (instigated or significantly accelerated) by the pandemic?
4. Is the change sustainable in light of a post-pandemic future?

These questions apply the three-component model (Lomax, 2019) that identifies the three key components as indicators of whether or not there was a change, whether the change improved the resiliency or capability of the system, and how strong the links between the change in the system and the cause of the change are. In summary, the aim was to identify which changes improved the ecosystems and are sustainable in a post-pandemic environment.

Figure 6: Change categorisation flow chart

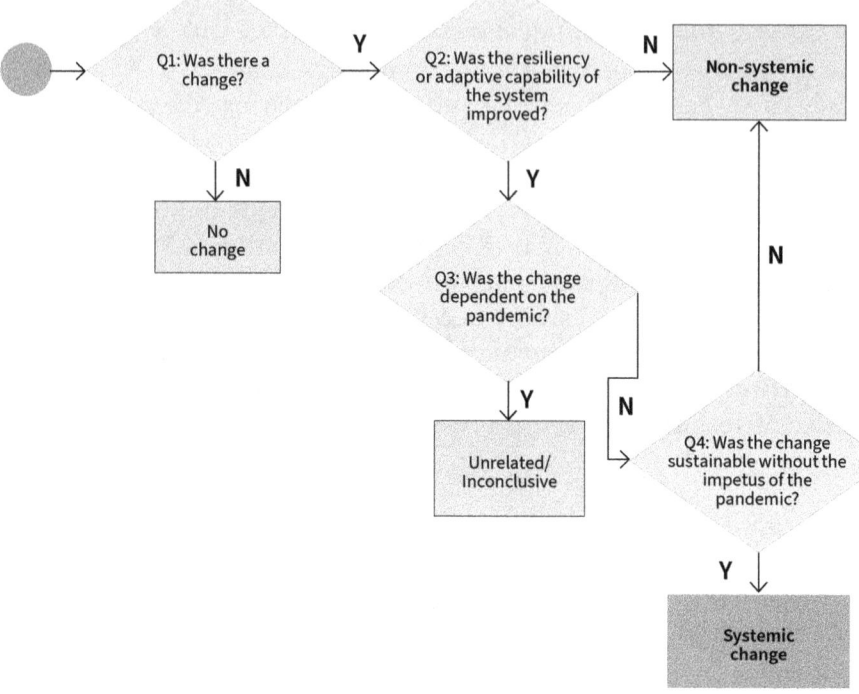

Figure 6 indicates the process followed in categorising the changes as systemic or non-systemic. These four questions will be referred to as Q1, Q2, Q3 and Q4 as labelled and are used to determine whether a change is systemic or transient. A change is only categorised as systemic if all four questions have a positive response.

Survey summary on changes to obstacles: The survey on changes in African innovation ecosystems due to the pandemic sought to determine which of these obstacles had led to positive or negative shifts in the ecosystem, if any. Figure 7 illustrates the results from the survey regarding changes to obstacles in African innovation ecosystems. The left-most bar represents the frequency with which an obstacle was identified in the pre-pandemic dataset. In contrast, the red and green bars respectively indicate relative deterioration of an obstacle and relative improvement of an obstacle.

Access to finance: According to the survey responses, access to finance

Figure 7: Changes to obstacles in African innovation ecosystems from the pre-pandemic dataset compared to the pandemic-survey dataset

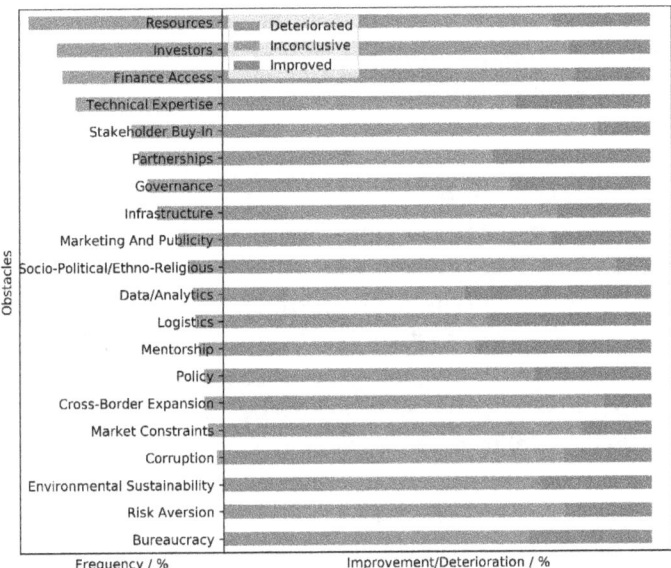

Note: Based on the survey – 'Changes to the African Innovation Ecosystem in the age of COVID-19'. Data collected between 2020-10-09 and 2020-10-25. 'Section 1: The Effect of COVID-19 on the Challenges Facing the African Innovation Ecosystem'.
Source: Authors' own.

was the challenge that became more difficult for the highest number of innovators, with about 50% of respondents indicating that financial access had become more difficult to attain. This was likely due to several factors that existed during the pandemic. For instance, the lockdown and social distancing protocols that were popular responses (OECD, 2020) simultaneously created economic conditions for profits to decrease across entire markets (Stats SA, 2020) and increased competition for the few funding activities that were available. This double-barrelled effect on the operating finances of any enterprise were experienced practically as a decrease in access to finances, and the smaller operators (which is the majority, given that most innovations are from start-ups and SMEs) were disproportionately affected (Kalemli-Ozcan et al., 2020; Stats SA, 2020). The pandemic produced numerous funding opportunities to support innovation practices (GDC, 2020; Golubski and Heitzig, 2020). However, these initiatives appeared mostly to be pandemic-related and therefore yielded a negative response to Q4 (sustainability), indicating that these were non-systemic changes to the innovation landscape. The availability of finances for innovation in Africa was a pre-existing condition, and the strain placed on all economies by the pandemic simply exacerbated the financing issue that is endemic to the innovation ecosystems in Africa, and it is likely to continue to be an important issue for the foreseeable post-pandemic future.

Corruption: The second most identified issue that became more of a hurdle in the course of responses to the pandemic was corruption. Though the pre-pandemic dataset did not indicate corruption as a major obstacle, literature indicated that legal systems were a factor that hinders innovation in Africa (McKinney, 2016). Corruption is an endemic problem to the existing African ecosystems, and while further opportunities for corrupt behaviour were likely facilitated by the responses to the pandemic, the corruption was not caused by the pandemic. In terms of the categorisation model, Q1 (whether there is a change) is inconclusive or negative, indicating that there was no change to the system due to the pandemic.

Market access: Another set of obstacles identified as most affected by the pandemic, according to the survey, were market constraints/access and logistics. The types of policies implemented to combat the pandemic exacerbated these problems. They were significantly worsened in the first two years of the pandemic due to the closing of borders, lockdowns, etc. (OECD, 2020). The impact on these issues gradually decreased as policies began to return back to their previous states. These changes were categorised as non-systemic as they did not improve the resiliency/capacity of the system (Q2) and were not sustainable in a post-pandemic environment (Q4).

These issues also showed some positive effects, particularly with regard to logistics. The improvement could have been due to the accelerated adoption of technologies such as e-commerce and the digitalisation of logistics (Jackson, 2020; UNDP, 2020a). The positive movement seen in the market constraints and logistics space was systemic according to the categorisation methodology, as there was a confirmed change that improved the adaptive capacity of the ecosystem that proved sustainable in a post-pandemic environment. In the pre-pandemic dataset, marketing, logistics and market constraints were identified as issues. However, they were not among the top five problems mentioned.

Partnerships: Partnerships were also negatively impacted during the pandemic. This was likely due to partners being preoccupied with the effects of the pandemic on their own operations. This is classified as a non-systemic change, as it was not beneficial to the system (Q2) and was not likely to be sustained beyond the pandemic (Q4). An interesting insight was that partnerships actually improved as well during the pandemic; partners were forced to improve their relationships in many cases in order to better weather the conditions induced by the pandemic on the innovation ecosystems. The positive changes in innovation ecosystems regarding partnerships, particularly in respect of improved communications, are systemic as there is a change that has sustainable benefits.

Data/analytics: The obstacle to innovation related to 'data and analytics' was identified as improving the most during the pandemic, which was corroborated by the literature (Liu, 2020). The pandemic had multiple effects on the data, analytics and artificial intelligence space, one of these being that decisions concerning responses to the pandemic need to be made quickly and accurately, which had increased the demand for data and analysis (Rao and Butterfield, 2020). Another possibly larger effect was due to the lockdown and social distancing protocols (OECD, 2020) used by governments to contain and slow the spread of the pandemic. The social distancing policies necessitated the use of technologies to maintain operations of business and government. Examples of this were the tracking and tracing systems for identifying spread vectors for the pandemic; this produced an enormous amount of data that needed to be analysed in order to warn potential carriers and those infected by the virus. This created an environment where data was generated en mass, and there was a primary drive to optimise business processes and operations, and a data-rich, resource-constrained environment in which the value of data science was readily observable (Some, 2020). The technologies and practices used were not novel; however, the adoption of these technologies was accelerated by the pandemic. This shift in practice towards data and analytics was one that is systemic as it had positive benefits to the resilience and adaptive capacity of the ecosystem while also being sustainable once the pandemic and its responses had passed.

Technical expertise: The obstacle of technical expertise was indicated as having both improved and deteriorated during the pandemic. The sudden need for technical expertise led to both a surge in technical expertise as well as a shortage. Another explanation for improved technical expertise was the widespread use of e-learning (Jackson, 2020) to facilitate education. The shift in the ecosystems towards more technical work and knowledge indicated that the requirements and technical knowledge are a systemic change that will persevere post-pandemic was a clear shift to higher demand and availability of technical skills, which improved the capacity of the ecosystem.

Bureaucracy: In the pre-pandemic dataset, bureaucracy was identified as an obstacle to the innovation ecosystems. However, it was ranked lower compared to the other identified obstacles. It is interesting to note that bureaucracy garnered more attention in the survey responses. Bureaucracy seems to have had both a positive and negative perception from the survey. There was a necessary increase in bureaucracy after the start of the pandemic, as a number of procedures and permits were put into place in order to enact the various response plans (OECD, 2020). This meant that the pandemic directly created more bureaucratic processes to be followed. The other effects of the pandemic included virtualisation and data analysis (Some, 2020), which led to improved tools to manage and administer the various processes. This likely gave mixed impressions to the various actors within the innovation ecosystems. While the procedures created due to due to the pandemic were non-systemic as they will not be sustainable in the post-pandemic environment (Q4), the improvements to the bureaucratic processes are systemic as they improved the resilience of the ecosystem while being sustainable.

Stakeholder buy-in: In the pre-pandemic dataset, stakeholder buy-in was identified as a significant obstacle to innovation ecosystems in Africa; this would be customers, investors and other ecosystem actors. The survey indicated that there were both positive and negative changes to stakeholder buy-in during the pandemic. According to the categorisation model, the buy-in was systemic as the system became more resilient and could be sustained. The survey suggested that digital buy-in increased due to changes in the environment because of the pandemic and the value that was realised from these technologies. The survey also indicated higher acceptance of technology among actors and customers. Buy-in can be thought of as a major change as all of the other changes in practices and obstacles were simply a matter of buying into a previously existing practice or technology. This systemic change in the view of the technologies used is something that will survive past the policies and responses to the pandemic itself and can be used to develop new innovative products and services.

Infrastructure: The survey indicates that infrastructure had become more critical but less of an obstacle. Infrastructure was identified in the pre-pandemic dataset as being an obstacle to innovation, which aligns with the literature (McKinney, 2016). The shift to using digital technologies during the pandemic restrictions led to higher requirements on electricity distribution and internet connectivity infrastructures which created problems for underserved areas, hence infrastructure became more of an issue (Chinye-Nwoko et al., 2020; Ndonga, 2012). However, the use of these same technologies allowed for others to overcome some of their infrastructural challenges. There are major infrastructural hurdles on the African continent, and the pandemic has highlighted some of those deficiencies while forcing innovation and behavioural change to work around these shortfalls. The permanent nature of infrastructure means that while the lack of infrastructure was a systemic obstacle, there were no systemic changes to infrastructure or its lack.

Obstacle change summary: Table 1 summarises the changes to the obstacles in the innovation ecosystems for small businesses and start-ups.

Table 1: Systemic categorisation model obstacle change summary

Changes in innovation ecosystem obstacles	Q1	Q2	Q3	Q4	Result
Access to Finance					
Funding opportunities	Y	Y	Y	N	Non-systemic change
Corruption	Y	Y	Y	Y	No change
Market Access					
e-commerce	Y	Y	Y	Y	Systemic change
Lockdowns	Y	N	Y	N	Non-systemic change
Partnerships					
Distracted partners	Y	N	Y	N	Non-systemic change
Improved communications	Y	Y	Y	Y	Systemic change
Data/Analytics					
Technology buy-in	Y	Y	Y	Y	Systemic change
Technical expertise	Y	Y	Y	Y	Systemic change
Bureaucracy					
Additional policies	Y	N	Y	N	Non-systemic change
Digitised practice	Y	Y	Y	Y	Systemic change
Stakeholder buy-in	Y	Y	Y	Y	Systemic change
Infrastructure	N	N	N	N	No change

Y represents a 'Yes' response and N a 'No'. Source: Authors' own.

Opportunities and suggestions

The survey elicited responses from many innovators around Africa with respect to solutions and recommendations for the future post-pandemic era. Among themes that emerged were suggestions that policies supportive of small and medium enterprises need to be developed within the African innovation ecosystems; the need to recognise and support developments in the virtualisation of processes and services, including for e-commerce, telemedicine, and other digital and ICT technologies; as well as the local manufacturing of products that are usually imported.

Small and medium enterprises are especially vulnerable during an economic crisis since they generally do not have access to as many resources as larger entities to adapt to changing conditions (International Trade Centre, 2020). The survey responses corroborate that small enterprises required assistance to survive the pandemic's economic climate through funding, technical expertise and mentorships. Furthermore, suggestions were made about improving the digital infrastructure footprint, digital literacy, education, technical expertise and addressing privacy matters in order to improve the buy-in and development of virtualisation of processes and services across Africa. Also, Africa would have to adopt better systems to increase resilience in handling future crises.

Innovation practices adopted in the age of the pandemic

The survey gathered information regarding changes in practices in the innovation ecosystems due to responses to the pandemic. Figure 8 outlines which changes in practice were experienced, and it was observed that, unsurprisingly, virtualisation was the most common change that occurred in the ecosystems, followed by online marketing and changes in operational strategy. The majority of changes identified by the respondents were correspondingly in the adoption of digital technologies, and this was corroborated by literature (Ajadi, 2020; Jackson, 2020; UNDP, 2020a; UNDP, 2020e).

In general, the virtualisation of operations and services has become an ubiquitous change with the advent of the pandemic (Soto-Acosta, 2020). According to the survey, virtualisation was the most significant change in practice, and the use of telemedicine, e-learning, and e-commerce was a subset of the virtualisation phenomenon. However, while these aspects appeared to be the most relevant to the innovators in start-ups and small businesses in Africa, virtualisation is a broader process that involves the movement of work processes to internet-based infrastructure, as well as remote work and attendance (e.g. for meetings), especially for knowledge workers. Figure 9

Figure 8: Changes observed in African innovation ecosystems

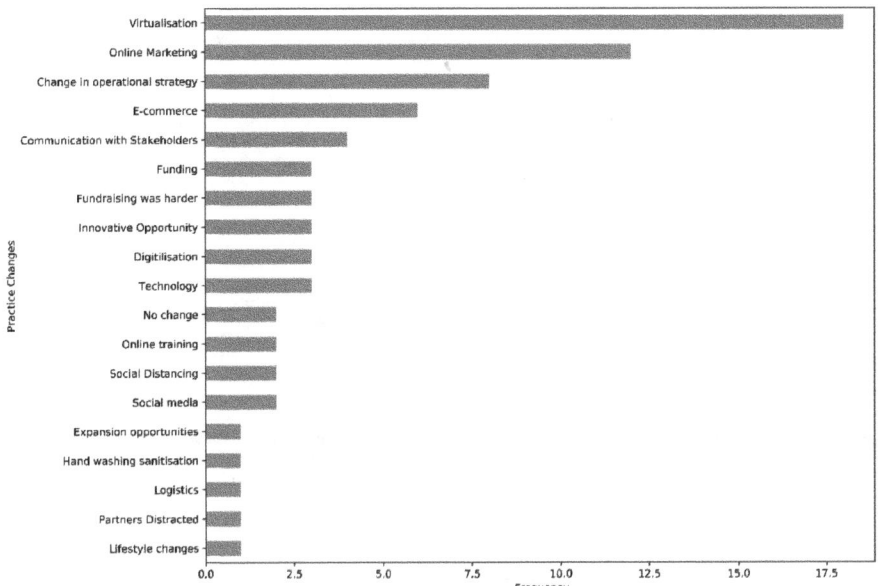

Notes: (1) Difference between 'Funding' and 'Fundraising got harder': Respondents who were being more general about changes to financing availability or methods responded under funding while respondents being more emphatic about non-availability of finance specifically are fundraising was harder. (2) 'No change' represents respondents who did not feel that there were any changes that they could observe in the innovation ecosystems.

Source: Based on survey 'Changes to the African Innovation Ecosystem in the age of COVID-19'. Data collected between 2020-10-09 and 2020-10-25. 'Section 3: The Effect of COVID-19 on the Practices within the African Innovation Ecosystem'.

depicts participant innovators' observations on the positive or negative impacts of virtualisation on African innovation ecosystems.

The responses to the survey indicate that the virtualisation of activities had improved the availability of partnerships, mentorships, technical expertise and marketing whilst also negatively impacting access to finance, logistics, bureaucracy, governance and infrastructure. Virtualisation requires a distributed and well-maintained technological network – which reinforces the need for adequate digital infrastructure. There appears to be a paradoxical view of how data and analytics were viewed through virtualisation. This could be attributed to the availability of technical resources to work with the large amount of data that virtualisation creates; if there had been sufficient technical resources, then there would have been a positive impact on the analytics. Governance and bureaucracy are ongoing problems as identified in the pre-pandemic datasets. The evolution of new systems, while making some aspects easier, may make systems more complex until integrated correctly with existing systems. On the

Figure 9: The effect of virtualisation on obstacles in African innovation ecosystems

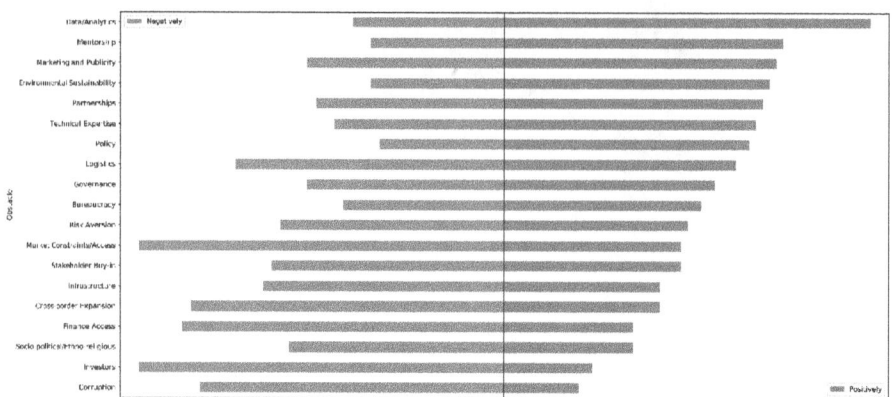

Source: Based on the survey – 'Changes to the African Innovation Ecosystems in the age of COVID-19'. Data collected between 2020-10-09 and 2020-10-25. 'Section 2: Virtualisation and the African Innovation Ecosystems'.

surface, there does not appear to be a reason why virtualisation would have negatively impacted logistics and corruption. For those who had not yet virtualised their services, virtualisation could have been seen as creating logistical problems for their product distribution and services as they would be reliant on physical presence, and if competitors and customers relied on virtualisation, then this could have been viewed as a negative. The issue of corruption is a very complex one, and questions such as 'Did corruption really get worse?' or 'Were the effects of corruption more readily apparent?' arise. In order to do justice to this issue, further research focusing on corruption will be necessary to understand the full origins of this perception.

The survey has shown that access to the marketplace was an endemic issue in African innovation ecosystems and has significantly worsened due to the policy efforts to contain and manage pandemic spread (OECD, 2020). The survey revealed that the logistics and obstacles to accessing markets have become worse, as a direct result of the restrictive policies (such as lockdowns and travel restrictions) applied during the pandemic (United Nations, 2020). E-commerce and online marketing are two of the key areas where practices changed during the pandemic. The use of e-commerce helps address many of the existing problems prevalent in African innovation ecosystems, such as access to the market and the types of resources and infrastructure required (Shahjee, 2015). Some of the more attractive benefits of e-commerce to African innovation ecosystems are the access to a larger marketplace and the decrease in operational costs (storefronts, etc.)

(Shahjee, 2015). The adoption of e-commerce is, however, not a silver bullet without drawbacks; there is a heavy reliance on existing logistic, electrical and communications infrastructure, which, if not adequately developed, cannot allow for the effective adoption of e-commerce (Ndonga, 2012).

The adoption of e-commerce as an adaptation mechanism during the pandemic may have been one driven by necessity, but in the long run, it may result in an enduring e-commerce culture. As stated by Jackson (2020, 1), 'Crisis accelerates change. Many people were forced to try e-commerce due to lack of alternatives, and once we get out of recession, many of them will stick to the new behaviour'. The categorisation model indicated that the change was systemic.

The systematic categorisation, however, also showed changes that did not seem to be systemic (see Table 2). The survey indicated a shift in practice from face-to-face learning to a transition towards e-learning during the pandemic. Literature indicates that e-learning was adopted more widely than before (Jackson, 2020). This increased use of educational technology was a direct response to policies surrounding the pandemic, indicating that the current popularity of e-learning is unlikely to continue. Mpungose (2020) indicates that there were various challenges that hindered disadvantaged students from realising the full potential of e-learning during the pandemic because of the digital divide. This was more prevalent in African countries such as South Africa, where there was a forced transit from face-to-face learning to e-learning (Mpungose, 2020). Our survey indicates that there was an adoption of e-learning in the early years of the pandemic. From the survey and the literature, it can be inferred that the adoption of e-learning was non-systemic as it has challenges that make it unsustainable in a post-pandemic environment (Q4).

The survey also indicated the use of telemedicine as an opportunity area and recommendation. Telemedicine was another area where there was a rapid growth in a short amount of time due to responses to the pandemic. The infectious nature of the coronavirus incentivised the medical community to embrace virtual consultation where there previously had been resistance to change (Jackson, 2020). The frequency of telemedicine increased significantly from a pre-pandemic base; however, in comparison to the total of all medical services that were performed, telemedicine may have constituted a very small portion. It seems reasonable to assume that the vast majority of medical practitioners did not adopt telemedicine as a solution as there were no policy shifts where regular medical services were limited. This supposition makes the immediate future of telemedicine unclear as it appears that the main obstacle to the adoption of telemedicine is regulation or governance, not just buy-in from practitioners (Oluwakemi, 2020). The survey and literature indicate that there was an appetite for telemedicine in the early stages of the pandemic outbreak. However, there was insufficient evidence to indicate that the change was sustainable (Q4); hence the turn to telemedicine with the advent of the pandemic can be considered non-systemic.

Respondents recommended the local manufacture of products as opposed to importation. Jayaram et al. (2020b) pointed to the pandemic as an opportunity for Africa to boost local manufacturing. There were multiple innovations (UNDP, 2020b, 2020d, 2020e) in the category of medical hardware out of necessity, as the medical infrastructure of the entire world was strained due to measures to control coronavirus spread, meaning that the supply of hardware from the usual suppliers was limited. These innovative operations are likely to have a lasting impact in a post-pandemic world if the cost of the products created by these initiatives remains competitive once market forces normalise. Some of the innovations were short term, such as the face shield and personal protective equipment (PPE) products that were in high demand during the height of the pandemic. However, that demand ceased in the post-pandemic period. The short-term innovations were not sustainable (Q4) without the impetus of the pandemic and were non-systemic changes. The longevity of the innovations that were manufactured locally once the stressful conditions of the pandemic ended depended entirely on whether the locally made products are able to compete with foreign imports. However, it is difficult to determine precisely how local innovations will fare in the post-pandemic world.

The categorisation model yielded an inconclusive result since the question of whether this change will be sustainable was not adequately answered. Effectively, some local manufacturing was a systemic change, and some was non-systemic.

The adoption of new technology was a theme that emerged from responses to the survey. There were a few innovations that used drones to perform a variety of tasks. In Cape Verde and Malawi, there were initiatives using drones to deliver light packages of medicine, samples or equipment, as well as disinfecting public areas to help combat the spread of the coronavirus (UNDP, 2020e). These types of applications are likely to continue in a post-COVID-19 environment since the logistical issues in remote areas will remain. Therefore, this type of innovation was categorised as systemic. However, the disinfection innovation was distinctly a demand-based application (non-sustainable Q4) which was a feature of the pandemic and, therefore, a non-systemic change in operations.

Along with the growth of data and analytics during the pandemic, the expansion of robotics, artificial intelligence and machine learning was also promoted. Examples of applications were medical chatbots and robots that assisted with diagnoses (UNDP, 2020c). These applications represented a systemic shift in methodology for medical first contact for a patient and further medical services, as these innovation types will maintain their value in the post-pandemic era. The adoption and dispersal of these technologies was limited by electrical and connectivity infrastructure as well as the basic digital literacy of the target consumers. Another invaluable area was the increase in the availability of various African languages on applications (UNDP, 2020c). This change has future applications in transforming the innovation landscape by addressing existing language barriers in Africa with respect to technology. The advances in artificial intelligence, machine learning and natural processing language were systemic changes used in chatbot applications (UNDP, 2020c) with the positive implication of adapting to use local African languages.

Table 2: Systemic categorisation model practice change summary

Change in innovation ecosystem	Q1	Q2	Q3	Q4	Result
Virtualisation					
e-learning	Y	Y	Y	N	Non-systemic change
Telemedicine	Y	Y	Y	N	Non-systemic change
e-commerce	Y	Y	Y	Y	Systemic change
Local Manufacturing					
Medical supplies	Y	Y	Y	N	Non-systemic change
Medical equipment	Y	Y	Y	N	Inconclusive
Technology					
Drone disinfection	Y	Y	Y	N	Non-systemic change
Drone delivery	Y	Y	Y	Y	Systemic change
Robots/AI applications	Y	Y	Y	Y	Systemic change
AI translation	Y	Y	Y	Y	Systemic change

Notes: Y represents a 'Yes' response and N a 'No'.
Source: Authors' own.

Discussion: Changes and continuities

African innovation ecosystems have undergone disruptions due to the pandemic – some of which highlighted certain pre-existing issues in the ecosystems. However, the pandemic brought about new issues and possibilities.

Prior to the pandemic, a number of key obstacles to innovation in Africa were identified in the pre-pandemic dataset. These obstacles corroborated the findings of existing literature and included resources (be it material or human), investors, access to finance, technical skills, infrastructure, stakeholder buy-in and partnership availability (Adesida et al., 2018).

The pandemic has been a driver of some changes in the African innovation ecosystem. However, one cannot rely on external shocks to catalyse change. There are many areas where the pandemic did not lead to transformative change. Among these pre-existing conditions that did not undergo transformational change were finance and infrastructure, which both continue to be major constraints to effective African innovation ecosystems. These issues were not amenable to quick fixes and will require a multiplicity of instruments (Abraham and Schmukler, 2017). In fact, building and deepening the financial sector in order to ensure that there are alternative funding products to scale innovations in Africa calls for systemic solutions. This must be a key element of African countries' agendas, given that finance has consistently been identified as a binding constraint to innovation (Adesida et al., 2018; Ayalew and Xianzhi, 2020). Addressing the finance challenge will require emphasis on providing incentives to the private sector and individuals to invest in innovation. There is also the need for African governments to serve as catalysts when needed, as well as a need for putting in place a robust policy and regulatory environment to sustainably build the financial sector over the long term. Similarly, the huge infrastructure deficit in most African countries calls for substantial investment over time and a robust policy environment. It is a gap that will require consistency in approach over a period of time. It requires significant resources, both capital and human, to fund, design, and build over time. At the time of data collection, the pandemic was still evolving. Solutions were largely focused on prevention and trying to minimise its impacts. It is therefore logical that the responses have not had any significant impact on the complex challenges of ensuring access to finance or dealing with the huge infrastructure gap in African countries. More importantly, the responses to the pandemic for the most part did not focus on seeking opportunities for a new beginning, new development vision and new policy-making.

For areas where there was systemic change, there is a need to consider implications for the future and policy-making. The pandemic created a favourable environment for virtualisation (Soto-Acosta, 2020), as well as the use of remote technologies due to the need for social distancing. Similarly, it increased the demand for local manufacturing (UNDP, 2020b, 2020d) as the local need for basic necessities such as personal protection equipment (PPE) increased when the pandemic brought global supply chains to a standstill (OECD, 2020).

Among the systemic changes that were observed was the accelerated adoption of virtualisation phenomena, particularly in the areas of remote working, AI, robotics and e-commerce, which were incorporated into the operations of many of the actors in the innovation ecosystem (Soto-Acosta, 2020). The adoption of drones for use in delivery will be a systemic change in logistics, especially in remote areas with poor road infrastructure.

However, the increased local manufacture of medical supplies (PPE, hand sanitiser, etc.) was a reflexive change in the innovation ecosystem; this change resulted from increased demand due to the pandemic and was non-systemic. They are products that did not need to be innovated further when the demand dropped drastically in the post-pandemic era. E-learning was also a non-systemic change and existing challenges still hinder the realisation of e-learning in Africa. Telemedicine was also a non-systemic change as the obstacles to the deployment of telemedicine (Chinye-Nwoko et al., 2020) have not been addressed. For these non-systemic changes, the status quo will likely return in the post-pandemic era.

The local manufacture of medical goods and equipment (respirators, etc.) is uncertain, as future market conditions will govern the longevity of these initiatives as well as the capacity of local producers (if any) to compete with established global manufacturers. The implementation of supportive policies is likely to be key to whether these changes in the innovation ecosystems will become systemic or not.

The survey and subsequent analysis revealed that these obstacles did not experience any systemic change resulting from responses to the pandemic. The changes in practices that became systemic (such as virtualisation and e-commerce) were not sufficient on their own to affect the large shifts needed to strengthen African innovation ecosystems over the long term.

With the understanding that the changes in the innovation ecosystems due to the pandemic are insufficient to fuel the strengthening of the ecosystems, the challenge currently before policy-makers is to find ways to ensure the transient changes become systemic over time. It will be important to implement policies that can extend and encourage the positive impacts of the new practices implemented during the pandemic.

The findings of the study lead us to a series of recommendations, including policy proposals. The focus of the recommendations is on addressing the constraints that continue to hinder innovation in Africa, as well as the need to seize the emerging opportunities resulting from the pandemic to ensure that the transient shifts become systemic as well as transformative.

First, *infrastructure* remains a hindrance, and it makes a major difference as to whether some changes remain transient or become systemic. Key areas include virtualisation and online education as well as telemedicine. As such, there is a need to prioritise infrastructure development, especially with respect to electricity and the internet. Also important will be the need to invest in developing quality educational materials for use in flexible and affordable e-learning across the continent in order to leverage the new technologies for skills development in light of the capacity deficit in critical areas in African countries.

Second, the issue of availability of or access to *finance* has always been the most identified constraint to innovation in Africa. It has become a systemic hindrance for the innovation ecosystems in Africa, and there was no systemic change in the issue of finance discernible from studying the responses to the pandemic. The momentum gained in funding during the pandemic can be made systemic if supported by policy-makers through the development of co-financing models between the public and private sectors and the creation of incentives such as tax rebates to facilitate funding for start-ups (Moore, 2019).

Third, policies that accelerate and improve *digital infrastructure* will allow the innovation ecosystems to maximise the value of the systemic changes have happened within Africa's innovation ecosystems as a result of the pandemic. The digital infrastructure of priority would be electricity and internet coverage (Moore, 2019).

Fourth, a robust educational policy can also contribute greatly to addressing the lack of *technical skills*, which poses significant constraints to innovation and development (Moore, 2019). The availability of the required technical skill is a major obstacle, and much study and analysis are required to develop effective educational policies and incentives that will facilitate the growth of the relevant skills in the innovation ecosystems.

Fifth, the temporality or the non-systemic nature of the changes – especially in manufacturing, online learning and telemedicine – can be addressed through policies. Efforts can be made through policies to attempt to shift the transient changes in manufacturing towards becoming more systemic. There is a need for policies that prioritise *local manufacturing* over imports, such as using fiscal incentives, lower taxation on locally produced goods and building an economic environment that is more business-friendly. The non-systemic changes in telemedicine and e-learning can also be made systemic by formulating more enabling policies and regulatory environments. A general challenge is that the cost of *access to digital systems* may be too high for a significant portion of the population, even if the infrastructure is fully available (Manyuchi and Ouma-Mugabe, 2020). A robust regulatory regime for public utilities is a must to promote access while ensuring economic returns for investors. Governments could also sponsor access to certain basic information or sites to which consumers would have a right to digital platforms for education, public health as well as other essential services.

Conclusion

The study affirms that the pandemic impacted African innovation ecosystems. The pandemic has triggered several innovations to directly respond to the pandemic itself, to the changes in the environment brought about by shifting government policies and regulations, as well as to innovation funding responses to the pandemic.

However, it is argued that it is important to distinguish between long-term systemic changes and shorter-term non-systemic changes. The latter may not be sustainable in post-pandemic conditions but may offer opportunities for purposeful policy attention.

Prior to the pandemic, there was a pre-existing set of endemic obstacles or challenges faced by innovators in African innovation ecosystems (Adesida and Karuri-Sebina, 2013; Adesida et al., 2018). This is supported by the evidence in the primary pre-pandemic dataset as well as confirmed by the existing literature. The new survey demonstrated that virtually all the key ecosystem obstacles still remain in spite of innovations implemented during the pandemic. However, there were systemic changes to some of the identified obstacles within the African innovation ecosystems, such as improvements to partnerships, mentorships, logistics, technical expertise and stakeholder buy-in. This was due to the heightened use of information and communications technology (WHO Africa, 2020) that allowed for effective communication at a distance and helped mitigate some of the difficulties placed on social and economic systems by the social distancing and lockdown protocols during the pandemic.

With the harsh market and economic conditions imposed by the responses to the pandemic, it was necessary to find methods and technologies to allow innovators to weather the storm. Some of these practices have led to systemic changes in the innovation ecosystems, such as the use of technology to perform remote services and communication. The survey and literature identified examples of how such systemic changes could lead to the growth and adoption of e-commerce technologies, drone usage, virtualisation, machine learning, artificial intelligence and natural language processing applications.

The practices deemed as non-systemic that emerged during the pandemic included the local manufacture of products that were in heightened demand during the pandemic, such as hand sanitisers, personal protective equipment, as well as e-learning and telemedicine platforms. Local manufacturing will need to be able to compete with global manufacturers now that demand (and competition) for these products has normalised during the post-pandemic period, and when the globalised competition has kicked into high gear. It is therefore not a given whether the opportunities or practices that were adopted are sustainable. Such transient dynamics may be insufficient on their own to signal significant shifts in the necessary strengthening of African innovation ecosystems (Adesida et al., 2018). However, they can still be leveraged to create improvements in the ecosystems by taking advantage of the opportunities that they represent. This will require purposeful use of policy and regulatory instruments, partnership incentives, and the prioritisation of the development and accessibility of digital infrastructure in order to strengthen the innovative and scale-up capabilities of innovators in Africa.

References

Abraham, F., and Schmukler, S. L. (2017). Addressing the SME Finance Problem. *Research and Policy Briefs*. World Bank. https://documents1.worldbank.org/curated/en/809191507620842321/pdf/Addressing-the-SME-finance-problem.pdf

Adesida, O., Karuri-Sebina, G., and Afonso, T. (2018). *Africa Innovation Summit (AIS), Kigali, 2018 Report*.

Adesida, O., Karuri-Sebina, G., and Resende-Santos, J. (Eds). (2016). *Innovation Africa: Emerging hubs of excellence*. Emerald.

Adesida, O., and Karuri-Sebina, G., (Eds.) (2013). Building innovation driven economies in Africa. *African Journal of Science, Technology, Innovation and Development* 5(1), 1.

AfDB. (2020). *African Economic Outlook 2020: Developing Africa's workforce for the future*. African Development Bank.

Ajadi, S. (2020, 20 July). COVID-19 and West Africa: Six key technology trends driving change. *GSMA*. https://www.gsma.com/mobilefordevelopment/blog/covid-19-and-west-africa-six-key-technology-trends-driving-change/

Anahory, P., and Adesida, O. (2014). *Africa Innovation Summit, Cape Verde, 2014 Report*.

Ashkenas, R. (2020, 16 September). Innovate with urgency — even when there's no crisis. *Harvard Business Review*. https://hbr.org/2020/09/innovate-with-urgency-even-when-theres-no-crisis

Ayalew, M. M., and Xianzhi, Z. (2020). The effect of financial constraints on innovation in developing countries: Evidence from 11 African countries. *Asian Review of Accounting*, 28(3), 273-308. https://doi.org/10.1108/ARA-02-2019-0036

Beech, P. (2020). These new gadgets were designed to fight COVID-19. *World Economic Forum*. https://www.weforum.org/agenda/2020/04/coronavirus-covid19-pandemic-gadgets-innovation-technology/

CCEF (Le Conseillers du Commerce extérieur de la France). (2020). *COVID-19 a Catalyst for Innovation*. https://www.cnccef.org/en/publication/covid-19-a-catalyst-for-innovation

Chinye-Nwoko, F., Effiong, U., and Ani, N. (2020, 28 July). Challenges and opportunities for telemedicine in Africa. *Mail and Guardian*. https://mg.co.za/africa/2020-07-28-challenges-and-opportunities-for-telemedicine-in-africa/

Davies, M. (2020). How will Africa manage the post COVID economy? *World Economic Forum*. https://www.weforum.org/agenda/2020/06/how-africa-manage-post-covid-economy/

Doruk, Ö. T., and Söylemezoğlu, E. (2014). The constraints of innovation in developing countries: Too many barriers to start ups? *10th International Strategic Management Conference*.

Edquist, C. (2001). The systems of innovation approach and innovation policy: An account of the state of the art. *DRUID Conference*, Aalborg, 12-15.

Egbetokun, A. A., Siyanbola, W., and Adeniyi., A. (2007). Indigenous innovation capability in sub-Saharan Africa: A review of the Nigerian situation. *Proceedings of the Fifth International Symposium on Management of Technology*, 1018-1022.

Forbes Africa. (2018). Rwanda: The emerging economy to watch. https://www.forbesafrica.com/economy/2018/12/05/rwanda-the-emerging-economy-to-watch/

Global Distributors Collective. (2020). COVID-19 funding opportunities. https://globaldistributorscollective.org/covid-19-funding

Golubski, C., and Heitzig, C. (2020). Africa in the news: New funding to fight COVID-19 in Africa, Somalia's prime minister voted out, and political updates in Mali and Côte d'Ivoire. *Brookings*. https://www.brookings.edu/blog/africa-in-focus/2020/08/01/africa-in-the-news-new-funding-to-fight-covid-19-in-africa-somalias-prime-minister-voted-out-and-political-updates-in-mali-and-cote-divoire/

Granstrand, O., and Holgersson, M. (2020). Innovation ecosystems: A conceptual review and a new definition, *Technovation*, 90-91, 102098.

Healey, N. (2020). Is there a bright future for telemedicine in a post-COVID world? *Medical Technology*. https://medical-technology.nridigital.com/medical_technology_aug20/telemedicine

IBM Communications. (2013). iHub. https://ihub.co.ke/ihubresearch/jb_BuildingAfricasInnovationEcosystemspdf2013-5-20-08-10-38.pdf

IDS. (2015, 16 February). Ebola and lessons for development. *IDS Practice Paper in Brief*. Institute of Development Studies. https://opendocs.ids.ac.uk/opendocs/bitstream/handle/20.500.12413/5849/ID557%20Online.pdf

International Trade Centre. (2020). *SME Competitiveness Outlook 2020: COVID-19: The Great Lockdown and its impact on small business*. International Trade Centre. https://www.intracen.org/uploadedFiles/intracenorg/Content/Publications/ITCSMECO202 0.pdf

Iizuka, M., Mawoko, P., and Gault, F. (2015). *Innovation for Development in Southern and Eastern Africa: Challenges for promoting ST&I policy*.

Jackson, T. (2020, 9 April). In COVID-19, Africa's tech start-up ecosystems face their gravest challenge to date. *Disrupt Africa*. https://disrupt-africa.com/2020/04/in-covid-19-africas-tech-startup-ecosystems-face-their-gravest-challenge-to-date/

Jackson, D. (2021). What is an innovation ecosystem? https://www.researchgate.net/profile/Deborah_Jackson2/publication/266414637_What_i s_an_Innovation_Ecosystem/links/551438490cf2eda0df30714f.pdf

Jayaram, K., Leiby, K., Leke, A., Ooko-Ombaka, A., and Ying, S. (2020a). Tackling COVID-19 in Africa: An unfolding health and economic crisis that demands bold action. *McKinsey and Company.* https://www.mckinsey.com/featured-insights/middle-east-and-africa/tackling-covid-19-in-africa

Jayaram, K., Leke, A., Ooko-Ombaka, A., and Ying, S. (2020b). Reopening and reimagining Africa. *McKinsey and Company.* https://www.mckinsey.com/featured-insights/middle-east-and-africa/reopening-and-reimagining-africa

Jenal, M. (2020, 26 January). Making sense of 'systemic change'. *Helvetas.org.* https://www.helvetas.org/en/switzerland/how-you-can-help/follow-us/blog/inclusive-systems/making-sense

Kalemli-Ozcan, S., Gourinchas, P.-O., Penciakova, V., and Sander, N. (2020, 25 September). COVID-19 and SME failures. *IMF Working Paper* no. 20/207. International Monetary Fund. https://www.imf.org/en/Publications/WP/Issues/2020/09/25/COVID-19-and-SME-Failures-49753

Kazeem, Y. (2019, 11 July). The explosion of tech hubs across Africa is showing no signs of slowing down. *Quartz.* https://qz.com/africa/1663602/how-many-tech-hubs-are-in-africa/

Liu, S. (2020). Demand for innovation accelerators post-COVID-19 in 2020. *Statista.* https://www.statista.com/statistics/1121625/impact-of-covid-on-innovation-demand/

Lomax, J. (2019). What is systemic change? Three components of a measurable definition. https://www.researchgate.net/publication/332227963_What_is_systemic_change_Three_ components_of_a_measurable_definition

Lorenz, A. E.-A. (2016). Firm-level innovation in Africa: Overcoming limits and constraint. *Innovation and Development.* https://www.tandfonline.com/doi/full/10.1080/2157930X.2016.1224619

Magezi, V. (2015). Technologically changing African context and usage of Information Communication and Technology in churches: Towards discerning emerging identities in church practice (a case study of two Zimbabwean cities). *HTS Theological Studies,* 71. http://www.scielo.org.za/scielo.php?script=sci_arttextandpid=S0259-94222015000300017

Manyuchi, A. E., and Ouma-Mugabe, J. (2020). Unlocking systemic barriers to health innovations for COVID-19 in Africa.

McKinney, Phil. (2016, 23 June). Innovation in Africa: Challenges and opportunities. *Phil McKinney.* https://philmckinney.com/innovation-africa-challenges-opportunities/

McKinsey. (2016, 18 June). Bridging global infrastructure gaps. *McKinsey and Company.* http://www.mckinsey.com/industries/infrastructure/our-insights/bridging-global-infrastructure-gaps

Moore, F. (1996). *The Death of Competition: Leadership and strategy in the age of business ecosystems.* Harper.

Moore, R. (2019). Tech start-ups will support Africa's growth. *Accenture*. https://www.accenture.com/_acnmedia/PDF-105/Accenture-Forbes-Advertorial-Tech-Startups.pdf

Mpungose, C. B. (2020). Emergent transition from face-to-face to online learning in a South African University in the context of the Coronavirus pandemic. *Humanities and Social Sciences Communication, 7*, 113.

Mudombi, S., and Muchie, M. (2014). An institutional perspective to challenges undermining innovation activities in Africa. *Innovation and Development, 4*(2), 313-326.

Muok, B. O., and Kingiri, A. (2015). The role of civil society organizations in low-carbon innovation in Kenya. *Innovation and Development, 5*, 207-223.

Mwiti, L. (2015). Science, technology and innovation in Africa: Not always rosy, but it is about to be. *Mail and Guardian*. http://mgafrica.com/article/2015-03-18-science-technology-and-innovation-in-africanot-always-rosy-but-it-is-about-to-be

Ndonga, D. (2012). E-commerce in Africa: Challenges and solutions. *African Journal of Legal Studies*, 243-268.

Ngomsi, C., Yatta, F., Pozhidaev, D., Kiwala, L., and Ndugwa, R. (2020). *COVID-19 in African Cities: Impacts, responses and policies*. https://www.tralac.org/documents/resources/covid-19/regional/3738-covid-19-in-african-cities-impacts-responses-and-policies-uneca-june-2020/file.html

Nhando, D. (2015, 30 October). 3 key challenges of implementing elearning in Africa. *eLearning Industry*. https://elearningindustry.com/3-key-challenges-implementing-elearning-in-africa

Organisation for Economic Co-operation and Development (OECD). (2020, 7 May). COVID-19 and Africa: Socio-economic implications and policy responses. http://www.oecd.org/coronavirus/policy-responses/covid-19-and-africa-socio-economic-implications-and-policy-responses-96e1b282/

Oluwakemi, S. (2020, 16 September). Africa needs telemedicine to overcome its healthcare challenges. *Africanews*. https://africanews.space/africa-needs-telemedicine-to-overcome-its-medical-challenges/

Oyelaran-Oyeyinka, B., Laditan, G. O., and Esubiyi, A. O. (1996). Industrial innovation in sub-Saharan Africa: The manufacturing sector in Nigeria. *Research Policy, 25*(7), 1081-1096.

Rao, A., and Butterfield, K. F. (2020, 23 July). 3 ways COVID-19 is transforming advanced analytics and AI. *World Economic Forum*. https://www.weforum.org/agenda/2020/07/3-ways-covid-19-is-transforming-advanced-analytics-and-ai/

Saluaudeen, A. (2020, 10 November). This $1 made-in-Africa Covid-19 test kit could revolutionise testing on the continent. *CNN*. https://edition.cnn.com/2020/11/10/africa/senegal-coronavirus-rapid-testing-spc-intl/index.html

Shahjee, R. (2015). The impact of electronic commerce on business organisation. *Scholarly Research Journal, 4*(27). http://oaji.net/articles/2017/1174-1484826380.pdf

Some, K. (2020, 19 July). The COVID-19 effect on data science and data analytics. *Analytics Insight*. https://www.analyticsinsight.net/the-covid-19-effect-on-data-science-and-data-analytics/

Soto-Acosta, P. (2020). COVID-19 pandemic: Shifting digital transformation to a high-speed gear. *Information Systems Management, 37*, 260-266.

Stats SA. (2020). Business impact survey of the COVID-19 pandemic in South Africa. *Statistics South Africa.* http://www.statssa.gov.za/publications/Report-00-80-01/Report-00-80-01June2020.pdf

Thurlow, J. (2020, 14 May). Coronavirus: Lockdowns across Africa creating major economic loss. *The Africa Report.* https://www.theafricareport.com/27774/coronavirus-lockdowns-across-africa-creating-major-economic-loss/

United Nations. (2020, 20 May). *Policy Brief.* https://www.uneca.org/sites/default/files/PublicationFiles/sg_policy_brief_on_covid-19_impact_on_africa_may_2020.pdf

United Nations Development Programme (UNDP). (2020a). E-commerce platform. *Africa Innovates* (32-33). https://reliefweb.int/sites/reliefweb.int/files/resources/Africa%20innovates%20-%2050%20homegrown%20African%20innovations%20tackling%20COVID-19%20%28Compressed%29.pdf

UNDP. (2020b). Ethical hand sanitiser factory. *Africa Innovates* (40-41). https://reliefweb.int/sites/reliefweb.int/files/resources/Africa%20innovates%20-%2050%20homegrown%20African%20innovations%20tackling%20COVID-19%20%28Compressed%29.pdf

UNDP. (2020c). Making hope contagious. *Africa Innovates* (68-69). https://reliefweb.int/sites/reliefweb.int/files/resources/Africa%20innovates%20-%2050%20homegrown%20African%20innovations%20tackling%20COVID-19%20%28Compressed%29.pdf

UNDP. (2020d). Purposeful PPE and facemask. *Africa Innovates* (66-67). https://reliefweb.int/sites/reliefweb.int/files/resources/Africa%20innovates%20-%2050%20homegrown%20African%20innovations%20tackling%20COVID-19%20%28Compressed%29.pdf

UNDP. (2020e). Robotics and drones services. *Africa Innovates* (8-9). https://reliefweb.int/sites/reliefweb.int/files/resources/Africa%20innovates%20-%2050%20homegrown%20African%20innovations%20tackling%20COVID-19%20%28Compressed%29.pdf

Voeten, J. J., and Naudé, A. W. (2014). Regulating the negative externalities of enterprise cluster innovations: Lessons from Vietnam. *Innovation and Development,* 4(2), 203-219.

WHO Africa. (2020). COVID-19 spurs health innovation in Africa. https://www.afro.who.int/news/covid-19-spurs-health-innovation-afric

Appendices

Appendix A: AIS and WHO data analysis

The WHO and AIS innovation datasets revealed the following information about the relative frequency with which different obstacles were encountered in the African innovation ecosystems.

Figure 10: Obstacles to innovation development and scale-up (pre-pandemic dataset)

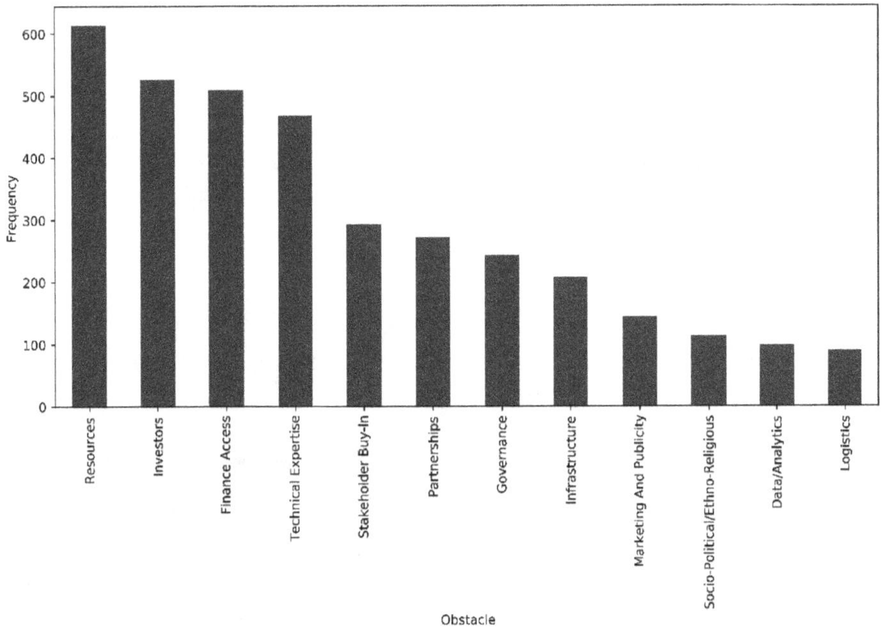

Source: Authors' own.

Appendix B: Changes to the African innovation ecosystem in the age of COVID-19 survey

A survey was performed in order to gauge the responses of various actors in African innovation ecosystems. The data were collected in the time period between 2020-10-09 and 2020-10-25. The survey had five question areas on effects of the pandemic as follows:

Q1) The effect of the pandemic on the challenges facing the African innovation ecosystems.

Figure 11 indicates which obstacles in African innovation ecosystems were exacerbated or alleviated during the pandemic response.

Figure 11: Deterioration and improvements of obstacles in the innovation ecosystems

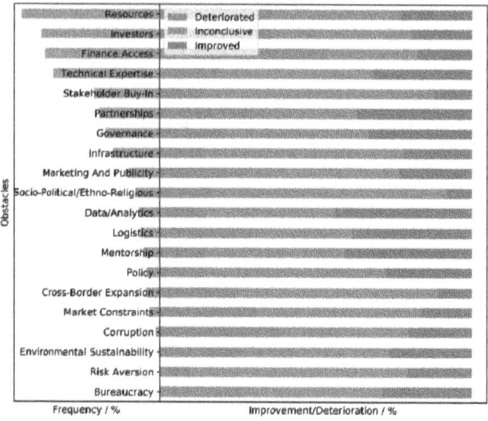

Q2) Virtualisation and African innovation ecosystems.
Figure 12 represents the observations regarding the impact of virtualisation on African innovation ecosystems.

Figure 12: The effect of virtualisation on obstacles in African innovation ecosystems

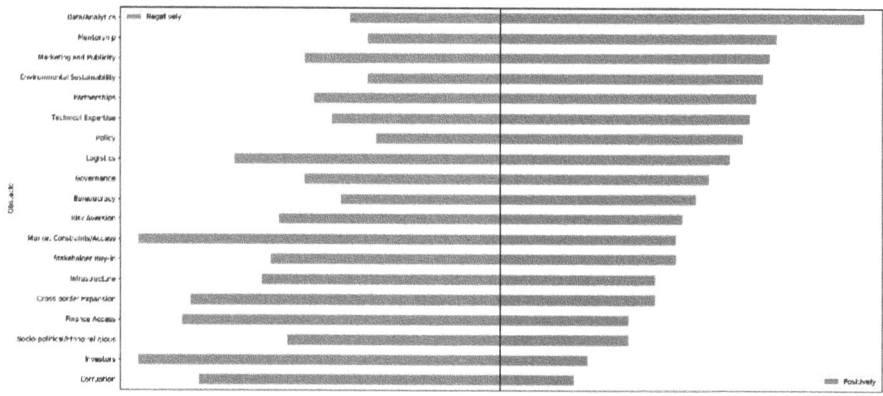

Q3) Practice changes
Figure 13 describes the observations regarding practices and policy on African innovation ecosystems.

Figure 13: Recommendation and opportunity areas

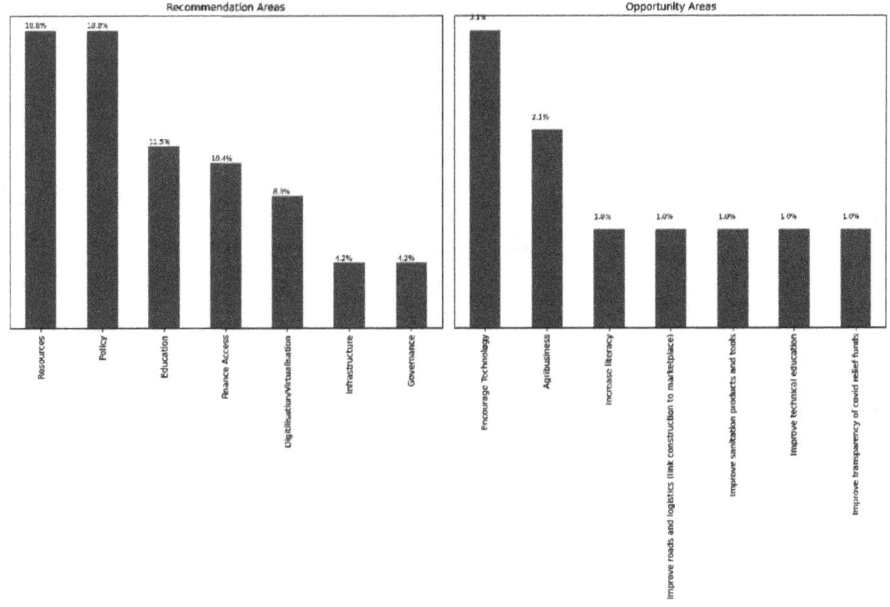

Figure 14: Identified practice changes during the pandemic

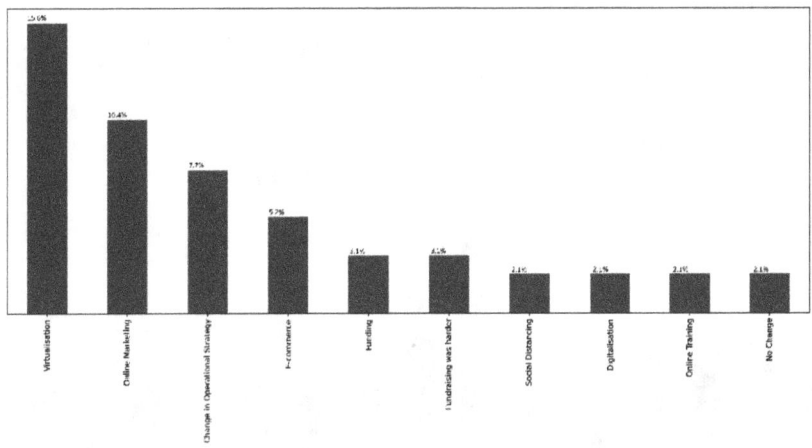

Q4) Policy changes.

Figure 15: Identified policy changes during the pandemic

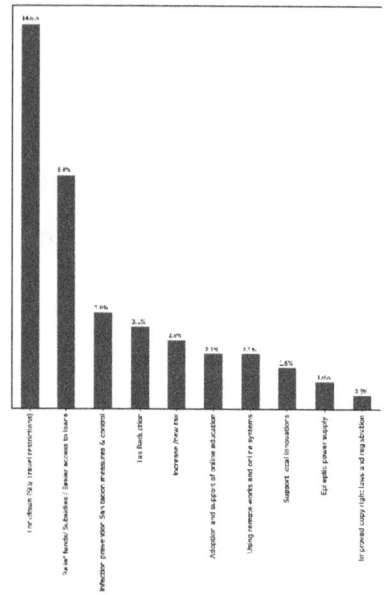

Q5) Recommendations and opportunity areas.

Figure 16 describes the recommendations and opportunity areas of the impact of the pandemic on the opportunity area.

Figure 16: Recommendations and opportunity areas

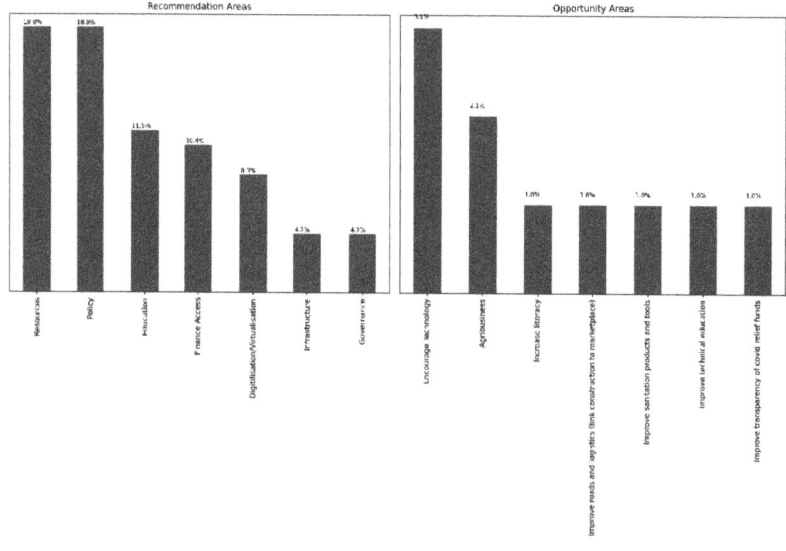

CHAPTER 4

Unlocking Systemic Barriers to Health Innovations in Africa

Albert Edgar Manyuchi and John Ouma-Mugabe

Introduction

The pandemic resulting form the rapid spread of the coronavirus unmasked Africa's ingenuity and innovative potential. Since the outbreak of the pandemic in early 2020, a wide range of innovations – technological, social, organisational, and policy – have emerged across the continent in both public and private sectors. The pandemic also stimulated scientific research in fields such as genomics and a surge of focus on epidemiological studies. Organisations such as the World Health Organization (WHO, 2020) and the European Investment Bank (EIB, 2020) documented or profiled various promising inventions and technologies to address the health dimensions of the pandemic. These inventions and technologies have often been tagged 'African COVID-19 innovations'. However, as we explain in this chapter, many, if not most, of the profiled 'African COVID-19 innovations' are still inventions with potential applications and technologies with the potential of 'entry' or deployment into national innovation systems in general and health systems in particular, but strictly do not qualify to be considered as innovations yet because they have not diffused or spread with social and economic impact or value. Thus, the word 'innovation' in the context of the pandemic has been used loosely by media, non-academic actors, as well as some think tanks and academics. This misled public policy for the pandemic and ignored problems in the innovation process.

This study provides a succinct analysis of different interacting technical, economic, social, policy, regulatory and institutional barriers to the dissemination of the pandemic's innovations. It attempts to answer two related questions: What were the main systemic barriers to the development, diffusion and deployment of innovations to tackle health challenges or aspects of the pandemic in Africa? And, what policy instruments and policy mixes unlocked the barriers and spurred the innovations that helped banish the pandemic from Africa? This chapter is about policy that was employed to unlock the systemic barriers to the diffusion and deployment of technologies and inventions that helped address the health effects of the pandemic. The study places emphasis on policies because the content of policies generally influences the dissemination of innovations. In this chapter, policy instruments refer to measures or actions that governments purposefully put in place to influence innovation processes and activities aimed at addressing health challenges associated with the pandemic.

The chapter is organised as follows: Section 2 provides an overview of the health and socio-economic challenges that the pandemic has caused and then discusses the challenge of innovation in African national health systems. It argues that African countries have tended to create a dichotomy between health and economy, where health is treated as a social sector, and the provision of healthcare is often considered as a social service that burdens the economy. This approach seems aligned to science, technology and innovation (STI) and industrial policy rationales founded on economistic framings such as 'economic competitiveness' and 'economic growth'. It misleads public policy and helps to keep countries' investments in STI and manufacturing misaligned to health security goals or imperatives. The pandemic, hopefully, has changed this and policy-makers in Africa will now appreciate that health and human well-being are foundations of economic competitiveness and security.

The third section outlines the conceptual approach of this study. Drawing on literature on national systems of innovation (NSI) and health innovation systems, the study frames or conceptualises barriers or impediments to innovations to addressing the health aspects of the pandemic as being systemic, embedded and interacting in the social, economic and health systems of nations. It is essential to unlock or remove the systemic and embedded barriers and speed up the diffusion and deployment of emerging innovations. We argue that countries need systemic policy measures supported by improved institutional configurations that are well aligned with each other.

Section 4 briefly presents the methodology and research questions of this study. In this section, the multi-methods of data collection, including in-depth individual interviews and focus group discussions with purposely selected informants and participants, are highlighted. In addition, the validation or quality assurance mechanisms, as well as limitations, are elaborated.

In Section 5, we map innovations for tackling the health aspects or challenges posed by the pandemic. The mapping was largely based on secondary sources, in particular reports by the WHO, the African Union (AU), the European Investment Bank and the media. While we do not claim that our secondary literature review is exhaustive, it is extensive and had the necessary depth to cover the subject under research. And finally, the findings of the study and the recommendations are provided in Sections 6 and 7, respectively.

The pandemic and innovation challenge in Africa

The pandemic arising from the rapid spread of the coronavirus in 2020 was a systemic and transformative crisis that has irreversibly affected health, social, economic and political activities around the world (Mugabe et al., 2020). It undermined prospects of attaining Africa's aspirations articulated in *Agenda 2063*[1] and global SDGs. In 2020, economic growth in Africa was projected to contract by 7.8% in GDP, particularly in small economies, and merchandise exports by 17% (UNCTAD, 2020). On the social front, the pandemic has disrupted social and religious activities, exacerbating mental ill-health and social unrest (Matthewman and Huppatz, 2020). Lockdowns and restrictions on international travel affected the mobility of people and goods, and regional integration and globalisation processes around the world (McNamara and Newman, 2020). The pandemic also widened social and economic inequalities, as more than 30 million school-going children were locked out of education during various lockdowns because they could not access digital learning.

Another formidable challenge posed by the pandemic related to the weakening of African national health systems and the worsening of the already huge burden of disease on the continent. The pandemic

---

[1] See African Union, *Agenda 2063: The Africa We Want*.

overstretched the capacity of most African national health systems. Recent study shows that in most African countries, health systems are relatively weak, as manifested in low budgets for health, poor infrastructure, limited health personnel and poor governance regimes (Mugabe et al., 2020). Few countries have hospitals with functional Intensive Care Units (ICUs) and health workers with specialised skills to treat illnesses associated with cancer, diabetes and other chronic diseases. Shortages of personal protective equipment (PPE), reagents and testing equipment, such as swabs, also plague these institutions.

Overall, the pandemic has disrupted social and economic activities and weakened national health systems. The pandemic may be both a cause and consequence of the fragility of health, socio-economic and ecological systems around the world. However, it offers countries, particularly those on the African continent, unique opportunities to find pathways out of the current health inequalities and the huge burden of disease. Innovation – the introduction and application of 'new' practices, products, processes and institutions (normative and agency types) – have been key in responding to epidemics and pandemics in the past (Niang et al., 2021). Hence, innovation (technological, social and organisational) is critically required for an effective response to pandemic outbreaks such as the coronavirus.

Noteworthy is the fact that the pandemic was a transformative crisis; that is, a crisis that causes positive and negative results as well as direct and indirect changes to people's ways of living. In addition, it was a transformational crisis in the sense that it stimulated a huge surge in political and public attention to the role of innovation in health. It reawakened national and international attention to the role of research and innovation (RandI) in health security. Media and research reports have stressed the importance of building the scientific research and innovation capabilities of countries to respond to pandemics in general and the effects of the coronavirus in particular (Mugabe, 2020). In a 2018 study, Quick (2018) emphasises the urgency of countries building scientific and technological preparedness for future epidemics and pandemics. Overall, building science and innovation capabilities, and perhaps even more important, utilising existing innovation capabilities to respond to the pandemic and future complex crises-related epidemics, need to be considered as part and parcel of countries' long-term efforts to build and/or strengthen their national systems of innovation (NSI) in general and national health systems in particular. This cannot be achieved through ad hoc, short-term, isolated policy interventions that are based on framings of innovation and innovation processes as linear, involving inputs and outputs of R&D (Stone and Lane, 2012). Indeed, innovation is a complex process characterised by nonlinearity and uncertainty, embedded in socio-political and economic contexts that are themselves dynamic (Kline, 1985). Thus innovation was key to ending the pandemic while ensuring that African health systems are strengthened and resilient to future pandemics and disease outbreaks.

In the next section, we outline the conceptual contours guiding this study and then propose a typology of barriers to the pandemic's innovations. The conceptual approach emphasises the systemic nature of both innovation processes and barriers to specific innovations in national health systems.

A conceptual outlook

Systems of innovation approach

The concepts of national systems of innovation (NSI) and national health innovation systems (NHIS) have gained currency in academic research and policy processes in many developed and developing countries (Lundvall et al., 2009; Mugabe, 2005). The NSI concept is increasingly used to frame STI policy design and governance in a growing number of African countries. Its usage can be traced in the national STI policy frameworks of Botswana, Ethiopia, Namibia, Kenya, South Africa, Seychelles and more countries in Africa (Muchie et al., 2003). The NSI has been designed as a 'network of institutions in the public and private sectors whose activities and interactions initiate, import, modify and diffuse new technologies' (Freeman, 1987). The network comprises interrelated policies, agencies and activities that spur the introduction, diffusion and application of new products, processes, practices and services to generate new value.

The NSI conceptual framing treats innovation as an interactive non-linear process involving various actors (in public and private sectors and civil society) and policy instruments. Innovation is viewed as an outcome of interconnected or networked systems of private companies (firms) or private individuals, research institutions, users or customers, financing agencies, training institutes, and policy and regulatory agencies operating within a national context (Mytelka and Smith, 2001).

Applying the NSI concept in policy-making has a number of advantages. First, it enables decision-makers to treat innovation as a process that involves social, cultural and political changes. Actors in innovation processes tend to be from a diverse range of backgrounds and play different roles in activities leading to the development, adoption and diffusion of technologies. Innovation is not an outcome of a single event or a product from an isolated person or agency. A systemic view of innovation requires policy-making to focus on long-term collective processes and not isolated projects of individual scientists and entrepreneurs.

Second, the NSI approach makes it possible for policy-makers to examine the whole 'environment' influencing technological and institutional change instead of narrowly or exclusively focusing on R&D inputs such as national Gross Expenditure on Research and Development (GERD) (Grobbelaar, 2006). The overall national context – including macroeconomic and political conditions – is a key determinant of firm-level or public institutional level efforts at innovation. The context influences inter-institutional linkages or relationships, particularly between public and private sector agencies. Policy and policy-making processes play essential roles in establishing conditions within which the actors (firms, public R&D institutes and universities) make decisions about innovation (Manzini, 2012). Policies generally create the mandate for these institutions. Policies can facilitate synergies between institutions and direct investments into these institutions as well as the innovative activities they undertake.

Third, the NSI approach puts emphasis on the role of learning and the building of learning capabilities. Innovation is a learning process, and firms, public institutions and countries are learners. According to Mytelka (2016, 27), '[l]earning and unlearning on the part of policy-makers, practitioners, users and producers of all sizes in an emerging or established innovation system are thus at the heart of the system's ability to respond to new challenges such as those resulting from the growing knowledge intensity of production, and the energy and environmental challenges that we are currently facing'.

It is important to place emphasis on dynamic national systems of innovation (NSI), that is, everchanging and adaptive systems of innovation are open and characterised by inflow and outflow of information, skills, knowledge, products and other forms of innovation (Etzkowitz and Leydesdorff, 2000). The openness of the NSI largely influences or determines its learning capabilities (Patrick et al., 1997). Less open innovation systems tend to be inimical to learning as they restrict the inflow of innovative ideas, new technology, new information and new skills. They do not adequately enable local firms and public institutes to be exposed to and learn from the external environment. More open NSI foster the inflow of new skills, information and technologies. Firms and public institutes in such systems interact more with foreign actors, thus acquiring new information and technologies.

The dynamism of an NSI is determined by the density and intensity of the interactions of its actors. A more dynamic NSI has dense and intensive actor interactions involving public and private sectors, and between producers and users. The interactions are both formal and informal, often stimulated by deliberate policy measures. Although problematic and limited, common approaches to measuring interactions within the NSI include co-publications, co-patenting and joint funding and joint implementation of R&D projects among various individuals and institutions (Bartels and Koria, 2014).

Governments play critical roles in the development of NSI. They are responsible for managing the formulation and implementation of policies for R&D, technology development and procurement, and technological innovation in general. Governments have the responsibility of financing R&D and innovation activities and regulating the development and procurement of new technologies. They are key actors in the NSI. Numerous studies show that the effectiveness of government policy interventions and financing influence the growth and dynamism of NSI (e.g. Lundvall, 2004). We note that African governments can play an important role in facilitating dynamic systems of innovation through developing and promulgating effective policies for innovation.

Issues pertaining to barriers to innovation are covered in a wide range of literature on NSI. Earlier work on NSI, such as Freeman (1981), Dosi et al. (1998) and Lundvall (1992), gave attention to issues of barriers to innovation with an emphasis on factors that impinge on countries' technological innovativeness and economic performance. Different kinds of barriers to innovation activities and the performance of NSI are categorised in the literature. For example, Dosi et al. (1998) focus on issues of institutional articulation and economic incentives and how different forms of intra- and inter-agency linkages influence innovation and technology diffusion at the firm and national levels.

In a recent study, Borras and Edquist (2019) argue that clearly identifying obstacles and barriers in the innovation system is a necessary first step for defining the scope and the nature of policy-making. They emphasise that the choice of policy instruments is critical in unlocking barriers in the innovation system. Policy instruments are purposive and used to influence the direction of innovation. Examples of policy instruments for innovation include economic instruments such as tax incentives for R&D, reduced interest rates and direct grants. Other forms of policy instruments are regulatory, for example, intellectual property rights and bioethical regulations and soft instruments that include public-private partnerships.

National health innovation systems

Drawing on and applying the NSI approach, a number of studies, such as Mugabe (2005) and Chataway et al. (2007), have proposed the notion of national health innovation systems to describe the interacting configurations of institutional actors, activities and policies at various levels of governance to spur innovation for and innovation in health. Chataway et al. (2007, 4) consider national health innovation systems to be

> *networks, which link groups from different sectors around a particular health problem [...] Existing health innovation networks are fluid and operate within and across national, sectoral and micro levels of systems of innovation. Collaboration is at the heart of these networks. While innovation requires a strong knowledge base – good research institutes and universities – that knowledge will not automatically be transferred upstream to the creation of products without strong links with other sectors and a dynamic interplay of users and producers of knowledge at different stages of the innovation cycle.*

Health innovation systems subsist in the NSI and are interdependent with other systems such as energy innovation systems, digital innovation systems, transport innovation systems and many others (Dinesh et al., 2016). In fact, there is a mosaic of interacting sub-systems of innovation in the NSI. Therefore, the challenge for innovation policy is to address systemic problems in the innovation process and not to fix isolated problems manifested in specific sectors (e.g. energy, information and communication technology (ICT), and health). For this reason, we argue that barriers to innovations for tackling the health dimensions of the pandemic were systemic and pervasive. They occured in or emerged from non-health sectors (e.g. energy and transport) but impinged on the realisation of health goals in the fight against the pandemic.

Having dealt with systems of innovations, in the next subsections, we propose a typology of innovations for the pandemic and a typology of systemic barriers to innovation. These typologies are suggested for illustrative purposes and are not rigid classifications of innovations and barriers to innovations.

Typologies of innovations for the pandemic

The typologies of innovations for the pandemic elaborated in this chapter are informed variously by existing literature. According to Chandy and Pranhu (2010), innovation typologies can be framed from the innovation concept, the customers targeted by the innovation, the firms implementing the innovation, the innovation features and innovation effects dimensions. In general, innovation typologies are premised on the national, regional (Navarro and Gibaja, 2012), sector and industrial (Sandven, 1996) units of analysis. A few attempts at providing an integrated and holistic framework have been made as well (Rowley et al., 2011). Deriving from these, we developed our typologies of innovations for the pandemic using a holistic approach, as shown in Table 1.

Table 1: Typologies of innovations for the pandemic

Nature of innovation	Radical innovation
	Incremental innovation
Type of Innovation	Product
	Process
	Organisational/Institutional
Effect of innovation	Economic
	Social
Innovations and knowledge	Science-based and informed
	Interactive learning
	Internationalised-unlimited to national level

Source: Authors' own.

Innovations to tackle or address health aspects of the pandemic fall in the following categories: technological (e.g. digital apps, ventilators, diagnostic kits, PPE and masks) and social and organisational (e.g. social/physical distancing). They were also incremental (e.g. improvement in or on an existing technology such as a mask) or radical (development and deployment of new vaccines or anti-viral drugs). Incremental innovations are about improving existing technologies and do not require huge leaps in knowledge production. The converse is true of radical innovations that involve radical changes in existing technological systems through new knowledge production and application. Radical innovations, defined as innovations that create revolutionary changes and generate far-reaching economic and social effects, tend to create an entirely new pathway or regime of technology, institutions and governance.

Social innovations are about changes in social institutions and practices. They generate new routines and/or modifications in existing practices or even a new social agency but do not necessarily have a direct impact on an existing technology or technological system.

Health innovations for the pandemic were scientific in the sense that they involved the production and use of new knowledge to enhance understanding of the coronavirus, for example, how it mutates in infected persons. They also included innovations in epidemiological studies that improved how such studies were conducted to reduce the rate at which the disease spreads.

In summary, innovations for the pandemic comprised a diversity of interacting technological (technical), organisational and social innovations in a national health system that were needed to address different aspects of the pandemic's challenges. The different aspects of managing the pandemic included (a) preventing the spread of the virus through measures such as wearing of masks, social distancing and sanitising, (b) testing to detect infections and tracing to establish the spread of the virus, (c) treating infected patients and (d) vaccines.

As stated before, not all the profiled or documented inventions were really innovations. Most of the so-called innovations were inventions that had not been deployed or proven to work; they were not commercialised and may never be commercialised. Therefore, the term innovation was loosely used in the context of profiling or documenting the pandemic. Given this, it is important to have a much more grounded and restrictive definition of innovations for the pandemic, which will provide a clear understanding of what constitutes an innovation.

Typology of barriers to innovation

What constitutes a barrier to innovation? It is an impediment to the development, introduction, diffusion and implementation of any type of innovation outlined in our typologies of innovations. While in other settings, barriers may be considered as enablers, we have not integrated this dimension to be able to pronounce them as such in this chapter. There are at least five groups or categories of barriers to innovations: technical, economic, social, organisational or institutional and policy/regulatory barriers (Parente and Prescott, 1994; Philibert, 2006; Zelenika and Pearce, 2011).

Technical barriers consist of hindrances to the development, diffusion and transfer or acquisition of a product or a process due to design complexity and/or inadequacy of scientific and technological knowledge.

Economic barriers include fiscal disincentives, high cost(s) of R&D, high costs of technology procurement and unfavourable macroeconomic conditions in general (Bartels et al., 2016).

Social barriers include resistance by individuals and/or communities, or society as a whole, to innovations due to perceived or real social risks. Perceived risks are 'imagined' negative consequences of a particular innovation – its introduction, diffusion and implementation. Because of the imagined negative consequences, individuals may reject or initially resist the adoption of an innovation (Chalmers, 2013).

Organisational or institutional barriers include entrenched norms, procedures and established routines or prevailing ways of doing things – that make it difficult for an agency (within the public and private sector) to develop and adopt as well as implement new technology or innovation. For example, the norms, procedures and routines may relate to how communication within an agency or between agencies is organised and managed. According to a wide range of literature on organisational behaviour and management, heavy bureaucratic structures with many levels of controls and approvals stifle creativity and innovation among employees. Organisational barriers also include entrenched business models, limited in-house skills and finances for and knowledge on the development and use of new technologies (Pourkiani et al., 2013).

Policy and regulatory barriers to innovation include an absence of R&D and innovation policy, incoherence and uncertainty in R&D and innovation policy, weak policy implementation capacity, absence or existence of weak technical standards, and fiscal and tax regulations that hinder investment or raise costs of investment in innovation. While ambiguous and/or weak intellectual property protection measures have traditionally been viewed as negatively affecting innovation, there is evidence that poor intellectual property regimes may have a neutral or positive effect on innovation. There are political considerations or factors that generate policy or regulatory barriers. Policy and regulations as outcomes of political negotiations and competition face resistance in implementation from certain political groups who may lose support from their constituencies if certain policy and regulatory interventions are instituted. Such groups tend to resist the implementation of certain policy and regulatory measures if they do not serve their political, ideological and even economic interests (Acemoglu and Robinson, 2000).

Barriers to the development, transfer and diffusion of an innovation or new technology or even the implementation or deployment of existing technologies tend to be systemic in the sense that they emerge from and are connected to various aspects of the NSI. Wieczorek and Hekkert (2012) focus on the systemic nature of barriers to innovation processes and activities in NSI. They argue for systemic policy instruments to address structural and functional NSI barriers to innovation:

> *The basic idea behind systemic instruments is that they aim to address problems that arise at the innovation system level and which negatively influence the speed and direction of innovation processes. These problems are often referred to as systemic weaknesses or systemic*

> *failures. They hinder the operation and development of the innovation system as a whole and the presence of these system failures is often considered to be a new policy rationale, replacing the neoclassical market failure. Examples include innovation networks that are either too weak or too strong, and poorly articulated demand for innovation or institutional capacity problems. (Wieczorek and Hekkert, 2012, 74)*

Mazurkiewicz and Poteralska (2017) also demonstrate that many of the barriers to technology transfer are systemic and require systemic policy interventions. They define barriers to technology transfer as any limitations that hamper the effective functioning of 'a technology transfer and research commercialization system and, as a result, block interactions between the R&D sector and enterprises, therefore impeding the development of innovative entrepreneurship' (Mazurkiewicz and Poteralska, 2017, 457). They provide the following categorisation of barriers: technical, organisational-economic and system barriers. These kinds of barriers interact systemically or have causal relationships.

Barriers to innovation are systemic and pervasive in the sense that their effects tend to spread across different sectors such as health, energy, water, transport and manufacturing. This is particularly so with institutional barriers related to poor linkages or disarticulation in the NSI, for example, the absence of a culture of cross-sectoral coordination among departments of health. ICTs and energy may lock digital health innovations out of healthcare in a country. A country with a poorly functioning or weak energy infrastructure was likely to have difficulties managing vaccination against the pandemic or even deploying digital applications in the diagnosis and epidemiological management of the disease.

Related to institutional barriers are impediments pertaining to policy incoherence. Foxon and Pearson (2008) examine policy processes for building sustainable innovation policy regimes. They put emphasis on measures that promote co-evolution of technology and policy processes, bringing together different policy goals (e.g. environmental sustainability) and innovation goals. Foxon and Pearson (2008) take a systems approach and stress that innovation and technology diffusion are systemic, dynamic and non-linear processes in which institutional and technological factors interact in uncertain ways.

Bartels et al. (2016) provide an analysis of barriers to innovation and innovativeness in Ghana using the NSI conceptual approach. They show how limited skills, low technological capabilities in ICTs, weak organisational capacities and institutional linkages, unsophisticated markets and deficits in fiscal policy interact in systemic ways to impede innovation and the building of innovation capabilities in the country. Weak interactions between government, private sector enterprises, and research institutes and universities are also identified as key barriers to innovation.

Desveaux et al. (2019) provide a good analysis of organisational and policy level barriers to health innovations. Their study centres on the 'plague of pilots' – 'where innovations fail to become part of the routine practice because of limited funding or ability to scale to broader sectors of the health care system.' They conclude: 'Context and culture drive changes in the use of technology, highlighting the central role that policy reform will play in the success (or failure) of the digital health agenda' and 'organizational factors, such as the capacity to innovate, readiness for the digital health innovation, availability of funding and extent of changes required to implement innovation, also influence the adoption process and thereby impact the uptake of digital health innovations in practice' (Desveaux et al., 2019, 2).

Given this, a barrier to innovation for the pandemic can be viewed as any systemic technical, economic, organisational, regulatory or policy, and social impediment to the development, commercialisation and diffusion of social and product innovations. The barriers were of a temporary nature.

Methodology

The preceding section is a review of the literature laying out the conceptual outlook of this chapter. It provides an appropriate framing for the analysis of barriers to innovations for the pandemic in Africa. The main research questions addressed in this study are:

1. What were the main systemic barriers to the development, diffusion and deployment of innovations to tackle health challenges or aspects of the pandemic in Africa?
2. What policy instruments and policy mixes would have unlocked the barriers and spurred the innovations to help banish the pandemic from Africa?

To answer these research questions, a review of secondary literature focusing on the typologies of innovations for tackling health challenges or aspects of the pandemic in Africa was done. The focused review specifically analysed case studies in recent academic papers in journals such as Nature and databases of the African Academy of Sciences (AAS) and Scopus. Although the search was not limited by years, the fact that the relevant papers dealt with the pandemic's innovations naturally and unintentionally emphasised searches from 2019 to 2022. Additional research on company and university websites highlighted in the reviewed literature was carried out.

Following the literature review exercise, mapping of different innovations for the pandemic was done guided by the typology proposed and using empirical information from published reports by organisations such as the WHO, AU and EIB. The mapping encompassed illustrative cases of ongoing R&D initiatives in African institutions. Some of the cases were illustrative of 'pipeline' or 'potential innovations'. A ranking of different innovations was done using the following criteria: the typology of the innovation, awareness of the existence and spread of the innovation, and stage of development and level of investment in the innovation. This was done by reviewing documentation (including reports and newspaper clippings). Results of the mapping exercise are presented in the next section.

Telephone and WhatsApp interviews were also carried out with purposively selected participants. These were persons considered to be leading the pandemic's response across many African countries, including Kenya (8 participants), Zimbabwe (6 participants), South Africa (12 participants), Côte d'Ivoire (5 participants). Four focus group discussions (FGDs) were conducted with participants from Botswana (4 participants), Uganda (4 participants), Senegal (4 participants) and Nigeria (4 participants), who discussed specific pandemic-related innovations. Participants in the FGDs also ranked specific innovations based on the following multi-criteria approach: alignment with national and local pandemic health emergency goals or priorities, the potential of the innovation to be rapidly commercialised or existence of a potential market for the innovation, scalability of the innovation and availability of skills and potential for capacity building in developing and using the innovation.

To complement data from FGDs, telephone interviews were conducted with key informants. These were nine purposively selected persons (three from the research community, two from private companies involved in the production of PPE and four policy-makers from departments of STI and trade in Kenya and South Africa). These interviewees were experts in their areas of work. In addition, using WhatsApp, opinions on and perceptions of barriers to specific innovations such as masks, social distancing and potential vaccines were gathered from 17 respondents randomly identified among post-graduate students at two universities in South Africa. The views of FGDs participants and post-graduate students were used to validate the findings from other respondents.

Data collection was stopped when saturation was reached, that is, when the same responses were given by a number of respondents, and no new insights could be gleaned from the responses. Data from these various sources were analysed, and summaries based on the data were written. These summaries were reviewed. The final summaries are presented as the findings in this chapter.

A study of this scope has some limitations. The participants were purposively recruited, and their responses may have been affected by desirability bias. This was minimised by using multi-research methods to collect the data. The number of study participants may be considered few. However, most of the selected participants were experts or knowledgeable in the subject under research. As a limitation, most participants were based in African countries. This may have limited the generalisability of the findings beyond the African continent.

Mapping health innovations for the pandemic

The initial months of the pandemic witnessed a huge surge of investments in scientific research and innovation processes to develop and deploy products, processes and practices to tackle the health aspects or challenges of the pandemic. Governments, private companies, individuals, research institutes and development assistance agencies were engaged in numerous initiatives to produce scientific knowledge on the coronavirus and the pandemic, manufacture of PPEs and other medical equipment such as ventilators, develop vaccines and a wide range of digital tools to address various aspects of testing, contact tracing and treatment. Firms, including small and medium enterprises (SMEs), were at the forefront of manufacturing PPEs and sanitisers. Research institutions and universities in many countries mobilised their faculties to undertake research on various aspects of the coronavirus, including epidemiological studies, and building data science on the pandemic. Community-based health interventions, including testing, tracing and treatment, were scaled up in some countries in Africa.

In August 2020, the African Union Development Agency-NEPAD (AUDA-NEPAD, 2020) produced a white paper on 'Harnessing Innovation and Emerging Technologies to Address the Impact of COVID-19 in Africa'. The paper profiled scientific research and innovation initiatives aimed at addressing the health impacts of the pandemic. Table 2 provides a summary of the initiatives.

Table 2: Examples of research and innovation initiatives for pandemic health impacts

Initiative category	Specific research and innovation focus	Institution/Country
SARS-CoV-2 Genome Sequencing	• Using genomics to develop candidate vaccines	University of Cape Town, South Africa
	• Production of PPEs using 3D printing	Addis Ababa University, Ethiopia
	• Production of face masks or shields using 3D-printing	University of Pretoria (MakerSpace Centre), South Africa
	• Ventilator prototypes	Harare Institute of Technology, Zimbabwe, Kenyatta University in Kenya
	• Use of robots in contact tracing and enforcement of social distancing measures	Ministry of Health, Rwanda Government of Tunisia
Health Diagnostics	• USD 1 less COVID-19 testing kit	Pasteur Institute, Senegal
	• Simple to use testing kit	Incas Diagnostics and the Kwame Nkrumah University of Science and Technology in Ghana
	• Swab tube dipstick	Makerere University in Uganda
	• Accessible web-based platform X-ray that scans lungs	Tunisian National Institute of Applied Sciences and Technology (INSAT)

Source: AUDA-NEPAD (August 2020).

In July 2020, the European Investment Bank released 'Africa's digital solutions to tackle COVID-19', which documents a variety of digital products, applications and practices that were developed to address health, social and economic challenges posed by the pandemic. To avoid including inventions that did not qualify as innovations, only digital innovations for health that were mentioned in this report are mapped in Table 3.

As stated earlier, Mugabe et al. (2020) also provide examples of various scientific initiatives and technological innovations with the potential to tackle the pandemic's health challenges. They described initiatives for the clinical trials and vaccine development, such as the 're-purposing' of the scientific capabilities and infrastructure accumulated by the South Africa AIDS Vaccine Initiative (SAAVI) to engage in the rapid development of coronavirus vaccines. The study also profiled efforts or programmes for harnessing the phytochemical potential of biodiversity and indigenous knowledge to develop health products to tackle the pandemic in Africa.

Table 3: African digital health innovations to tackle the pandemic

Type of innovation	Overview of health usage or utility	Innovator/Institution/Country
Contact tracing applications	• Msafari, application for tracing movements of people who have contracted the coronavirus or have been in contact with infected persons on public transport	Fablab, an innovation hub, in Kenya
	• Wiqaytna, mobile phone contact tracking application that cross checks movements of persons who are supposed to be in quarantine	Government of Morocco
	• PGuard robot circulates in Tunis and other cities equipped with speakers and cameras to broadcast safety instructions and monitor compliance with social distancing and mask-wearing requirements	Enova Robotics, a private company, in Tunisia
Health system applications	• Zipline drones used to collect test samples from health facilities in rural areas and deliver them to medical laboratories in urban centres in Rwanda and Ghana	Zipline (USA Company) with contracts with government institutions or departments in Ghana and Rwanda
	• Humanoid robots used to screen 50-150 people per minute, monitor patients and help minimise physical contact, also deliver medicines and food to patients' rooms, thus helping to protect health workers	Government of Rwanda in partnership with the United Nations Development Programme (UNDP)
	• mHero, healthcare software that helps to connect ministries of health centres and health workers in rural areas. It is a two-way mobile phone communication system that was used during Ebola epidemics in Liberia, Guinea, Sierra Leone and Uganda	Implemented in 16 African countries, including Kenya, South Africa, Ghana and Rwanda
	• Wellvis app is an application allowing users to self-assess their coronavirus risk category based on their symptoms and exposure history. Also enables individuals to make digital health appointments with payment online	Ethiopia, Uganda and South Africa are examples of countries that implemented the innovation
	• WHO health alert on WhatsApp, proactive communication tool providing the public with information on measures to prevent spread and exposure to the pandemic	

Source: EIB (2020).

Other examples of promising pandemic-related health innovations included the diagnostic kit developed and released by the Kenya Medical Research Institute (KEMRI). Building on accumulated scientific and technological capabilities for HIV and tuberculosis (TB) diagnostics research, KEMRI innovated and released kits for rapid testing of COVID-19; Cobas 6800 viral load testing equipment. The South African National Bioinformatics Institute (SANBI) sequenced the whole genome of SARS-CoV-2 isolated from a patient with COVID-19. This somewhat innovatively helped provide the data necessary to determine the COVID-19 variants in South Africa. In addition to these research and innovation efforts, some African countries (e.g. South Africa and Kenya) participated in the Johnson and Johnson international clinical trials for a COVID-19 vaccine. South Africa was involved in several COVID-19 vaccine trials. For example, the University of the Witwatersrand participated in two COVID-19 vaccine trials; the Novavax product called NVX-CoV2373 and the Oxford COVID-19 vaccine trial, which uses the ChAdOx1 COVID-19 vaccine.

The World Health Organization (WHO) Regional Office for Africa issued a statement on 29 October 2020 providing an analysis of the health technology innovations that had been stimulated by the pandemic in Africa. The analysis concluded that Africa accounts for 12.8% of the 1000 or so new or modifications of existing technologies that have been developed worldwide to target different areas of the COVID-19 response (WHO, 2020). It showed that digital innovations or ICT-driven innovations comprised a large share of the African health innovations, accounting for about 58% of the total innovation. 3D printing-related innovations accounted for 25% and robotics made up 10.9% of the innovations deployed to address health challenges related to the pandemic in Africa. Most of these innovations were introduced or deployed in South Africa (13%), Kenya (10%), Nigeria (8%) and Rwanda (6%) (WHO, 2020).

The next section focuses on systemic barriers to the dominant promising health innovations for the pandemic in Africa. While three clusters of innovations were highly rated to be critical and penetrating in African health systems (WHO, 2020), the barriers identified by respondents and FGD participants are described, and their systemic nature is analysed below.

Systemic barriers to health innovations

Much of the existing Africa-specific literature does not explicitly deal with barriers to health innovations. However, there is innovation literature that deals with barriers in general. Table 4 shows the barriers to innovation highlighted in existing literature as well as the findings on barriers to health innovations from the study participants. Since the findings on barriers to health innovations are the focus of this chapter, they are further explained.

Table 4: Barriers to health innovations

Barriers to innovation and systematic barriers to health innovations highlighted in existing literature	Systematic barriers to health innovations from respondents
Economic cost of the innovation	Access to information
Cost of the innovation	Digital literacy
Lack of financing	Weak or poor infrastructure
Organisational rigidities	Policy and regulatory barriers
Skills shortages	High cost of procurement
Information asymmetries about the technology	Social resistance
Lack of market information	
Unresponsive customers	
Government regulations	

Source: Authors' own.

There were six main (highly rated by interviewees and participants in the FGDs) systemic or interacting barriers to health innovations for tackling the pandemic in Africa: (a) limited access to information on the innovations; (b) low levels of digital literacy; (c) weak infrastructure, particularly limited and unreliable supply of electricity; (d) weak policy and regulatory regimes; (e) high economic costs of procuring and deploying the innovations in low-income or poor households/communities; and (f) social resistance to innovations, particularly anticipated resistance to coronavirus vaccines and therapeutics.

From the reviewed literature, we noted that other barriers to health innovations included weak links between research institutions and industry and low levels of funding of scientific research on the pandemic in many African countries. Some of the potential testing kits developed by African institutions such as KEMRI in Kenya were likely to be stunted innovations because there were no explicit strategies to commercialise them, and institutional arrangements for getting private companies to invest in mass production was weak. Related to this was low funding for R&D which created discontinuity in scientific research, such as the SARS-CoV-2 genome sequencing efforts which could have served as pathways to vaccine development in Africa. We elaborate on each of the six main barriers below.

Access to information

Limited (or lack of) access to information on the various health innovations and their applications was highlighted as one of the major barriers to their diffusion and deployment in tackling the pandemic. Most of the study participants noted that people and health workers in rural areas of Africa do not have information on the existence of the different digital innovations for the pandemic. Some interviewees and respondents held the view that even in urban areas, there was limited information on the various digital innovations. This viewpoint was also expressed in existing literature, such as in the EIB and AUDA-NEPAD reports. Because many individuals and households did not have information (on the existence and applications), digital health innovations were under-utilised in the fight against the pandemic.

The information problem was associated with poor or weak marketing by private innovators and weak support by governments in publicising the innovations of private individuals and companies. According to one interviewee, 'governments are not actively prospecting for and promoting technologies or inventions that can be used to manage the pandemic and other diseases in Africa. They wait for newspapers and other forms of media to market new innovations.'

Digital literacy

The spread and utilisation of digital health innovations, both in healthcare systems and households, was limited by low levels of digital literacy. The use of self-assessment applications such as Wellvis (a healthcare application that individuals could use to diagnose themselves and contact medical emergency workers) was largely undermined or constrained by illiteracy among households, particularly in low-income rural areas. According to EIB (2020) and several interviewees, many of the self-assessment or self-diagnosis tools for the pandemic were not easily accessible to illiterate people, particularly the elderly in rural areas.

Weak or poor infrastructure

In countries or regions and households with low or poor electricity access and mobile phone penetration as well as internet connectivity, digital health innovations did not diffuse rapidly and were not effectively deployed to address regional health needs in general, including the pandemic. These countries and communities found difficulty managing the vaccines when they were finally available on the market. According to the EIB (2020, 20) report, 'a lack of electricity and internet are major challenges identified in the interviews, in remote areas and in cities. [...] The second significant issue is the lack of internet servers, data centers and electricity supporting the digital technology in place or in development'. Study participants in FGDs identified poor or limited access to electricity as a major barrier to the use of digital innovation in health systems and households in many African countries.

Policy and regulatory barriers

The absence of coherent, holistic policy measures and weak implementation of existing STI policies, as well as weak regulatory frameworks for health innovation, stood in the way of harnessing new medical technologies to fight the pandemic in Africa. African Academy of Science (2020) and Mugabe et al. (2020) discussed how weak regulatory frameworks affected clinical trials and registration of medicines and medical products. According to Mugabe et al. (2020, 22), 'regulatory mechanisms and frameworks for health R&D in general and clinical trials in particular are weak in most African countries. Costs – time and money – of clinical trials are relatively high in some countries. Institutional arrangements for regulating – including approval – health R&D and clinical trials in particular – are weak. Multiple agencies and ambiguous procedures make it cumbersome to get approvals for health R&D as well as clinical trials. This may undermine the continent's efforts to participate in global vaccine initiatives and related R&D. It acts as a disincentive for private industry to engage with public health R&D and clinical trials'.

In South Africa, any application for a clinical trial for a vaccine has to receive Medical Control Council approval, the ethics approval board, and register with the Department of Health before it is given a unique number in the South African National Clinical Trial Register. The application then goes through monitoring and periodic review, and finally, it has to be submitted to SAHPRA, which through its Medicinal Evaluation and Research Unit, will determine whether to register the vaccine. This process takes a relatively long time, is cumbersome, and would have been a barrier to, for example, vaccine approval and distribution in the country, if it had been followed to the letter indiscriminately.

High costs of procurement

The economic costs of some of the pandemic's health innovations were relatively high for some countries and communities, particularly for poor or low-income households. Study participants identified high costs as a barrier to the spread and use of various health innovations, including approved quality masks and PPE in general. Some countries experienced shortages of PPE because of the relatively high costs of importing them and the lack of domestic capabilities to produce them locally. According to some interviewees, some producers of PPE and high-quality masks complained of small fragment markets for durable medically approved PPE.

Social resistance

Some of the health innovations such as masks, social distancing practices and potential vaccines, faced social resistance-related barriers during the pandemic. Social resistance was often associated with misinformation or lack of information about the safety and utility of some health innovations (e.g. vaccines and diagnostics). According to some interviewees and all participants in the FGDs, the pandemic's innovations most likely to have faced social resistance were social distancing, mask-wearing and vaccines when they were available in Africa.

Measures to unlock systemic barriers to the pandemic's innovations

Overall, the main identified barriers to developing, diffusing and deploying health innovations to tackle the pandemic were not technological but related to infrastructure (energy and connectivity), policy and regulations, social and economic, weak institutional articulation or linkages, literacy and information access. These barriers affected the dominant innovations, which were digital ones, in the fight against the pandemic. To remove or unlock these barriers required a wide range of interventions beyond traditional STI policies and programmes. In this section, we suggest some of the most feasible measures for removing the barriers or impediments to health innovations.

The identified barriers to health innovations for the pandemic were embedded in countries' national systems of innovation and interacted in various systemic ways. For example, low levels of digital literacy were, in part, due to poor education and training and a lack of exposure to digital technologies as much as they were exacerbated by weak or poor internet connectivity. Weak internet connectivity was, in large measure, related to weak infrastructure, including poor access to electricity. Barriers such as poor or limited access to electricity and internet connectivity tended to affect innovation processes and activities, thus impeding the generation or production (not just the spread and deployment) of new innovations.

Thus, because of their systemic nature, measures to address or remove the barriers need to be systemic in order to have an effect on NSI in general and health innovation systems in particular. This approach, drawing on a study by Borras and Edquist (2019), is based on the view that a mix of holistic policy instruments and related institutional arrangements are needed to remove or unlock barriers to innovation. As stated before, in this chapter, policy instruments refer to measures or actions that governments purposefully instituted in order to influence innovation processes and activities aimed at addressing health challenges associated with the pandemic.[2]

The range of policy instruments available to governments to unlock barriers to innovations for tackling health challenges associated with the pandemic was relatively wide, in the sense that it covered social, economic and fiscal, regulatory, manufacturing and industrial, R&D, education and training and other facets of public policy. In this regard, the challenge for governments lay in choosing instruments that could be implemented effectively and efficiently during the crisis and uncertain times of the pandemic. The choice of policy instruments should ideally have been informed by criteria such as state capability and flexibility for adjustment based on policy learning.

To address the information access deficits and social resistance barriers identified in this study, respondents noted that governments should have considered invoking and using access to information provisions in national constitutions. Most national constitutions have such provisions requiring state agencies to ensure that citizens have access to information, particularly on issues of public emergency and/or concern. To implement access to information provisions and help remove information barriers to health innovations for the pandemic, governments should have designed and launched public information and awareness programmes for approved digital innovations and treatments, including vaccines and medicines. Such programmes should have focused on raising awareness of the availability, utility and applications of various approved pandemic-related innovations. In practice, they would involve the use of media, including print, radio and television, to communicate messages or information on available innovations. Community innovation outreach and demonstration activities led by relevant government departments, private firms and individuals involved in developing specific innovations would also have helped to disseminate information on and build public understanding of how to use

---

2   For a more elaborate and broad definition of policy instruments, see Borras and Edquist (2019).

such innovations to address health challenges such as those related to the pandemic.

Removing barriers associated with the high economic costs of procuring and deploying appropriate innovations required dedicated fiscal or financial instruments. Governments needed to consider establishing national COVID-19 innovation funds that would provide positive incentives to individuals, households and even community-based agencies to procure approved health innovations, such as testing kits. These innovation funds could have comprised of cash grants, interest-free loans, cash transfers and loan guarantees that innovators could have accessed in order to help scale and mass produce their products. For example, South Africa, among a few African countries, provided cash transfers to cushion selected groups of vulnerable persons from the effects of the pandemic.

A related measure pertained to industrial policies that helped repurpose private industrial activities, which were necessary in leveraging existing innovation capabilities to address production or manufacturing challenges. Financial instruments that enabled small and medium enterprises (SMEs) to access financial means to help produce PPEs and other products were needed to strengthen local and national health systems.

To address weak or poor infrastructure barriers, including electricity and internet connectivity, African governments and private sector actors in collaboration with international partners need to urgently explore possibilities of fast-tracking connectivity to various sources of energy (such as solar). Poor access to reliable electricity hinders the use of different digital innovations and keeps local health systems at the periphery of technological change. One approach to addressing this challenge is to establish national schemes that enable households and communities, particularly in rural areas, to procure solar and other off-grid sources of electricity cheaply and in more rapid ways. Community-based energy facilities that are developed and managed by local cooperative groups, including women's associations, should be encouraged through various fiscal incentives and technical capacity building programmes.

In order to strengthen existing policy and regulatory frameworks, governments of African countries need to urgently conduct critical reviews or assessments and revisions of existing national policies, legislation and regulations for clinical trials, and registration of health products to make them flexible enough to allow for rapid innovation, including using various public procurement mechanisms to promote domestic or endogenous manufacturing of pharmaceuticals. African countries need to invest in policy learning, drawing lessons from experiences of countries such as

India and South Korea that have been able to improve efficiencies in clinical trials and procurement as well as local manufacturing of health products.

Overall, the pandemic was a transformative process that required transformative responses. As such, the focus should have been on exploiting technological convergences and innovations that produce systemic outcomes. A holistic approach based on NSI approaches was essential. Notably, the need for fewer silos between systems (health, industry, education) and the establishment of a more coherent well-capacitated NSI is necessary. Single technologies or innovations were unable to fix the pandemic and its health consequences. Investments in carefully chosen mixes of innovation activities and processes were needed. As stated earlier, such action depended on mixes of policy instruments that supported research and development, technology incubation, scaling up technology production or manufacturing and quality of technical standards.

Conclusions

This chapter shows that the pandemic stimulated a surge in various health innovations in Africa. Most of the innovations were digital, involving various applications for testing and tracing as well as monitoring and surveillance to control the spread of the coronavirus. Some African countries deployed modern technologies such as robotics in their health systems to help curb the spread of the virus and contain the disease. There were also scientific research initiatives and clinical trials in some countries in the process of vaccine development. However, these initiatives were undermined by various barriers, including information access deficits, low levels of digital literacy, weak policy and regulation measures, and poor institutional arrangements. Fiscal and non-fiscal measures, including various mixes of policy instruments, were proposed to unlock the barriers in order to harness the potentials of the innovations to tackle health aspects of a pandemic such as the coronavirus outbreak.

We recommend the nexus between health and industrialisation or manufacturing for future research, as it is under-studied in Africa. There is scant empirical research on how industrial change (or industrial development) can aid (transform) public health, particularly in terms of reducing the costs of local manufacturing of medicines and medical equipment. Empirical data and evidence-based policy analysis are needed to help improve the integration of health considerations into national industrial policies and programmes and to stimulate industrial production for health and well-being. Such research would generate and provide evidence to policy-makers and practitioners in health and industrial sectors to help fast track innovations that address epidemics and health emergencies such as the pandemic. It will help unlock barriers to technological innovation in national health systems and promote ways and means of narrowing inequalities related to access to health innovations.

African countries were exposed to a wide range of technological and non-technological opportunities in the fight against the pandemic. Seizing these opportunities required deliberate and urgent policy and programmatic actions, including technology assessment and procurement given the high demand for technologies to fight the pandemic in the face of growing techno-nationalism (i.e. a process whereby states became inwardly looking and prioritised their citizens and persons resident in their countries and were less concerned about non-citizens). Any efforts at promoting invention, technology development and innovation to address pandemics or other health-related concerns should be informed by the specific needs or demands of African innovation systems in general and health innovation systems in particular. Like other continents, African innovation systems are diverse, evolving and characterised by differentiated strengths and weaknesses. Different African countries have different absorptive technological capabilities. However, there have been similarities in the nature of the barriers to health technologies and innovations for the pandemic. Measures for promoting these health innovations should be cast in the broader context of unlocking the barriers and strengthening national innovation systems.

References

Acemoglu, D., and Robinson, J. (2000). Political losers as a barrier to economic development. *American Economic Review*, 90(2), 126-130. https://doi.org/10.1257/aer.90.2.126

African Academy of Science (2020). *Research and Development goals for COVID-19 in Africa*. African Academy of Sciences.

AUDA-NEPAD. (2020). *Harnessing Innovation and Emerging Technologies to Address the Impact of COVID-19 in Africa*. African Union Development Agency.

Bartels, F. L., and Koria, R. (2014). Mapping, measuring and managing African national systems of innovation for policy and development: The case of the Ghana national system of innovation. *African Journal of Science, Technology, Innovation and Development*, 6(5), 383-400. https://doi.org/10.1080/20421338.2014.970427

Bartels, F., Koria, R., and Vitali, E. (2016). Barriers to innovation: The case of Ghana and implications for developing countries. *Triple Helix*, 3(12). https://doi.org/10.1186/s40604-016-0040-y

Borras, S., and Edquist, C. (2019). *Holistic Innovation Policy: Theoretical foundations, policy problems, and instrument choices.* Oxford University Press.

Chalmers, D. (2013). Social innovation: An exploration of the barriers faced by innovating organizations in the social economy. *Local Economy,* 28(1), 17-34. https://doi.org/10.1177/0269094212463677

Chandy, R. K., and Prabhu, J. C. (2010). Innovation typologies. In: *Wiley International Encyclopedia of Marketing.* https://doi.org/10.1002/9781444316568.wiem05012

Chataway, J., Chaturvedi, K., Hanlin, R., Mugwagwa, J., Smith, J., and Wield, D. (2007). *Building the Case for National Systems of Health Innovation.* ESRC Innogen Centre.

Desveaux, L., Soobiah, C., Bhatia, S., and Shaw, J. (2019). Identifying and overcoming policy-level barriers to the implementation of digital health innovation: Qualitative study. *Journal of Medical Internet Research,* 21(12), e14994. https://doi.org/10.2196/14994

Dinesh, A., Sundararaman, T., Madhaven, H. and Joseph, K. J. (2016). Building inclusive health innovation systems: Lessons from India. *Cadernos de Saúde Pública,* 3(2). https://doi.org/10.1590/0102-311X00045215

Dosi, G., Freeman, C., Nelson, R. R., Silverberg, G., and Soete, L. (Eds). (1998). *Technology and Economic Rheory.* Pinter.

European Investment Bank (EIB). (2020). *Africa's digital solutions to tackle COVID-19.* EIB. www.eib.org

Etzkowitz, H., and Leydesdorff, L. (2000). The dynamics of innovation: From national systems and 'mode 2' to a triple helix of university–industry–government relations. *Research Policy,* 29(2), 109-123. https://doi.org/10.1016/S0048-7333(99)00055-4

Freeman, C. (1981). *Technological Innovation and National Economic Performance.* Aalborg University Press.

Freeman, C. (1987). *Technology and Economic Performance: Lessons from Japan.* Pinter.

Foxon, T., and Pearson, P. (2008). Overcoming barriers to innovation and diffusion of cleaner technologies: Some features of a sustainable innovation policy regime. *Journal of Cleaner Production,* 16, S148-S161. https://doi.org/10.1016/j.jclepro.2007.10.011

Grobbelaar, S. S. (2006). R&D in the national system of innovation: A system dynamics model. PhD thesis, University of Pretoria.

Kline, S. (1985). Innovation is not a linear process. *Research Management,* 28(4), 36-45. https://doi.org/10.1080/00345334.1985.11756910

Lundvall B-Å. (1992). *National Systems of Innovation: Towards a theory of innovation and interactive learning.* Pinter.

Lundvall, B-Å. (2004). National innovation systems: Analytical concept and development tool. www.researchgate.net/publication/24081600

Lundvall, B-Å., Joseph, K., Chaminade, C., and Vang, J. (2009). Innovation systems and developing countries: An introduction. In: B-Å. Lundvall, K. Joseph, C. Chaminade and J. Vang (Eds), *Innovation Systems and Developing Countries: Building domestic capabilities in a global setting.* Edward Elgar.

Manzini, S. T. (2012). The national system of innovation concept: An ontological review and critique. *South African Journal of Science,* 108(9-10), 1-7. https://doi.org/10.4102/sajs.v108i9/10.1038

Matthewman, S., and Huppatz, K. (2020). A sociology of Covid-19. *Journal of Sociology,* 56(4), 675-683. https://doi.org/10.1177/1440783320939416

Mazurkiewicz, A., and Poteralska, B. (2017). Technology transfer barriers and challenges faced by R&D organizations. *Proceedia Engineering,* 182, 457-465. https://doi.org/10.1016/j.proeng.2017.03.134

McNamara, K. R., and Newman, A. (2020). The big reveal: COVID-19 and globalization's great transformations. *International Organization,* 74(S1), E59-E77. https://doi.org/10.1017/S0020818320000387

Muchie, M., Gammeltoft, P., and Lundvall, B.-Å. (2003). *Putting Africa First: The making of African innovation systems.* Aalborg University Press.

Mugabe, J. (2005). Health innovation systems in developing countries: Strategies for building scientific and technological capacities. Background study prepared for the World Health Organization (WHO) Commission on Intellectual Property Protection, Innovation and Health.

Mugabe, J. (2020). Global solidarity in science and innovation will stop COVID-19 and speed the SDGs. STRINGS. http://strings.org.uk/global-solidarity-in-science-and-innovation-will-stop-covid-19-and-speed-the-sdgs/

Mugabe, J. O., Kulohoma, B. W., Matoke-Muhia, D., Ubalijoro, E., Fagbamigbe, F. A., Maura, G., Gitaka, J., Thorn, J. P. R., Badu, K., Muchie, M., Dukhi, N., Ndung'u, T., Muposhi, V. K., Bouhaouala-Zahar, B., Sogbanmu, T., and Kapulu, M. (2020). Securing Africa's health sovereignty: Why investing in science and innovation matters. *AAS Open Res,* 3, 52. https://doi.org/10.21955/aasopenres.1115135.1

Mytelka, L. (2016). Innovation systems approaches in a time of transition. In: J. Francis, L. Mytelka, A. Van Huis and N. Röling (Eds), *Innovation Systems: Towards effective strategies in support of smallholder farmers.* Centre for Tropical Agriculture (CTA).

Mytelka, L., and Smith, K. (2001). *Innovation Theory and Innovation Policy: Bridging the gap.* United Nations University Institute for New Technologies (UNU-INTECH).

Navarro, M., and Gibaja, J. J. (2012). Typologies of innovation based on statistical analysis for European and Spanish regions. In: B. T. Asheim and M.D. Parrilli (Eds), *Interactive Learning for Innovation.* Palgrave Macmillan. https://doi.org/10.1057/9780230362420_11

Niang, M., Dupéré, S., Alami, H., and Gagnon, M.-P. (2021). Why is repositioning public health innovation towards a social paradigm necessary? A reflection on the field of public health through the examples of Ebola and Covid-19. *Global Health,* 17, 46. https://doi.org/10.1186/s12992-021-00695-3

Parente, S., and Prescott, E. (1994). Barriers to technology adoption and development. *Journal of Political Economy,* 102(2), 298-321. www.jstor.org/stable/2138663

Patrick, Y., Chau, K., and Tam, K. (1997). Factors affecting the adoption of open systems: An exploratory study. *MIS Quarterly,* 21(1), 1-24. https://doi.org/10.2307/249740

Philibert, C. (2006). *Barriers to Technology Diffusion: The case of solar thermal technologies.* Organization for Economic Co-Operation and Development (OECD) and the International Energy Agency (IEA).

Pourkiani, M., Farahabadi, H. S., and Komak, M. D. (2013). Organizational innovation, barriers and factors. *European Online Journal of Natural and Social Sciences,* 2(3), 724-731. https://european-science.com/eojnss/article/view/494

Quick, J. (2018). *The End of Epidemics: The looming threat to humanity and how to stop it.* Scribe.

Rowley, J., Baregheh, A., and Sambrook, S. (2011). Towards an innovation-type mapping tool. *Management Decision*, 49(1), 73-86. https://doi.org/10.1108/00251741111094446

Sandven, T. (1996). *Typologies of Innovation in Small and Medium Sized Enterprises in Norway.* Studies in technology, innovation and economic policy report. STEP.

Silva, M., João, L., and Raposo, M. (2007). *Barriers to Innovation faced by Manufacturing Firms in Portugal: How to overcome it?* Munich Personal RePEc Archive. University of Beira Interior.

Stone, V. I., and Lane, J. P. (2012). Modeling technology innovation: How science, engineering, and industry methods can combine to generate beneficial socioeconomic impacts. *Implementation Science* 7, 44. https://doi.org/10.1186/1748-5908-7-44

UNCTAD. (2020). *Assessing the Impact of COVID-19 on Africa's Economic Development.* United Nations Conference on Trade and Development.

WHO. (2020). COVID-19 spurs health innovation in Africa. World Health Organization, Regional Office for Africa. www.afro.who.int

Wieczorek, A., and Hekkert, M. (2012). Systemic instruments for systemic innovation problems: A framework for policy makers and innovation scholars. *Science and Public Policy*, 39(1), 74-87. https://doi.org/10.1093/scipol/scr008

Zelenika, I., and Pearce, J. M. (2011). Barriers to appropriate technology growth in sustainable development. *Journal of Sustainable Development*, 4(6). https://doi.org/10.5539/jsd.v4n6p12

CHAPTER 5

Revisiting Resource-Based Development Strategies in the Post-Pandemic Era

Keun Lee

Introduction

Natural resources account for 20% of world goods trade and dominate the exports of many countries. Natural resource or mineral exports and growth are topics highlighted in economic history.[1] Many scholars argue that, on the one hand, natural resource exports can create a growth boom.[2] On the other hand, natural resource abundance may impede growth.

Some countries in the Global South (e.g. several of the Arab Emirates, Malaysia and Botswana) have managed to harness the potentials of natural resources and maintain both strong investment and economic growth. The economic histories of Latin American countries, such as Bolivia and Ecuador, also show some periods of a boom in natural resource exports leading to

---

1   Natural resource exports are defined as exports of agriculture, minerals and fuels (Sachs and Warner, 1997). Mineral exports are defined as only fuels and primary metals (Sachs and Warner, 1999).
2   With regard to the former, De Ferranti et al. (2002) cited the history of successful natural resource-abundant countries, such as Canada, Australia, Sweden and Finland. According to standard economic theory, the wealth effects associated with natural resources should lead to increased investment and economic growth in the long run.

growth.³ In contrast, another strand of literature argues that natural resource abundance is a curse for the economy.⁴ The example of Dutch disease is a classic example of the direct negative effect of resource abundance – the discovery and exploitation of natural gas led to several incidences of economic difficulty in the Netherlands since the 1960s. Gylfason (2001) stated that natural resource abundance might hurt growth by harming trade, and Sachs and Warner (1997) found that economies with a high ratio of natural resource exports to GDP tended to grow relatively slowly.⁵

Given the debates or contrasting views on resource-based development, this chapter revisits this issue in the post-pandemic era. The disruption of global value chains (GVCs), which started at the onset of the pandemic through lockdown restrictions affecting the mobility of goods and people, has extended into the post-pandemic period. These disruptions pose both new difficulties and opportunities for emerging countries seeking new modes of development and catching-up. An OECD (2020) report observes that beyond the health risks, the shock of the rapid spread of the pandemic to African economies came in three waves: (i) lower trade and investment from abroad, including China, in the immediate term; (ii) a demand slump associated with the lockdowns in the European Union; and (iii) a continental supply shock affecting domestic and intra-African trade. Overall, the pandemic further shaken commodity-driven growth models in Africa that had largely failed to create more and better jobs or improve well-being. Further, Rudahindwa and Van Huellen (2020) observe that the pandemic has demonstrated the fragility of globally dispersed supply networks and reinvigorated an interest in regional networks.

---

3   In Bolivia, revenue from natural resource exports rose from 11% to 23% of Gross Domestic Product (GDP) over a nine-year period between 1975 and 1984. In Ecuador, revenue from primary exports rose by 19% of GDP in just two years (between 1972 and 1974). In Mexico, revenue from oil exports increased by 6% of GDP between 1978 and 1983 (Sachs and Warner, 1999).

4   Blum and Leamer (2004) asserted that natural resource abundance is a curse rather than a blessing. Leite and Weidmann (1999) suggested that capital-intensive sectors involving natural resources are a major source of corruption. Paldam (1997) explained that natural resource abundance is, as a rule, accompanied by booms and busts.

5   Gylfason (2001) explained that natural resources bring risks, with an economy becoming restricted to low-skill and natural-resource-intensive industries. He also found evidence that nations with abundant natural capital tend to have more corruption and less trade, foreign investment, education and domestic investment than other nations. Leite and Weidmann (1999) discussed the direct and indirect effects of natural resources. Poelhekke and Van der Ploeg (2009) also analysed the direct effect of natural resource abundance on economic growth and its indirect effects through the volatility of unanticipated output growth associated with price changes of resources. They found that the direct effect can be positive but can be swamped by the negative effect resulting from volatility.

Whatever alternative modes are possible, one common point of a new departure would be the need to rely more on domestic or regional resources for a more resilient pattern of development, where possible. The same OECD report also argues that strategies to recover from the crisis should include a strong structural component to reduce dependence on external financial flows and global markets and develop more value-adding, knowledge-intensive and industrialised economies. In this context, it is worthwhile to revisit the prospect of resource-based development strategies. Further, given that high-end manufacturing sectors imply higher entry barriers for most emerging economies at the middle-income stage, the possibilities of high-value-addition in resource-based sectors should be explored.

In fact, a paper by Lebdioui et al. (2020) suggests that Malaysia and Chile are showing some signs of growth beyond the middle-income trap,[6] owing their success not to manufacturing but to several resource-based sectors, such as petroleum, rubber and palm oil sectors in Malaysia, and salmon, fruits, wine and forestry in Chile. These sectors are not just domestic market-oriented but export-oriented, and further, they are not exporting crude resources but processed or high value-added exports. These cases point to the possibility of resource sectors serving as the engine of export-oriented growth in resource-rich countries, including those in Africa.

Successful catching-up through specialisation in resource-based sectors is consistent with the argument that the latecomers should identify low-entry barrier sectors in the international division of labour (Lee, 2013). These resource-based sectors represented such low-entry barrier sectors for many resource-rich emerging economies. Somewhat differently from the early arguments by Latin American scholars (Perez, 2008) that emerging economies could utilise resource-based development to leapfrog into emerging technologies, such as IT, it may be argued that the resource sectors could be the ultimate leading sectors generating intra-sectoral diversification and deepening in value chains, and not just transitional sectors leading diversification into non-resource sectors.

This chapter explores the possibility and strategies for resource-based development (RBD) in the post-pandemic era, and it will focus on three enabling conditions for resource-based development.

First, it will be argued that upgrading by resource sectors requires a specific 'getting prices wrong' style industrial policy, in particular, given the

---

6   The middle-income trap is defined as the per capita GDP of a country/region remaining within 20%–40% for several decades (World Bank, 2010, 2012).

possibility of a different kind of resource curse; a price boom reinforcing the prevailing export of crude or unprocessed commodities (e.g. crude palm oil) but discouraging the desired transition to the export of processed commodities (Sato, 2016). 'Getting prices wrong' by taxes, subsidies, or regulation may be necessary, like in the example of the successful manipulation of export taxes on crude versus processed palm oil in Malaysia (Oikawa, 2016).

Second, the eventual emergence of locally controlled firms plus local ownership of resources may be an important ingredient for long-term success with RBD, although the sources of initial learning importantly include foreign actors and foreign direct investment (FDI). This is consistent with early insight by Amsden (1989) that foreign investments and multinational corporations (MNCs) can be important channels to access foreign knowledge but tend to interfere with the eventual growth of indigenous technological capabilities. It is also consistent with the non-linear, or the 'In-Out-In Again' pattern of the GVC participation (Lee et al., 2018). The idea was that at the initial stage of growth by a latecomer, increased participation in GVC is necessary to learn foreign knowledge and production skills. In the functional upgrade at the middle-income stage, effort must shift to seek separation and independence from existing foreign-dominated GVCs so as to increase domestic value-added. Finally, after establishing their local value chains, latecomer firms and economies may have to seek reintegration into the GVCs, which emphasises the transient separation from GVC at the middle-income stages so as to increase domestic value-added and to develop technological capabilities.

The third factor would be macroeconomic policies, in particular in relation to exchange rates, to facilitate the export orientation of resource sectors. This factor is related to the question of why it is so difficult to expand manufacturing and manufactured exports in resource-rich developing countries. This is referred to as the barrier of the resource curse and associated vicious cycles. First proposed in Ramanayake and Lee (2018), this barrier arises due to the negative effect of undervaluation on the dollar-based earnings from primary exports. The problem is that the more a currency is undervalued in countries that are highly dependent on natural resource exports, the less are their earnings in dollars, while exports of natural resources are not responding much to the changes in exchange rates (given their low elasticity). This finding underscores a policy dilemma for resource-rich countries aiming to diversify into manufacturing. While they need undervaluation of local currency to promote manufactured exports, undervaluation has an immediate negative effect on economic growth through its negative effect on earnings from natural resource exports. While dual exchange rates may be one obvious way to overcome this dilemma, other solutions can also be explored, such as a bold policy move to adopt the non-exchange rate-linked, asymmetric support for the resource sector, for example, preferential loans, entry controls (licensing) and subsidies.

Following the exploration of the three enabling conditions for resource-based development, Section 2 of the chapter provides a discussion of the related literature on growth strategies in the South, with a focus on resource-based development. The following sections discuss each of the three issues raised above. In other words, Section 3 covers the subject of macroeconomic issues in promoting the resource sector as an export-oriented industry. Section 4 discusses the importance of local ownership as a necessary condition for success with resource-based development. Section 5 discusses the role of industrial policy in boosting the resource-based sector, especially in the context of regional developmentalism. Finally, Section 6 concludes the chapter with a summary and some policy discussions for Africa in a post-pandemic context.

Debates on development trajectories: Primacy of manufacturing vs alternatives

Most of the literature emphasises the primacy of manufacturing in catching-up, stressing that no country has reached a high-income status without first developing manufacturing. However, my view is that the manufacturing to service sequence is just one of the options for latecomers (Malerba and Lee, 2021). There exist alternatives, including leapfrogging into newly emerging sectors (new IT services), advanced resource-based sectors, a combination of services and manufacturing taking advantage of the technologies of the new millennium, and green technologies, to name a few. This flexible approach is consistent with an evolutionary economics perspective which considers economic catch-up as not deterministic but a dynamically evolving process, always seeking new niches and taking advantage of new windows of opportunity associated with not only hard-core innovations but also new business models (Malerba and Lee, 2021).

Africa has struggled with developing its manufacturing sector for several reasons. The continent is characterised by weak manufacturing, premature tertiarisation leading to a high presence of micro-enterprises and weak export bases (African Export-Import Bank, 2017, 14–34). Such difficulties must have been caused by a combination of several factors or unfavourable initial conditions, such as colonial experiences, frequent civil wars and political instability, or food shortage and hunger. Regarding financial markets, the high policy rates prevailing in Africa for controlling inflation or sterilisation purposes has led to de facto crowded-out loans to SMEs. High transaction costs and fragmented financial markets have also kept interest spreads between deposit and loan rates very high (Nissanke, 2019).

Thus, the cost of obtaining bank credits and loans is often prohibitively high for most domestic firms in African countries; for example, lending (nominal) interest rates were very high in 2018 coming in at 19.8% in Uganda, at 32.3% in Malawi, and at 26.7% in the Democratic Republic of Congo, according to World Bank data.[7] Typical commercial banks tend to charge interest rates of as high as 30% (Seibel, 2002). This is very high even in terms of real interest rates,[8] in view of the tolerable inflation rates and low-interest rates applied to savings deposited into banks in some countries like Uganda (Lee, 2019). This situation is unfavourable for private investment and reflects the asymmetric power and dominance of the lender over the borrower and of the banking sector, owned by foreign MNCs, over the manufacturing sector. If both sides have equal power, then interest rates for savings should also be high. In other words, financial markets are oligopolistic and imbalanced in terms of the power of supply and demand and may be in a state of market failure. Such a situation may justify government intervention, including the regulation of interest rates. The fact that the banking sector is earning extra rents associated with oligopoly is the opposite of the desirable state of a productive sector enjoying rents. This is opposite to past situations in Germany, Japan or Korea where the banking sector 'served' the real (manufacturing) sectors by providing a stable supply of so-called 'growth money,' at affordable rates for the German, Japanese and Korean economies to realise structural transformation with manufacturing as the pillar sector (Lee, 2019; Nissanke, 2019).

Further, in many African countries, exports are unresponsive despite competitive exchange rates (undervaluation). This situation is expected because competitive exchange rates work to boost exports only in an economy with a strong manufacturing basis. Moreover, Ramanayake and Lee (2018) found a negative effect of undervaluation on growth in mineral-exporting groups; if the currency is undervalued in countries that depend substantially on natural resource exports, then less income is earned in

---

7   The source is the World Bank data on lending interest rate (%) in sub-Saharan Africa available at: https://data.worldbank.org/indicator/FR.INR.lend
8   The same World Bank data show the following ranges of real interests rates: 21.0% in Democratic Congo (2019), 24.0% in Malawi (2018), 14.6% in Uganda (2018).

terms of dollars because natural resource exports are often insensitive or inelastic to exchange rates.

In sum, the typical conditions of already-free capital mobility and already-privatised banking sectors in Africa indicate that promoting manufacturing is difficult. Given the liberalised financial system, undervaluation of currency leads to capital flight and thus to decrease of domestic savings available for investment. Control of interest rates to boost investment in industrial sectors is also not that feasible under the private (or foreign) dominance of commercial banking. The situation in Kenya, where an interest ceiling was implemented fairly recently, shows such a dilemma (Lee, 2019).

If domestic effort to promote exports is limited, then foreign direct investment (FDI) is certainly an option. However, attracting FDI in the manufacturing sector has not been easy either in many African countries, except in a few (e.g. Ethiopia) that receive FDI flow from Asia, including China. Further, the pandemic has weakened FDI in Africa.[9] In this case, a radical or innovative idea for a country, such as Uganda, might be to leapfrog into IT services or smart agriculture and bypass the manufacturing stage (Lee et al., 2014). A preceding case of leapfrogging happened in India, which bypassed manufacturing to leapfrog into IT service as its engine of growth (Lee, 2019). Agriculture is increasingly being recognised no longer as a traditional industry but rather as a high-technology sector that belongs to the so-called 'sixth industry', a combination of primary, secondary and tertiary industries.[10] The sixth industry is combined with IT or digital technologies as it braces for the benefits of new innovations that have been associated in recent years with the 4IR (Fourth Industrial Revolution). Broadly, not only agriculture but also other resource-based activities may be a more attractive sector to FDI than manufacturing in several African economies in terms of comparative advantages.

Furthermore, even some success in FDI-based manufacturing tends to remain in low-value-added activities, and is eventually subject to a growth slow-down or middle-income trap situation (Lee and Ramanayake, 2018). Even manufacturing in Malaysia, Thailand and Mexico is not safe from

---

9   On the general effect of the pandemic on FDI, see the UNCTAD report at https://unctad.org/press-material/impact-coronavirus-outbreak-global-fdi. Specifically in Africa, see: https://www.tralac.org/blog/article/14720-covid-19-to-curtail-fdi-flows-to-africa-in-2020-how-to-mitigate-the-effects-in-the-long-term.html#:~:text=The%20coronavirus%20(COVID%2D19),to%2040%20percent%20in%202020

10 As one of the many sources of the term 'sixth industry', please refer to: https://japancrops.com/en/prefectures/tokyo/sixth-industry/

the middle-income trap symptoms (Lee, 2019), although these economies have been considered to have achieved some success benefitting from participation at the GVC (Baldwin, 2016, 250–254). As discussed in Lebdioui et al. (2020), the IT industry in Malaysia is only a mixed success in terms of upgrading, although it used to be the dominant export sector. The mixed success of IT manufacturing can be attributed to a combination of a lack of explicit industrial policy and of a critical mass of locally owned firms vis-à-vis continuing dominance of MNCs in the sector. Again, the dominance of MNCs implies less room for state intervention and less interest in building local capabilities, local suppliers and local linkages. In the IT manufacturing sector in Malaysia, the government adopted a rather 'minimalist' approach, mainly providing basic infrastructure and government services and promoting FDI by offering tax incentives and low wages (Rasiah, 2017).

The initial outcome was the successful growth of low value-added labour-intensive FDI-led manufacturing. However, the long-term sustainability of such a strategy was not certain because Malaysia also faced rising wage rates, while other neighbouring countries offered lower wages to attract FDI. In other words, the IT sector in Malaysia was not innovative enough to compete against high-wage innovators from the top economies and, at the same time, their wages were already too high to compete against low-wage manufacturers. This is the typical symptom of the middle-income trap (World Bank, 2012), and some studies had discussed such a possibility with regard to Malaysia (Rasiah, 2006; Yusuf and Nabeshima, 2009). Malaysia's shares in global high-tech exports have decreased in the past decade, and Malaysia is losing its labour-cost advantage to neighbouring countries (e.g. Vietnam). In the meantime, technology diffusion and domestic linkages have remained constrained by the lack of technology transfer by MNCs in Malaysia (Cherif and Hasanov, 2015; Raj-Reichert, 2019). Some countries in Africa would also be subject to this risk of the middle-income trap, such as South Africa and Mauritius (Lee et al., 2021).

Given this background, we are now set to explore the possibility of resource-based development.

Overcoming the double resource curse

Over time, many developing countries have become increasingly reliant on export revenues from minerals as their primary source of foreign exchange earnings. Table 1 lists the 20 countries with the highest mineral-export contributions as a percentage of total merchandise exports in 2010, also reporting this share for these countries in 1996 and 2005. It can be noted that almost half of them are from Africa. Many of these countries have low human development index (HDI) scores, drawing attention to the potential for earnings from the mining sector to contribute to poverty reduction. In particular, in Chile, Ghana and Brazil, mining businesses contribute to poverty reduction and improve social development indicators more than non-mining ones (International Council on Mining and Metals [ICMM] 2012). The ICMM suggests that the mining sector's contribution is important for sustaining development, especially in developing countries. According to the ICMM report in 2012, the nominal value of world mineral production was nearly four times higher than it was in 2002, which implied more earnings from the same amount of production.

Table 1: Reliance on export of metallic minerals

Rank by country (2010)	Mineral export contribution as % of total merchandise exports in 1996	Mineral export contribution as % of total merchandise exports in 2005	Mineral export contribution as % of total merchandise exports in 2010
1 Botswana	58.70%	86.50%	83.70%
2 Zambia	79.40%	64.00%	83.60%
3 Dem. Rep. of the Congo	72.40%	70.20%	78.30%
4 Mongolia	60.30%	70.10%	77.60%
5 Suriname	68.00%	64.30%	75.40%
6 French Polynesia	69.20%	55.30%	67.10%
7 Chile	47.70%	56.50%	65.90%
8 Guinea	77.10%	84.00%	65.20%
9 Peru	48.30%	57.90%	62.70%
10 Mauritania	36.10%	49.30%	60.40%
11 Northern Mariana Islands	3.30%	4.50%	58.90%
12 Mozambique	6.10%	66.90%	57.00%
13 Mali	8.50%	37.20%	54.80%
14 Sierra Leone	30.60%	58.20%	54.30%
15 Papua New Guinea	24.50%	39.20%	54.00%
16 Namibia	36.20%	41.20%	53.40%
17 Nauru	73.10%	25.20%	50.80%
18 Armenia	23.90%	39.80%	50.60%
19 Jamaica	49.70%	68.50%	49.60%
20 Cuba	15.10%	39.20%	47.70%

Notes: Reproduced from ICMM (2012); Mineral (non-fuel) exports in 2010 as a percentage of total merchandise exports (UNCTAD data); from Ramanayake and Lee (2018). African countries highlighted.

Given the large contribution of natural resource exports for many developing countries, examining the effect of currency undervaluation or overvaluation on mineral exports is important. UNCTAD (2005) highlights the fact that the real exchange rate reflects the underlying relative movement of prices at home and abroad. Generally, currency undervaluation, depreciation, or devaluation increases the competitiveness of exports and makes imports more expensive. Currency overvaluation or appreciation makes imports cheaper and exports more expensive. Rodrik (2008) found that currency undervaluation stimulates economic growth and export expansion, particularly in developing countries.[11] Actually, the currencies of developing countries tend to be undervalued in terms of the estimation approach of Rodrik (2008). By enhancing the sector's profitability in such a situation, undervaluation works as a second-best policy that compensates for the negative effects of these distortions. High profitability promotes investment in tradable sectors, which subsequently expand and promote economic growth. Setterfield (2010) asserted that developing countries obtain significant growth benefits by maintaining a low value of their currencies relative to competing developing countries. Yeyati and Sturzenegger (2007) claimed that an undervalued currency boosts output and productivity growth. Korinek and Servén (2010) also asserted that currency undervaluation can raise growth through learning-by-doing externalities in tradable sectors.

Nevertheless, the 'undervaluation is good' growth argument has also been criticised (Aguirre and Calderon, 2005; Williamson, 2012).[12] Aguirre and Calderon (2005) explained that although small or moderate undervaluation enhances growth, large undervaluation hurts growth. Haddad and Pancaro (2010) claimed that undervaluation causes high and destabilising liquidity growth and inflation, which leads to financial instability, with undervaluation working for low-income countries only in the medium term. Therefore, whether undervaluation is beneficial or harmful to growth remains debatable.

Given this background, it is worthwhile delving deeper into the effects of undervaluation on economic growth in mineral exporting countries. Currencies have been increasingly undervalued rather than overvalued in most mineral-exporting countries such as Botswana, Guinea, Mauritania, Papua New Guinea and Peru, countries with shares of mineral exports in total exports of more than 40% (Ramanayake and Lee, 2018). Thus, examining whether currency undervaluation is truly responsible for

---

11 Countries with per capita income below USD 2,500.
12 Williamson (2012) demonstrated that undervalued currencies are likely to improve the current account surplus, stimulating capital flows out of the country instead of in, thus impeding investment from entrepreneurs and, ultimately, economic growth.

declining growth in these mineral-exporting countries is meaningful. But, the findings of Ramanayake and Lee (2018) indicate that undervaluation hurts economic growth in mineral-exporting countries.[13] This study compared two different samples of countries: manufacturing-exporting countries and natural-resource-exporting countries.[14] The results suggest that while the degree of undervaluation has a positive but insignificant impact on growth for manufacturing exporters, the effect on natural resource exporters is negative and significant.[15] The results indicate that currency overvaluation may be beneficial for economic growth in mineral-exporting countries. The interpretation was that undervaluation exerts significant effects only in the presence of a strong manufacturing base and an adequate level of capabilities. This finding is consistent with the fact that if a currency is more undervalued in countries that are highly dependent on natural resource exports, then they earn less income in terms of dollars, given that natural resource exports are inelastic to changes in exchange rates.

This finding underscores a policy dilemma for resource-rich countries aiming to eventually diversify into manufacturing. While they need undervaluation to promote manufactured exports, such a policy stance has immediate adverse effects on economic growth through its negative effect on dollar-based earnings from natural resource exports. In countries with no such capacity in manufacturing but primarily reliant on mineral exports, crisis-driven devaluation does not boost exports sufficiently and thus recovery tends to be slow or prolonged, with the countries ending up with more foreign debts, which is consistent with the situation of the so-called middle-income trap (Bresser-Pereira et al., 2020; World Bank, 2012).

Undervaluation's failure to produce significant effects underscores the difficulties facing economic growth in mineral-exporting economies and

---

13   This study uses cross-country panel data with data averaged over five-year periods from 1986 to 2012. The samples of manufacturing- and natural-resource-exporting countries are pooled together in the analysis, with dummy variables for manufacturing and natural resource exporters (along with their interactions with the main explanatory variables) included to allow for different effects across the two samples.

14   The natural-resource-exporting sample consists of only mineral-exporting countries (excluding giant oil exporters) that had a share of mineral exports in total exports of 40% or more in 2010. The manufacturing-export sample includes countries where manufacturing exports constituted at least 70% of their total goods exports (in at least one of the two years, 1999 or 2001). The global average of this percentage corresponds to an average of 68% over 1999–2003, as reported by UNCTAD (2005).

15   This positive but insignificant effect is consistent with Ramanayake and Lee (2015), who found that undervaluation significantly affects growth in high-income countries but not in middle- or low-income countries.

thus the dilemma of the so-called resource-based development model. Countries get caught up in a vicious cycle, and the means to stop the cycle remain unclear. It can be called the 'double resource curse' in the sense that these countries face not only the original curse of low growth but also the curse of not being able to promote manufacturing even by the undervaluation of local currencies.

It then implies that managing exchange rates alone is not a solution for long-term growth in these countries. One way out of this vicious circle is to make their resources more processed rather than to export unprocessed resources, which make them high value-added or even manufactured goods, for example, wines rather than grapes. That is what happened in the resource-based export sector in Chile and Malaysia (Lebdioui et al., 2020); Chile exports wines rather than grapes, processed vegetables and fruits and furniture rather than woods, whereas Malaysia exports condoms rather than rubber, palm oils rather than palms and refined oils and products than crude oils. The prices of these processed products are more sensitive to exchange rates, with a higher price elasticity than unprocessed materials. Then, undervaluation or depreciation to more export linkage can be established.

Such transformation, of course, requires the development of technological capabilities, a more pressing concern (Lee et al., 2014; Lee and Mathews, 2012). Broadly, regarding this barrier of the double resource curse, one possible means of exiting such a bad equilibrium would be for a big push or leapfrogging, which can be combined with a bold policy move to adopt non-exchange rate-linked, asymmetric support for the manufacturing sector, such as preferential loans, entry controls (licensing) and tariffs. Again, Malaysia may offer an example.

Interestingly, Malaysia's efforts to stimulate resource-based exports (e.g. palm oils) were met with counter-attacks from the incumbent firms (Lebdioui et al., 2020). For instance, Malaysia's exports of processed palm oil in the 1970s were blocked by the European common market, which practised tariff escalation to ensure that refining capacity would remain in Europe. In order to counter the EU import duty structure, the Malaysian government had initially decided to introduce an export duty on crude palm oil production. After further tariffs escalation in the EU in the 1990s, from about 100% in the 1970s to more than 200% in the 1990s (Gopal, 2001), most market deals for Malaysian processed palm oil were signed through government-to-government partnerships under so-called barter arrangements.[16] As a result of this barter trade that enabled securing export markets, palm oil refining activities in Malaysia considerably increased and became the most competitive internationally within ten years, achieving both economies of scale and scope. Another incentive for processed palm oil against crude oil was higher export taxes on crude oil and lower taxes for more processed oil, which made domestic prices of crude and processed oil deviate from the international market prices (Oikawa, 2016).

Then, the eventual solution was Malaysia's execution of a hostile takeover of three British palm oil and rubber plantation conglomerates listed in the London stock exchange by Malaysian public capital in 1981 (Oikawa, 2016). While we will deal with this issue of ownership in the next section, it can be said that such upgrading into exporting processed palm oil, rather than crude oil, would not have been possible if there was no change of ownership from foreign to local. In the following sections, we will turn more to these two issues, namely local ownership and industrial policy.

Local ownership as an eventual requisite for upgrading in GVCs

This section deals with one of the most delicate issues in development, namely the role of foreign versus domestic ownership in upgrading through GVC participation. Our proposition is that the eventual emergence of locally controlled firms plus local ownership of resources may also be an important ingredient for long-term success with RBD, although the sources of initial learning importantly included foreign actors and FDI. This is consistent with early insight by Amsden (1989) that foreign investments and MNCs can be important channels to access foreign knowledge but tend to interfere with the eventual growth of indigenous technological capabilities.

Such a view is also consistent with the recent finding of the 'In-Out-In Again' pattern of the GVC participation in Lee et al. (2018). The idea was that at the initial stage of growth by a latecomer, increased participation in GVC is necessary to learn foreign knowledge and production skills. In the functional upgrade at the middle-income stage, effort must shift to seeking separation and independence from existing foreign-dominated GVCs so as to increase domestic value-added. Finally, after establishing their local

---

16   Barter grade is a system of trade in which participants in a transaction directly exchange goods or services for other goods and services of equivalent value without the use of money.

value chains, latecomer firms and economies may have to seek reintegration into the GVC, which emphasises the transient separation from GVCs at the middle-income stages so as to increase domestic value-added and to develop technological capabilities.

The case of resource sectors in Malaysia may offer some lessons about the importance of local ownership. In both the rubber and palm oil sector in Malaysia, the plantations were all foreign-owned in the early days going back to the colonial period, and there was no interest in increasing domestic value-added compared to foreign value-added. The largely European-controlled plantation companies preferred to export crude palm oil and did not see many gains in relocating their vegetable oil processing facilities in Malaysia. After the initial entry point into the foreign-dominated GVCs during colonial times, Malaysia broke up those foreign-led GVCs through the nationalisation of ownership as it executed a hostile takeover of three British palm oil and rubber plantation conglomerates listed in the London stock exchange by Malaysian public capital in 1981 (Lebdioui, 2019b; Oikawa, 2016). The interest in processing palm oil and natural rubber locally has increased since then. In addition, in the rubber sector, a large difference in purchasing behaviour can be noted between domestic and foreign firms. Foreign-owned firms have fewer forward and backward linkages to other manufacturers in the Malaysian economy than domestically owned firms.

The petroleum sector of Malaysia was initially dominated by multinational oil companies, which remained the main providers of upstream technology in the early periods of resource exploitation, especially given the context of Malaysia's technology-demanding offshore and deep-water fields. To overcome such a situation, the government of Malaysia established a state-owned enterprise, Petronas, in 1974, which became possible by proclamation of the Petroleum Development Act (PDA) and the associated Production-Sharing Contracts (PSC). The objective of the PDA was to gain greater national control over petroleum resources, to provide affordable petroleum resources to the local market to form the basis for capital and energy-intensive industries and to encourage production linkages in both upstream and downstream activities (Nordas et al., 2003). Petronas, the state-owned oil corporation, has also gradually developed capabilities and upgraded into higher-value activities.

The government also initiated a holistic approach to industrial policy combining local content requirements, tax incentives, skills transfer (through technical and specialised universities), state-led investments and opportunities for learning by doing (Lebdioui, 2019a). These tools have been successful in enhancing the industrial capabilities of local suppliers by allowing local firms to benefit from more stable intra-industry relationships, exposure to best practices, quality standards, as well as marketing capabilities. This holistic approach led to the accumulation of the capabilities needed for knowledge-intensive activities along the petroleum value chain.

Petronas was an essential vehicle for such an industrial policy drive as it ran a programme like the Petronas Vendor Development Programme to bring up local suppliers. Petronas' partners are required to pay Petronas an annual research contribution, the 'Research Cess', to promote joint R&D (PSC, Arts 9.1 and 9.2). Thus, the growth of local companies followed that of Petronas, and 74% of the total value of contracts in upstream activities in the petroleum sector was granted to local companies by 1995 (Tordo and Anouti, 2013). Given the key role in promoting production linkages through several initiatives, it is doubtful whether similar value addition results would have been achieved if international oil corporations controlled the sector. Petronas itself has grown into a fully integrated international oil and gas company, which operates in over 30 countries. It is now on the list of the global Fortune 500 companies.

The role of ownership can also be discussed in terms of the upgrading path from OEM to ODM and OBM, in that along these three stages, ownership increases from simple ownership of production equipment and facility (OEM: own equipment manufacturing) to ownership of (product) design (ODM; own design manufacturing) and finally to own brand (OBM: own brand manufacturing). Despite the effectiveness of OEM as a method of catching-up at an early stage of economic growth, this mode is a somewhat uncertain long-term strategy because foreign vendor firms may move their production orders to other low-wage production sites (Lee and Mathews, 2012).

Currently, a similar trend is underway among flower producers in East Africa because foreign vendor firms buy flowers not only from Kenya but also from neighbouring countries that are catching up with Kenya. In this respect, OEM firms should prepare long-term plans in their transition to original design manufacturing (ODM) and finally to original brand manufacturing (OBM). ODM firms carry out most of the detailed product design, and their customer firms continue with marketing functions. Meanwhile, OBM firms undertake to manufacture, design new products, R&D for materials, processing of products, and sales and distribution for their own brands. The path from OEM to ODM to OBM has become the standard upgrade process for latecomer firms (Lee, 2019).

The transition to OBM is difficult and rare even in East Asia (Lee, 2019). However, a successful case can be found in Uganda in Africa. Good African

Coffee, a coffee company established in 2013 by an entrepreneur from Uganda named Rugasira, has been successful in the global market with its brands and sales network in Europe and North America. This case is very unusual and exceptional in Africa because this company exports not crude or unprocessed coffee but high-valued processed branded coffee. However, an interesting aspect of this case is that the company skipped the OEM stage and attempted OBM from the beginning. In a sense, this is a case of leapfrogging that bypassed the earlier stage of OEM. Actually, the company started by selling its own brand of coffee in retail supermarkets in foreign countries with packing performed abroad. Only after several years did the company gain the capacity of packaging in Uganda. This case is similar to several Korean companies, such as Hyundai Motors, which started selling cars with its own brands but with foreign-made engines and transmission and only later progressed to localising production of engines and transmission. This case may imply that the agri-food industry and processing segment of the primary sector industry can also be a compelling option for industrial development in Africa.

Modified examples of such upgrading in African flower firms include producing long-lasting flowers with specific scents and using a small number of pesticides, which require innovation. A transition to OBM in the flower industry will require African firms to enter into marketing and to set up their own outlets with their own brands in Europe. Such a transition to ODM or OBM is difficult but serves as a narrow path to the middle- or even high-income status. In a sense, Botswana is attempting to find a niche by targeting the middle-level quality of diamond cutting and polishing, which lies above that of the small stones produced in China and India and below that of the specialised stones produced in Belgium and Israel (Morris et al., 2012).

In this stage, public policy should focus on two kinds of upgrading: entry into new industries and upgrading to high-valued segments in existing industries, which involves upgrading the overall industrial structure (Lee, 2019). Short-cycle technology-based sectors are candidate niches for latecomers. The main issue is determining how to break into medium short-cycle technology-based products or the high-valued segment of existing sectors. Effective targets for such import substitution entry are the products that these countries used to import at high prices because of the oligopolistic market structure dominated by incumbent exporting countries or firms. A compelling example is China's telephone switch development in the 1980s and 1990s (Lee et al., 2012). These lessons have implications for African countries, such as Nigeria, which produce oil without refining and export mostly as crude oil. These countries can build additional oil refineries, which are sectors corresponding to mature or medium short-cycle technologies. This task is possible because the technology required to build oil refineries is old, mature and easily available at a cost. The process resembles Korea's entry into steel making through a state-owned enterprise in the early 1970s.

The above-mentioned technological development models share the common element of involving access to foreign knowledge through diverse channels. Foreign knowledge is critical because latecomers' catching-up effort frequently becomes risky, time-consuming and costly without it. The diverse channels of knowledge, access and learning generally include such modes as training in foreign firms and institutes, OEM, licensing, joint ventures, co-development with foreign specialised R&D firms, hiring of individual scientists or engineers, reverse brain drain, overseas R&D centres, strategic alliances, and international mergers and acquisitions (Lee, 2013). Successful technological development by latecomers involves government support, access to foreign knowledge and private firms' effort. The weights and specific roles of the three elements differ by sector and level or stage of economic development.

Breaking the vicious circle/equilibrium by industrial policy

The discussion in the preceding section suggests that the issue of local ownership and room for industrial policy are closely intertwined in the sense that it is not easy to impose such intervention on foreign-owned firms, which are dominant in resource sectors in Africa. While that is an important aspect, the role of industrial policy goes beyond that, as it can break the 'bad' equilibrium. An example is the diamond sector in Botswana.

The diamond sector has been the key sector contributing to the rise of Botswana from a low-income to a middle-income country. An important trigger was the special deal between the Botswana government and the foreign actor (in this case, an MNC) through which local firms had been able to evolve from being simple commodity producers to diamond cutting and polishing processors since the 1980s (Lee, 2019). The path for such an upgrade was not smooth but took a long time. A change came in 2005 when De Beers, a global diamond jewellery company, and the Botswana government entered into a big deal to promote local processing industries (Morris et al., 2012). The government took advantage of its bargaining power in the specific year of 2005 when the 25-year mining license of De Beers was due for renewal. The government persuaded the multinational jewellery company to help Botswana create a viable cutting and polishing industry. It was a condition for the licence to be renewed for another 25 years (Morris et al., 2012). Until then, De Beers used to say that Botswana had no comparative advantage in the processing sector compared to those in India (Morris et al., 2012).

After the new contract was signed, the government encouraged leading cutting and polishing companies (16 in total) to establish factories in Botswana and to transfer required skills to local firms and workers. Now, a challenge for the next stage is to keep moving up the value chain from crude diamond production to cutting and polishing and then to polished dealing, jewellery manufacturing and marketing and sales to reach the high value-added segment in the value chain.

Further, upgrading by resource sectors requires specific 'getting prices wrong' style industrial policy. Research by Sato (2016) indicates the possibility of a different kind of resource curse, where a price boom for minerals reinforces the prevailing export of crude or unprocessed commodities (e.g. crude palm oil) but discourages the desired transition to exporting processed commodities. In this case, 'getting prices wrong' by taxes, subsidies or regulation may be necessary, like the successful manipulation of export taxes on crude versus processed palm oil in Malaysia (Oikawa, 2016).

Another channel to promote the resource sector in Africa can be 'regional developmentalism,' proposed by Rudahindwa and Van Huellen (2020) and Rudahindwa (2018) and inspired by the new developmental state paradigm, which advocates for gradual rather than full-fledged trade liberalisation, and endorse more significant state intervention to steer productive capacity development and the establishment of regional value chains relying on regional, rather than international, markets. A rationale and motivation for regional developmentalism is the recognition that conventional trade liberalisation and indiscriminate economic integration, such as the agreement to establish an African Continental Free Trade Area (AfCFTA), which aims to create a continental market for goods and services, has not led to trade diversification into higher value-added segments of supply chains, and thus the region continues to be heavily dependent on a primary commodity with devastating consequences for the balance of payment position of involved countries, in particular those in the ECOWAS (Economic Community of West African States) region.

Causes for such disappointing outcomes are not just slow progress in tariff reduction or often-cited supply-side bottlenecks but also fundamental asymmetry in global economic power structures (Rudahindwa and Van Huellen, 2020). For instance, typical agri-food chains, including the global cocoa-chocolate or coffee chain, are characterised by a high concentration of buyer power in the hands of a few MNCs, which makes it difficult for newcomers to enter (Cramer, 1999; Gereffi, 1994; Gibbon, 2001; Talbot, 2009).

Specifically, key players in the segments, such as grinders who process cocoa beans into intermediate products, branders who manufacture consumable end products and merchandise them, and large supermarket chains, are all highly concentrated, with a handful of MNCs holding more than 50% of the global market share (Gilbert, 2007; TCC, 2010; UNECA, 2013). Further, many advanced countries impose tariffs with the rates increasing progressively with the degree of cocoa processing, posing an effective barrier to entry. Given these structural asymmetries, a radical response would be a takeover of oligopolistic MNC or FDI firms in the value chains by indigenous agency, as happened in Malaysia (see the preceding section).

Or, one of the alternative routes for new entrants into a global value chain can be via regional markets (Nissanke, 2019; UNECA, 2013). Actually, the latest pandemic crisis has demonstrated the fragility of globally dispersed supply networks and reinvigorated interest in regional networks (Rudahindwa and Van Huellen, 2020). Regional markets can provide necessary linkages and niche markets for the infant industries to develop, whereby local firms are able to build up capabilities in regional markets that are less demanding in terms of standards and competition (Humphrey and Schmitz, 2004; Rudahindwa and Van Huellen, 2020).[17] Specific infant industry protection measures may include tariffs, import quotas and subsidised government loans. Rudahindwa (2018, 47) argues that these measures could be accommodated under the WTO Enabling Clause, which is designed to benefit regional trade agreements involving less developed countries, as well as GATT 94 article XVIII, which includes special measures for the protection and the nurturing of infant industries in poor developing countries.

Specific support for the coffee farmers by the Vietnamese government is pointed out as one of the factors for the rise of coffee sectors in Vietnam at the expense of market shares by coffee from Africa (Marsh, 2007).[18] While credits to farmers were offered at a very high rate of 15% in Africa, the state-owned development bank VBARD in Vietnam supplied farmers with credit in very favourable arrangements, including several clauses to protect farmers

---

[17] However, as Rudahindwa and Van Huellen (2020) observe, despite West Africa being the single largest region to contribute to global cocoa bean supply (75% of the world's cocoa is produced in West Africa), only 2% of the USD 100 billion cocoa industry is generated in the region and cocoa beans are largely exported with no or little processing for value addition (TAFAC, 2019). Paradoxically, West Africa and the African continent in general are among the fastest growing markets for consumer chocolate and cocoa containing foodstuff, whereby the rising demand is satisfied in great parts through imports from outside the region (89% of chocolate imports originate from outside the region).
[18] After 1990, Africa's coffee production dropped by an average of 1.5% per year while the growth in the Asian market was 4.1% per year (Dube and Vargas, 2013).

during difficult market conditions, such as an adjustment of loan repayment terms or freezing of repayment for up to three years when the price of coffee drops (Marsh, 2007). One factor for the advance of the coffee sector in Vietnam and Brazil is a mix of governmental policies helping farmers and producers as well as new inventive ways such as the increased density of productive hybrid varieties, irrigation and improved mechanical harvesting, combined with proactive industry organisations (Technoserve, 2003).

In sum, targeted industrial policy in the context of the regional developmentalism paradigm may promote export-led and resource-based industrialisation by building up productive capacity and related regional value chains to reverse the adverse effects of the international economic order on lower- and middle-income countries.

Summary and concluding remarks

Given the debate on the resource curse and resource-based development, this chapter revisits this issue in the context of the pandemic and prospects for the post-pandemic era. Disruption of GVCs in the post-pandemic era poses both additional difficulties and new opportunities for emerging countries seeking new modes of development and catch-up. Such a new mode can be something more reliant on domestic resources for a more resilient pattern of development if it is possible. Successful catch-up by specialising in those resource-based sectors is consistent with Lee's (2013) argument that the latecomers should identify low-entry barrier sectors in the international division of labour; these resource-based sectors have represented such low-entry barrier sectors for many resource-rich emerging economies.

In this sense, many resource-rich African countries can be said to have a certain advantage in resource-based activities, and the only problem is that they still tend to export unprocessed or raw materials. Such a situation is in contrast to the experiences of several countries on other continents that have managed to develop high value-added, export-oriented, resource-based sectors, pursuing RBD. This chapter suggested the following generic lessons extracted from other countries' examples that can be useful for African countries, although these should be further tailored to the specificities of each country, taking into account the multidimensional unfolding of the impacts from the pandemic (e.g. weakening of FDI, closures of many local businesses and limited ability for countries to use their exchange rates).

Briefly, this chapter identified the following three enabling conditions for resource-based development. First, upgrading by resource sectors requires specific 'getting prices wrong' style industrial policy. Second, the eventual emergence of locally controlled firms plus local ownership of resources may also be an important ingredient for long-term success with RBD, which is consistent with the early insight by Amsden (1989) and the recent observation about the 'In-out-In Again' pattern of the GVC participation in Lee et al. (2018). The third issue is how to overcome the 'double resource curse' that developing countries face; not only the original curse of low growth but also the curse of not being able to promote manufacturing even by the undervaluation of local currencies.[19] One solution is to promote high value-added or processed products by bold policy moves to promote innovation-based upgrading combined with non-exchange rate-linked, asymmetric support for the resource sector, such as preferential loans, entry controls (licensing) and subsidies.

These strategies can be further refined and implemented in view of several structural barriers, such as prohibitively high interest rates associated with an oligopolistic banking sector dominated by foreign banks, the concentration of high-end value chains by foreign MNCs, and high tariffs by advanced economies against processed foods and other commodities. Some of these are the consequences of the past liberalisation, and in this sense, African countries also suffer from the liberalisation-caused middle-income trap, like Latin American countries (Bresser-Pereira et al., 2020). Such vicious circle or equilibrium may require an effort and interventions to break up the equilibrium, such as establishing indigenously owned banks (including development banks), hostile take-over of foreign-held high-end value chains (as happened in the palm oil sector in Malaysia), and 'getting prices wrong' type industrial policy to disrupt asymmetry in power relations.

Overall, this study implied that there can be several alternative ways to promote economic development in emerging economies, despite the initial dominance of FDI and MNCs (Malerba and Lee, 2021). The first, mainly experienced in East Asia (e.g. Taiwan, South Korea), is based on the idea of catching-up by developing technological capabilities in short-cycle technology manufacturing sectors (Lee, 2013).[20] The second option

---

[19] As a matter of fact, despite the fact that the pandemic resulted in further depreciation of currencies of typical African countries, the situation is not helping any manufacturing in Africa, rather many local firms have been closed down.

[20] Lee (2019) points out that at the middle-income stages, Korea and Taiwan went through a different path by specialising in sectors with 'short-cycle' technologies in contrast to advanced economies that specialise in 'long-cycle' technology-based sectors (Lee, 2013). In sectors and activities that are based on short-cycle technologies, the extensive experience of firms in front-running countries is no longer considered an advantage because frontier technologies tend to be disrupted and change radically and frequently.

of specialisation for latecomers is not in manufacturing but in IT services, such as mobility, e-commerce, games, mobile payments, travel, music and entertainment, and other app-based services, with a prime example of success in India. As discussed in the context of Africa (Lee et al., 2014), these are also low-entry-barrier sectors, given that these IT-related services are also short-cycled, similar to IT manufacturing. The third or resource-based option is what has been discussed in this chapter, which was a gradual way to exercise consistent industrial policy to promote local capabilities – an option that focused more on the technological capabilities around resource-based industries rather than resource rents alone. It strongly relies on a strong process of linkage development to get out of the middle-income trap. My contribution to this debate is the analysis of this route with the example of the resource-based sectors in various countries.

References

African Export-Import Bank. (2017). *Transforming African Trade*. African Export-Import Bank.

Aguirre, A., and Calderon, C. (2005). Real exchange rate misalignments and economic performance. *Central Bank of Chile Working Papers*, no. 315.

Amsden, A. H. (1989). Asia's next giant: How Korea competes in the world-economy. *Technology Review*, 92(4), 46-53.

Baldwin, R. (2016). *The Great Convergence*. Harvard University Press.

Blum, B., and Leamer, E. E. (2004). Can FTA suspend the law of gravity and give the Americas higher growth and better income distribution? http://eml.berkeley.edu/~obstfeld/e281_sp03/leamer.pdf

Bresser-Pereira, L. C., Araujo, E. C., and Peres, S. C. (2020). An alternative to the middle-income trap. *Structural Change and Economic Dynamics*, 52, 294-312.

Cherif, R., and Hasanov, F. (2015). The leap of the tiger: How Malaysia can escape the middle-income trap. *IMF Working Paper* WP/15/131. IMF.

Cramer, C. (1999). Can Africa industrialize by processing primary commodities? The case of Mozambican cashew nuts. *World Development*, 27(7), 1247-1266.

De Ferranti, D., Perry, G. E., Lederman, D., and Maloney, W. (2002). *From Natural Resources to the Knowledge Economy: Trade and job quality*. World Bank Latin American and Caribbean Studies.

Dube, O., and Vargas, J. F. (2013). *Commodity Price Shocks and Civil Conflicts: Evidence from Columbia*. Oxford University Press.

Gereffi, G. (1994). The organization of buyer-driven global commodity chains: How U.S. retailers shape overseas production network. In: G. Gereffi and M. Korzeniewicz (Eds), *Commodity Chains and Global Capitalism*. Praeger.

Gibbon, P. (2001). Upgrading primary production: A global commodity chain approach. *World Development*, 29(2), 345-363.

Gilbert, C. L. (2007). *Value Chain Analysis and Market Power in Commodity Processing with Application to the Cocoa and Coffee Sectors*. Commodity Market Review: CMR.

Gopal, J. (2001). The development of Malaysia's palm oil refining industry: Obstacles, policy and performance. PhD thesis submitted, Imperial College, London.

Gylfason, T. (2001). Natural resources, education, and economic development. *European Economic Review*, 45(4), 847-859.

Haddad, M., and Pancaro, C. (2010). *Can Real Exchange Rate Undervaluation Boost Exports and Growth in Developing Countries? Yes, but not for long*. World Bank.

Humphrey, J., and Schmitz, H. (2004). Chain governance and upgrading: Taking stock. In: H. Schmitz (Ed.), *Local Enterprises in the Global Economy: Issues of governance and upgrading* (349-382). Edward Elgar.

International Council on Mining and Metals (ICMM). (2012). *The Role of Mining in National Economies: Mining's contribution to sustainable development*. ICMM.

Korinek, A., and Servén, L. (2010). Undervaluation through foreign reserve accumulation: Static losses, dynamic growth. *World Bank Policy Research Working Paper* no. 5250. World Bank.

Lebdioui, A. (2019a). Local content in extractive industries: Evidence and lessons from Chile and Malaysia. *Extractive Industries and Society*. https://doi.org/10.1016/j.exis.2019.05.001

Lebdioui, A. (2019b). Economic diversification and development in resource-dependent economies: Lessons from Chile and Malaysia. PhD thesis, University of Cambridge.

Lebdioui, A., Lee, K., and Pietrobelli, C. (2020). Local-foreign technology interface, resource-based development, and industrial policy: How Chile and Malaysia are escaping the middle income trap. *Journal of Technology Transfer*, 46(3), 660-685. DOI: 10.1007/s10961-020-09808-3.

Lee, K. (2013). *Schumpeterian Analysis of Economic Catch-Up: Knowledge, path-creation, and the middle-income trap*. Cambridge University Press.

Lee, K. (2019). *The Art of Economic Catch-up: Barriers, detours and leapfrogging in innovation systems*. Cambridge University Press.

Lee, K., Lee, J., and Lee, J. (2021). Alternative pathways to growth beyond the middle-income stage and national innovation systems (NIS): Balanced, imbalanced, catching-up, and trapped NIS. *World Development*, 144, 105472.

Lee, K., Mani, S., and Mu, Q. (2012). Explaining divergent stories of catch-up in the telecommunication equipment industry in Brazil, China, India, and Korea. In: F. Malerba and R. Nelson (Eds), *Economic Development as a Learning Process* (21-71). Edward Elgar.

Lee, K., and Mathews, J. (2012) Firms in Korea and Taiwan. In: J. Cantwell and E. Amman (Eds), *The Innovative firms in the Emerging Market Economies* (223-245). Oxford University Press.

Lee, K., Juma, C., and Mathews. J. (2014). Innovation capabilities for sustainable development in Africa. In: C. I. Monga and J. Y. Lin (Eds), *The Oxford Handbook of Africa and Economics*. Oxford University Press.

Lee, K., and Ramanayake, S. (2018). The adding-up problem and wage-productivity gap in exports of developing countries: A source of the middle-income trap. *European Journal of Development Research*, 30(5), 769-788.

Lee, K., Szapiro, M., and Mao, Z. (2018). From global value chains (GVC) to innovation systems for local value chains and knowledge creation. *The European Journal of Development Research*, 30(3), 424-441.

Leite, C., and Weidmann, J. (1999). *Does Mother Nature Corrupt? Natural resources, corruption and economic growth*. IMF African and Research Department.

Malerba, F., and Lee, K. (2021). An evolutionary perspective on economic catch-up by latecomers. *Industrial and Corporate Change*. https://doi.org/ 10.1093/icc/dtab008

Marsh, A. (2007). Diversification by smallholder farmers: Vietnam robusta coffee. *Marketing and Finance Working Document* no. 19. FAO.

Morris, M., Kaplinsky, R., and Kaplan, D. (2012). *One Thing Leads to Another: Promoting industrialisation by making the most of the commodity boom in sub-Saharan Africa*. Lulu.

Nissanke, M. (2019). Exploring macroeconomic frameworks conducive to structural transformation of sub-Saharan African economies. *Structural Change and Economics Dynamics*, 49, 103-116.

Nordas, H. K., Vatne, E., and Heum, P. (2003). The upstream petroleum industry and local industrial development: A comparative study. NHH Brage. http://hdl.handle.net/11250/164495

Organisation for Economic Co-operation and Development (OECD). (2020, 7 May). COVID-19 and Africa: Socio-economic implications and policy responses. OECD Policy Responses to Coronavirus (COVID-19).

Oikawa, H. (2016). Resource-based industrialization of the Malaysian palm oil industry. In: Y. Sato and H. Sato (Eds), *Varieties and Alternatives of Catching-up* (247-276). Palgrave Macmillan.

Paldam, M. (1997). Dutch disease and rent seeking: The Greenland model. *European Journal of Political Economy*, 13(1), 591-614.

Perez, C. (2008). A vision for Latin America: A resource-based strategy for technological dynamism and social inclusion. *Globelics Working Paper Series* no. 2008-04. The Global Network for Economics of Learning, Innovation and Competence Building System (Globelics).

Poelhekke, S., and Van der Ploeg, F. (2009). Volatility and natural resource curse. *Oxford Economic Papers*, 61(4), 727-760.

Raj-Reichert, G. (2019). The electronics industry in Indonesia and its integration into global supply chains. *ILO Working Papers* 995052493402676. International Labour Organization.

Ramanayake, S. S., and Lee, K. (2015). Does openness lead to sustained economic growth? Export growth versus other variables as determinants of economic growth. *Journal of the Asia Pacific Economy*, 20(3), 345-368.

Ramanayake, S.S., and Lee, K. (2018). Differential effects of currency undervaluation. On economic growth in mineral- vs. manufacture-exporting countries: Revealing the source of the vicious procyclicality in the resource-cursed South. In: J. Niosi (Ed.), *Innovation Policy, Systems and Management*. Cambridge University Press.

Rasiah, R. (2006). Explaining Malaysia's export expansion in palm oil and related products. In: *Technology, Adaptation, and Exports: How some developing countries got it right*. World Bank.

Rasiah, R. (2017). The industrial policy experience of the electronics industry in Malaysia. In: J. Page and F. Tarp (Eds), *The Practice of Industrial Policy: Government–business coordination in Africa and East Asia*. Oxford University Press.

Rodrik, D. (2008). The real exchange rate and economic growth. *Brookings Papers on Economic Activity*, 2, 365-412.

Rudahindwa, J. B. (2018). *Regional Developmentalism through Law: Establishing an African economic community*. Routledge.

Rudahindwa, J. B., and Van Huellen, S. (2020). Regional developmentalism in West Africa: The case for commodity-based industrialization through regional cooperation in the cocoa-chocolate cector. *SOAS Department of Economics Working Papers* 239. University of London.

Sachs, J. D., and Warner, A. M. (1997). Sources of slow growth in African economies. *Journal of African Economies*, 6(3), 335-376.

Sachs, J. D., and Warner, A. M. (1999). The big push, natural resource booms and growth. *Journal of Development Economics*, 59, 43-76.

Sato, Y. (2016). Curse or opportunity? A model of industrial development for natural resource-rich countries on the basis of Southeast Asian experiences. In: Y. Sato and H. Sato (Eds), *Varieties and Alternatives of Catching-up: Asian development in the context of the 21st century*. Palgrave Macmillan.

Seibel, H. D. (2002). *Coffee Finance in Kenya: How to undermine rural finance and development*. Development Research Center, University of Cologne.

Setterfield, M. (Ed.). (2010). *Handbook of Alternative Theories of Economic Growth*. Edward Elgar.

Talbot, J. M. (2009). The comparative advantages of tropical commodity chain analysis. In: J. Bair (Ed.), *Frontiers of Commodity Chain Research*. Stanford University Press.

Technoserve. (2003). *Business Solutions to the Coffee Crisis*.

TCC. (2010). *TCC Cocoa Barometer 2010*. Tropical Commodity Coalition (TCC).

Tordo, S., and Anouti, Y. (2013). *Local Content in the Oil and Gas Sector: Case studies*. World Bank.

UNCTAD. (2005). *Transnational Corporations and the Internationalization of R&D, World Investment Report 2005*. United Nations.

UNCTAD. (2013). *Economic Development in Africa Report. Intra-African Trade: Unlocking private sector dynamism*. United Nations.

UNECA. (2013). *Economic Report on Africa 2013. Making the Most of Africa's Commodities: Industrializing for growth, jobs and economic transformation*. United Nations Economic Commission for Africa.

Williamson, J. (2012). Some basic disagreements on development. Panel at the High-Level Knowledge Forum for Rethinking Development Policy held by KDI and the World Bank in Seoul.

World Bank. (2010). Escaping the middle-income trap. In: *World Bank East Asia and Pacific Economic Update: Robust recovery, rising risks* (27-43). World Bank.

World Bank. (2012). *China 2030: Building a modern, harmonious, and creative high-income society*. World Bank.

Yeyati, E. L., and Sturzenegger, F. (2007). Fear of appreciation. *World Bank Policy Research Working Paper* no. 4387. World Bank.

Yusuf, S., and Nabeshima, K. (2009). Can Malaysia escape the middle-income trap? A strategy for Penang. *World Bank Policy Research Working Paper* no. 4971. World Bank.

SECTION II

PROBLEM-SPECIFIC POLICY RESPONSES

CHAPTER 6

Harnessing Innovation in the Informal Food Services Sector

Insights for public policy

Il-haam Petersen, Nazeem Mustapha, Nicole Dunn-van Rheede and Glenda Kruss

Introduction

Across the globe, the pandemic impacted negatively on livelihoods, increased unemployment and deepened poverty, especially in the Global South, and particularly severely for those citizens already marginalised and vulnerable (FAO, 2020; Mahler et al., 2020; Yaya et al., 2020). In Africa, historically, millions of households and individuals have sought their livelihoods in the informal sector, often in response to economic crises, with the growth in the informal sector widely believed to be a counter-cyclical 'shock absorber' (Khambule, 2020). Under the restrictions of the pandemic, the informal sector was not insulated from the economic shocks and global volatility resulting from 'lockdown strategies' to prevent the spread of the coronavirus and may have even been more severely impacted than the formal sector (Koveos, 2020; Rogan and Skinner, 2020).

In South Africa and many other countries in Africa, informal food trade in townships and peri-urban areas accounts for a large proportion of informal economic activity and is critical to food access for the poor

(Petersen and Charman, 2017; Tawodzera, 2019). Hence, the negative impact of the pandemic on the survival of informal food enterprises constituted a double burden, impacting not only livelihoods but also household food security.

There is growing evidence globally that the typical government responses to mitigate the economic and social impacts of the pandemic failed to reach the most vulnerable. Where informal enterprises are included, government policy tends to focus on formalisation strategies, to bring the informal sector within business regulatory frameworks. The way in which informality is typically understood, as a binary opposite and as a temporary linear process towards formality, was not helpful in informing policy responses to the pandemic's crisis with the greatest likelihood of promoting inclusive development.

This chapter raises critical questions about the approach underpinning government policy and the extent to which it can mitigate livelihood risk and alleviate the negative impact on the most vulnerable citizens. Rooted in a neoliberal approach to informality, approaches typically focus on identifying the drivers of informality and strategies to overcome the barriers to formality. A neoliberal account assumes that informality is a form of 'grassroots entrepreneurship' that arises because poorly designed laws and regulations allow and incentivise non-compliance (Crush and Young, 2019). Many states design their policies based on this premise, focused on reforming the legal and regulatory systems to incentivise compliance and wider participation.

In contrast, we argue that creating pathways for economic recovery post-pandemic requires public policies that engage with the realities and persistence of the informal sector, and significantly, with the ways in which innovation is so central to the very nature of informality and can be harnessed towards enterprise growth and inclusive development. Based on an empirical analysis of informal micro-enterprises providing food services, our chapter draws on and contributes to the large body of research on the informal sector in South Africa. It focuses on a critical dimension that this research typically hints at but does not explore in detail: the innovative activity that is so critical to the survival and growth of informal micro-enterprises.

The chapter argues that promoting innovation in the informal sector should have been a key part of any strategy to mitigate the impact of the pandemic on the most vulnerable. Often such strategies focus on how barriers to innovation can be removed so that informal enterprises can increase their output. The chapter adopts a different approach and focus. It explores how informal enterprises progress onto better business evolution pathways that help them grow in complexity through their innovation activities. The 'complexity' of an enterprise refers to the degree of structure, which can vary from simple enterprises with a single product and single ownership to enterprises with many varied product ranges and greater management, organisational, or technological structures. We argue that this is an important avenue to promote the inclusion of informal food enterprises in a way that also strengthens local food systems more effectively in a post-pandemic economy.

Section 2 examines the literature on innovation in the informal food sector, focusing on the impact of the pandemic. It proposes an analytical distinction to identify degrees of (in)formality rather than mutually distinct formal and informal sectors (Mbaye and Gueye, 2020, 22) and considers the role of innovation in stimulating changes in informality states. Section 3 describes the methodology of the research on which the chapter is based. Given that the informal economy is highly complex and deeply embedded in specific environments (Crush and Young, 2019), Section 4 situates the analysis and provides a detailed description of the informal food micro-enterprises in the study area, including the production value chain, networks and nature of innovation. Section 5 explores how informal food micro-enterprises respond to crisis events through innovation for their survival or growth and their complex, multiple evolutions or cycles towards manifesting different levels of informality over time. Section 6 presents policy insights to support innovation and economic inclusion, focused on promoting learning in informal enterprises and stronger systemic linkages towards better business evolution pathways.

Understanding innovation in informal food enterprises to promote inclusive change

Drawing on a brief overview of the literature on the informal food sector in South Africa, this section provides insight into the emergence and dynamics of the informal food trade in townships and rural areas. The gap in understanding the nature and role of innovation in informal food businesses is highlighted. Building on insights from the emerging literature on innovation in the informal sector, we propose a framework for exploring how informal food businesses use innovation to continually adapt and evolve to stay competitive and survive under difficult socio-economic conditions. A different approach to understanding (in)formality, one that sees it as a non-linear process involving a multitude of states, underpins our approach.

Research on the informal food sector in South Africa

The pandemic has stimulated a renewed focus on the role of the informal sector in food security (Moore, 2020; Mottaleb et al., 2020). One major strand of the literature focuses on informal food production in smallholder agricultural enterprises (Amadu et al., 2020; Kahsay et al., 2020; Mdemu et al., 2020; Mora et al., 2020). Another is on strengthening food security programmes, whether public or private (de Amorim et al., 2020; de Araújo and Calazans, 2020; Kinsey et al., 2020).

Our focus is on the most prevalent informal sector, informal food trade in urban and peri-urban townships and rural settlements (Crush and Caesar, 2014; Petersen and Charman, 2017; Rogan and Skinner, 2018). The chapter draws on an emerging literature in South Africa that provides the kind of analysis required to understand its dynamics of emergence and persistence (Charman and Petersen, 2018; Fourie, 2018; Rogan and Skinner, 2017, 2020).

Crush and Young (2019) argue that while informal food trade in Africa tends to be a 'last refuge' for the most marginalised, these enterprises are a site of entrepreneurial agency, energy and innovation. More detailed studies are available that illustrate this creative tension through contextually embedded and historically specific research. Based on a micro-enterprise survey in Mpumalanga, for example, Mahadea and Khumalo (2020) argue that internal factors within the informal enterprise, such as entrepreneurial factors or education and training, are greater hurdles to their success than external market factors. They urge a greater focus on understanding the internal entrepreneurial limitations to growth and sustainability, and hence, on how to promote value co-creation through collaborative networks, dynamic interaction and resource integration. Petersen and Charman (2018) emphasise the contribution of informal food enterprises to local economic development in KwaZulu-Natal, as well as local food security, in culturally relevant ways. They highlight a distinctive feature: the role of the family and the household as employees in shaping the dynamics of these micro-enterprises, as enablers of daily operations, but potential blockages to growth, given precarity and excessive family demands that may impact on success. Tawodzera (2019) used the Hungry Cities Partnership survey data (Joubert et al., 2018; Skinner and Haysom, 2016; Skinner, 2019) to show that the motivation for starting an enterprise is primarily necessity-driven (BER, 2016) – to obtain money to survive. His work contributes an approach to understanding the structures and dynamics of food vendor enterprises in a rich, detailed manner.

Contextually embedded research on innovation in informal food enterprises

Missing in this literature on the informal food sector is a dedicated focus on innovation and on the creative and dynamic nature of these micro-enterprises, which are continually adapting and evolving their economic activities as a competitive and survival strategy.

The emerging innovation studies literature that shows how crucial innovation is for the survival of informal sector businesses in Africa provides useful insights through novel analytical frameworks for understanding innovation at the local level (De Beer et al., 2013; Mustapha et al., 2021); sectoral studies (Kraemer-Mbula and Wunsch-Vincent, 2016; Konté and Ndong, 2012); policy analysis (Koczberski et al., 2018); investigations of clustering (Mytelka and Farinelli, 2000; Jegede et al., 2020; Jegede and Jegede, 2018); and econometric studies (Fu et al., 2018; Mendi and Mudida, 2018). The innovation studies literature points to the need for greater attention to the role of innovation, particularly in promoting learning towards upgrading informal micro-enterprises and linking them into value chains for growth and sustainability. Mendi and Mudida (2018), for example, explore the effect of innovation in formal enterprises in Kenya which had started out as informal enterprises and found that the informal phase of the business was crucial for learning and upgrading, with many going on to become successful exporters. A recent study measuring innovation in informal micro-enterprises in one local area in South Africa shows that the rate and intensity of innovation in the informal sector are high, but the typical nature of the innovation activities is very different from what we find in formal, larger businesses (CeSTII, 2020a, 2020b, 2020c). The emerging evidence suggests distinctive patterns of innovation in informal enterprises that enable them to adapt rapidly to changing circumstances and experience few 'real' barriers to their innovative behaviour.

Innovation in informal micro-enterprises, including those in food, tends to be necessity-driven (BER, 2016) in response to a need to keep the enterprise operating, to meet basic needs such as feeding the family or sending children to school, rather than opportunity-driven, that is, by a desire to exploit opportunities to grow the business (Petersen and Kruss, 2021). The innovations tend to be non-technological and take 'forms of imitation' (Kraemer-Mbula et al., 2019, 6). Kraemer-Mbula et al. (2019) explain why it is so important to develop technological and organisational capabilities to absorb and modify technologies and products, even if only new to the firm and incremental:

> [T]he fact that innovation takes the forms of imitation does not make it any less important economically. It may be the necessary condition for the business to maintain a competitive position in the local market. At a more aggregated level it will be central to the capacity of these firms to generate needed employment and contribute to industrial production. (Kraemer-Mbula et al., 2019, 6–7)

Based on an analysis of informal food service enterprises in a South African township, Petersen and Kruss (2021) show the limitations of necessity-driven innovation strategies for linking into formal value chains and highlight the importance of learning and entrepreneurial strategies that include linkages with formal knowledge producers based on models aligned with locally embedded institutions.

Promoting locally embedded modes of innovation in informal enterprises requires very different types of policy intervention than the norm in the South African national system of innovation. Current policy practice, typically based on a 'neoliberal' approach (Crush and Young, 2019), seeks to promote the progression of informal businesses to the formal sector. Our research argues for the adoption of a conceptual approach that recognises the rich variety of informality embedded in local contexts and systems and the significance of innovation as a driver of micro-enterprise dynamics to inform more inclusive and developmental interventions.

Researching innovation and informality in informal food micro-enterprises: Potential for new policy insights

Distinguishing degrees of informality to recognise heterogeneity. The limited research on the nature of entrepreneurial activity in the informal sector suggests it is more useful to consider a multitude of formality states rather than a linear process or a simple change that takes place when the business becomes registered.

Formality/informality are better conceptualised as interchangeable stages along a continuum, instead of binary opposites on a linear, uni-directional trajectory (Benjamin and Mbaye, 2012; Mbaye et al., 2015). Hence, an enterprise's degree of formality or informality cannot be defined based on a single binary criterion. Understanding this multiplicity of (in)formality levels can provide policy insights into the role of innovation in business evolution in the informal sector, considering that innovation tends to be motivated by necessity-driven strategies (BER, 2016; Petersen and Kruss, 2021).

Mbaye and Gueye (2020) create an appropriate set of criteria for measuring the degree of informality/formality of a business, based on empirical data drawn from over 1,500 informal businesses in six major cities in West and Central francophone Africa. They propose that because there are contextually determined degrees of formality and informality, a diverse array of classification criteria should be used. Table 1 reflects a set of criteria based on Mbaye and Gueye's classification criteria adapted for our study in relation to the nature of the informal food sector in South Africa.

Table 1: Criteria for identifying the degree of informality of a business

No.	Criteria	Description of criterion
1	Firm size	Criterion 1 is fulfilled if the business employs fewer than five people. It captures the size of firms, with fewer than five employees being characteristic of small enterprises. This can be further broken down to several levels: own-account workers are those with one employee (the owner), nano-enterprises are those with two to three employees, and small enterprises are those with four to five employees.
2	Registration status	Criterion 2 is fulfilled when the business indicates that it is not registered with any public authority. Several modalities of registration are considered: registration with tax authority, registration with the department of commerce, and registration as importer/exporter.
3	Taxation	Criteria 3 is met if the business does not pay any form of tax, based on actual revenue.
4	Maintenance of financial statements	Criterion 4 is fulfilled when the business records that it does not maintain regular, accurate accounts and financial statements. This includes that here are no certified statements, no annual accounts, and no registry of revenue or expenditure.
5	Access to land	Criterion 5 is met when the business records that it does not operate from fixed premises. The premises could be mobile, using the operator's home or public space as a working premise.
6	Access to external finance	Criterion 6 is met when the business has not received a bank or microfinance loan within the last five years.
7	Employee benefit	Criterion 7 is met if employees are not registered with a social security scheme such as health, retirement, or accident coverage.

Source: Adapted from Mbaye and Gueye (2020, 28).

Considering the current policy emphasis on business registration as a key indicator of formality, it is important to examine and understand the variety of specific attributes or conditions that can support sustainable formalisation.

Innovation and informality. For informal enterprises, the state of informality itself, in addition to current crisis events, creates the context for change in the business. The role of innovation is investigated by exploring the relationship between events prompting innovation in an informal food enterprise, that is, 'innovation events' and the evolution towards manifesting the different levels of informality over time. Innovation events may include personal or financial crises events such as experiencing financial loss, being a victim of crime, becoming ill or being involved in an accident. Innovation events are of interest because they illuminate the link between innovation and business resilience or evolution. Studying responses to crisis events becomes even more important in the context of the pandemic that gave rise to increasing financial and personal distress. When informal micro-enterprises innovate to overcome these kinds of events, does this contribute to a change in business evolution? Specifically, does the innovation contribute to a change in the state of informality/formality, as illustrated in Figure 1?

Figure 1: The relationship between innovation, innovation events and levels of formality

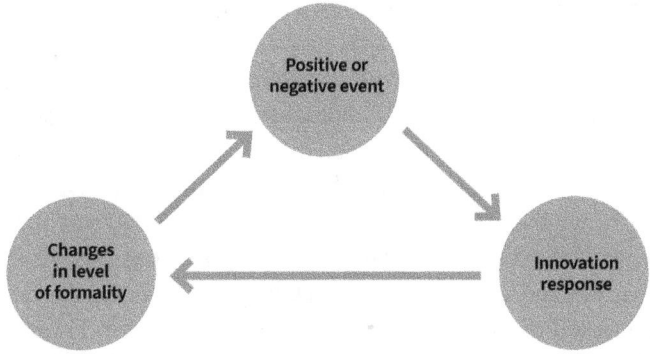

Source: Authors' own.

Here, the expanded definition of innovation introduced in the latest version of the Oslo Manual was used, as it was found to be suitably comprehensive and inclusive of researching and measuring innovation in the informal sector:

> *[I]nnovation is a new or improved product or process (or a combination thereof) that differs significantly from the unit's previous products or processes and that has been made available to potential users (product) or brought into use by the unit (process). (OECD, 2018, 32)*

In the following sections, this chapter goes on to situate the context in which the informal food enterprises operate and then to investigate the relationship between events prompting innovation for survival or growth and the evolution of informal food service micro-enterprises. We argue that this provides a sound basis to identify insights into the kinds of policy mechanisms that may be effective drivers of innovation in informal food micro-enterprises. This kind of transformative policy focuses on achieving environmental and social benefits alongside economic objectives, which can inform the design and implementation of an inclusive and sustainable policy that is critical to promoting food security and livelihoods in a post-pandemic world (Akon-Yamga et al., 2021, 1).

Case study design and methodology

This section outlines the methodological and theoretical frameworks used in the study. The chapter is based on a larger study, the Innovation in the Informal Sector (IIS) project, which aimed to experiment with ways to measure innovation in the informal sector using a mixed methods approach.[1] This approach was preferred as it enables both breadth and depth in understanding complex concepts and processes such as innovation in the informal sector. A baseline study was conducted in a predominantly peri-urban area, Mpumuza ('Sweetwaters'), located in the second-most populous region of South Africa, KwaZulu-Natal. One of the key factors informing the selection of this study area is that the municipality has established an informal sector business chamber as part of its informal sector policy. The baseline study was based on a quantitative survey and case study research. One case study, focused on business upgrading in informal food services enterprises, was used to inform the analysis in this chapter. Informal food services were found to be the most dominant economic activity in the study area and were the primary economic activity of almost a third (27%) of the informal businesses in our study. The decision to focus the case study on food services was also informed by preliminary analysis of the data obtained via the survey and digital storytelling workshops, which showed

---

[1] The Innovation in the Informal Sector (IIS) Survey was conducted in 2019 by a team of researchers based at the Centre for Science, Technology and Innovation Indicators (CeSTII) at the Human Sciences Research Council. The survey covered a two-year period, 2017 and 2018. The results were formally released on 30 March 2021. A more detailed description of the methodology, and its advantages and limitations, can be found in the IIS project outputs (CeSTII 2020a, 2020b, 2020c), which can be accessed via CeSTII's webpage (www.hsrc.ac.za/en/media-briefs/cestii), and in Mustapha et al. (2021).

the innovativeness and dynamism of the informal food businesses and thus their suitability for the purposes of this chapter.

Using the LIPS framework to design a survey of innovation in the informal sector at the local level

A survey of innovation in the informal sector has to take into account the typical size of informal sector businesses, which tend to be survivalist and micro, and the local nature and spatial dynamics of informal sector industries. For this task, this study adopted a local innovation and production systems (LIPS) methodological framework (Cassiolato et al., 2017; Cassiolato and Lastres, 2020). LIPS can be defined as:

> *Group(s) of economic, political and social agents localised in the same area, performing related economic activities, in which formal and informal interdependence and consistent linkages usually result in cooperation and learning processes, with a potential to generate the increase of productive and innovative capabilities. (Lastres and Cassiolato, 2005, 7)*

The LIPS framework places the unit of analysis in the set of agents, at the collective level, going beyond the individual organisations (enterprises), sectors, or production chains, establishing a close relationship between the territory and the economic activities (Cassiolato et al., 2017). Thus, it allows for data collection and analysis that goes beyond a national innovation systems approach. With an emphasis on the impact of the socio-economic context on production and innovation, and vice-versa, a LIPS framework aligns well with the analysis proposed in the informal sector literature. It also provides a meaningful way to delineate an empirical study unit.

Our approach builds on and adapts the LIPS framework by factoring in specificities of the informal sector in South Africa (de Beer et al., 2013; Fourie, 2018; Kraemer-Mbula and Wunsch-Vincent, 2016; Rogan and Skinner, 2018). The adapted LIPS framework includes a broad range of new actors within the system, such as informal financing and education and training actors, informal forms of linkages among these actors, as well as the peculiarity of the socio-cultural, political, institutional and technological landscape. Figure 2 illustrates the LIPS framework as applied in the IIS project.

Mixed methods participatory approach

First, we designed a quantitative innovation survey of all informal businesses in a selected study area, based on an Oslo-Manual design, adapted by drawing on the South African literature on the informal sector, as well as our own empirical qualitative work in other settings. Following best practice guidelines for conducting a Small Area Census (Charman et al., 2017), a small area, Ward 1 and surrounds in Msunduzi, was selected as the empirical focus. This methodology fits well with the LIPS approach in that it selects a contiguous local area and identifies all the informal businesses within that area for the innovation survey.

With the use of mobile technology, the IIS questionnaire was administered through face-to-face structured interviews with informal sector business owners at their business premises and at times convenient for them, yielding a sample of 996 businesses.

Second, case study research was used to enable a more in-depth exploration of the nature of innovation. A total of 271 (27%) of 996 informal businesses included in the 2017-18 IIS Survey reported food production and services as their main economic activities. Of these 271 businesses, 232 (or 85.6%) had successful innovations within the reference period under study. A small group of 13 food businesses, who indicated that they had engaged in innovation, was selected for semi-structured interviews to add to the survey data collected from them. These interviews were conducted with the business owners, face-to-face and telephonically, depending on their availability and preference. The aim was to investigate the history of the business, how it developed over time and the nature and role of innovation and learning.

The analysis of innovation events in Section 5 draws on a set of digital stories of informal businesses created at two separate workshops in Msunduzi[2] and Philippi,[3] a township area with similar socio-economic conditions. Digital storytelling is a community-based participatory research technique found to be suitable for research with hard-to-reach communities and for exploring complex concepts and processes such as innovation (see Lambert, 2013). Participants were recruited via local expertise, and in total 15 digital stories focused on the same guiding topic were created: Tell me a TRUE story of a time when you did something different in the way that you run your business and what happened. This guiding topic was selected as a way to communicate the complex concept of 'innovation' in such a way that it could be easily understood by the informal business owners. The freedom of reflection provided by the workshop environment allowed for in-depth illumination of the nature of changing business, critical events and

---

2   Conducted in Sweetwaters, from 27 to 31 May 2019.
3   Conducted in Cape Town, from 24 to 28 September 2018.

the nature of innovation. The guiding topic conveyed a broad understanding of innovation, informed by the *Oslo Manual* (OECD, 2018) definition of innovation and reinforced through in-depth discussions in the digital storytelling workshops. The digital stories – typically a four to five-minute video clip – were factual and narrated by the informal business owners in their own words. The transcripts of the digital stories were analysed to facilitate an in-depth understanding of learning and innovation activities.

The analysis of innovation events contributes to building an understanding of how informal businesses respond to personal and financial crises events, specifically how they may use innovation to respond to such events and progress along their business evolution pathways. Therefore, although this study was conducted before the pandemic, it provides potentially useful insights into how informal food businesses may be supported to overcome similar pandemic-related personal and financial challenges.

A case study of informal food services in Msunduzi, South Africa

This section presents a contextual background of the study area and analyses the nature of innovation activity in the informal food local innovation and production system based on the survey data. These results provide insight into the locally embedded nature of the innovation and production activities in the study area.

The study area, one municipal ward in Msunduzi, had a population of approximately 18,500 people, with a working-age population of 59% (Census, 2011; Community Survey, 2016) and a slightly larger proportion of females (52%). Despite consistent economic growth in recent years, unemployment and poverty levels remain high, particularly in townships and peri-urban settlements, where unemployment rates may exceed 70% (Pietermaritzburg Msunduzi Integrated Development Plan, 2018). Local community members are thus compelled to seek livelihood opportunities in the informal sector.

Similar to other township areas, informal food accounted for a large proportion of economic activities. In general, barriers to entry into food services are low, requiring little start-up capital and medium- to low-level skills (Bhorat et al., 2016, 6), making food services an attractive livelihood option in a resource-poor context.

A description of the informal food enterprises

The analysis in this section is based on the survey data, which included 271 informal food businesses. Most (65.7%) of these informal food enterprises started out of necessity due to unemployment, and more than a third (36.9%) to meet the basic needs of the family. A large proportion also indicated that they decided to open a food business because they liked the activity (43.2%) and/or because they had the skills required (26.9%). These businesses were typically older than five years, with a large proportion, between 20% and 25%, older than ten years. Most (81.5%) of the business owners had at least an intermediate (grade 9) or junior certification or equivalent. Less than a third (29.9%) reported that they completed school (grade 12) (see Table 2).

Retail trade was reported as the main economic activity for most of the informal food enterprises, with 50.2% trading in groceries and beverages, and 12.2% in livestock, poultry or fresh produce. A large proportion (65.7%) of these informal traders were spaza shops (i.e. 111 of 169 enterprises). Informal food and related services, including businesses selling fast-foods/take-aways and baked goods, and those providing catering services, accounted for 31.7% of the informal food enterprises. A very small proportion (4.1%) reported farming as their main economic activity. The remaining 1.8% provided cooling services to the informal traders, a crucial service that enables the businesses to store their perishable goods in cold storage. These businesses were relatively new, between one and three years old. In line with common practice in the informal sector, some of the food businesses engaged in secondary economic activities, such as doing beadwork or carpentry or selling clothing.

Table 2: Description of employees in 2018

	Total employees (2018)	Employees who completed school (2018)	Paid employees (2018)	Employees who are family (2018)	Female employees (2018)	Male employees (2018)	Increase in employees from 2017-2018
Retail in livestock, poultry and fresh produce	14 (1.3)	3 (0.3)	7 (0.8)	4 (0.4)	5 (0.5)	6 (0.5)	1 (0.1)
Food and related services	217 (2.5)	119 (1.6)	164 (2.1)	64 (0.9)	94 (1.1)	101 (1.2)	52 (0.6)
Retail in groceries and beverages	316 (1.9)	114 (0.8)	177 (1.2)	102 (0.8)	95 (0.6)	156 (0.9)	95 (0.6)
Other services (to informal traders)	17 (3.4)	10 (2.5)	16 (3.2)	5 (1.0)	6 (1.2)	11 (2.2)	3 (0.6)
Total food businesses	564 (2.1)	246 (1.1)	364 (1.5)	175 (0.8)	200 (0.7)	274 (1.0)	151 (0.6)

Note: The average number of employees is included in brackets. Data source: CeSTII 2017-18 IIS Survey.

Most (62.4%) of the food businesses operated from home, either from a separate or dedicated space within the home. Some operated from mobile structures, including 12.8% of the food services businesses and 20.7% of the informal traders selling groceries and beverages. Few operated from a dedicated external structure, whether attached to the owner's home or on the property (3.7%), another person's home (3.0%), a non-residential building (1.5%), a taxi rank (4.4%), a footpath or street (4.1%) or a market (0.7%).

In such a resource-poor area, it is expected that access to basic services and facilities would be low. While many of the informal food businesses had access to piped water within the structure (38.7%) or on-site (41.3%), sanitation services were not as well developed, as only a third had access to a flushing toilet within the structure (32.5%) or offsite (13.3%). A large proportion (44.6%) reported access to other types of facilities.

Employment growth was minimal, and most of the food businesses employed only one or two people (see Table 2). The businesses accounted for about a quarter of the employment levels (26.2%) and the total turnover reported by informal businesses in the study area in 2018. Altogether, the 271 businesses reported an annual turnover of ZAR 6,903,353 in 2018, with an average of ZAR 27,949 per business.

The informal food production value chain and networks supporting innovation

A simple production value chain for the informal food sector in Msunduzi links formal and informal food producers, food retailers and food services, and businesses supporting informal traders in the local area. Marketing of products is generally performed within the production unit and is primarily through word of mouth (81.5%), very similar to the general trend (81.1%) in the study area.

For illustrative purposes, Figure 2 selects informal fast-food/take-aways and catering businesses as the main production unit at the centre of the food services LIPS. The production value chain of the informal food enterprises is mapped out in the lower half of the diagram. The diagram also includes specific service providers and other businesses, such as competitors and business clusters that form part of the local system. The main actors that typically play a role in supporting innovation are mapped in the upper half of the diagram. The innovation support organisations include formal education and training organisations, informal training support, formal and informal intermediary actors such as informal trader associations, and formal and informal sources of finances such as commercial banks and stokvels.[4] It is possible to draw similar diagrams depicting each of the other two food services categories – retail in livestock, poultry and fresh produce, and retail in beverages and groceries – as the main production units in the centre, and map their specific actors and networks.

Figure 2: Informal food services local innovation and production system in Msunduzi, with the informal food-related service businesses in the centre

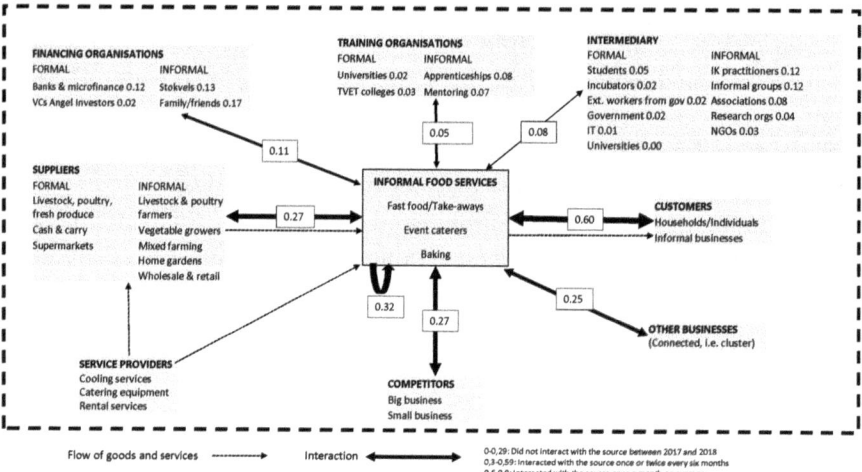

Source: Authors' own.

The overall profile of the consumer base for the informal food sector reflects that of the informal sector in general in Msunduzi, with the majority of the consumer base drawn from individual households (94.5%). A large proportion (44.3%) of the customers were located within the local neighbourhood, comparable to the average of 39% for all businesses in the study area, illustrating the importance of local embeddedness that appears to be a general non-industry-specific feature of informality.

The main suppliers were businesses (35.4%) and households (52.8%). Only 7.4% of suppliers were from informal business sources, similar to that for all informal businesses in the area (9.0%). Typically, formal suppliers to the informal food businesses would be low-price retailers in the local area or nearest town or within the main city in the province (32.8%). Few suppliers

---

4 A stokvel is a savings scheme where the members of the savings scheme pool their savings by providing regular payments into the fund. Each member receives a lump sum payout after a predetermined period of saving.

were found at a distance from Msunduzi, with only 3.0% found somewhere else in the country and 0.4% outside the country.

Innovation in the informal food enterprises

In general, analysis of the innovation activities in the informal food businesses shows that most (85.6%) engaged in some form of innovation activity, resulting in product (67.2%) and process innovations (81.5%) that were mainly new to the local area (27.7%) or the local industry (26.6%). Here, a process innovation refers to 'a new or improved business process for one or more business functions that differs significantly from the firm's previous business processes and that has been brought into use by the firm' (OECD, 2018, 34). And a product innovation 'is a new or improved good or service that differs significantly from the firm's previous goods or services and that has been introduced on the market' (OECD, 2018, 34).

High rates of innovation of a specific nature were found, with innovation activity driven mainly by the need to respond to changing customer demand. Figure 3 shows that the most frequently reported innovation activity[5] is responding to customer demand, based on their feedback (71.7%), followed by acquiring tools, machinery and equipment (56.1%) – such as buying a fryer to allow for the sale of hot chips – and finding new suppliers of raw materials and tools (50.6%), mainly in the proximity of the business locale. The importance placed on innovating to respond to customer demand more effectively was higher for the food enterprises than the average for all informal enterprises in the study area (68.2%). This may be because of the nature of business in food retail and food services, where there is a relatively high rate of customer interaction compared with other industries. Changes to buildings, vehicles or other infrastructure were also more important for the food enterprises (33.2%) than other businesses in the study area (24.8%). Finally, a common innovation activity was described as 'happy accidents', that is, unexpected discoveries during production (37.5%). The food enterprises reported that the innovation often 'just happened by chance' as the businesses engaged in their everyday business operations.

Learning while conducting everyday business operations, through customer feedback and experimentation – learning by using (71.6%) and doing (52.0%) – were valued most. Learning through imitating other

---

5   Based on the *OECD Oslo Manual* (2018, 33) guidelines: '(i)nnovation activities include all developmental, financial and commercial activities undertaken by a firm that are intended to result in an innovation for the firm'.

businesses (44.3%) was higher in the food businesses than in most other informal businesses in the study area. In general, interaction within the local system was very weak and, in relation to knowledge actors and intermediaries such as NGOs, almost non-existent.[6] Only 15.5% of the food businesses used the internet or cellphone applications, and this relatively low-level use of readily available technology was the same for the average informal business.

Figure 3: Innovation activities in the informal food enterprises, compared to the total

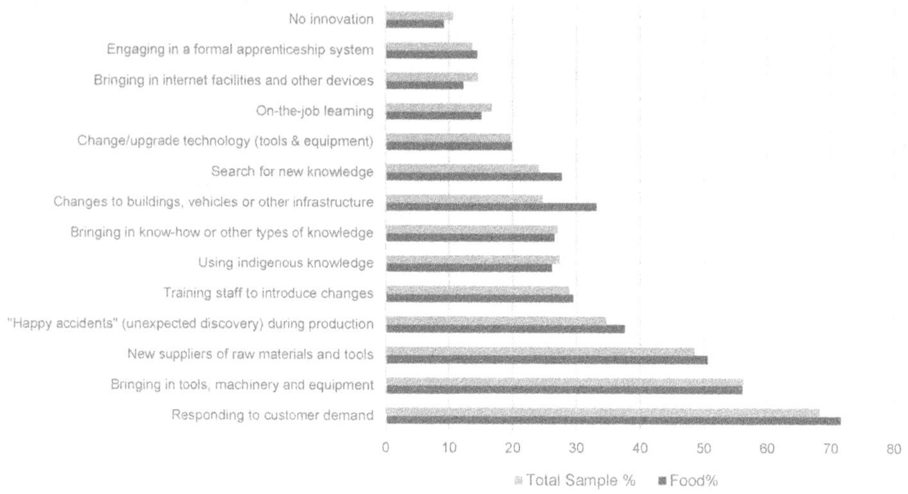

Data source: CeSTII 2017-18 IIS Survey.

In summary, the informal food services enterprises, with their low barriers to entry, offer viable livelihood opportunities for individuals in the local area who have relatively low levels of education. These micro-enterprises operate from home and were started mainly out of necessity and a need to provide for the basic needs of the family, which is in line with other research on informal food enterprises (Skinner and Haysom, 2016; Skinner, 2019; Tawodzera, 2019). Most businesses were relatively established, having been

---

6   The strength of interaction between the informal food micro-enterprises and other key actors that may support innovation was assessed by using responses to a question in the 2017-18 IIS Survey on the frequency of interaction with a set of possible sources of information. The strength of interaction was measured on a scale ranging from 'did not interact' (0) to 'interacted more than once a month, on average' (1). Data source: CeSTII 2017-18 IIS Survey.

in operation for over five years. These findings, together with similar trends found in other studies (Chiliya and Roberts-Lombard, 2012), indicate that the informal food micro-enterprises are a sustainable field of economic activity and are not just established as temporary relief from unemployment. The fact that the food businesses serve mainly individuals and households in the local area indicates their significance in providing low-income consumers with access to affordable food options, which became even more important during the early days of pandemic outbreak and should continue post-pandemic when unemployment and poverty in the area deepen.

A concern is that although the informal food micro-enterprises have been operating for so long, most do not contribute significantly to employment growth in the local area. The businesses also tended to remain necessity-driven, with uncertain levels of income.

The analysis of their innovation activities indicates a weak, customer-driven, and very locally embedded system, reflecting the prevalence of forms of local learning and capability building mainly from customers, and to a lesser extent, suppliers and other businesses. Nevertheless, in that they enable informal food enterprises to survive over time, these innovations are critical, and if correctly supported, may lead to better learning strategies that support business evolution and growth of opportunity.

Innovation and business evolution in the context of informality and uncertainty

This section first analyses the heterogeneous nature of formality in the informal food enterprises in Msunduzi. Second, it explores the links between innovation and the heterogeneous nature of formality. Third, the role of innovation is investigated by exploring the relationship between crisis events prompting innovation in an informal food enterprise and the evolution towards manifesting different levels of informality within the local innovation and production system over time.

A multiplicity of (in)formality levels
Many informal enterprises reported a desire to become 'a formal business' when the conditions are 'right'. As one of the informal food service enterprises explained, premature formalisation can be risky:

> [Y]ou have to consider the money you make and if you are still going to be able to cover the things you have to, if you now also have to pay for tax, that is the tricky part [...] because with the money that

we make, we still need to keep the business and our homes running. (Informal food service enterprise VID1119)

The criteria proposed by Mbaye and Gueye (2020) were used to explore the specific conditions of (in)formality as a starting point to identify potential business evolution pathways (Table 1). The specific criteria identified, based on a set of proxies selected from the 2017-18 IIS survey and interview data,[7] are included in Table 3. Each informal food business was classified according to the number of criteria they met. Six levels of informality were possible, ranging from completely formal (Level 0, no criteria met) to completely informal (Level 6, all criteria met).

Table 3: Survey proxy indicators for levels of informality

Criteria	Survey and interview data proxy
Firm size	How many people were working in the business?
Registration status	Is your business registered?
Taxation	No proxy (no data available)
Maintenance of financial statements	Does your business have a bank account?
Access to land	Business Location
Access to external finance	During the two years (2017 to 2018), how often did you interact with the following sources of information in your innovation activities? Commercial banks, microfinance banks.
	Did you receive any financial support?
Employee benefit	No proxy (no data available)

Source: Authors' own.

All of the food enterprises displayed some degree of informality, with the majority (51%) classified as mostly informal or completely informal. The other half displayed higher degrees of formality, of which a large proportion was classified as semi-informal.

---

7   Of the 271 informal food enterprises covered by the survey, 38% were excluded from the proxy identification due to missing data. The analysis is thus based on a total of 167 food businesses.

Using the in-depth qualitative data, the formalisation processes of each informal food enterprise were then analysed.[8] As shown in Figure 4, different patterns of business evolution may exist. For the informal food enterprises, having fixed premises was most important and was typically the first condition necessary for building the business. The importance of business premises is illustrated in this example provided by an informal fruit and vegetable trader in Philippi:

> *I [...] started mobile vegetable selling. I carried a crate on my head and knocked on every door. It was not easy when hot, and neither were conditions better in the cold and wet winter [...] Things improved marginally when I bought a trolley. It enabled me to carry more and to reach far. Soon I realised the trolley got stuck in mud when it rained, and I struggled to push it. The heat of the sun still affected my products in summer [...] I had to find a way of getting out of the challenges and grow my business [...] I had to find a permanent trading place! [...] I immediately started building my vegetable vending stall [...] Now my life has changed. I have a permanent place. I stock more. I am able to send my kids to school, buy clothes and food, pay rent and send my mother some money. I have been trading at this spot for five years now. (Informal food enterprise PH1)*

Most of the businesses that reached a higher degree of formality, beyond becoming an employing business, reported that they put better financial management procedures in place and/or used a business bank account. Only a small proportion of the businesses reported business registration as the first step, while others only registered after other conditions were met. Significantly, although a business may have fulfilled a criterion at one point in time, this is not permanent and may change at a later point, as this quote illustrates: 'I used to have a bank account, but I no longer use it as it is expensive' (Informal food enterprise VID571).

The analysis thus suggests that there is more than one pathway through which informal enterprises evolve towards formalisation. Further research is needed to better understand the complex multiplicity and identify the specific pathways that informal enterprises may follow.

---

8   This total includes four informal food businesses operating in a peri-urban area in another major province in South Africa. The digital stories of these four businesses were produced at a digital storytelling workshop conducted as part of the research project.

Figure 4: Business evolution in the informal food enterprises

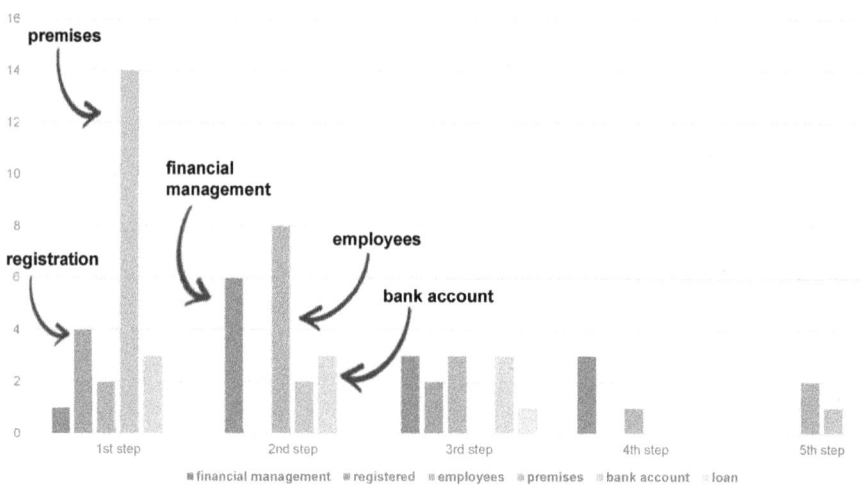

Source: Authors' own.

Innovation events and shifts in (in)formality

The digital storytelling workshops provided useful insights to deepen understanding of the nature of innovation, including the key drivers. An analysis of seven digital stories revealed a trend: key innovations were introduced in response to major events such as debt due to financial loss, losing goods due to a burglary or the business owner becoming ill. Here, these events are referred to as 'innovation events'. Innovation events are distinct from the events that prompted the start of the business or an 'entrepreneurial event', although the nature of the events may be the same. For example, the absence of bookkeeping records may have a negative effect on the firm being able to access finance from formal sources, and poor management capability or presence could result in business failure from under-supervised staff, prompting innovation responses. The events triggered a change, an innovation response that often contributed to a degree of business evolution in terms of a change in degrees of informality. The typical trajectory is illustrated in Figure 5.

By aggregating analysis across all the digital stories, two types of innovation events can be identified: events related to financial distress and events of a personal nature (Table 4). A business may experience a major event once or a recurrence of the same type of innovation event. For example, a 'tuckshop' business in our sample, after establishing a fixed location and employing one person, took a step to Level 3 of formality by

Figure 5: An illustration of innovation events that shift informality levels

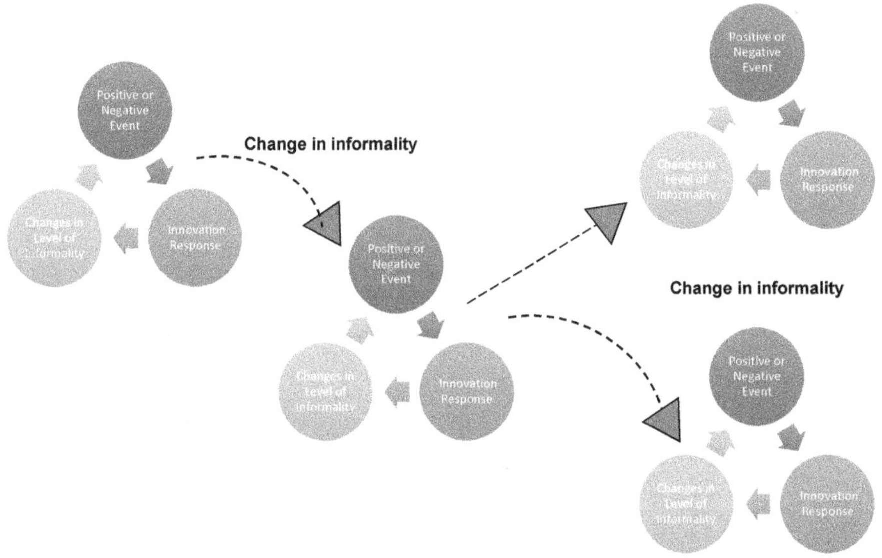

Source: Authors' own.

introducing new forms of financial management. In response to financial loss due to poor management, the business owner bought a cash register and introduced new financial management systems to better monitor transactions and record daily sales. As the business owner explained, the new financial management systems 'helped keep track of products that were selling and those that weren't, so we could make informed decisions on which products we could have on special the next month'. The innovation event was a stimulus for learning and change within the business, linked to a change in the level of formality.

Insights on informality, innovation and business evolution

Innovation events shape the future trajectory of any group of informal enterprises, depending on the starting state and the local environment. The innovation event could be of a positive or negative nature, but it is the resultant innovation response that ultimately causes the shifts in informality that contribute to business resilience and growth.

These cycles can take place several times and involve multiple cycles of innovation events (Figure 5), which may lead to increases or decreases in levels of informality. For example, to reduce costs, the owner may decide to close a business account (leading to increasing informality) or formalise to access business finance (leading to an increase in formality). One event

Table 4: Innovation events, innovation and the effect on informality across the informal food businesses

	Detail	Innovation response	Innovation outcome	Effect on informality
Informal food businesses in Msunduzi and Phillipi				
Financial	Debt	Added goods or services based on customer demand	More customers	Added employees
	Debt	Different way of doing things	Improved the efficiency of the business	Moved to better premises
	Debt	Different way of doing things	Increased profits due to improved business management, with stock monitoring and transaction tracking to better tailor sales based on customer behaviour	Improved financial management
	Financial loss due to food not selling	Added goods or services based on customer demand	More customers	None reported
Personal	Police raided store	Added goods or services	The added service helped the business survive	None reported
	Car accident	Added goods or services and Different way of doing things	More customers and different business offerings, therefore more sustainable	Added employees
	Illness	Different way of doing things	Improved quality of business offering	Financial management
	Burglary	Different way of doing things	Market differentiation	Registered the business
Non-food informal businesses in Msunduzi				
Personal	Was arrested	Different way of doing things	Improved the business through the introduction of safety equipment	None reported
	Illness	Different way of doing things	Professionalised the business	Moved to better premises

Source: Authors' own.

could also lead to an innovation response that helps the business leapfrog, skipping more than one level to a higher level of formality. The converse applies, particularly in the case of a major disruption such as a pandemic, and given the resource-poor local contexts in which businesses operate. While the change in informality ostensibly is growth across different levels from least informal to completely formal, the specific pathways cannot be inferred from the limited data analysed in this chapter. The pathways businesses follow are more complex and crooked, with movement from higher to lower levels of informality and back again, depending on circumstances and innovation events. This back and forth movement goes hand-in-hand with the learning process within the business.

What the analysis makes abundantly clear is that the attainment of formal registration is not, by itself, a guarantee of sustainability or growth. Formal registration may be driven by a specific aim of acquiring new business opportunities, for example, from public suppliers, but the informal business may choose to let that registration lapse at a later point in time. The analysis suggests that for an informal business to evolve into a successful formal business, it needs to have acquired several attributes, defined by its level of informality: it must employ people regularly, it must keep records, it needs management capabilities and so on.

It would be useful to determine how widely applicable the set of informality criteria is through further research in other settings to test the robustness of these findings. Such a set of criteria for (in)formality would be of great practical value to the policy-maker who wishes to ignite growth and evolution in informal sector businesses. The analysis using the current set of proxies allows for the identification of the state of informality of classes of informal businesses, which, combined with a greater understanding of how business evolution proceeds as a result of innovation events, provides fresh insight into what is required for dynamic, sustainable growth.

The next section is based on this conclusion, that the type of policy intervention that seeks to promote the desired change must be based on an understanding of the level of informality and the type of innovation events that prevail in any local innovation and production system.

Policy insights to support innovation and economic inclusion of informal micro-enterprises in local food systems post-pandemic

In this section, we attempt to draw out potentially useful insights for policy promoting resilience and inclusion in local food systems. Informal food services are crucial for food security in African countries, particularly for low-income households were the hardest hit by the pandemic. The extraordinary personal and financial crises that this pandemic visited upon the world test the ability of informal food businesses to respond in ways that can ensure their survival or growth.

Based on research on innovation in informal food businesses in South

Africa, this chapter provides valuable insights into how informal food businesses engage in innovation in response to personal and financial crises. We show how innovation, often triggered by personal and financial crises, shapes the learning and business evolution pathways of informal businesses, contributing to their resilience. We refer to crisis events that stimulate innovation as 'innovation events'.

Although this research was conducted before the pandemic, an understanding of how innovation takes place in the context of crisis events is an empowering tool to the policy-maker whose concern is to promote resilience and inclusion in local food systems. For example, in South Africa, many informal food traders reported financial losses due to lockdown regulations restricting food trade in informal settlements. A strict curfew was introduced in 2020, and the sale of alcohol was also prohibited, affecting the livelihoods of informal taverns. Many responded by selling alcohol illegally, at a higher price. Based on insights from our case study, another response may be to diversify, to sell foods in demand but not readily available in the local area, at prices affordable to local consumers.

Government social relief initiatives and support programmes would be important to support informal business owners to respond in ways that contribute to their sustainability. However, promoting resilience in local food systems post-pandemic requires a reconsideration of conventional policy approaches to the informal sector and policy intervention at different levels.

First, it is necessary to reconsider the assumptions underpinning policy aimed at promoting the graduation of informal food businesses to viable formal businesses. Our research indicates that business evolution paths are not linear, as often assumed. Informal food businesses follow complex pathways and move between multiple levels of (in)formality, and innovation is central to this process. The chapter, therefore, argues that the complex trajectory that businesses follow in their quest for formalisation is an area that requires policy targeting itself, particularly in relation to the kinds of economic restructuring triggered by the pandemic. Policy-makers need an approach that recognises the complex pathways informal enterprises take to reach what may be called 'sustainable formalisation'. This requires the development of policy tools that are able to effect change based on the specific state of a business, instead of the blunter instruments developed from the uni-dimensional process of formalisation through registration, based on a binary notion. A key aim of policy should be to support informal businesses to build 'formalisation capability'. Rather than shifting informal businesses towards becoming 'declared' and 'accountable to the state', they should be supported to evolve towards a set of conditions that enable them to operate sustainably in the formal sector. Fundamental to this is an understanding of the role innovation plays in that process.

The analysis shows that what matters most in informal businesses is how they respond to personal or financial crises through innovating. This may be part of the reason that innovation rates tend to be high in the informal sector. However, informal business owners are often not aware of the value of innovation, and their innovation strategies tend to be reactive. A simple intervention would be to promote an understanding of the value of innovation for business growth and resilience, through skills development programmes, for example.

Such interventions are crucial for building the capabilities of informal businesses. However, promoting sustainable business evolution trajectories does not only depend on building internal innovation capabilities.

Second, a policy aim should be to promote the informal sector as a learning environment that enables innovation activities that lead to progressive outcomes. As our research shows, the innovation response of an informal business involves a process of learning that may lead to a change in business evolution that may be progressive but could easily be regressive. Examples include policy interventions promoting better engagement with knowledge actors such as technical and vocational colleges, and education and training NGOs, and with formal suppliers to create opportunities for stronger linkages and learning opportunities in local innovation and production systems. Linkages with formal suppliers could be facilitated through the construction of distribution centres closer to local businesses, allowing easier and cheaper access to goods for informal businesses. Another option would be for local government to promote knowledge sharing between informal food enterprises and other businesses, including their competitors. Education and training NGOs are important partners for local government because they play a crucial role in supporting skills development and promoting learning linkages among informal businesses (Petersen and Kruss, 2021).

Third, the policy approaches should recognise that the innovation and production activities of informal businesses are deeply embedded in the specific environment in which they emerge. Instruments designed to cope with the the pandemic needed to take this fact firmly into account.

Therefore, to bring about transformative change in production and innovation within local food systems requires systemic structural change (Crush and Young, 2019) through building forward and backward linkages across value chains, stronger learning networks and physical facilities to support the specific forms of learning needed. But also through providing basic (serviced) infrastructure for trading in the local area, building stronger support structures to address crime and so on. Such a policy response necessitates stronger interaction and coordination across different levels of government – vertically, across local, regional and national government departments, and horizontally, across mandates, such as for small business development, innovation, and education and training.

Conclusion

This chapter's contribution to the debate on how to harness innovation in the informal sector for inclusive local economic development post-pandemic lies in the proposal to shift away from the policy emphasis on formality as a goal. Rather, policy-makers, particularly at the local government level, acting in partnership with other relevant government departments, should focus on promoting and supporting business evolution pathways that foreground learning towards conditions that may eventually lead to progressive business evolution pathways.

Investigating mechanisms that could be responsible for driving growth in complexity in informal businesses becomes a key area of attention for further research in the field and for post-pandemic policy design. The chapter explored the link between innovation and informality as a first step in this direction. The evidence presented is compelling and could inform strategies to mitigate the negative economic impact of the pandemic. However, it is certainly not comprehensive. Therefore, further research in other settings and economic domains would be of great value to test the findings and extend policy insights.

A useful aspect of the research is how well it lends itself to policy experimentation. For example, the proxies developed to describe levels of informality allow for an application of policy interventions at the local level that are testable through links to well-defined outcomes. This is an area where policy-makers and researchers may engage in joint interventions at the local level, with an approach that is collaborative and inclusive.

While the ultimate goal of formalisation is a convenient tangible milestone for policy intervention, the economic disruption wrought by the pandemic highlights the need for a shift in focus towards building sustainable, profitable businesses, which requires the promotion of innovation in the informal sector through stimulating learning networks, as a central policy goal.

References

Akon-Yamga, G., Daniels, C. U., Quaye, W., Ting, B. M., and Asante, A. (2021). Transformative innovation policy approach to e-waste management in Ghana: Perspectives of actors on transformative changes. *Science and Public Policy*, 1(11). DOI: 10.1093/scipol/scab005.

Amadu, F. O., McNamara, P. E., and Miller, D. C. (2020). Understanding the adoption of climate-smart agriculture: A farm-level typology with empirical evidence from southern Malawi. *World Development*, 125(104692), 1-22.

Benjamin, N. C., and Mbaye, A. A. (2012). *The Informal Sector in Francophone Africa: Firm size, productivity, and institutions*. Africa development forum. World Bank Group.

Bureau for Economic Research (BER). (2016). *The Small, Medium and Micro Enterprise sector of South Africa*. (Research Note No 1.). University of Stellenbosch.

Bhorat, H., Rooney, C., and Steenkamp, F. (2018). Understanding and characterising the services sector in South Africa. In: R. Newfarmer, J. Page and F. Tarp (Eds), *Industries without Smokestacks: Industrialisation in Africa reconsidered* (275). Oxford University Press.

Cassiolato, J. E., and Lastres, H. M. M. (2020). The framework of 'local productive and innovation systems' and its influence on STI policy in Brazil. *Economics of Innovation and New Technology*, 29(7), 784-784. DOI: 10.1080/10438599.2020.1719650.

Cassiolato, J. E., Lastres, H. M. M., Szapiro, M., and de Matos, M. G. (2017). Local production and innovation systems in Brazil: A balance of 20 years. *RedeSist Working Paper TD DIT-No. 04/2017*. www.redesist.ie.ufrj.br

CeSTII. (2020a). *Innovation in the Informal Sector Survey Statistical Report: Baseline survey in Sweetwaters, KwaZulu-Natal, 2017-2018*. Human Sciences Research Council.

CeSTII. (2020b). *Innovation in the Informal Sector Project: Textiles case study report*. Human Sciences Research Council.

CeSTII. (2020c). *Innovation in the Informal Sector Project: Food case study report*. Human Sciences Research Council.

Charman, A. J. E., Petersen, L. M., Piper, L. E., Liederman, R. and Legg, T. (2017). Small area census approach to measure the township informal economy in South Africa. *Journal of Mixed Methods Research*, 11(1), 36-58.

Charman, A., and Petersen, L. (2018). Informal micro-enterprises in a township context: A spatial analysis of business dynamics in five Cape Town localities. In: F. Fourie (Ed.), *The South African Informal Sector: Creating jobs, reducing poverty*. HSRC Press.

Chiliya, N., and Roberts-Lombard, M. (2012). Impact of level of education and experience on profitability of small grocery shops in South Africa. *International Journal of Business and Economics Research*, 3(1), 462-470.

Crush, J., and Caesar, M. (2014). City without choice: Urban food insecurity in Msunduzi, South Africa. *Urban Forum*, 25, 165-175.

Crush, J., and Young, G. (2019). Resituating Africa's urban informal food sector. *Urban Forum*, 30, 377-384.

de Amorim, A. L. B., Ribeiro Junior, J. R. S., and Bandoni, D. H. (2020). National school feeding program: Strategies to overcome food insecurities during and after the COVID-19 pandemic. *Brazilian Journal of Public Administration*, 54(4), 1134-1145.

de Araújo, F. R., and Calazans, D. L. M. E. S. (2020). Management of food security actions during the COVID-19 pandemic. *Brazilian Journal of Public Administration*, 54(4), 1123-1133.

de Beer, J., Fu, K., and Wunsch-Vincent, S. (2013). *The Informal Economy, Innovation and Intellectual Property: Concepts, metrics and policy considerations* (Vol. 10). WIPO.

Food and Agriculture Organization of the United Nations (FAO). (2020). *Impact of COVID-19 on Informal Workers*. http://www.fao.org/documents/card/en/c/ca8560en

Fourie, F. (Ed.). (2018). *The South African Informal Sector: Creating jobs, reducing poverty*. HSRC Press.

Fu, X., Mohnen, P., and Zanello, G. (2018). Innovation and productivity in formal and informal firms in Ghana. *Technological Forecasting and Social Change*, 131, 315-325. DOI: 10.1016/j.techfore.2017.08.009.

Jegede, O. O., and Jegede, O. E. (2018). Determinants of innovation capability in the informal settings: The case of Nigeria's clustered ICT microenterprises. *OpenAIR, Working Paper* 12. African Innovation Research.

Jegede, O. O., Oluwale, B. A., Ogunjemiluia, E. M. and Ajao, B. F. (2020). From start up to scale up: Indicators showing the role of knowledge sharing in clustered microenterprises in Nigeria. In: M. Muchie and A. Baskaran (Eds), *Science, Technology and Innovation Indicators: Lessons from development experience in Africa* (315-342). Africa World Press.

Joubert, L., Battersby, J., and Watson, V. (2018). *Tomatoes and Taxi Ranks. Running our cities to fill the food gap*. African Centre for Cities, University of Cape Town.

Kahsay, S. T., Reda, G. K., and Hailu, A. M. (2020). Food security status and its determinants in pastoral and agro-pastoral districts of Afar regional state, Ethiopia. *African Journal of Science, Technology, Innovation and Development*, 12(4), 333-341.

Khambule, I. (2020). The effects of COVID-19 on the South African informal economy: Limits and pitfalls of government's response. *Loyola Journal of Social Sciences*, 34 (1), 91-110.

Kinsey, E. W., Kinsey, D., and Rundle, A. G. (2020). COVID-19 and food insecurity: An uneven patchwork of responses. *Journal of Urban Health*, 97, 332-335.

Koczberski, G., Curry, G. N., Bue, V., Germis, E., Nake, S., and Tilden, G. M. (2018). Diffusing risk and building resilience through innovation: Reciprocal exchange relationships, livelihood vulnerability and food security amongst smallholder farmers in Papua New Guinea. *Human Ecology*, 46, 801-814.

Konté, A., and Ndong, M. (2012). The informal ICT sector and innovation processes in Senegal. *African Journal of Science, Technology, Innovation and Development*, 4(3), 61-97.

Koveos, P. (2020). COVID-19, Economic crisis and the informal sector. *Journal of Developmental Entrepreneurship*, 25(2), 1-3.

Kraemer-Mbula, E., and Wunsch-Vincent, S. (Eds). (2016). *The Informal Economy in Developing Nations*. Cambridge University Press.

Kraemer-Mbula, E., Lorenz, E., Takala-Greenish, L., Jegede, O. O., Garba, T., Mutambala, M., and Esemu, T. (2019). Are African micro-and small enterprises misunderstood? Unpacking the relationship between work organisation, capability development and innovation. *International Journal of Technological Learning, Innovation and Development*, 11(1), 1-30.

Lambert, J. (2013). *Digital Storytelling: Capturing lives. Creating community.* Routledge.

Lastres, H. M., and Cassiolato, J. E. (2005). Innovation systems and local productive arrangements: New strategies to promote the generation, acquisition and diffusion of knowledge. *Innovation: Management, Policy, and Practice*, 7(2-3), 172-172.

Mahadea, D., and Khumalo, S. (2020). Understanding the internal and external constraints to growth of microenterprise entrepreneurship in a South African provincial context: A case of Mpumalanga-Mkhondo. *Journal of Developmental Entrepreneurship*, 25(2).

Mahler, D. G., Laknerr, C., Aguilar, R. A. C., and Wu, H. (2020, 20 April). The impact of COVID-19 (Coronavirus) on global poverty: Why sub-Saharan Africa might be the region hardest hit. *World Bank Blogs.* https://blogs.worldbank.org/opendata/impact-covid-19-coronavirus-global-poverty-why-sub-saharan-africa-might-be-region-hardest.

Mbaye, A. A., and Gueye, F. (2020). Conceptualising the informal sector: Analysis and application to francophone Africa. In: A.A. Mbaye, S.S. Golub and F. Gueye (Eds), *Formal and Informal Enterprises in Francophone Africa: Moving toward a vibrant private sector* (21-41). International Development Research Centre (IDRC).

Mbaye, A. A., Ekomié, J-J., Saha, J. C., Kobou, G., Charmes, J., Benjamin, N., Golub, S. S., Haughton, D., Cissé, R., Diop, I. T., Gueye, F., Diop, A. N., Doucouré, F. B., and Diallo, N. A. (2015). *Secteur informel, environnement des affaires et croissance économique : Une analyse comparative de l'Afrique de l'Ouest et du Centre.* International Development Research Centre (IDRC). https://idl-bncidrc.dspacedirect.org/handle/10625/54414

Mdemu, M., Kissoly, L., Bjornlund, H., Kimaro, E., Christen, E. W., van Rooyen, A., Stirzaker, R., and Ramshaw, P. (2020). The role of soil water monitoring tools and agricultural innovation platforms in improving food security and income of farmers in smallholder irrigation schemes in Tanzania. *International Journal of Water Resources Development*, 36(1), s148-s170.

Mendi, P., and Mudida, R. (2018). The effect on innovation of beginning informal: Empirical evidence from Kenya. *Technological Forecasting and Social Change*, 131(C), 326-335.

Moore, M. (2020). Food insecurity, health privilege and COVID-19. *Home*, 30(17), 1-5.

Mora, O., Mouël, C. Le, Lattre-Gasquet, M. De, Donnars, C., Dumas, P., Réchauchère, O., Brunelle, T., Manceron, S., Marajo-Petitzon, E., Moreau, C., Barzman, M., Forslund, A., and Marty, P. (2020). Exploring the future of land use and food security: A new set of global scenarios. *PLoS ONE*, 15(7), 1-30.

Mottaleb, K. A., Mainuddin, M., and Sonobe, T. (2020). *COVID-19 induced economic loss and ensuring food security for vulnerable groups: Policy implications from Bangladesh.* PLoS ONE, 15(10), 1-21.

Msunduzi Municipality (2018). *Integrated Development Plan.* Msunduzi Municipality.

Mustapha, N., Petersen, I., Bortagaray, I., Jegede, O., and Kruss, G. (2021). Measurement of innovation in the informal sector in Africa: The importance to industrial policy. *Innovation and Development*. DOI: 10.1080/2157930X.2021.1887614.

Mytelka, L., and Farinelli, F. (2000). Local clusters, innovation systems and sustained competitiveness. *UNU/INTECH Discussion Paper*.

Organisation for Economic Co-operation and Development (OECD)/Eurostat. (2018). *Oslo Manual 2018: Guidelines for Collecting, Reporting and Using Data on Innovation, 4th Edition, The measurement of scientific, technological and innovation activities*. OECD Publishing. https://doi.org/10.1787/9789264304604-en

Petersen, L. M., and Charman, A. J. E. (2017). The scope and scale of the informal food economy of South African urban residential townships: Results of a small-area micro-enterprise census. *Development Southern Africa*, 35(1), 1-23.

Petersen, L. M., and Charman, A. J. E. (2018). The role of family in the township informal economy of food and drink in KwaMashu, South Africa. *International Journal of Sociology and Social Policy*, 4(3).

Petersen, I., and Kruss, G. (2021). Universities as change agents in resource-poor local settings: An empirically grounded typology of engagement models. *Technological Forecasting and Social Change*, 167, 120693.

Rogan, M., and Skinner, C. (2017). *The Nature of the South African Informal Sector as Reflected in the Quarterly Labour-Force Survey, 2008-2014*. University of Cape Town.

Rogan, M., and Skinner, C. (2018). Employment in the South African informal sector: Interrogating trends, identifying opportunities. In: F. Fourie (Ed.), *Tackling Unemployment and Poverty in South Africa: The contribution of the informal sector*. HSRC Press.

Rogan, M., and Skinner, C. (2020, 8 August). Support for women informal workers is urgent as pandemic unfolds in South Africa. *The Conversation*. https://theconversation.com/support-for-women-informal-workers-is-urgent-as-pandemic-unfolds-in-south-africa-144136

Skinner, C., and Haysom, G. (2016). *The informal sector's role in food security: A missing link in policy debates?* (Discussion paper no. 6). Hungry Cities Partnership.

Skinner, C. (2019). Contributing and yet excluded? Informal food retail in African cities. In: J. Battersby and V. Watson (Eds), *Urban Food Systems Governance and Poverty in African Cities*. Routledge.

Tawodzera, G. (2019). The nature and operations of informal food vendors in Cape Town. *Urban Forum*, 30, 443-459.

Yaya, S., Otu, A., and Labonté, R. (2020). Globalisation in the time of COVID-19: Repositioning Africa to meet the immediate and remote challenges. *Globalisation and Health*, 16(51), 1-8.

CHAPTER 7

Enabling Inclusive Technological Change through Transformative Policies

Frugal innovations from medical device manufacturing firms in South Africa

Sanghamitra Chakravarty and Peter Knorringa

Introduction

The lack of affordable and appropriate medical devices to serve the needs of developing countries has been a global health concern (WHO, 2010a) long before the pandemic. Most medical devices meant for developing countries are designed by firms in high-income countries who innovate primarily for their home markets (WHO, 2010b). This market gap for frugal medical devices, largely unaddressed by Western multinational firms, offers an opportunity for innovative firms in developing countries. South Africa, with its growing medical device manufacturing sector, well-established science and technology infrastructure, and world-class universities with high-level biomedical research capacity, is well positioned to tap into this market gap. Studies suggest that the sector offers significant potential to contribute to South Africa's National Development Plan (NDP), which aims to eliminate poverty and reduce inequality by 2030 (SAMRC – PATH, 2014). This chapter offers complementary micro-level perspectives, making connections with existing macro and sectoral studies; and, in addition, focusing on pathways to accelerate capability accumulation and inclusive technological change.

The pandemic has highlighted three aspects of healthcare delivery in developing countries. First, it put frugal health technologies at the centre stage of the response to the pandemic, particularly in the initial stages of the crisis. Frugal innovation has been conceptualised as good enough, functional, and significantly cheaper products for resource constrained settings (Weyrauch and Herstatt, 2017; Zeschky et al., 2014), developed in bottom-up processes driven by necessity (Basu et al., 2013). At the height of the pandemic, frugal approaches around healthcare were observed to exhibit characteristics of re-purposing, reusing and rapid deployment, in addition to affordability (Harris et al., 2020). Numerous frugal innovations emerged, from low-cost ventilators to temporary hospital facilities with re-purposed equipment and infrastructure, giving developing countries with limited resources ways to deal with the crisis. Frugal approaches were rapidly and resourcefully deployed during the pandemic, not only in developing countries but also in the richest[1] (Harris et al., 2020; Corsini et al., 2021). For developing countries on tight budgets, it has reaffirmed the urgent need for frugal health technologies for inclusive healthcare delivery.

Second, geopolitical uncertainties and global trade conflicts gave rise to a call for technology sovereignty (Edler et al., 2020), bringing to the forefront the need to enhance regional capabilities, self-reliance and resilience. International policy debates on access to healthcare have not yet focused sufficiently on building local innovation and manufacturing capabilities in Africa, though there has been a slight shift. For example, access to medicines in Africa is focused around funding procurement of essential medicines from Asian manufacturers (Mackintosh et al., 2016). Africa's medical device needs have, so far, mainly been met through imports of equipment designed for high-income countries and through international donations, and a disproportionate percentage remains nonfunctional or broken[2] (Howitt et al., 2012; Marks et al., 2019; Perry and Malkin, 2011; WHO, 2010a). The World Health Organization observes that addressing

---

[1] Such as the design of a ventilator made with primarily off-the-shelf components already existing in the NHS supply chain in the UK (Harris et al., 2020) and re-purposing full-face scuba masks into Continuous Positive Airway Pressure (CPAP) ventilators in Italy (Corsini et al., 2021).

[2] https://www.npr.org/sections/goatsandsoda/2016/09/08/492842274/rage-against-the-busted-medical-machines?t=1621597274176

disparities in access is a complex challenge dependent on a variety of factors[3] and not singularly related to local production (WHO, 2012). Rooted in a historical political economy approach and offering a different perspective, Mackintosh et al. (2016) argue that to tackle the acute healthcare needs of Africa, the development of industrial production and related capabilities in pharmaceuticals are necessary elements. The onset of the pandemic in 2020 contributed to an intermittent disruption of most global value supply chains. In South Africa, the supply of reagents normally sourced internationally was disrupted due to a rise in global demand, fluctuation in exchange rates and restricted transport. The South African government responded with funding support to strengthen the local manufacture of reagents, diagnostic kits and ventilators to address shortages, tapping into research capabilities built over decades.

Third, the 'shocking imbalance'[4] in the global distribution of vaccines provided evidence that the availability of technology does not ensure its equal access; nor does having production capability, as was the case with India, ensure its efficient and timely delivery. Inclusive healthcare requires coordinated action across policy domains as well as capabilities.

In the post-pandemic era, this chapter focuses on pathways to strengthen existing capabilities in medical device firms in South Africa for both public health security and economic development. One of the fundamental challenges facing policy-makers in developing countries is aligning inclusive development with technological progress and innovation (Cozzens, 2008; Cozzens and Kaplinsky, 2009; Kaplinsky, 2011; Srinivas, 2012). Technological change is a contextual process (Srinivas and Sutz, 2008), and in specific sectors, it has shown to be the nucleus of economic and social transformation for industrialising countries (Kim, 1997; Srinivas, 2012). Medical devices could be such a high potential sector for South Africa, intersecting industrialisation and improvement of its own healthcare delivery as well as having an impact on global health.

Using three cases of medical device manufacturing firms in South Africa, this chapter analyses firm-level innovation capabilities and processes at various stages of innovation generation, production and diffusion to the market. It is based on primary data collected in phases between July 2018 and September 2019, as well as secondary data. Follow-up online

---

3   Such as business environment, financing mechanisms, regulations and policies (WHO, 2012).
4   https://www.who.int/director-general/speeches/detail/director-general-s-opening-remarks-at-the-media-briefing-on-covid-19-9-april-2021

interviews to gauge firm resilience to the pandemic were carried out during the pandemic. Our research follows a non-linear abductive methodology involving systematic combining of framework, theories, fieldwork and case analysis (Dubois and Gadde, 2002). Two key sources that have influenced our analysis are Srinivas (2012) and Bell and Figueiredo (2012). First, in our framework, the innovation processes are viewed as a 'web of three interlinked relationships' (Srinivas, 2012) involved in the generation, production and diffusion of innovation, similar to the concept of technology systems determining technological change (Carlsson and Stankiewicz, 1991). Second, the evaluation of innovation capabilities is based on Bell and Figueiredo (2012), who have integrated technological capabilities and organisational capabilities in their study of capabilities accumulation in innovative firms in developing countries. Bell and Figueiredo propose a 'revealed capability' approach where the innovation activity, understood in terms of increasing novelty and significance (from basic, intermediate, advanced to world-leading or innovation frontier)[5]; and the associated elements of capabilities (knowledge base, production and organisational) are matched (see Figure 1 and Figure 4 below).

Anchored in these theoretical groundings, our chapter makes several contributions. First, the empirical evidence suggests that the firms in this study have intermediate to advanced innovation capabilities demonstrated by the development of frugal innovations, which are fundamentally new products suitable not only for the local market but also for export. Despite the complex challenges of a resource constrained environment and an emerging sector, these firms have successfully designed and commercialised product innovations. Second, the high level of innovation activity does not always match the equivalent technological and organisational dimensions as expected from our reference framework (Bell and Figueiredo, 2012). A likely explanation of this could be due to frugal processes and the creative ability of firms in developing countries of 'doing more with less' (Radjou et al., 2012). Further, as frugal products, they point towards a different direction of innovation than global incumbents and new pathways of technological change (Romijn and Caniëls, 2011). Third, the evidence shows that while the firms have been supported by the state in some activities to an extent, they have not been direct recipients of large R&D grants. Fourth, all three firms have contributed to varied levels of inclusive technological change through innovation generation, production and diffusion processes. Fifth

---

5   In terms of novelty and along similar lines as the *Oslo Manual*.

and last, the data suggest that within the context of South Africa, innovation procurement of frugal medical devices not only enables domestic firms but creates access for those solely dependent on public healthcare. In order to accelerate the pace of inclusive technological change, future policies may take these findings into account.

The chapter is structured as follows: first, it provides a background of the medical device manufacturing and innovation in South Africa, including initiatives in pandemic management. A literature review follows – it is divided into four subsections and explores the concepts of and relationships between frugal innovation, inclusion in healthcare, evolving policy perspectives and innovation capabilities in developing country firms. Next the methodological approach and the three case studies are presented, followed by a discussion of the findings with respect to innovation capabilities, inclusive technological change suggesting possible policy directions. The final section of the chapter offers a conclusion and future research direction.

Background: South African medical devices sector – innovation and manufacturing

South Africa has a small but growing medical devices manufacturing sector that has recently received attention from the state. Some industry-level studies have been carried out (DTI-Deloitte, 2014; SAMRC-PATH, 2014). The perception is that South Africa is uniquely placed to develop its medical device manufacturing and, through it, improve its healthcare as well as bring economic benefits, all contributing towards the National Development Plan 2030 (SAMRC-PATH, 2014). However, success would be dependent on political commitment and aggressive policies, the key recommendations being the strategic alignment of core healthcare device areas and technology focus, establishing and enforcing local standards and a regulatory framework; and developing a transparent public procurement process (SAMRC-PATH, 2014). The South African Medical Device Industry Association (SAMED), consisting largely of importing companies, has also funded a similar sectoral study (SAMED-KPMG, 2014). The country has many world-class universities and a legacy of frontier level research on healthcare and biomedical engineering. Many cutting-edge medical device innovations have emerged from universities and public research organisations and are at various levels of development. Some of these can be categorised as frugal. One such example is a cost-effective and non-occlusive solution for rheumatic heart treatment being developed by Strait Access Technologies (SAT), a University of Cape Town (UCT) start-up. Another example is the

UmbiFlow – a cheaper alternative to the conventional 2D ultrasound with Doppler mode to track foetus health developed by the Council for Scientific and Industrial Research (CSIR) and the South African Medical Research Council (SAMRC).

At the onset of the pandemic in 2020, as governments across the world tried to urgently build internal capacities for diagnostics test kits and essential equipment like ventilators, many initiatives were undertaken by the South African government. They involved public research organisations and universities as well as the private sector. The Department of Science and Innovation (DSI), SAMRC and Technology Innovation Agency (TIA), awarded ZAR 18 million (USD 1.2 million) funding to enhance national research and production capabilities of reagents and diagnostic kits (Department of Science and Innovation, 2020). Another important response to the pandemic was the National Ventilator Project – a national effort to design, develop and manufacture ventilators. This project was initiated by the Department of Trade, Industry and Competition (DTIC) and managed by the South African Radio Astronomy Observatory (SARAO)[6] with technology support from CSIR.[7] One of the products developed under this project was the Continuous Positive Airway Pressure (CPAP-100) device. The fact that this was an affordable device and could be operated by nurses with minimum training suggests that it is a frugal innovation.[8] Part of its production was carried out by the South African Emergency Ventilator Project (SAVE-P) – a local consortium, and purchased via the Solidarity Fund set up by the government. SAVE-P is constituted of a group of manufacturing companies and expert professionals working together to redesign CPAP machines with existing locally available technology. Table 1 is a compilation of some of the initiatives in South Africa to manage the need for diagnostic kits, reagents and ventilators during the height of the pandemic.

Many medical device innovations also emerged from private manufacturing firms in the country, which are the focus of this chapter and discussed in the case studies below. While South Africa imports medical devices worth USD 670 million annually, local manufacturing comprises mainly IVD (in vitro diagnostic) products, implants (orthopaedic, cardiac, dental, etc.) and surgical devices, most of which are exported (WHO, 2013,

---

6   https://www.sarao.ac.za/media-releases/
    sarao-mandated-to-manage-the-production-of-respiratory-ventilators/
7   https://www.csir.co.za/csir-supports-national-covid-19-response-locally-developed-ventilator
8   https://www.sarao.ac.za/wp-content/uploads/2020/06/Fact-Sheet-CPAP-ventilator-2.pdf

2016). Its domestic market, as in all emerging countries, is dominated by multinational corporations selling mainly imported products (WHO, 2012). For small firms in the local manufacturing sector, competition from international companies is one of the key deterrents for manufacturing (WHO, 2013, 2016). The innovation system offers challenges of resource constraints and bureaucratic inefficiencies. Many enabling institutions are in the process of restructuring and transition. The South African Health Products Regulatory Authority (SAHPRA), which is the central authority governing the import, purchase, use, etc., of medical devices, was established in 2015, following the passing of the Medicines and Related Substances Amendment Act 14. Previously, the Technology Innovation Agency (TIA) was also restructured to improve innovation funding. Unlike in countries with a well-developed medical devices sector, there are few ISO 13485 certified contract manufacturers, an essential requirement for the sector.

In recent years, many academic articles have also shone light upon various facets and challenges of the medical devices sector in South Africa. For example, de Jager et al. (2017) characterise domestic collaborations in medical devices using bibliometric analysis. They suggest a need for translational partnerships (i.e. including academia, healthcare and industry) as pivotal for enabling commercialisation. Investigating technology transfer and absorptive capacities of local manufacturing firms, Ramaoka (2020) observes that from the key channels of external technology sources such as FDI, embodied technology and joint ventures, partnerships were more exploitative (technology purchasing) rather than explorative or involving knowledge sharing. Saidi and Douglas (2018) note that while the establishment of a comprehensive regulatory framework such as SAHPRA is a milestone development, this transition poses formidable challenges for the industry. In focusing on innovative manufacturing firms and a micro-level qualitative approach, we complement these sectoral studies and this academic literature with a fresh perspective.

Literature review

Frugal innovation and inclusion

Despite its undeniable contributions to development, the impacts of technological change on developing countries have not always been positive. Inequalities in innovation generation and diffusion have led to increased global social justice challenges (Papaioannou, 2011), increasing relative poverty among vulnerable sections of society in the Global South. Development studies scholars have drawn attention to the complex relationship between innovation, technological change, poverty and inequality, to show how in a highly interconnected and globalised world, technological change has reproduced and magnified, rather than reduced prevailing inequalities (Arecona and Sutz, 2003; Cozzens and Kaplinsky, 2009; Kaplinsky, 2011; Lazonoick and Mazuccato, 2013). Product innovation, particularly in healthcare, is a space where inequality plays out prominently (Cozzens and Kaplinsky, 2009). For example, the 10/90 gap highlights that only 10% of global health research expenditure is devoted to the health needs of developing countries, which account for 90% of the global disease burden (Global Forum for Health Research and WHO, 2004). Just as partnerships such as the International AIDS Vaccine Initiative (IAVI) have tried to bring new science and technology closer to the needs of the poor (Chataway and Smith, 2006), the Priority Medical Devices Project was initiated by World Health Organization to address the total lack of affordable context-specific devices for low- and middle-income countries (WHO, 2010a).

Frugal innovation has been positioned as enabling more inclusive development and is popularly understood as 'doing more with less and for more people' (Prabhu, 2017; Radjou et al., 2012). In this chapter, we identify frugal innovations in medical devices as products that are significantly cheaper and more appropriate[9] for resource constrained settings. These are driven by underlying frugal processes making significant cost reduction and suitability to context possible.

While a more exhaustive discussion on the various discourses around frugality is beyond the scope of this chapter, the prominent debates that have shaped our methodology and arguments are elucidated here. First, the term 'frugal innovation' is not commonly used amongst local firms in South Africa. 'Inclusive innovation' is more widely used and relevant given the pervasive inequalities in the society; and implies broadly similar phenomena, notwithstanding differences in philosophical lineages (Onsongo and Knorringa, 2020). Second, the discourse around how frugal innovation relates to inclusive development remains ideologically polarised and lacks detailed empirical evidence (Knorringa et al., 2016). The initial discourse dominated by business literature, focused on benefits of frugal innovation from a product perspective and the latent purchasing power of

---

9   Referring to features like ruggedness (performance is not easily affected by high temperatures, humidity, etc., requiring less infrastructure to house); operation (simple to operate, not requiring specialised skills which may be scarce); using fewer utilities and consumables; and maintenance (locally serviced, including ease of availability of parts and consumables).

Table 1: Examples of pandemic-related initiatives to address medical device needs in South Africa

Project/area	Technology/manufacturing	Key supporting agencies
Diagnostic reagents – Local manufacture of nucleic acid isolation kits for nasal and oropharyngeal swab samples.	Council for Scientific Research (CSIR) that will work closely with several spin-off companies.	Department of Science and Innovation, South African Medical Research Council, and Technology Innovation Agency
Application-ready RT-PCR reagents – Cost-effective technology for production of Taq DNA polymerase, a key ingredient in RT-PCR reagents previously developed by CSIR.	CSIR and CapeBio Technologies (Pty) Ltd; technology licensing to CapeBio.	
Diagnostic reagents – Develop and produce highly stable synthetic DNA and RNA molecules containing all of the commonly used target sequences used for SARS-CoV-2 nucleic acid detection, as well as internal control sequences to check for the integrity of the nucleic acids.	Biopharming Research Unit (BRU) of the University of Cape Town.	
Antigen-based rapid test for detecting acute cases – Point of care diagnostic designed to directly detect the COVID-19 spike glycoprotein S1 in saliva to determine currently acute infection.	Medical Diagnostech (Pty) Ltd	
Rapid test kit – Detecting the SARS-CoV-2 viral antigen in PoC or near-patient settings.	Mintek, other South African institutions and biotech companies as partners.	
Aptamer based diagnostic kit – Building on long-term HIV research, the project will leverage an in-house developed algorithm to identify several aptamers against any target, viral, or bacterial protein for more sensitive, accurate, and cost-effective diagnostics.	University of Western Cape, Aminotek and Amasu Technologies, and Medical Diagnostech (Pty) Ltd.	
Design of loop-mediated isothermal amplification (LAMP) rapid diagnostic test to run on both open RT-PCR platforms and closed ParaDNA PoC platform for rapid testing.	Gknowmix (Pty) Ltd., a spin-off from SAMRC, initially supported under Newton Fund (UK) for development of diagnostic testing and screening of breast cancer.	
Setting up of a new manufacturing facility based on recombinant proteins from Nicotiana benthamiana for a serology test to detect antibodies in blood at Cape Biologix, Mauritius. Also establishing laboratory and climate-controlled hydroponic grow rooms.	Cape Bio Pharms, a spin-off from Biopharming Research Unit of University of Cape Town.	European Investment Bank, Foundation for Innovative New Diagnostics
National Ventilator Project where stream 1 addresses the need for non-invasive Continuous Positive Airway Pressure (CPAP) ventilators – a device used for COVID-19 patients in the initial stages of infection suffering from respiratory distress. Stream 2 focuses on ventilator demand for a smaller number of critically ill patients.	CSIR, South African Emergency Ventilator Project (SAVE-P), Siemens, Akacia Medical, and others.	South African Radio Astronomy Observatory (SARAO), Department of Trade, Industry and Competition (DTIC), Solidarity Fund, Siemens

Source: Authors own based on press releases of: CSIR (2020); Denel (2020); Department of Science and Innovation (2020); SARAO (2020); Siemens (2020); University of Cape Town (2020).

the poor (Prahalad, 2006), has drawn sharp criticism from development scholars (Arora and Romijn, 2011; Knorringa et al., 2016; Meagher, 2017; Papaioannou, 2014). Much of this initial frugal literature ignored local participation and capability building as part of the innovation process and a necessary step in inclusive development. Inclusive innovation, scholars argue, should explicitly conceive development in terms of active inclusion of those who are currently marginalised, satisfying one or more of the following: inclusion in terms of relevance, in terms of development, ease of absorption and impact on livelihoods (Foster and Heeks, 2013). Inclusion is a multidimensional concept, and innovations should meet the principles of global justice of equitable participation, not only in their diffusion but also in the way they are generated (Papaioannou, 2014). Third and last, firm-level capability building and transformation of production processes, which lie at the heart of economic development (Chang and Andreoni, 2021; Chang, 2014), have not been taken into consideration in the frugal innovation discourse. These debates and gaps in literature have informed our analysis of inclusive technological change, as discussed in the methodology section (below).

Inclusion in healthcare: The institutional triad

The pandemic has made evident how providing healthcare in a more inclusive and equitable manner is a highly complex issue, particularly for governments in developing countries. High innovation and industrial capability in the health sector is by no means a guarantee for improving health outcomes. Pre-pandemic lessons from India and Brazil suggest that inclusion in healthcare is not possible without coordinated policies to ensure access. India, often referred to as the 'pharmacy to the world', accomplished an impressive level of innovation and industrial capability. However, despite being a major pharmaceutical exporter, India has not been very successful in meeting its own health needs (Srinivas, 2012, 2016). In contrast, Brazil, since adopting the Unified Health System (Sistema Único de Saúde or SUS) in 1988, progressively brought together industrial development, science technology initiatives, and the healthcare needs of its citizens through a series of policy interventions such as the National Medicine Policy and National Policy of Pharmaceutical Care (Aragão et al., 2016). In view of these complexities, Srinivas (2012) suggests the health sector be viewed as a 'web of three interlinked relationships' consisting of industrial production, the system of delivery, and that of consumption, and makes the following observation:

> *Markets for health technologies have several unique characteristics, such as limited information and autonomous choice, blurred distinctions between producers and users [...], risks of use, and particular cultural traits. [...] neither patients nor health professionals but third-party payers [...] may be the buyers of the end products. [...] This collective aspect of consumption and demand shapes late industrial technological advance and constrains how states can reconcile economic and social goals. (Srinivas, 2012, 3–4)*

Rather than viewing health technologies solely from the innovation perspective/supply-side or from the health policy/demand side, Srinivas suggests that institutions of the triad are in dynamic co-evolution, interacting with each other and requiring the consistent intervention of the state to maintain a 'comfortable equilibrium' (Srinivas, 2012, 9). This is analogous to the concept of technology systems understood as a network of agents within an institutional infrastructure involved in the generation, diffusion and utilisation of technology (Carlsson and Stankiewicz, 1991) and determining technological change. This heuristic is adapted to our research context for analysing inclusive technological change. In contrast to the triad as production, delivery and consumption (which was mainly in view of pharmaceuticals and especially generics studied by Srinivas), in this chapter, we have adapted the three vertices of the triad as innovation generation, production and diffusion. Further, we are specifically looking at frugal innovations emerging from innovative South African SMEs which are appreciative of resource constraint environments typical in developing countries. We focus on the extent to which these firms play a role in innovation generation (design and development of frugal medical devices), and along with their local production and use, catalyse a nucleus of more inclusive technological change.

What is evident from the above discussion is that attaining inclusivity in healthcare requires a coordinated effort across different policy domains. The three vertices of the framework also indicate the three stages of innovation design to delivery, with each stage dominantly influenced by a particular policy domain such as science, technology and innovation policy; industrial policy; and health policy. Figure 1 illustrates the adapted institutional triad and the associated policy domains.

Emerging policy perspectives

Exploring extant literature, we identify three emerging policy trends relevant to our research context. First, industrial policy has resurfaced in mainstream development discourse and with it the importance of building manufacturing capabilities (Andreoni and Chang, 2019; Chang and Andreoni, 2021). Second, over the past few decades, the understanding of how science, technology and innovation (STI) can be harnessed for economic growth and social benefits has evolved, and so has policy-making. Starting from a narrow R&D focus, recent recommendations for innovation policies have proposed greater attention to inclusion (Chataway et al., 2014) and are targeted towards transformative change for addressing social and environmental challenges (Schot and Steinmueller, 2018). Thus, on the one hand, there is an understanding that innovation should drive economic transformation towards desirable social change, while on the other hand, there is the idea that innovation policy should strongly target economic diversification and structural change (Uyarraa et al., 2020). Third, there is renewed policy interest in the demand side of innovation and public procurement of innovation (PPI) as an integrated component of innovation and industrial policy (Edler and Georghiou, 2007; Edquist and Zabala-Iturriagagoitia, 2012; Uyarra and Flanagan, 2010; Uyarra et al., 2020). PPI is being viewed as an instrument that can harmonise the competing policy agendas of transformative innovation policy and industrial policy (Uyarra et al., 2020). However, the primary objective of state procurement is to address human needs or societal problems, and stimulating new product development or diffusion of innovation from procuring organisations are secondary objectives (Edquist and Zabala-Iturriagagoitia, 2012; Uyarra and Flanagan, 2010). Early empirical studies have suggested that long-term state procurement is more efficient in stimulating innovation compared to R&D subsidies (Geroski, 1990; Rothwell and Zegveld, 1981), with Aschhoff and Sofka (2009) highlighting the role of universities; Malerba (2007) that of experimental customers; and Uyarra and Flanagan (2010) recommending 'innovation friendly' procurement for tackling trade-offs between conflicting policy goals.

Closer to our geographical context, in sub-Saharan Africa, there has been a renewed interest in science policy and funding in recent years, but with greater recognition that science needs to be aligned with pressing social challenges (Chataway et al., 2019) and that research excellence should not be limited to publications (Kraemer-Mbula et al., 2020). The study of the sectoral ecosystem in collaboration with PATH (SAMRC-PATH, 2014) had also observed that despite high research capacity in healthcare and biomedical field, 'research is almost exclusively publication driven rather than also focusing on innovation and product R&D' and commercial exploitation of IP remains low (SAMRC-PATH, 2014, 7). Neoliberal policies and a free market environment have led to insufficient industrial growth and premature deindustrialisation in many African countries. Kraemer-Mbula and Monaco (2020) argue that industrial policy must follow a bottom-up approach by strengthening innovation capabilities of small-scale firms, including those in the informal sector. One key issue in developing countries, as is in the case of South Africa (Kruss and Lorentzen, 2009; OECD, 2007), is that too much policy attention is concentrated in public research organisations and universities; and dedicated to radical or disruptive innovations (Bell and Figueiredo, 2012). Without adequately supporting the productive base towards incremental or design innovations and accumulation of capabilities, it creates an imbalance of complementarities (Bell and Figueiredo, 2012). Nevertheless, what is evident from the innovations experienced during the recent pandemic, is that the research capacity built over decades made it possible for South Africa to quickly respond to the needs of the pandemic. Recognising the importance of imitative, frugal, and incremental innovation, as well as design and engineering activities, within its developmental context, South Africa's recent White Paper on Science, Technology and Innovation (DST, 2019) has also adopted a broader conceptualisation.

The white paper also proposed to strengthen the focus on demand-side innovation through co-funding, public procurement and sectoral innovation funds, working in collaboration with other government departments. Public procurement is a highly technical (and political) process requiring consideration of both immediate costs and of health priorities as part of longer-term development goals and of building innovation capabilities (Chataway et al., 2016). For medical device frugal innovations in cases where no equivalent product exists or procurement was based only on imported standardised products, this can be even more complicated. It may involve adjustment or introduction of standards and regulations, a time-consuming and long drawn out process.

Innovation capabilities in developing country firms

Developing countries are posed with the challenges of industrial transformation in an environment of highly regulated global policies – a context very different from how the now industrialised countries built their technological prowess and wealth (Chang, 2002). Recent studies by the World Bank have also made similar observations, suggesting that innovation in developing countries is several times more challenging as compared to the already industrialised (Cirera and Maloney, 2017). Intellectual property

Figure 1: Institutional triad and interconnected processes influencing inclusive technological change

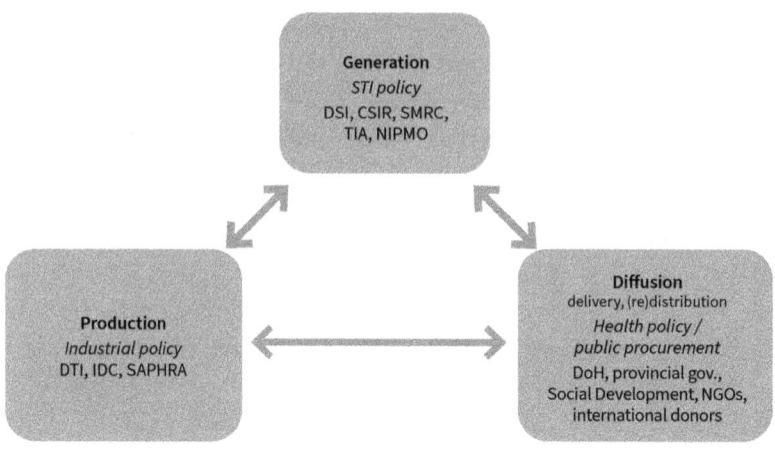

Source: Adapted from Srinivas (2012).

regimes rigidly enforced by multilateral agreements like TRIPS[10] has led to 'intellectual monopoly capitalism' (Pagano, 2014), benefitting firms from the Global North while creating barriers to entry for indigenous firms in industrialising countries. Accumulation of capabilities in firms in developing countries may lead to different types of products, processes and organisational configurations from that found in developed countries, and new patterns of technological change may emerge (Bell and Figueiredo, 2012; Romijn and Caniëls, 2011).

One of the most widely adopted classifications of technological capabilities was developed by Lall (1992) based on functions (investment, production, linkages) and their degree of complexity (routine, adaptive, replicative, innovative/risky), reflecting the deepening of knowledge over time. While the use of the term 'technological capabilities' implies both production and innovation capabilities and the ability to organise these activities, some authors like Bell and Pavitt (1993) distinguish between production capabilities (improving productivity) and innovation capabilities (new products, processes closer to frontier level). Subsequently, Dutrénit (2000, 2004), in her study of a Mexican firm, emphasised the importance of organisational capabilities, which until then were studied in firms in

---

10   Trade-Related Aspects of Intellectual Property Rights, World Trade Organization.

developed countries. The concept of organisational capabilities is primarily explained by the resource-based view of the firm highlighting distinctive competences that cannot be easily transferred or imitated (Nelson and Winter, 1982; Penrose, 1959). Defined using various other terms such as core competences (Prahlad and Hamel, 1990) or dynamic capabilities (Teece and Pisano, 1994), organisational capabilities are understood as the firm's ability to integrate, build and reconfigure internal and external resources. Bell and Figueiredo (2012) draw from the technological capabilities literature (from the works of Katz, Lall, Hobday, Figueiredo and others) but also integrate it with literature on organisational capabilities (Dutrénit), which was earlier more prevalent in the study of firms in developed economies (Teece, Pisano and others). They propose the analysis of innovation capability accumulation through a 'revealed capability' approach, understood in terms of increasing novelty and significance of innovation activity; and matching the associated elements of capabilities. Figure 2 represents the path of innovation capability building (Bell and Figueiredo, 2012), suggesting that with increasing levels of innovation activity represented by the technological dimension, firms also build organisational capabilities (Dutrénit, 2000). As discussed above, this understanding has been used as a broad reference in the analysis of individual dimensions of innovation capabilities.

Figure 2: Innovation capability accumulation. Changing emphasis on 'technological' and 'organisational' dimensions

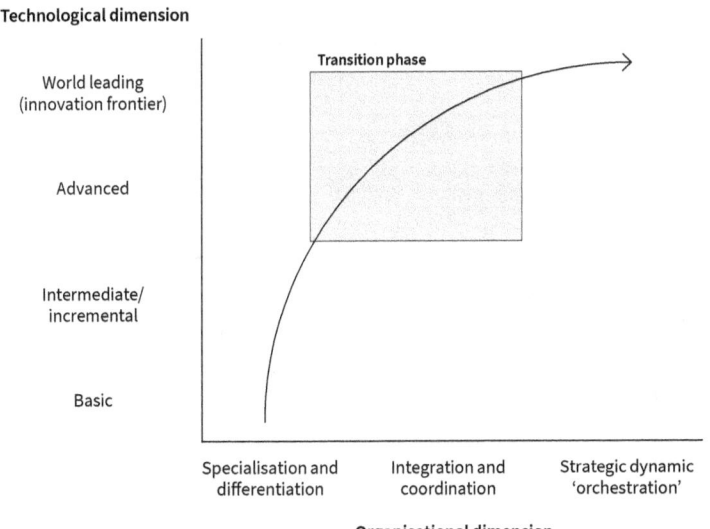

Source: Bell and Figueiredo (2012); adapted from Dutrénit (2000).

Methodology and framework

The purpose of this chapter is to understand the innovation profiles of small and medium medical device manufacturing firms in South Africa and in what way these firms can be better supported to enable inclusive technological change. The research methodology follows a non-linear abductive process involving systematic combining, where the analytical framework, theories, fieldwork and case analysis are considered to be intertwined (Dubois and Gadde, 2002), as illustrated in Figure 3. The foundation of this methodology is the constant revisiting of the various types of interrelated research activities or 'matching'. The search for theories and emerging publications was continued in parallel to data collection. Data were analysed throughout the process of redirecting the research enquiry. The initial analytical framework, which was largely based on the notion of solely technology capabilities and sectoral innovation systems, was refined based on new literature. The two most relevant pieces of literature found during this process were the works of Srinivas (2012), which offered an analytical framework for viewing the interconnectedness of the innovation processes influencing inclusive technological change; and Bell and Figueiredo (2012) for analysing innovation capabilities. We applied a case study analysis in a qualitative and explorative manner, which is best suited for a complex and understudied phenomenon that cannot be easily explained by a single established theoretical lens (Yin, 2014).

Figure 3: Methodological approach of systematic combining

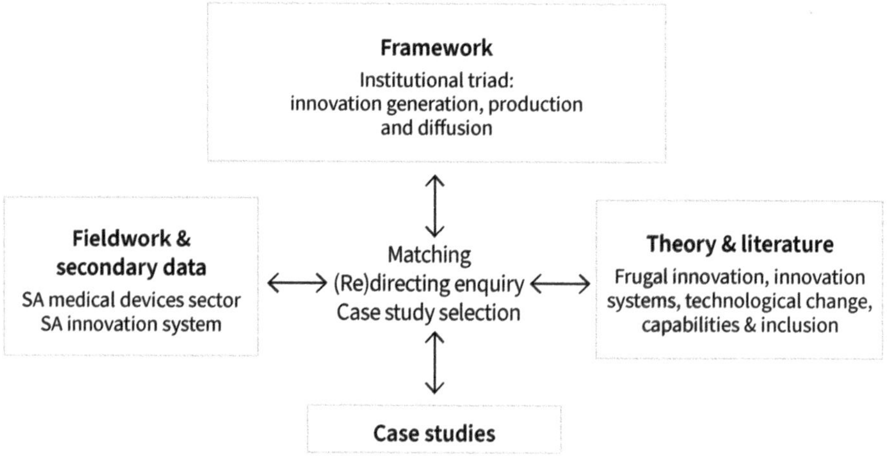

```
                    ┌─────────────────────────────┐
                    │         Framework           │
                    │    Institutional triad:     │
                    │ innovation generation,      │
                    │  production and diffusion   │
                    └─────────────────────────────┘
                                 ↑↓
┌──────────────────┐                            ┌──────────────────────┐
│   Fieldwork &    │         Matching           │  Theory & literature │
│  secondary data  │ ←→ (Re)directing enquiry ←→│ Frugal innovation,   │
│ SA medical       │    Case study selection    │ innovation systems,  │
│ devices sector   │                            │ technological change,│
│ SA innovation    │                            │ capabilities &       │
│ system           │                            │ inclusion            │
└──────────────────┘                            └──────────────────────┘
                                 ↑↓
                         ┌───────────────┐
                         │ Case studies  │
                         └───────────────┘
```

Source: Adapted from Dubois and Gadde (2002).

In order to analyse in what way the activities of the firm are driving inclusive technological change, we adapt the concept of an institutional triad (Srinivas, 2012), illustrated in Figure 1. For innovation capability, we follow the 'revealed capability' approach (Bell and Figueiredo, 2012) to match the novelty and significance of innovation activity with the associated elements of technological and organisational capabilities. Figure 2 and Table 4 provide a broad reference to interpret innovation capability, integrating the technological dimension having two components (knowledge base and production capabilities) and organisational capabilities.

Case study selection

Local medical device firms were identified from desk research, with industry association websites being the key information sources.

From about 20 firms initially selected, 15 were interviewed. The final selection of the three case studies, guided by their theoretical relevance (Glaser and Strauss, 1967), was based on the following criteria. Firms

- must have clinically tested products in the domestic market, indicating that these products could be preferred over competing products due to their 'frugal' characteristics;
- must have product innovations developed with sufficient internal effort as indicated by R&D investments, technical personnel, etc.;
- must have local production set up;
- should be in mature/growth stage, indicating they are sustainable economic entities with cash-flow; and
- should be available and willing to share information and be part of the study.

These selection criteria were developed by matching the cases with the analytical framework, and the case studies were 'found' during the course of the research (Ragin and Becker, 1992) through this process. The application of these criteria resulted in the selection of the three cases shown in Table 2.

The purpose of selecting multiple case studies was not simply to overcome any weakness of specificity or to enhance validity (Eisenhardt, 1989; Yin, 2014) but to analyse the variations and common thread among them as they are influenced by similar national policies and thus not entirely independent.

Table 2: Characteristics of case study firms

Firm	Product profile	Maturity	Size	Market
Shonaquip	Several design and engineering based products	Mature	Large	Primarily domestic. Growing export
Sinapi Biomedical	5–6 design and engineering based products	Mature	Large	Domestic with substantial export
eMoyo Technology	Two new technology and software-based products	Growth	Medium	Primarily export

Note: Size (Full-time employees): 1-30 – Small; 31-60 – Medium; Over 61 – Large. Maturity: Early Stage: No product in market; Growth Stage: Few Products in market, more in pipeline; Mature Stage: Products in market, few in pipeline.
Source: Authors' own.

Data collection and sources

At the outset, extensive desk research was carried out to understand the sector and the systemic challenges and opportunities of the innovation system in general. Primary data were collected in three phases over several months of fieldwork between July 2018 and September 2019. Informed consent was obtained from the firms to use the data for academic and policy purposes. Additional online interviews were carried out in November 2020 to get insight into how the firms were doing during the pandemic, as well as to clarify and reconfirm information. Each case study consisted of two or more semi-structured interviews supported by an innovation survey, both built along similar lines. The survey was drawn up by adapting the Community Innovation Survey (CIS) and following guidelines of the OECD Oslo Manual (OECD, 2018). The broad line of enquiry for interviews was spread out into four quadrants: background/evolution, product innovation, process/operations, and experience and challenges. All interviews were audio-recorded for transcription. The duration of a single interview was approximately an hour forming the key data source to capture the stories and underlying layers of complexity not achievable in a survey. Also, it was anticipated that these were small teams headed by the owner/entrepreneur who may not have the time to complete surveys or may assign the task to someone not fully knowledgeable. With this understanding, the most important source was the interviews. Table 3 shows the data sources for each of the case studies. It is relevant to mention that the broader study involved about 40 interviews with firms, academics and government officials. Those that are not directly related to the three selected case studies have enhanced overall understanding and influenced the data analysis by revealing information and experiences which would not have emerged from these three cases alone.

Table 3: Overview of primary and other data sources for case studies

Firm	Interviewee	Collection	Duration	Other key data sources
Shonaquip	Founder	Sept. 2019 Dec. 2020 (online) Oct. 2019	160 min Full-day interaction at ISS, The Hague	• https://shonaquipse.org.za/Innovation Survey • Driver-Jowitt (2017) • Publications and impact reports shared by Shonaquip • Scheffler (2009) • WHO (2006) • Accelovate Design Challenge: Innovative Postural Support Solutions for Wheelchair Users in Low-Resource Settings https://reprolineplus.org/system/files/resources/wheelchair-design-report-2015.pdf
Sinapi Biomedical	Founder and MD International Sales Manager Professor, Obstetrics and Gynaecology, Stellenbosch University	Feb. 2019 Aug. 2020 (online) Nov. 2020 (online) Sept. 2019	240 min	• https://sinapibiomedical.com/ • https://www.globalhealth.northwestern.edu/about/improving-sample-collection-for-accurate-tb-diagnosis-a-qa-with-sinapi-biomedical.html • Technical documents shared after interview
eMoyo Technologies	Founder	March 2019 Sept. 2019 Nov. 2020 (online)	210 min	• https://emoyo.net/ • Innovation Survey • Company documents • Swanepoel et al. (2013) • Visagie et al. (2015)

Source: Authors' own.

Analysis of data

The core objective was to analyse the process of technological change from a firm-level perspective; in what ways these processes were already inclusive; and how they could be further enabled through policies for transformative change. To do so, we have analysed (a) innovation capabilities of the firms and (b) inclusion at each stage of the innovation process. The analysis of innovation capability was conducted in two steps: first, understanding the product portfolio and second, the illustrative elements of capabilities. The first was used to understand the level of innovation activity as well as the orientation of the firms, which was useful in understanding in what ways they were inclusive at the level of generation of innovations. We examined the product portfolio: What kind of products were the firms innovating? Could one or more of these products find application in the domestic market, or was it solely innovating for Western markets? Did it have any product which specifically catered to domestic health challenges? How were these developed? Who were the firms collaborating with?

The understanding of innovation comes from the Oslo Manual (2005)[11] and the extensive discussions in the works of Bell and Figueiredo (2012). The typologies of innovation level used in this analysis are summarised in Table 4 along with the corresponding organisational dimension. We have also given some indication of the quantity of human capital as we feel it is an important element of the firms' economic impact and of technological change. Lastly, in our analysis, we take a cross-sectional view of the innovation capabilities and not accumulation over time. Also, the firms in our study have not emerged as having simple production capabilities having primary manufacturing capabilities.

Table 4: Classification of innovation activity

Innovation level	Technological dimension	Organisational dimension
World-leading (Innovation frontier)	Overtaking incumbent innovators at the international frontier by cutting-edge innovation in products, production and organisational processes and systems.	Strategic dynamic orchestration
Advanced	Catching-up with the international technological frontier and closing in on leading global incumbents, with differing directions of innovation.	Advanced integration and coordination
Intermediate/ Incremental	Relatively complex improvements and modifications to products, process organisation and systems.	Integration and coordination
Basic	Minor adaptations and improvements, close to imitation adoptions.	Specialisation and differentiation

Source: Adopted from Bell and Figueiredo (2012).

Both in the interview and survey, special attention was paid to capturing the behaviour/orientation of the firm in the context of frugal innovation. Firms were questioned about product characteristics (affordability, appropriateness), main markets, customers, etc., to identify if any of their key products could be categorised as frugal innovations. Firms were assumed to offer frugal innovations if one or more of their products met all of the following criteria: (a) significantly cheaper than available options, (b) more appropriate for the local context in terms of features and (c) were used or have been used in the domestic market as evidence of being the preferred option. Table 5 draws out the parameters used in the analysis of inclusive technological change.

---

11 In levels of novelty such as innovation being 'new to the firm', 'new to the market', 'new to the world'.

Table 5: Inclusion at each stage of innovation process/micro level technological change

Stage	Criteria
Generation	Product portfolio relevant for the domestic market Collaborative development of products with local stakeholders
Production	Local production and manufacturing (as opposed to simple assembly) Local procurement of some materials, supplies and machinery
Diffusion	Use in the domestic market to replace imported products Use in government healthcare delivery and services

Source: Authors' own.

As with data collection, the analysis of data was carried out over time, beginning soon after the completion of the first stage of fieldwork. For each firm, after transcription of the first interview, an initial description was drafted into the lines of enquiry or pillars mentioned earlier. With each additional interview, these pillars were strengthened with more information. Going back to the firms multiple times helped to gauge the consistency of information as well as wean out important issues which were repeated in more than one interview, based on which the data was reinterpreted and the description refined. Several descriptions of the cases have been written depending on research sub-questions, with the narrative in the current chapter written to fit our analytical framework. A substantial part of technical information was extracted from secondary sources such as company websites, social media pages, newspaper articles, press releases, YouTube videos and websites of partnering organisations. These also helped to corroborate statements made by the firms about their products and collaborations in order to double-check findings from the interviews (Miles and Huberman, 1994).

Case studies

This section introduces the three case studies of local firms in South Africa that have successfully designed and brought frugal innovations to the market. The case studies highlight firm-level innovation capabilities and patterns of technological change. The narrative is structured as much as possible along the lines of our analytical approach of the three stages of the innovation process; generation, production and diffusion, which we use as a proxy for micro-level technological change. For detailed frugality analysis of innovations from these firms refer to Chakravarty (2022).

Case I: Shonaquip: Assistive mobility devices, hybrid model, addresses national social objectives

Shonaquip (Pty) Ltd, based in the Western Cape province, designs and manufactures paediatric wheelchairs for children who need more postural support than a traditional wheelchair. While the company was formally registered in 1992, its inception was years earlier, born out of Shona McDonald's personal need in trying to find a solution for her daughter born with cerebral palsy. Imported adult wheelchairs were not only expensive and inappropriate for use in unforgiving terrains, but they are also unfit to provide postural support to children, with their use leading to secondary disabilities, sometimes more complex than the primary. Shonaquip's product portfolio has a range of positioning and mobility devices as well as wheelchair cushions and therapy equipment. In addition to being more appropriate for African settings, a standard Shonaquip device costs less than one-third of imported devices and can be repaired and maintained locally.

The first wheelchairs were developed in collaboration with the Biomedical Engineering Department at the University of Cape Town. Subsequently, in 1996 with a grant from Nelson Mandela Children's Fund, the Madiba Buggy (named after Mandela), the first standardised paediatric wheelchair with postural support and adjustable modular seating that could be used on uneven terrain, was designed. The company follows a highly collaborative and bottom-up innovation process, where its design team works together with a gamut of other stakeholders, including users, therapists and caregivers. There are domestic and international collaborations for learning and development. Some international partnerships include the Stanford Design for Extreme Affordability and Accelovate, a global health programme funded by USAID.

Shonaquip has a full production unit with 75 employees, 30% of whom have some form of disability but work fully integrated into an inclusive environment. Shonaquip has ISO 9001 certification and is setting up a testing laboratory ISO 17025 with an ISO 7176-8 certified testbed modified for testing wheelchairs for low resource settings that have longer wheelbases than regular devices, as such a facility does not exist in Africa and testing overseas is prohibitive.

Shonaquip operates as a hybrid social enterprise with other entities to broadly create a more inclusive ecosystem for children with disabilities. These other entities include the Uhambo Foundation, Champions of Change Trust for lobbying and awareness and a private college.

Shonaquip's primary client is the South African government, Departments of Health, Education and Social Development. As it is rooted as a social enterprise, the company sets its profit margins as low as possible so that public budgets have optimum reach. In addition to the domestic market, the company also exports to other developing countries, including within Africa. While the company has received some grants from the Small Business Enterprise Development Agency (SEDA) and Technology Innovation Agency (TIA) and several awards, both nationally and internationally, the key to its sustainability is a hybrid business model where prices can be cross-subsidised as well as being part of the public procurement. McDonald has been part of an international committee of the WHO for developing guidelines for manual wheelchairs in low-resource settings. The initiation into the tender system stemmed from McDonald's relationship with champions within the provincial Western Cape government having a shared vision. Prior to the mid-nineties, there was no dedicated government funding for assistive devices and the science behind seating was little understood. Over the years, and not without the relentless lobbying of many, South Africa has passed several regulations such as the Integrated National Disability Strategy White Paper, 1997; National Rehabilitation Policy, 2000; and Standardisation of Provision of Mobility Assistive Devices in South Africa, 2003. These policy changes have provided a conducive environment for Shonaquip to grow and its devices to reach children who need them most.

Case II: *Sinapi Biomedical: Affordable, high-quality devices for domestic market and export, many addressing national healthcare challenges*

Sinapi Biomedical is a Stellenbosch based medical device manufacturing company managed by founder Chris de Villiers, who has an engineering background and diverse industrial experience. While it was started some years earlier, Sinapi has been fully operational since 2006. It has designed and successfully commercialised several products such as a chest drainage, urinary drainage, feeding cup, uterine balloon tamponade and a TB sputum container. One of Sinapi's most innovative and successful products, which has contributed to the growth of the company, is the chest drainage. The product has found commercial success not only in South Africa, which has a high incidence of patients with gunshot wounds, but is also used in Europe. One of its recent innovations costing a fraction of imported alternatives is the Ellavi, a uterine balloon tamponade device for treating postpartum haemorrhage (PPH), a common cause of death after childbirth across Africa.

Sinapi has a strong research, design and engineering team that works collaboratively with government bodies, academics, surgeons and healthcare workers. Each product is matured and perfected through numerous iterations throughout the design, development and trial process with inputs from various stakeholders. For some products, Sinapi has been funded by the South African Medical Research Council (SAMRC) for clinical trials that were carried out by Stellenbosch University in both Western and Eastern Cape hospitals. Important international partnerships include those with PATH (an international global health non-profit that played a pivotal role in the design and commercialisation of the Ellavi) and Center for Innovation in Point-of-Care Technologies for HIV/AIDS (C-THAN) in Northwestern University, USA. Sinapi has complex manufacturing capabilities conforming to FDA's GMP standards and ISO 13485 and ISO 11135 accredited facilities. It also offers contract manufacturing services. The company employs over 150 people, including many technical personnel.

Sinapi has a domestic market selling directly to hospitals in South Africa and through distributors as well as a large international market. For public health, due to the high volumes of sales, it plans to offer the Ellavi at a subsidised cost. Sinapi is a mainstream company but invested in developing affordable products to make healthcare accessible and has partnerships with non-profit organisations. While the company has received some grants from international donors, the Technology Innovation Agency (TIA) and Department of Trade, Industry and Competition (DTIC), its main source of funds, are commercial banks. Sinapi has also received recognition in Grand Challenge Canada for its work.

Case III: eMoyo Technologies – new technology products, demonstrated in national health programme, export-based

eMoyo is a new technology-based manufacturing company founded by Dr Dirk Koekemoer. The company, based in the Gauteng province, was formally registered in 2013 but has existed as other entities for several years before. Koekemoer is a medical doctor with a strong belief in telemedicine for efficient healthcare delivery, and this is reflected in eMoyo's product line. The company has two key products, with the initial development and launch of some of the products happening before eMoyo was formally registered. One of the company's products is a portable lung function testing machine (ORCAwave Spirometer) for use in occupational health respiratory testing of people exposed to irritants affecting pulmonary function. The other is a portable audiometer called the KUDUwave that offers an alternative to traditional audiology. KUDUwave comes in the form of headphones by enabling fully booth-free operation for screening and diagnosis of hearing loss. Using proprietary software and cloud-enabled features, it can connect patients in remote locations and find applications in telemedicine.

eMoyo employs about 34 people, of which almost one-third work in design and development. To meet the necessary skill set, the company recruits people from South Africa and other countries in Africa. R&D efforts are continuously resulting in improvements in product features, software, calibration, etc. The company has recently developed a slightly differentiated version of the KUDUwave to be sold at a slightly lower cost for the local market. Most R&D is internal to the firm, and no domestic research collaborations currently exist. However, there have been partnerships for clinical trials such as with the University of Pretoria, University of Cape Town, etc. eMoyo has ISO 13485 certified production facilities and some high-value manufacturing, including an in-house 3D printing facility. A large part of eMoyo's components and supplies is based on imports, either due to unavailability or unreliability of local procurement. However, some critical technology services such as high precision milling and extrusion are obtained locally.

For the South African market, eMoyo conducts screening programmes in schools in partnership with NGOs, but otherwise, there are few sales. Due to limited uptake in the domestic market, eMoyo is primarily export-based. The products find a ready market in Europe and particularly in the US, where eMoyo has set up a branch. However, its products are highly relevant to the local context, and for KUDUwave, its application has been demonstrated. Between 2015 and 2016, the KUDUwave was used in the government's multi drug-resistant-TB programme to track ototoxicity or hearing loss, which is a side effect of TB drugs. eMoyo has been set up largely from personal funding sources. The Technology Innovation Agency (TIA) and Department of Trade, Industry and Competition (earlier DTI) have funded the application of provisional patents and for obtaining CE Mark.

Results and discussion

Innovation capabilities
All three firms investigated in this chapter have one or more products that can be classified as frugal innovations. These are also fundamentally new products against functional or stripped-down versions of existing solutions, indicating that these firms have successfully designed and brought to market new-to-the-world innovations at their respective levels of technological complexity. Table 6 (below) presents the analysis of the innovation capabilities of the three firms. Applying the framework adopted from Bell and Figueiredo (2012) and exploring the illustrative elements of capability shows some deviations and unique patterns. For example, in the case of

Shonaquip, the elements of the technological dimension seem closer to an intermediate level – as much of the R&D is highly collaborative, keeping the internal technical team lean. Further, its production base is in the process of ISO 13495 certification. However, the organisational dimension of capability demonstrates many aspects of an advanced level, such as strategic orchestration of not only Shonaquip's own activities but across its many hybrid structures. In the case of Sinapi, its level of innovation activity and the illustrative elements of capability can all be classified as advanced, closely fitting all typologies of the framework. In the case of eMoyo, the level of innovation activity from its product characteristics and R&D spending can be classified as frontier level. However, having been formally established only in 2013, the firm is in the growth stage, still developing its internal structures and organisational capabilities. It may also be relevant to mention here that eMoyo's shows characteristics of a new technology business firm (NTBF) with products that can be classified as disruptive. Therefore, it faces the challenges of being a forerunner in the market. The data suggest that the level of innovation activity, as expressed by the product characteristics and their commercial success, does not always match the equivalent technological or organisational dimensions of our reference framework (Bell and Figueiredo, 2012). One explanation for this could be due to frugal processes and the creative ability of 'doing more with less'.

Table 6: Analysis of innovation capabilities

Level of innovation activity	Illustrative elements of capability	
	Technological dimension	*Organisational dimension*
Shonaquip		
Intermediate and showing a movement towards an advanced level of innovation. This is because some products have recently received CE certification, and the production base is in the process of ISO 13485 certification. However, products are new, developed in a highly collaborative and bottom-up process and not creative imitations; they are path creating (frugal) products suggesting a new direction of innovation. High levels of organisational capabilities not expected at this level of innovation activity observed.	*Human capital and knowledge base* 75 employees with a lean three-member internal team of industrial designers and engineers. External collaborations in different functional areas such as product development, the introduction of standards, etc., with a multitude of users at the individual level; as well as international and domestic institutional knowledge-sharing and generating collaborations.

Production base ISO 9001 certified manufacturing and in process of securing ISO 13485. Setting up a testing laboratory ISO 17025 with an ISO 7176-8 certified testbed modified to test rural wheelchairs with longer wheelbases. | Strategic dynamic 'orchestration'. Ability to strategically orchesrate activities by sensing and seizing opportunities and threats, reconfiguring assets and organisational structures to innovate profitably. This is more managerial than technical. Demonstrated through periodic organisational changes, hybrid model, many collaborations, policy advocacy, etc., to reach organisational goals. |

Sinapi Biomedical		
Advanced. Design, development and manufacture of complex products with CE certification, which have also been adopted in Western markets. Different (frugal) directions of innovation.	*Human capital and knowledge base* 150 people employed through a highly selective recruitment process showing a preference for people with strong cognitive skills. Within this is a nine-member internal team of various types of design and development engineers as well as many technical persons in the area of quality and supervision. External collaborations in different functional areas such as R&D, clinical trials, etc., with doctors, clinicians, nurses and health practitioners; as well as international and domestic institutional knowledge-sharing and generating collaborations. *Production base* ISO 13485, ISO 9001 certified, FDA approved GMP manufacturing, ISO 11135 certified sterilisation plant, primary manufacturing facility with injection moulding and extrusion, Class 100 000 cleanroom for assembly.	Advanced integration and coordination demonstrated by domestic and international supplier network, sales and distribution network, product design, development integrating many knowledge sources, periodic organisational changes and restructuring.
eMoyo Technologies		
World-leading/innovation frontier but with some advanced characteristics. Design, development and manufacture of potentially disruptive innovations which are easily absorbed in US market as reverse innovations, but also have great value as frugal innovations in developing countries. However, the firm is still viewed to be in a 'growth stage' with some characteristics of new technology business firms due to the highly innovative nature of its products.	*Human capital and knowledge base* More than one-third of its 34 employees work in research, design and development. Some external collaborations exist in different functional areas, such as clinical trials with domestic research organisations and with foreign universities. *Production base* ISO13485 certified with a large part of the manufacturing done in-house, including 3D printing of components.	Advanced integration and coordination demonstrated by domestic and international supplier network of speciality components, sales and distribution network including an overseas office.

Source: Authors' own.

Inclusive technological change

Using our parameters for inclusion at various stages of the innovation process (Table 5), we have qualitatively analysed inclusive technological change as a result of the activities of the firms. The innovations developed by these firms are generated and clinically tested in a bottom-up process with the participation of people from the field who were deeply appreciative of ground realities. For firms like Sinapi and Shonaquip, this process is highly inclusive and collaborative. In the case of eMoyo, much of the understanding emerges from the experiences of the founder, who is a medical doctor, and R&D is largely internal to the firm. However, during the early stages of development, as well as for clinical trials, there has been involvement with experts from local universities. Therefore, it is also inclusive in some respects. All three firms have received government support for one or more activities (clinical trials, provisional patent application, certification, etc.). However, this is a small component of their overall product development costs. All three of the firms have well-established manufacturing and production facilities; source materials from domestic and international markets; and together have created over 250 jobs. Since the medical devices sector is still emerging, there are gaps in necessary technology infrastructure, such as specialised testing facilities. Each firm faces different challenges, which, to some extent, are related to the kind of product they manufacture and their specific infrastructure needs. While Sinapi has a highly sophisticated production base and also a well-established supplier base, eMoyo carries out a high degree of manufacturing in-house due to difficulties in building reliable domestic service providers. To overcome the lack of suitable domestic testing services and prohibitive testing costs overseas, Shonaquip is trying to set up an in-house ISO 17025 with an ISO 7176-8 certified testbed.

One or more products from all three firms have been diffused in the domestic market, assisting more efficient healthcare delivery in South Africa. In the case of Shonaquip, because its products lie in the domain of national initiatives and due to the company's hybrid model, the government is the primary client and has played a critical role in the diffusion process. 70% of Sinapi's products are sold in the domestic market, largely to private hospitals. However, it also participates in government tenders, and some of its products, such as the Ellavi, will be sold to the government at a differential cost due to the large volume of sales expected. In the case of eMoyo, it is primarily export-based due to insufficient local sales. However, one of its products, the KUDUwave, has been successfully used in the Department of Health's decentralised multi-drug resistant TB programme. An overview of the analysis is illustrated in Table 7.

Typically, medical device frugal innovations would emerge from a point that existing devices may be too expensive or not suitable for conditions found in developing countries (usually both); or a product may simply not exist. Further, since a large percentage of people in these countries are dependent on public healthcare, even if frugal innovations are available but not part of the public healthcare delivery or reimbursed by private insurance, it is unlikely people would be able to afford them, and they would be lost to those who need them most. The empirical evidence, as summarised in Table 5, suggests that the activities of all three firms first have brought about inclusive technological change in different degrees.

Table 7: Analysis of inclusive technological change at each stage of the innovation process

Firm/Stage	Shonaquip	Sinapi Biomedical	eMoyo Technologies
Generation	Highly inclusive with all products emerging from specific unmet local needs and developed collaboratively in a bottom-up user-centric process involving a multitude of individuals and organisations, local as well as international.	Highly inclusive with all products addressing important domestic needs as well as having global relevance. The process of product development is collaborative and bottom-up, involving local as well international organisations.	Inclusive in some aspects as both its products are relevant for improving efficiencies in domestic healthcare delivery. However, there are some challenges to their large-scale adoption. Product development has been largely internal to the firm, but there have been domestic collaborations over the years for clinical trials.
Production	Highly inclusive as most procurement is done locally. Work environment is highly inclusive.	Highly inclusive as there is substantial local procurement, network of suppliers, and it provides employment to over 150 people.	Inclusive in some aspects: Most materials are imported, and production is in-house, but some very critical precision components are sourced locally. Production facility re-purposed to manufacture special masks with CE Mark for domestic needs during the pandemic.
Diffusion	Highly inclusive with primarily a domestic market and catering to the government, hybrid model and differential pricing to optimise access to those who need it.	Inclusive with a large domestic market. Sales mainly to private hospitals and to government through tenders. Differential pricing planned for Ellavi to public healthcare due to large volume of sales.	Inclusive in some aspects. Primarily export and some local sales. However, one of its main products has been used in government healthcare programmes and for demonstration by NGOs in schools.

Source: Authors' own.

It is important to mention here that all three firms were affected during the pandemic or responded to market needs in different ways. Shonaquip developed a Powered Air-Purifying Respirator (PAPR), which offers a flow of pure air for comfortable working, especially for frontline healthcare workers. The product has a P3 virus filtration system, a transparent full view visor to enable lip reading and works for eight hours without charging. The cost of making the initial prototypes was crowdfunded through the BackaBuddy Campaign. Shonaquip is in the final stages of certification from the NRCS (National Regulator for Compulsory Specifications) certification. eMoyo, which sources a large part of its supplies internationally, had to stop production intermittently. The firm re-purposed its facilities to manufacture high-quality CE certified masks for the domestic market.

Policy implications

This study offers a fresh perspective for policy actions intersecting medical devices, industrialisation and inclusion. The medical device sector is a highly sophisticated and regulated industry, requiring accredited specialised testing infrastructure, ISO certification expertise and certified facilities. Multiple actors and institutions shape design, production and delivery of innovation.

Therefore, the full impact of innovation investments would not be possible without the harmonisation of policies across institutions and actors. While the concept of 'innovation chasm' is very much adopted by South African policy-makers in the context of research commercialisation, the production and redistribution of innovation are viewed less within a unified lens. The 'institutional triad' approach could be a useful heuristic. As the empirical evidence shows, the firms in this study have been supported directly or indirectly by the state to some extent at various stages of the innovation process. However, R&D or innovation grants do not form a substantial component of the funding sources of firms in this study. One reason for this could be because STI funding, as noted in Section 3, is more geared towards state-of-the-art research within public research organisations and universities and less towards the private sector (Kruss and Lorentzen, 2009; OECD, 2007). This is typical in developing countries where public resources are concentrated in building capabilities in centralised organisational structures to create radical technology and less on firms that are dispersed and at the lower end of the innovation spectrum (Bell and Figueiredo, 2012).

This structural divide has several implications. First, as pointed out in Section 3, a slower pace of capabilities accumulation at the productive base creates an imbalance of complementarities (Bell and Figueiredo, 2012). For a vibrant industry to emerge with a critical mass of innovations, in addition to high technology, incremental innovation and product innovations centred around design and engineering with quick time to market is needed. Second, it is important to recognise that while some frugal innovations could be based on new platform technologies and new architectural innovation (Lim and Fujimoto, 2019; Rao, 2013), this is not the norm. Most do not emerge from radical technologies; but from incremental innovations or from product design and engineering. Many innovation studies have demonstrated the economic importance of incremental innovations emerging from the firm's engineering departments building on the existing knowledge base, not reflected in formal R&D budgets (Enos, 1962; Hollander, 1965). Consequently, a 'policy mix' (Bell and Figueiredo, 2012) that directly supports SMEs' incremental or design innovations, in addition to existing R&D funding initiatives, could boost the sector. It may also be important to recognise that drivers of innovation within academia and for firms are different, with speed and time to market being critical for the economic sustainability of the latter.

Another aspect where policy intervention would be critical relates to improved public health through access to these frugal medical devices and the indirect impact of innovation procurement on small domestic firms. In South Africa, where more than 80% of the population is dependent on the public health system, the primary way to ensure that frugal innovations reach those who need them most is only possible through public procurement. Without a preferential local procurement policy in place, many local companies struggle to compete with cheaper imports. Key components adding to the cost of domestic products where policy can play a critical role include testing infrastructure, accreditation and registration. One of the key recommendations of the SAMRC–PATH (2014) study was also the development of a more transparent public procurement process. As discussed in Section 3.3, public procurement of innovation and innovation-friendly procurement mechanisms proposed as a mechanism of integrating the top-down approach of transformative innovation policies with the narrow focus of innovation policy (Uyarra et al., 2020; Uyarra and Flanagan, 2010) could be one of the key policy interventions. Some of the mechanisms could be in the form of government becoming the 'experimental user' of new technologies and products (Malerba, 2007; Uyarra and Flanagan, 2010), supporting clinical trials in public hospitals, etc. Table 8 summarises the key discussion points and possible policy directions.

Table 8: Summary of discussion and possible policy directions

Generation: STI Funding
- Currently: (a) Resources concentrated in building capabilities at public research organisations and spin-offs in high-technology areas; (b) Less attention to building firm-level capabilities in innovative SMEs creates imbalance in complements (Bell and Figueiredo, 2012).
- Recognise: (a) Innovation drivers for academia and firms differ (SAMRC-PATH; 2014); (b) High economic impact is also possible from process, engineering and incremental innovations (Enos, 1962; Hollander, 1965).
- Future direction: (a) Mixed portfolio including technology transfer, new technologies, incremental innovations, import, etc. (Srinivas, 2008); (b) Specialised funding schemes for innovative SMEs with a focus on design and incremental innovations (DST, 2019).

Manufacturing and production: Industrial policy
- Currently: An emerging sector with several enabling agencies and initiatives in formation/transition (Saidi and Douglas, 2018).
- Recognise: (a) Medical device in South Africa represents a technology intense sector in resource constrained setting with competition from firms in HIC with efficient innovation systems; (b) Innovative SMEs as 'nucleus' of inclusive technological change.
- Future direction: (a) Capability building in innovative SMEs as a bottom-up industrialisation process (Kraemer-Mbula and Monaco, 2020); (b) Upgrade/create specialised SandT infrastructure for testing, metrology, certification, etc. (SAMRC-PATH, 2014).

Access and diffusion: Public health and procurement
- Currently: No preferential procurement, higher cost of registration versus imports.
- Recognise: Frugal innovation users depend on public services, and access would not be possible without public procurement.
- Future direction: Enhance demand-side innovation policies (DST, 2019). More innovation-friendly procurement (Uyarra and Flanagan, 2010); government as 'experimental user' (Malerba, 2007).

Source: Authors' own.

Conclusion

The crisis resulting from the pandemic has reaffirmed the urgent need for affordable and appropriate (frugal) medical devices to meet the healthcare needs of developing countries, as well as the need to enhance regional capabilities for public health security. Our purpose in this chapter was to demonstrate through a review of literature and empirical evidence that enabling innovative medical device manufacturing firms in South Africa offers an opportunity for both economic and social development. In contrast to earlier literature, this study has approached the problem from a micro-level perspective to analyse the stages of the innovation process that are influenced by different policy domains and are not always well-coordinated. Firm-level studies of African SMEs are rare, and the ways in which firms innovate remains a 'black box' in the minds of policy-makers (Lorentzen, 2009). This chapter has carried out a micro-level analysis of three medical device manufacturing firms in South Africa and proposed policy recommendations to accelerate the accumulation of capabilities.

The evidence highlights that in designing and successfully bringing to market frugal medical devices, these firms are not only enabling new pathways of technological change but also ones that are more inclusive. While these suggest more than an intermediate level of innovation activity in these firms, the equivalent complexities in technological or organisational structures do not always match that proposed in extant literature. It is likely that these differences are due to 'frugal processes' and the creative ability of 'doing more with less'. However, these firms operate in a space dominated by international players coming from high-income countries and resource-rich environments. The question that arises in a highly competitive global environment is: Could these frugal processes become a barrier to the firm's growth? And what kind of policies are needed to prevent that from happening? Future research could explore these questions. The prompt deployment of funding and technology support by the South African government during the pandemic to address shortages through local manufacturing was evidence of the country's capabilities as well as political commitment. During the post-pandemic era, this momentum should be carried forward to strengthen existing capabilities for both public health security and economic development.

References

Andreoni, A., and Chang, H. (2019). The political economy of industrial policy: Structural interdependencies, policy alignment and conflict management. *Structural Change and Economic Dynamics*, 48, 136-150. DOI: 10.1016/j.strueco.2018.10.007.

Aragão, E., Guimarães, J. M., and Loureiro, S. (2016). The dissemination of local health innovations: Political economy issues in Brazil. In: M. Mackintosh, G. Banda, P. Tibandebage and W. Wamae (Eds), *Making Medicines in Africa: The political economy of industrializing local health* (166-182). Palgrave Macmillan.

Arocena, R., and Sutz, J. (2003). Inequality and innovation as seen from the South. *Technology in Society*, 25(2), 171-182.

Arora, S., and Romijn, H. (2011). The empty rhetoric of poverty reduction at the base of the pyramid. *Organization*, 19(4), 481-505.

Aschhoff, B., and Sofka, W. (2009). Innovation on demand – Can public procurement drive market success of innovations? *Research Policy*, 38(8), 1235-1247. DOI: 10.1016/j.respol.2009.06.011.

Basu, R., Banerjee, P., and Sweeny, E. (2013). Frugal innovation: Core competencies to address global sustainability. *Journal of Management for Global Sustainability*, 1(2), 63-82. DOI: 10.13185/JM2013.01204.

Bell, M., and Figueiredo, P. N. (2012). Building innovative capabilities in latecomer emerging market firms: Some key issues. *Innovative Firms in Emerging Market Countries*, 24-109.

Bell, M., and Pavitt, K. (1993). Technological accumulation and industrial growth: Contrasts between developed and developing countries. *Industrial and Corporate Change*, 2(2), 157-210.

Carlsson, B., and Stankiewicz, R. (1991). On the nature, function and composition of technological systems. *Journal of Evolutionary Economics*, 1(2), 93-118. DOI: 10.1007/BF01224915.

Chakravarty, S. (2022). Resource constrained innovation in a technology intensive sector: Frugal medical devices from manufacturing firms in South Africa. *Technovation*. https://doi.org/10.1016/j.technovation.2021.102397

Chang, H. (2002). *Kicking Away the Ladder*. Anthem.

Chang, H. (2014). Hamlet without the prince of Denmark: How development has disappeared from today's 'development' discourse. In: D. Held, C. B. Rogers and R. Charles (Eds), *Global Governance at Risk* (129-148). Polity.

Chang, H., and Andreoni, A. (2021). *Bringing Production Back into Development: An introduction*. https://discovery.ucl.ac.uk/id/eprint/10124056.

Chataway, J., Banda, G., Cochrane, G., and Manville, C. (2016). Innovative procurement for health and industrial development. In: M. Mackintosh, G. Banda, P. Tibandebge and W. Wamae (Eds.), *Making Medicines in Africa: The political economy of industrializing local health* (224-242). Palgrave Macmillan.

Chataway, J., Dobson, C., Daniels, C., Byrne, R., Hanlin, R., and Tigabu, A. (2019). Science granting councils in sub-saharan Africa: Trends and tensions. *Science and Public Policy*, 46(4), 620-631.

Chataway, J., Hanlin, R., and Kaplinsky, R. (2014). Inclusive innovation: An architecture for policy development. *Innovation and Development*, 4(1), 33-54. DOI: 10.1080/2157930X.2013.876800.

Chataway, J., and Smith, J. (2006). The international AIDS vaccine initiative (IAVI): Is it getting new science and technology to the world's neglected majority? *World Development*, 34(1), 16-30.

Cirera, X., and Maloney, W., F. (2017). *The Innovation Paradox: Developing-country capabilities and the unrealized promise of technological catch-up*. World Bank. https://openknowledge.worldbank.org/handle/10986/28341

Corsini, L., Dammicco, V., and Moultrie, J. (2021). Frugal innovation in a crisis: The digital fabrication maker response to COVID-19. *R&D Management*, 51(2), 195-210. DOI: 10.1111/radm.12446.

Cozzens, S. E. (2008). Equality as an issue in designing science, technology, and innovation policies and programs. In: W. Østreng (Ed.), *Confluence: Interdisciplinary communications 2007/2008*. Centre for Advanced Study at the Norwegian Academy of Science and Letters.

Cozzens, S. E., and Kaplinsky, R. (2009). Innovation, poverty and inequality: Cause, coincidence, or co-evolution? In: B. Lundvall, K. L. Joseph, C. Chaminade and J. Vang (Eds), *Handbook of Innovation Systems in Developing Countries* (57-82). Edward Elgar.

CSIR. (2020). CSIR supports national COVID-19 response with locally developed ventilator. Press release. https://www.csir.co.za/csir-supports-national-covid-19-response-locally-developed-ventilator

Dahlman, C., and Westphal, L. (1982). Technological effort in industrial development: An interpretive survey of recent research. *World Bank Reprint Series*, REP263. World Bank.

Daniel, L. (2020, 7 December). SA company gets R900 million to develop rapid covid-19 test – using tobacco plants. *Business Insider SA*.

Denel. (2020). Local ventilator projects are reaching critical stages. Press release. http://www.mechemdemining.com/press-article/LOCAL-VENTILATOR-PROJECTS-ARE-REACHING-CRITICAL-STAGES/232

de Jager, K., Chimhundu, C., Saidi, T., and Douglas, T. S. (2017). The medical device development landscape in South Africa: Institutions, sectors and collaboration. *South African Journal of Science*, 113(5-6), 1-8.

Department of Science and Innovation. (2020). Minister Blade Nzimande on funding awards to South Africa coronavirus COVID-19 testing ability. Press release. https://www.gov.za/speeches/south-africa-covid-19-testing-ability-6-jul-2020-0000#

Driver-Jowitt, S. (2017). A hybrid revolution enabling a sustainable response to social problems through multiple entities: A case study on Shonaquip. Master's thesis, Stellenbosch University.

DST. (2019). *The 2019 White Paper on Science, Technology and Innovation*. Government of South Africa.

DTI -Deloitte. (2014). Research to guide the development of strategy for the medical devices sector of South Africa. Deloitte for Department of Trade and Industry, Government of South Africa.

Dubois, A., and Gadde, L. (2002). Systematic combining: An abductive approach to case research. *Journal of Business Research*, 55(7), 553-560.

Durand, C., and Milberg, W. (2019). *Intellectual Monopoly in Global Value Chains*. Routledge.

Dutrénit, G. (2000). *Learning and Knowledge Management in the Firm*. Edward Elgar.

Dutrénit, G. (2004). Building technological capabilities in latecomer firms. *Science, Technology and Society*, 9(2), 209-241.

Edler, J., and Georghiou, L. (2007). Public procurement and innovation – Resurrecting the demand side. *Research Policy*, 36(7), 949-963. DOI: 10.1016/j.respol.2007.03.003.

Edler, J., Blind, K., Frietsch, R., Kimpeler, S., Kroll, H., Lerch, C., and Walz, R. (2020). *Technology Sovereignty: From demand to concept*. Fraunhofer ISI.

Edquist, C., and Zabala-Iturriagagoitia, J. M. (2012). Public procurement for innovation as mission-oriented innovation policy. *Research Policy*, 41(10), 1757-1769. DOI: 10.1016/j.respol.2012.04.022.

Eisenhardt, K. M. (1989). Building theories from case study research. *Academy of Management Review*, 14(4), 532-550.

Enos, J. L. (1962), Invention and innovation in the petroleum refining industry. In: *The Rate and Direction of Inventive Activity: Economic and Social Factors* (299-322). National Bureau of Economic Research.

Foster, C., and Heeks, R. (2013). Conceptualising inclusive innovation: Modifying systems of innovation frameworks to understand diffusion of new technology to low-income consumers. *European Journal of Development Research*, 25(3), 333-355.

Geroski, P. A. (1990). Innovation, technological opportunity, and market structure. *Oxford Economic Papers*, 42(3), 586-602.

Glaser, B., and Strauss, A. (1967). *The Discovery of Grounded Theory: Strategies for qualitative research*. Sociology Press.

Global Forum for Health Research, and World Health Organization. (2004). *The 10/90 Report on Health Research 2003-2004*. Global Forum for Health Research.

Harris, M., Bhatti, Y., Buckley, J., and Sharma, D. (2020). Fast and frugal innovations in response to the COVID-19 pandemic. *Nature Medicine*, 26(6), 814-817.

Hollander, S. (1965). *The Sources of Increased Efficiency: A study of DuPont Rayon plants*. MIT Press.

Howitt, P., Darzi, A., Yang, G., Ashrafian, H., Atun, R., Barlow, J., and Conteh, L. (2012). Technologies for global health. *The Lancet*, 380(9840), 507-535.

Kaplinsky, R. (2011). Schumacher meets Schumpeter: Appropriate technology below the radar. *Research Policy*, 40(2), 193-203.

Katz, J. M. (1987). *Technology Generation in Latin American Manufacturing Industries*. Palgrave Macmillan.

Kim, L. (1997). *Imitation to Innovation: The dynamics of Korea's technological learning*. Harvard Business School Press.

Knorringa, P., Peša, I., Leliveld, A., and van Beers, C. (2016). Frugal innovation and development: Aides or adversaries? *European Journal of Development Research*, 28(2), 143-153.

Kraemer-Mbula, E., and Monaco, L. (2020). Informality and innovation: An avenue towards bottom-up industrialisation for Africa? In: J. Charmes (Ed.), *Research Handbook on Development and the Informal Economy* (363-386). Edward Elgar. DOI: 10.4337/9781788972802.00026.

Kraemer-Mbula, E., Tijssen, R., Wallace, M. L., and Mclean, R. (2020). *Transforming Research Excellence: New ideas from the Global South*. African Minds.

Kruss, G., and Lorentzen, J. (2009). The South African innovation policies: Potential and constraint. In: *BRICS and Development Alternatives* (163-190). Anthem.

Lall, S. (1992). Technological capabilities and industrialization. *World Development*, 20(2), 165-186.

Lazonick, W., and Mazzucato, M. (2013). The risk–reward nexus in the innovation–inequality relationship: Who takes the risks? Who gets the rewards? *Industrial and Corporate Change*, 22(4), 1093-1128.

Lim, C., and Fujimoto, T. (2019). Frugal innovation and design changes expanding the cost-performance frontier: A schumpeterian approach. *Research Policy*, 48(4), 1016-1029. DOI: 10.1016/j.respol.2018.10.014.

Lorentzen, J. (2009). Learning by firms: The black box of South Africa's innovation system. *Science and Public Policy*, 36(1), 33-45.

Mackintosh, M., Banda, G., Tibandebage, P., and Wamae, W. (Eds). (2016). *Making Medicines in Africa: The political economy of industrializing for local health*. Palgrave Macmillan.

Malerba, F. (2007). Innovation and the dynamics and evolution of industries: Progress and challenges. *International Journal of Industrial Organization*, 25(4), 675-699.

Marks, I. H., Thomas, H., Bakhet, M., and Fitzgerald, E. (2019). Medical equipment donation in low-resource settings: A review of the literature and guidelines for surgery and anaesthesia in low-income and middle-income countries. *BMJ Global Health*, 4(5), e001785.

Meagher, K. (2017). Cannibalizing the informal economy: Frugal innovation and economic inclusion in Africa. *European Journal of Development Research*, 30(1), 17-33.

Miles, M. B., and Huberman, A. M. (1994). *Qualitative Data Analysis: An expanded sourcebook* (2nd edn). Sage.

Nelson, R. R., and Winter, S. G. (1982). *An Evolutionary Theory of Economic Change*. Belknap.

Organisation for Economic Co-operation and Development (OECD). (2007). *OECD Reviews of Innovation Policy. South Africa*. OECD.

OECD/Eurostat. (2018). *Oslo Manual 2018: Guidelines for collecting, reporting and using data on innovation* (4th edn). OECD Publishing. https://doi.org/10.1787/9789264304604-en.

Onsongo, E. K., and Knorringa, P. (2020). Comparing frugality and inclusion in innovation for development: Logic, process and outcome. *Innovation and Development*, [ahead-of-print].

Pagano, U. (2014). The crisis of intellectual monopoly capitalism. *Cambridge Journal of Economics*, 38(6), 1409-1429.

Papaioannou, T. (2011). Technological innovation, global justice and politics of development. *Progress in Development Studies*, 11(4), 321-338.

Papaioannou, T. (2014). How inclusive can innovation and development be in the twenty-first century? *Innovation and Development*, 4(2), 187-202.

Penrose, E. T. (1959). *The Theory of the Growth of the Firm*. Blackwell.

Perry, L., and Malkin, R. (2011). Effectiveness of medical equipment donations to improve health systems: How much medical equipment is broken in the developing world? *Medical and Biological Engineering and Computing*, 49(7), 719-722.

Prabhu, J. (2017). Frugal innovation: Doing more with less for more. *Philosophical Transactions of the Royal Society of London. Series A: Mathematical, Physical, and Engineering Sciences*, 375(2095), 1-22. https://www.jstor.org/stable/44678469

Prahalad, C. (2006). *The Fortune at the Bottom of the Pyramid: Eradicating poverty through profits* (1st edn). Pearson.

Prahalad, C. K., and Hamel, G. (1990). The Core Competence of the Corporation. University of Illinois at Urbana-Champaign's Academy for Entrepreneurial Leadership Historical Research Reference in Entrepreneurship.

Radjou, N., Prabhu, J. C., and Ahuja, S. (2012). *Jugaad Innovation* (1 edn). Jossey-Bass.

Ragin, C. C., and Becker, H. S. (1992). *What is a Case?* Cambridge University Press.

Ramaoka, S. T. (2020). Technology transfer and capabilities in the medical device industry of South Africa. Master's thesis. University of Johannesburg.

Romijn, H. A., and Caniëls, M. C. J. (2011). Pathways of technological change in developing countries. *Development Policy Review*, 29(3), 359-380.

Rothwell, R., and Zegveld, W. (1981). *Industrial Innovation and Public Policy: Preparing for the 1980s and the 1990s*. Pinter.

Saidi, T., and Douglas, T. S. (2018). Medical device regulation in South Africa: The medicines and related substances amendment Act 14 of 2015. *South African Medical Journal*, 108(3), 168-170.

SAMED – KPMG. (2014). Industry overview and economic impact assessment for the South African medical technology industry: Prepared for the South African Medical Device Industry Association (SAMED).

SAMRC – PATH. (2014). Developing an ecosystem to support the local medical device and diagnostics industry in South Africa: Recommendations from an international perspective. South African Medical Research Council.

SARAO. (2020). Request for information in support of the national ventilator project. Press release. https://www.sarao.ac.za/request-for-information-in-support-of-the-national-ventilator-project/

Scheffler, E. (2009). What is an appropriate wheelchair? *Western Cape Rehabilitation Centre*. https://www.wcrc.co.za/docs/34/What%20is%20an%20appropriate%20wheelchair.pdf

Schot, J., and Steinmueller, W. E. (2018). Three frames for innovation policy: R&D, systems of innovation and transformative change. *Research Policy*, 47(9), 1554-1567.

Siemens (2020). Siemens South Africa joins forces with the national ventilator project community in response to the COVID-19 pandemic. Press release. https://press.siemens.com/za/en/pressrelease/siemens-south-africa-joins-forces-national-ventilator-project-community-response-covid

Srinivas, S. (2012). *Market Menagerie: Health and development in late industrial states.* Stanford University Press.

Srinivas, S. (2016). Healthy industries and unhealthy populations: Lessons from Indian problem-solving. In: M. Mackintosh, G. Banda, P. Tibandebage and W. Wamae (Eds), *Making Medicines in Africa: The political economy of industrializing local health* (183-199). Palgrave Macmillan.

Srinivas, S., and Sutz, J. (2008). Developing countries and innovation: Searching for a new analytical approach. *Technology in Society*, 30(2), 129-140.

Swanepoel, D. W., Maclennan-Smith, F. and Hall, J. W. (2013). Diagnostic pure-tone audiometry in schools: Mobile testing without a sound-treated environment. *Journal of the American Academy of Audiology*, 24(10), 992-1000. DOI: 10.3766/jaaa.24.10.10.

Teece, D., and Pisano, G. (1994). The dynamic capabilities of firms: An introduction. *Industrial and Corporate Change*, 3(3), 537-556.

University of Cape Town. (2020). UCT spin-off receives millions in European funding. Press release. https://www.news.uct.ac.za/article/-2020-12-22-uct-spin-off-receives-millions-in-european-funding

Uyarra, E., and Flanagan, K. (2010). Understanding the innovation impacts of public procurement. *European Planning Studies*, 18(1), 123-143.

Uyarra, E., Zabala-Iturriagagoitia, J. M., Flanagan, K., and Magro, E. (2020). Public procurement, innovation and industrial policy: Rationales, roles, capabilities and implementation. *Research Policy*, 49(1), 103844. DOI: 10.1016/j.respol.2019.103844.

Visagie, A., Swanepoel, De W., and Eikelboom, R. H. (2015). Accuracy of remote hearing assessment in a rural community. *Telemedicine and e-Health*, 21(11), 930-937. DOI: 10.1089/tmj.2014.0243.

Weyrauch, T., and Herstatt, C. (2017). What is frugal innovation? Three defining criteria. *Journal of Frugal Innovation*, 2(1), 1-17. DOI: 10.1186/s40669-016-0005-y.

World Health Organization (WHO). (2006). *Report of a Consensus Conference on Wheelchairs for Developing Countries*. https://www.who.int/disabilities/technology/Wheelchair%20Consensus%20Conference%20Report_Jan08.pdf

WHO. (2010a). *Medical Devices: Managing the mismatch: An outcome of the priority medical devices project*. WHO.

WHO. (2010b). *Landscape Analysis of Barriers to Developing or Adapting Technologies for Global Health Purposes*. WHO.

WHO. (2012). *Local Production and Technology Transfer to Increase Access to Medical Devices: Addressing the barriers and challenges in low- and middle-income countries*. WHO.

WHO. (2016). *Towards Improving Access to Medical Devices through Local Production: Phase II: Report of a case study in four sub-Saharan countries*. WHO. https://apps.who.int/iris/handle/10665/206545

Yin, R. K. (2014). *Case Study Research* (5th edn). Sage.

Zeschky, M. B., Winterhalter, S., and Gassmann, O. (2014). From cost to frugal and reverse innovation: Mapping the field and implications for global competitiveness. *Research Technology Management*, 57(4), 20-27. DOI: 10.5437/08956308X5704235.

CHAPTER 8

Endogenous Pharmaceutical Innovation

Epistemological perspectives from Benin and South Africa

Ogundiran Soumonni and Aimé Sègla

Introduction

The main objective of this chapter is to present some of the main epistemological controversies that have arisen during the pandemic and to reflect on those as a basis for proposing a theoretically informed conceptual framework that could better inform policy interventions to advance pharmaceutical innovation in Africa. In particular, we underscore the contested nature of various knowledge claims of having a proven treatment globally and attempts in selected African countries to propose possible solutions of their own. While people across the world have been implored to comply with emerging governmental regulations, which were said to have been informed by expert advice, it quickly became clear that all experts were not in agreement with the measures. These scientific controversies consequently spilt out into popular discourse in an atypical manner.

However, the moral predicament that accompanied the global pandemic, namely that between wealth accumulation and the preservation of human lives, required ethical knowledge to help make judgements about it. In the Southern African context, for instance, one of the key axioms of Ubuntu philosophy in general, and with respect to 'traditional African medicine' in particular, *'feta kgomo o tshware motho'* (preserving the life and dignity of a human being must supersede the accumulation of wealth) in the Sepedi language, offers us a clear ethical direction (Ramose, 2005). Additionally, serious contestations relating to the validity of the very knowledge bases and methodological approaches from which various solutions have been proposed have been no less contentious. They, therefore, underscore the need to better understand the status of the knowledge available in Africa, clarify ambiguous terminology about it, and identify the extent to which it could contribute to worldwide efforts to significantly mitigate the effects of the pandemic during the post-pandemic era.

One of the most widespread controversies during the pandemic emerged around the announcement of a cure by Didier Raoult, a prominent French microbiologist and expert in 'drug repositioning', who declared that a combination of the anti-malarial hydroxychloroquine and the antibiotic azithromycin could cure the disease (Sayare, 2020). Raoult's claims in the media and in a scientific article in March 2020, were by May of the same year prominently rejected by a subsequently retracted article in the prestigious medical journal, *The Lancet*, which claimed that, based on randomised clinical trials, there was no association between using either chloroquine or hydroxychloroquine (HCQ) on the one hand, and health benefits to COVID-19 patients on the other (Mehra et al., 2020). Thus, while discrediting the scientific basis for the efficacy of HCQ on methodological grounds and even suggesting that it was harmful, the US-based researchers, Mehra et al. (2020), later withdrew their article in response to charges that they had used a suspicious and unverifiable dataset.

This type of epistemological debate also played itself out in the Global South, with respect to proposed treatments based on natural or herbal medicines, as opposed to synthetic pharmaceutical treatments, suggesting an irreconcilable fault line between them. However, a Chinese researcher from the Department of Traditional Medicine at Zhejiang University warned in *The Lancet* that despite an official announcement of the approval of three widely used herbal medicines to treat COVID-19 symptoms in April 2020, such drugs carried their own risks and should therefore not be used without sufficiently rigorous scientific testing (Yang, 2020). That public statement in favour of scientific rigour by a Chinese natural medicine researcher need not be seen as either ad hoc or exceptional, however. It may instead be better understood through the observation by Hwang (2020) that China has a fairly well-integrated medical system, whereas South Korea's is strictly bifurcated between 'traditional medicine' and 'Western' medical health services.

In Africa, the media prominently featured claims by the president of Madagascar that the Artemisia plant-based medication, COVID Organics (CVO), has strong healing properties. The Cameroonian Archbishop of the city of Douala, Samuel Kleda, reported a successful treatment based on a herbal mixture that targets associated respiratory ailments, and South Africa assembled its best scientific minds to direct its response to the pandemic (Tangwa and Munung, 2020). The Malagasy case, in particular, generated a lot of controversies, in part, because of the confrontational style of the country's president in the face of what he viewed as an international dismissal of African knowledge and because of the perception by many public commentators of the implausibility of medicinal treatment for the virus coming from an impoverished country. In contrast, the posture of Samuel Kleda, who has studied herbal medicines for three decades, was much more modest. He sought to clarify the difference between his healing approach, which helps to eliminate or alleviate symptoms, and that of a conclusive cure, thereby calling for collaboration with scientific researchers and other health experts to ensure greater efficacy (Sina, 2020). In a similarly inclusive vein, South Africa's president called for complementary efforts with 'traditional medicine' to fight the pandemic in his Heritage Day speech in September 2020, stating the following:

> *In as much as we join the international community and search for diagnostics and therapeutics, we are also looking at the real and important contribution indigenous knowledge systems, particularly traditional medicine can play in improving the life outcomes of our people. (RSA, 2020)*

It is important to note, however, that historical evidence suggests that what is widely characterised as two distinct traditions of medicine actually have a more intertwined record than is generally recognised by observers, and concerning epidemics, in particular. In a recent book, the Pulitzer Prize-winning African-American author, Isabel Wilkerson, revived the memory of Onesimus, an enslaved African, who told his captor of an inoculation procedure against smallpox in his native West Africa that saved 97.5% of the 240 people who adopted it during a similar epidemic in Boston, Massachusetts, in 1721 (Wilkerson, 2020). Unfortunately, even though this method became the basis for standard vaccinations in the US, Wilkerson notes that Onesimus was neither compensated for his contribution nor even freed from his status of enslavement, thereby highlighting the grossly unethical dimension of this medical knowledge transfer from Africa to America. These initial insights are intended to frame the broad contours of the epistemological challenge for endogenous innovation in the pharmaceutical industry that we discuss in subsequent sections.

Background

Two premises ground our study. The first is the moral challenge that the pandemic presented with respect to the preservation of human life vis-à-vis wealth accumulation. Second, the pandemic led the public to raise important epistemological questions about available knowledge resources to resolve the health crisis, which had serious implications for the role of endogenous innovation in the pharmaceutical industry. In other words, an ethical imperative rather than an economic one takes precedence in our use of the endogenous innovation concept. It is nevertheless critical to briefly clarify the concept of pharmaceutical innovation to better appreciate the ethico-epistemological considerations thereof.

A classification scheme provided by Djellal and Gallouj (2005) subdivides medical innovation into three subgroups, namely: (1) biomedical or bio-pharmacological innovation, which includes novel medicines and pharmaceutical substances; (2) technological systems that offer healthcare and biological analysis; (3) 'soft', 'invisible', or intangible medical innovation involving therapeutic strategies, care protocols, etc. The first subgroup, bio-pharmacological innovation, may further be based on either synthetic medicine (also labelled 'conventional' or 'orthodox' medicine) or phytomedicine (or plant-based medicine). However, Iwu (2002) provides the useful clarification that the related term, phytopharmaceuticals, refers to chemically isolated plant substances that are usually treated like their synthetic equivalents by most governments, which is not necessarily the case for other phytomedicines, whose active ingredients are exclusively contained in plant materials or extracts that may result in polyvalent therapeutic action.

Although the study, identification, standardisation, quality control and production of phytomedicines have become the explicit focus of the growing domain of pharmacognosy within pharmaceutical science (Dhami, 2013), the implicit inference is that the process of drug discovery in synthetic medicine is well established. However, in a study about the means by which medical expertise progresses, Nelson et al. (2011) demonstrated that while many biomedical scientists believe that increased scientific research (learning by searching) leads to improvements in practice, such expected scientific breakthroughs are empirically relatively rare. Conversely, they argue, learning by doing and using in clinical practice, as well as the cumulative observation of physicians and patients over time, are sometimes more significant sources of medical innovation than can be obtained via either in vitro (test tube) research or animal research, or even exclusively through randomised clinical trials, which are considered to be the highest benchmark for evaluating the effectiveness of a new intervention. Phrased differently, even though the scientific paradigm and the practice paradigm are interrelated, it is not unusual for a high degree of scientific understanding to have little bearing on practice and conversely, that ongoing practices may be acknowledged as being effective, but with minimal scientific understanding as to exactly why (Nelson et al., 2011).

An argument for the relative importance of the practice paradigm vis-à-vis the scientific paradigm in producing useful knowledge in the context of the pandemic underpinned the epistemological claims made by the French microbiologist, Didier Raoult. Indeed, in a March 2020 co-authored paper, the authors claimed a 100% success rate in treating patients with both HCQ and azithromycin, based on a single-arm protocol (rather than the more rigorous double-blind testing against a placebo), but issued a proviso in the conclusion, arguing that the context of the pandemic temporarily justified publishing the findings despite the small sample size of 36 patients and other methodological shortcomings (Gautret et al., 2020). A detailed, 10-point rebuttal was subsequently published by the Dutch clinical epidemiologist, Frits Rosendaal, who argued that even if the study had been based on an uncontrolled case series of patients who were treated, the failure to unequivocally establish the effectiveness of the clinical treatment or to present its adverse effects rendered the conclusions both unjustified and negligent (Rosendaal, 2020).

Beyond the methodological shortcomings relative to the ideal practice, of which he was well aware, Raoult insisted in the face of intense criticism that many significant achievements in health had never been validated by stringent randomised controlled trials (RCTs) and that it would be unethical to deny a drug whose effectiveness was 'visible' to ill patients (Sayare, 2020). Nevertheless, by July 2020, a number of French doctors and patients, as well as a group that represents 500 infectious diseases specialists, filed professional misconduct complaints against Raoult, accusing him of continuing to promote the HCQ/azithromycin combination despite its potentially deleterious side effects and the lack of sufficiently rigorous clinical trials to substantiate its benefits (AFP, 2020).

That contestation within the broad scope of synthetic medicine is important to reflect upon because several African countries, such as Benin and Burkina Faso, began clinical trials to establish the relative efficacy between the HCQ/azithromycin combination and a phytomedicine, Apivirine, developed by a Beninese researcher, with Burkina Faso indicating its ability to produce 200,000 tablets of HCQ per day, depending on the outcome of the tests (Nabaloum, 2020). In response to a number of proposed African medicinal solutions, however, a Burkinabé epidemiologist wrote an article in the widely circulated continental news magazine, Jeune Afrique, challenging the president of Madagascar, as well as the Beninese inventor of Apivirine, to publish the results of their trials rather than relying on rhetoric to make their respective cases due to the risk of diffusing highly toxic medicines (Kouanda, 2020).

Thus, epistemological debates about a highly specialised field, contemporary medicine, were prominently thrust into the public eye in a manner that is seldom witnessed. Nevertheless, given that a large proportion of Africans straddle between synthetic and culturally embedded medicine due to the cost-prohibitive access to the former on the one hand, and greater social ease with the latter on the other hand, a keen appreciation for the epistemological questions of the type enumerated above are of contextual relevance.

***

To proceed, we first seek to clarify some semantic ambiguities with respect to terms that are used in different ways in the literature, to provide a greater degree of precision in how we operationalise the concepts in our chapter. We then propose a conceptual framework that offers a way of understanding the various components and interrelationships that make up endogenous innovation as it applies to our topic of investigation. Third, we present the findings of two mini-case studies, which then underpin some recommendations that could help guide the activities of policy-makers and other practitioners in a more evidentiary manner.

Issues, controversies, problems

Our starting point is to clarify commonly used, but often conceptually vague, terminology that relates to scientific knowledge in general, medical knowledge in particular, and the manner in which they are grounded in ethical principles. To begin with, the terms 'indigenous knowledge' or 'traditional knowledge' are typically used in contrast with 'modern' or 'Western' knowledge. However, Hountondji (1994) has argued that this bifurcation is unsatisfactory because it suggests a radical separation between the old and the new and reflects a barely masked assumption of a priority of Western cultures over the supposedly static, undifferentiated, and ultimately marginalised non-Western ones. Furthermore, in the face of continuing interactions over long periods of time, it is rarely clear when 'indigenous' knowledge becomes 'modern' and vice versa. It is in large measure, to circumvent and overcome this ambiguity, that we choose to employ the terms 'endogenous knowledge' and 'endogenous innovation' that we have already referred to, and that will be made clearer below.

From the point of view of what is commonly understood to be 'modern science', Nelson (1974) assessed the extent to which the 'indigenous science community' in latecomer economies had a significant role in technology adaptation and ultimately technological leadership. Richard Nelson, therefore, clearly considers domestic 'modern' scientists to simultaneously be 'indigenous' scientists who exist even in 'less developed countries' and whose R&D efforts, beyond their techno-economic benefits, could be seen as a way to influence scientific values in a given country. From this vantage point, the nomenclature of 'indigenous knowledge' applies both to the community that operates outside of Western-style institutions (themselves originally influenced by non-Western traditions) and those that operate within it. An excellent illustration of the simultaneous interpretation of such 'indigeneity' was given by the Chinese pharmaceutical scientist, Youyou Tu, in her 2015 Nobel Prize lecture, which detailed how thoroughly she and her team interrogated ancient Chinese medical documents, folk remedies and herbal medicine practitioners, using contemporary techniques, in order to develop an effective anti-malarial drug based on Qinghao plants (or Artemisia family herbs) (Tu, 2016).

Another practical experience relayed by Abayomi Sofowora, the highly regarded author of the pedagogical book, *Medicinal Plants and Traditional Medicine in Africa* (first published in 1982), is highly instructive in this regard. A long-time professor of pharmacy and a high-level advisor to the World Health Organization (WHO), he recalled an applicant for a prestigious academic post at an elite national university in Nigeria who repeatedly referred to other Nigerians with considerable knowledge of medicinal plants outside the academic setting as 'indigenous', to the great annoyance of the selection panel (Sofowora, 2010). That particular response conveys Sofowora's view that competence and belonging to two different epistemic communities by a person from a given locale does not make him or her any more or any less 'indigenous'. It also reflects our perspective that the critical exchange, both within and between such communities, as in the Chinese and Nigerian examples, is the crux of endogenous knowledge. We discuss this in greater detail below.

Epistemological perspectives on endogenous knowledge
The eminent South African philosopher Mogobe Ramose has famously demonstrated that the philosophy of Ubuntu/Botho is consistent with its cognate concepts in the remainder of Southern Africa and in much of the African continent. With respect to medicine, in particular, we lean on his insight that the term *'bongaka'* in Sepedi, Setswana and Sesotho refers to the medical institution that informs the morally binding nature of the conduct between the doctor and the patient in African cultural settings (Ramose, 2005). In Ramose's assessment, it is first based on the acknowledgement that human life and integrity must prevail over wealth generation (usually symbolised by a metaphysical ritual), and only after does the prescription of an appropriate herbal medicine proceed. He, therefore, draws the compelling conclusions that in the African philosophical understanding under consideration, positivist or 'value-free' conceptions of both law and economics are rejected in favour of establishing harmony between the physical and the psychic/communal dimensions. This perspective consequently has implications for the diagnosis and treatment of diseases, as well as the overall organisation of medical practice (Ramose, 2005).

Another study of plural medical systems in mid-20th century Bechuanaland (present-day Botswana) by the medical historian, Julie Livingston, emphasises the 'productive misunderstandings' that arose from the encounter between the culturally based medical system and the one introduced in the colonial context (Livingston, 2007). However, we find her account of the significant innovation that continued to occur in Tswana medicine due to the expansion of its own biomedical epistemology to account for evolving phenomena to be more compelling from an integrative point of view. It is useful to note parenthetically in this regard that two extant private firms in the contemporary city of Gaborone in Botswana, named Bongaka Pharmaceuticals and Bongaka Health Care, may be predominantly based on synthetic medicine, but their names simultaneously capture the holistic concept of 'healing', as understood in the surrounding socio-cultural and linguistic setting. With respect to plant-based drug development initiatives in neighbouring South Africa (to which this cultural understanding extends itself), the STS scholar, Geri Augusto, uses the notion of 'transepistemic research' to offer persuasive conceptual and strategic direction for mutual cognitive acknowledgement, complementary understanding and identification of shared interests between two seemingly distinct knowledge traditions (Augusto, 2005, 201).

Furthermore, this perspective finds a strong echo as the basis of the concept of 'endogenous development' that was most ably and comprehensively articulated by the late, preeminent historian from Burkina Faso, Joseph Ki-Zerbo. In *La natte des autres: Pour un développement endogène en Afrique*, Ki-Zerbo stressed the significance of drawing from a historically and culturally based knowledge heritage in order to help address present-day challenges, but in critical exchange with more recent knowledge, both locally generated and adopted from elsewhere (Ki-Zerbo, 1992). Among the chapters in the book are three dedicated to medicine (Gbodossou, 1992; Hodouto, 1992; Sawadogo, 1992), including one on the creation of a centre for the 'judicious integration' of conventional and culturally based, holistic approaches to medicine by the Beninese medical doctor, Erick Gbodossou, who is equally trained in both traditions. With respect to the quest for effective knowledge, irrespective of traditions, however, it is useful to refer to Louis Pasteur, the celebrated 19th-century French microbiologist, chemist and inventor (of vaccines, among other inventions), who famously stated in 1888 that 'Science has no nationality because knowledge is the patrimony of humanity, the torch which gives light to the world'. While Pasteur may have been referring to a particular conception of scientific rationality, his cross-cutting statement was suggestive of deference to the validity of knowledge rather than to the national origins of its holder. Nevertheless, the renowned 20th-century Austrian philosopher of science, Paul Feyerabend, would go much further in 1975, chastising some of his fellow European philosophers for their gratuitous use of the term 'Voodoo' [sic] as the quintessential antithesis of science, stating that:

> *Nobody knows it, everybody uses it as a paradigm of backwardness and confusion. And yet Voodoo [sic] has a firm though still not sufficiently understood material basis, and a study of its manifestations can be used to enrich, and perhaps even to revise, our knowledge of physiology.* (Feyerabend, 2010, 30)

The contemporary relevance of this discourse, from the perspective of the holders of this African-derived knowledge system in Haiti and in the specific context of the pandemic, is highly noteworthy. Given the inadequacy of the public health system in the small Caribbean country, many communities turned to their Vodun priests and priestesses for preventative and medicinal natural herbal remedies. In a widely circulated investigation by Reuters, it was reported during the pandemic that these knowledge holders converted their temples into isolation centres in which their treatments were administered (Paultre and Sanon, 2020).

A study of a similar context on the African side of the Atlantic by the noted Beninese historian, Élisée Soumonni, provides the insight that while healing practices and ritual ceremonies in culturally embedded medical systems are connected, several European commentators on the smallpox pandemic that occurred in 19th-century Benin only emphasised rituals, thereby 'mistaking form for content' (Soumonni, 2012, 39). In the context of the pandemic, the archaeologist Akinwumi Ogundiran proposes a revisitation of how, over a millennium of managing the smallpox disease, the Yoruba of West Africa (present in modern-day Nigeria, Benin, Togo, Sierra Leone and the diaspora in the Americas) incorporated sacred groves that could serve as isolation centres against epidemics into their ancestral urban planning (Ogundiran, 2020). Furthermore, Sègla (2015) describes the process of smallpox inoculation in greater detail and presents evidence to suggest that the process of vaccination in general, though incorporated into initiation ceremonies, had been known to the Yoruba at least since 500 CE.

More specifically, however, Soumonni (2012) points out that metaphysical/physical correspondences are known among the knowledge-holders and draws our attention to the original 1967 publication of an impressive, though non-exhaustive, compilation of 3,529 Yoruba medicinal plants by the French anthropologist, Pierre Verger, entitled *Awǫn ewé ǫsanyin: Yoruba medicinal leaves*. In consulting an expanded version of that work, we note that not only did Verger (1997) assign Latin-based scientific names to the specimens (based on analyses done in African and European laboratories), there were also multiple Yoruba names for some of the individual species or combinations of plants, depending on their diverse uses.

Beyond the medical knowledge heritage described above, there is a substantial amount of information relating to an African contribution to global medicine from time immemorial. In discussing the origins of Western medicine, for example, Newsome (2007) provides evidence that some of the earliest medical writings in the Nile Valley in antiquity, which subsequently heavily influenced Ancient Greece, such as the Edwin Smith papyrus and the Ebers papyrus, did include religious commentary, but were certainly replete with details about herbal pharmacology, intestinal disease, dermatology, obstetrics and physical diagnosis that are consistent with 'objective and scientific medicine'. Finch (2007) further presents proof of medical skill in other parts of the continent that were comparable to that of the West at the same time. For instance, Banyoro surgeons, primarily in modern-day Uganda, were observed performing Caesarean sections in 1879 (published in the *Edinburgh Medical Journal* in 1884); and the Zulu in modern-day South Africa had precise knowledge of the uses of at least 700 medicinal plants, some of which were subsequently adopted in the Western pharmacopoeia.

In his review of a book on 'native' African medicine among the Mano of present-day Liberia, the pioneer African-American historian, Carter G. Woodson, underscored the study's finding that the Mano society's medical practitioners distinguished between rational treatments of diseases and metaphysical rites, despite instances in which both were used simultaneously (Woodson, 1941). These Mano 'traditional doctors' had a clear knowledge of anatomy and physiological processes and had developed an effective system of quarantine for smallpox, which involved isolating patients in a 'sick bush' (Finch, 2007).

It is therefore not surprising that in a medical historical study of eight 19th-century European-trained West African medical doctors, Adeloye (1974) reported that three of them (Africanus Horton, Obadiah Johnson, and Sodeinde Leigh-Sodipe) wrote successful theses on the basis of their documentation and classification of extant medical knowledge in their region of origin. A fourth doctor, Oguntola Sapara, used his own financial resources and spent time investigating West African herbal medicine, and used that knowledge to help in the fight against local epidemics such as smallpox, tuberculosis and the bubonic plague that emerged in the early 20th century (Adeloye, 1974). Likewise, the Black South African medical doctor, William Anderson Soga, qualified in Glasgow, Scotland, in 1883, and subsequently praised the effectiveness of 'traditional medicine' in treating fractures, but was also critical of what he considered to be the unscrupulous behaviour of some 'traditional diviners' (Mayosi, 2015, 636).

The cursory presentation above of culturally embedded African scientific medicine across the length and breadth of the continent, in both ancient and relatively recent times, is intended to demonstrate that it cannot arbitrarily be divorced from 'modern' medicine as though the latter were alien to Africa. Thus, while accepting the pluralistic basis of knowledge, including the metaphysical, historical, cultural and more instrumental scientific dimensions, our specific interest in this chapter is in articulating the epistemological foundations of endogenous knowledge for innovation, which are also plural. Said differently, in this chapter, we are more interested in the content of embodied knowledge in a manner that is potentially transferable across cultures and epistemic communities in interaction than merely in its symbolic form.

Epistemological perspectives on endogenous innovation

Given our clarification of 'endogenous knowledge' in the previous section, we now extend it to the notion of 'endogenous innovation' as a conceptual framework that had already been anticipated in Ki-Zerbo's theory of endogenous development and combine it with insights from the contemporary innovation systems framework. In fact, Gu and Lundvall (2006) have used the term 'endogenous innovation', from a systemic point of view, in connection with China's aspiration to 'harmonious development', which they argue is rooted in its ancient contributions to global science and technology, as well as its Confucian philosophical heritage. Our use of the term is analogous to this sense, although more substantively grounded in historical and philosophical perspectives on innovation than were presented in their article. Consequently, our approach can be understood as bringing the more critically oriented social studies of science and technology (STS) outlook together with the more programmatically driven innovation studies approach to bear on the challenges the pandemic presented in Africa.

Nevertheless, irrespective of whether we are referring to endogenous knowledge that is primarily culturally embedded or that which mainly emerges from the dominant global mode, the challenge of endogenous innovation in relation to pharmacology and medicine remains daunting. In her study of a South African start-up pharmaceutical company, iThemba Pharmaceuticals, that unsuccessfully sought to undertake drug discovery based on 'mainstream' synthetic chemistry, rather than the 'bioprospecting' of botanical knowledge, Pollock (2019) succinctly summed up the endogenous innovation challenge as follows:

> What if South Africa were to become a prominent place not just of raw materials, test subjects, and end users but of the basic science of pharmaceutical knowledge making? Synthesizing Hope is unusual in combining attention to global health and attention to postcolonial science, two spheres that are not often thought about together. In global health literature, scientists working in postcolonial contexts like Africa receive scant attention. Most global health research assumes that rich countries are the main, if not unique, source of knowledge making and that this knowledge flows 'south'. (Pollock, 2019, 1)

Likewise, an earlier study by Foster (2017) on the Hoodia plant, which is well known to the San people of Southern Africa, underscored the extended negotiations among the knowledge-holding communities, the Council for Scientific Research (CSIR) of South Africa and international companies with respect to patenting, benefit-sharing and other concerns. However, that attempt at endogenous innovation through an interaction between different knowledge traditions and among diverse actors was not successful either. While the books by Anne Pollock and Laura Foster shed enlightening insights in relation to the tensions associated with endogenous pharmaceutical innovation from a humanistic, STS perspective, we proceed to map out, in a more explicitly policy-relevant manner, potential pathways to the viable attainment of that aspiration.

Conceptual framework: Endogenous pharmaceutical innovation

In this section, we present a theoretically informed conceptual framework that is intended to explicitly elucidate some of the pathways that could engender an innovative and locally relevant yet competitive pharmaceutical industry in Africa in the short, medium and long term. The main theoretical paradigms that we weave together are innovation systems, pharmaceutical innovation and endogenous development. Informed by these perspectives, we propose the three main dimensions of our framework below.

Endogenous technological innovation

In this dimension, we elevate the technological component of innovation with respect to the capabilities of domestic firms and organisations in the pharmaceutical industry. We begin with the importance of scientific knowledge, in particular, to the long-term growth and development of the industry, which is consistent with the insights of endogenous growth and endogenous innovation in the neoclassical economics tradition, as well as in the evolutionary economics and innovation system approaches (Nelson and Romer, 1996). We, therefore, use the term 'original innovation' to refer to the novel scientific knowledge derived from laboratory-based R&D, and that represents one key contribution to the progress of medical know-how (Nelson et al., 2011).

We also use it in reference to the type of knowledge acquired in an explicitly African cultural and linguistic setting, but which is acknowledged to be highly specialised, such as 'traditional doctors' who have specific expertise as botanists with a deep and expansive knowledge of the effectiveness, toxicity, preparation and dosage of medicinal plants (Sofowora, 2010). It is notable that in his preface to Sofowora's book (published in both English and French), the equally pioneering Beninese professor of pharmacy, Edouard Adjanohoun, lamented the fact that despite their abundance (200,000 out of 300,000 identified plant species are in the Global South), the only medicinal plants that African students were being taught about were those that had been featured in textbooks from industrialised countries (Adjanohoun, 2010). Adjanohoun, therefore, called for greater resources to be directed toward related teaching and research on this rich plant heritage in Africa.

The next component of endogenous technological innovation is termed 'secondary innovation', which Wu and Li (2015) refer to as the sequential process by which firms in 'latecomer' economies first acquire mature production or manufacturing capabilities and progressively upgrade their technological capabilities, but with the primary intention of closing the gap in productivity with those countries that frequently capture market opportunities based on knowledge at the frontiers of science. However, given that the treasure trove of knowledge that is required for pharmaceutical innovation has been accumulated in many parts of the Global South and Africa, in particular, over centuries and even millennia, we consider that long-term effort at exploration, experimentation and application to be consistent with the notion of original innovation. Based on this premise, the uni-directional, forward-looking 'catch-up' basis for secondary innovation becomes bi-directional in our conceptual framework for the reasons below.

In the first instance, as Lee et al. (2018) point out, catching-up firms can only develop successful domestic brands by overcoming steep challenges in the face of incumbents' positions in the relevant global value chain. The difficulty at upgrading is even more severe in the pharmaceutical industry due to the much more stringent patenting that is a result of the significant R&D investment costs by dominant firms, which are typically on the order of five times more than in other manufacturing industries (2 to 3% of revenues in the latter versus 10 to 20% for pharma), as well as to prevent the relative ease of imitation, according to Scherer (2010). Hwang (2020) further corroborates the argument that given the strong hierarchy by leading pharmaceutical firms in the global value chain (GVC), very few latecomer firms have been competitive on the basis of their domestic innovation in synthetic medicines and that phytomedicines, therefore, offer a window of opportunity to decouple the home-grown industry from the GVC on the basis of its local knowledge and demand. This possibility offers a basis for our proposed bi-directionality.

In the African context, a study on herbal medicine in Ghana by Essegbey and Awuni (2016) demonstrates that its practitioners are primarily located in the informal or popular sector, but are gradually registering their enterprises, improving their manufacturing processes and upgrading their quality assurance levels. According to the authors, intellectual property protection is generally informed by social norms of secrecy, and when formal, it is limited to trademarks, partly because the standards of technological capabilities for patenting are too stringent for most local enterprises to meet (Essegbey and Awuni, 2016). However, if further supported, as in the GVC-related example above, this also represents an opportunity to build manufacturing capabilities based on original, culturally embedded phytomedicinal knowledge.

We now introduce a third component of the endogenous technological innovation dimension, termed 'tertiary innovation', which has been used to explain the innovative deployment of existing products and services in the context of the green energy industry (Soumonni and Ojah, 2022). Tertiary innovation can also be likened to learning by doing and using in clinical practice, which according to Nelson et al. (2011), includes an evaluation-selection process involving not only formal randomised clinical trials but also a multiplicity of other dynamic evaluation methods that ultimately contribute to the development of new treatments and to fundamental biomedical understanding.

To illustrate the relevance of the sub-categories above to the development of phytomedicines, which are produced by extracting, purifying, concentrating, fractionally distilling, or subjecting plant materials to similar physical or biological processes, the three generations identified by Okigbo and Mmeka (2006) are a useful guide, namely: the first, in which botanical plants are used in mainly unprocessed form; the second, in which pure molecules are extracted to be used as therapeutic agents, for example, quinine; and the third in which the formulation of medicines is based on randomised, double-blind clinical trials and toxicological studies. While each subsequent generation reflects a greater degree of scientific precision, it is important to note that all three have their independent search (original innovation), production (secondary innovation) and innovative diffusion models (tertiary innovation).

For synthetic medicine, a more recently published set of commentaries led by the president of the International Union of Immunological Societies, the Kenyan immunologist, Faith Osier, provides us with a glimpse of the technological capabilities that the 15 represented countries have deployed in responding to the pandemic (Osier et al., 2020). Each of the countries' immunologists worked closely with public health officials, epidemiologists, clinicians and other experts, to better understand and manage the new disease. At the level of tertiary innovation, which mainly required the rapid deployment of adopted technologies, all countries embarked on a vibrant public information campaign, most boosted their testing capacity, a few (namely Cuba) had highly effective track and trace programmes, and many specifically reported undertaking clinical research to better understand the local dynamics of the disease (e.g. Senegal and South Africa) (Osier et al., 2020).

Epistemic pharmaceutical communities
In the second dimension of our conceptual framework, we adopt the notion of 'epistemic communities', which has been found to be relevant to health policy by Löblová (2018) in its reference to actors across society who have expertise in a given domain, and organise themselves around their shared knowledge, normative principles, notions of validity and common policy objectives. While our use of the term overlaps with the more widely known 'communities of practice', we nevertheless employ the former because of our emphasis on the high degree of professional competence, critical self-awareness and intentional networking to achieve common objectives. In the first instance, we identify the epistemic community whose activities revolve around synthetic medicine, whether as medical doctors, public health researchers, pharmacists, pharmaceutical researchers, or policy-makers. With respect to South Africa's pharmaceutical industry, for example, the arena is characterised by Suleman and Gray (2017) as consisting primarily of formal public and private sector actors engaging in the acquisition and distribution of generic and imported medicines. This constitutes for us the relevant cluster from which the synthetic medicine epistemic community emerges.

Second, in his contribution to Joseph Ki-Zerbo's seminal book on endogenous development in Africa, writing on the subject of medicinal plants, Sawadogo (1992) reported the manner in which he had assembled anthropologists, sociologists, ethnobotanists and culturally embedded doctors in order to select and harvest certain widely utilised medicinal plants (tertiary innovation). His laboratory research team subsequently extracted their active ingredients, developed appropriate dosages, investigated their effects on physiological functions with the aim of scaling up the production of the phytomedicines (secondary innovation), and finally, sought to engage in fundamental research for a more rigorous understanding of complex phenomena that had not yet been explained (original innovation) (Sawadogo, 1992). We, therefore, identify these actors across disciplines as forming another epistemic community that revolves around phytomedicine.

Third, we identify a 'transepistemic' community that is informed by common aims between different traditions (in our case, the synthetic and phytomedicinal approaches) whose actors jointly develop innovation models and are keenly conscious of the epistemological challenges that may impede the desired equitable outcomes (Augusto, 2005). It is also consistent with the notion of 'transdisciplinarity' in the endogenous development framework, which according to Laleye (1992), invites dispersed knowledge holders from different horizons to be willing to subordinate some of their discipline-centric preferences (without sacrificing freedom of critique) to sharpened solidarity with respect to resolving fundamental societal challenges. In this regard, we cite PROMETRA International (research, education and advocacy organisation on 'African traditional medicine' headquartered in Dakar, Senegal), which collaborates with the well-respected and historically African-American Morehouse School of Medicine in Atlanta, USA (Braithwaite et al., 2020; Gbodossou, 1992). Their integrative research on preventive and complementary solutions made promising interventions during the Ebola epidemic and the COVID-19 pandemic (MSM, 2021; PROMETRA, 2021).

We should note, however, that the basis for this hybridity is a reflexive and critical complementarity between them, rather than a static or deontological (rule-based) knowledge regime. Sofowora (2010), for instance, is of the view that the rationale for illnesses is the main difference between the two approaches to medicine, with culturally embedded medicine often attributing this to spiritual or metaphysical causes as much as to physical causes, while synthetic medicine focuses primarily on the physical dimension and to a lesser extent, psychological complications. Abayomi Sofowora nonetheless concedes that even certain practices that may initially appear to be arbitrary (e.g. plucking medicinal leaves at different times of the day) are actually consistent with established scientific findings that demonstrate the variation of secondary metabolytes in some plants, or changes in composition in others, during the course of the same day.

On the other hand, Tangwa (2007) argues that patients who consult practitioners of culturally embedded medicine typically do so only after they have exhausted well-known home remedies and that most such practitioners rely on herbal plants, whereas any need for specific spiritually based healing, per se, is relatively unusual. Godfrey Tangwa, a bioethicist, therefore challenges the type of comparison of 'Western scientific medicine' (allopathic or synthetic medicine) and 'African traditional medicine' (culturally embedded medicine) that insists that the latter should be subordinated to the former without rigorously ascertaining what the bases for their complementarity might be. However, he points out that while in medical research, a promising drug can only be validated on rigorous, methodological grounds, medical therapy (whether culturally based or allopathic) is governed by an ethical standard that prioritises the health of the patient. This ethos may then justify the use of a promising drug that is yet to be conclusively proven, on humanitarian grounds (Tangwa, 2007).

For his part, Ogungbemi (2007) contends that to the extent that esoteric or supernatural claims are made by certain practitioners of culturally embedded medicine, or conversely, if practitioners of allopathic medicine categorically dismiss their counterparts in the former group, then such attitudes would be unproductive. Citing an example of a clinic in Bulawayo, Zimbabwe, in which allopathic doctors referred patients to their culturally embedded doctors for psychosomatic disorders and behavioural problems, Segun Ogungbemi, a philosopher, thus concludes that when those who have knowledge of curative and preventive medicine are open to dialogue and critique, then the potential for contributing to healthcare is magnified.

Thus, outlooks on the manner in which synthetic medicine and phytomedicine might be jointly used in practice range from sympathy with culturally embedded medicine but subject to scientific verification (Sofowora), to opposition to the establishment of any type of what Augusto (2005) calls 'cognitive hierarchy' (Tangwa and Gbodossou), to a rejection of the esotericism of culturally embedded medicine on the grounds that it is anachronistic (Ogungbemi). As can be seen, these epistemological perspectives by experts in their respective fields do not fall along disciplinary lines but are based on their judgement of the relative strengths and weaknesses of the two main approaches. Our explication of the first two dimensions of our framework is depicted in Figure 1, with each of the nine boxes depicting possible pairs of a type of technological innovation and a given epistemic community that could use it to achieve a desired innovative outcome.

The most appropriate paths (boxes), or various combinations of paths, that could enable the achievement of collective goals in a given society are then informed by historical path dependence, which we proceed to discuss in the third dimension.

Historical path dependence
Although having diverse interpretations in the policy theory literature, our use of the term 'path dependence' is consistent with the proposition by Ingram et al. (2007) that policies toward politically powerful target groups will be highly favourable if they have a positive social construction, but

Figure 1: Conceptual framework: Endogenous pharmaceutical innovation

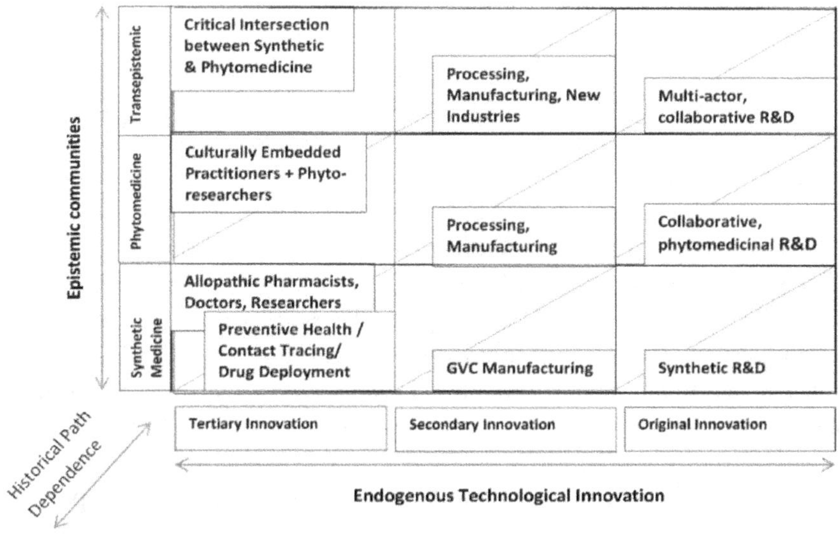

		Tertiary Innovation	Secondary Innovation	Original Innovation
Epistemic communities	**Transepistemic**	Critical Intersection between Synthetic & Phytomedicine	Processing, Manufacturing, New Industries	Multi-actor, collaborative R&D
	Phytomedicine	Culturally Embedded Practitioners + Phyto-researchers	Processing, Manufacturing	Collaborative, phytomedicinal R&D
	Synthetic Medicine	Allopathic Pharmacists, Doctors, Researchers / Preventive Health / Contact Tracing / Drug Deployment	GVC Manufacturing	Synthetic R&D

Historical Path Dependence →

Endogenous Technological Innovation →

Source: Authors' own.

less explicit if they are viewed negatively ('contenders'). On the other hand, politically weak target groups that benefit from a positive social construction ('dependents') will get positive rhetorical support, but only minimal or modest substantive support, while weak groups that have a negative social construction ('deviants') tend to be burdened with a disparate proportion of policy-backed sanctions (Ingram et al., 2007). Therefore, an understanding of the degree of political power that the epistemic groups that we proposed have, as well as the way in which they are typically viewed by policy-makers, can serve as predictors of the degree of support (substantive or rhetorical) or sanction that they ultimately receive.

For example, herbal medicine and associated therapeutic practices in Africa were long characterised as 'retrograde' during colonial rule, and later, by the health community based on synthetic medicine (Okigbo and Mmeka, 2006). However, through the efforts of pharmaceutical researchers and gradual recognition by various governmental bodies and international organisations such as the WHO, phytomedicine has received official recognition as having the potential to help meet the shortfall in the delivery of health services by the state and private sector. Thus, plant medicine has moved from the position of a 'deviant' that is explicitly sanctioned to a 'dependent' that is accepted to varying degrees but remains politically weak.

Nonetheless, our use of the term 'historical path dependence' is intended to go beyond the preliminary, though valuable, assessment of its use in the social construction framework. It underscores the need to have a more rigorous epistemological engagement between the 'subordinated' or 'defeated' substantive knowledge of politically weak epistemic communities and the justificatory claims of those that are powerful. This approach is specifically informed by the historically grounded imperative of endogenous development, which we have already defined above, but is now more specifically applied to the first two dimensions of our framework.

With respect to endogenous technological innovation, Ki-Zerbo (1992) supports the view that it can be inspired by restoring in the younger generation the inventive spirit that drove the development of magnificent accomplishments in ancient times and further deepened by reviving the old foundations of that knowledge. Nevertheless, he insists that one should not confuse the 'traditional' in the sense that it merely ought to be 'preserved' or remain unexamined, with the 'endogenous', which implies the capacity to adopt and improve upon extant knowledge, in particular, that which is embedded in African languages, cultures and values, through contemporary scientific R&D and related methods.

The conceptual elucidation of the otherwise loosely used terms in quotation marks above is emblematic of one of the pillars of the endogenous development theoretical framework by Ki-Zerbo (1992), namely, a selective epistemological secession from dominant paradigms that may employ words with normatively and teleologically charged meanings. To further buttress the point, the words 'traditional' and 'orthodox' are synonymous in English language thesauri (as they are in French ones). Yet, the former is widely used to refer to culturally embedded medicine, while the latter refers to allopathic medicine. This leads us to the crucial question posed by Tangwa:

> *In what sense can a system on which only 20% of a population depends for their healthcare needs be considered as 'mainstream' while that on which more than 80% depends, and have depended for centuries, be considered as unconventional/unorthodox? (Tangwa, 2007, 48)*

Likewise, the terms 'native', 'indigenous', 'modern', 'conventional' and so on are not necessarily neutral. Their use may vary widely depending on a given author's own presuppositions, their contextual relevance, or perhaps, politically significant meanings. This, in large part, explains why we have opted for the more theoretically grounded term 'endogenous' that happens to be much more widespread in the French-speaking literature but which enables us to explicitly grapple with the dynamics of interaction among diverse knowledge traditions across space and time.

Beyond this call for terminological and semantic caution, however, the detailed study of epistemic tensions regarding the knowledge of plants in the 17th and 18th century Cape region (in what is now South Africa) by Augusto (2007) draws our attention to a number of crucial insights that can enable us to bridge the apparent impasse. One is her usage of the concept of 'cognitive injustice' to demonstrate the manner in which the overwhelming majority of flora and fauna, that had been identified and classified by Khoikhoi, Sankwe and Nguni-speaking societies, were appropriated by European naturalists who typically bestowed their personal names (in Latinised form) on the plants.

Another is the notion of 'epistemic openness', which Geri Augusto uses to show how certain persons from groups such as the Malay, Surinamese, Akan (from present-day Ghana and Côte d'Ivoire) and the BaKongo (from modern-day DRC, Republic of Congo and Angola), who found themselves enslaved in the Cape, brought with them ethnobotanical knowledge that they drew upon and exchanged with others in their new environment. She also points out that products like tobacco, thought of as medicinal plants or as valuable drugs, were brought to the Cape from the Caribbean by Dutch colonists (Augusto, 2007). Augusto (2017) also reminds us that tobacco was one of the quintessential 'plants of bondage' that were cultivated by subjugated Africans and Native Americans. Nevertheless, the imposition of this plant never succeeded at deterring the survival of desirable food and medicinal plants, whether camouflaged on plantations ('limbo plants') or grown in maroon communities ('liberation flora') throughout the Americas (Augusto, 2017).

Given the temporal and spatial scale of the knowledge flows described above, a very recent and epistemologically significant pandemic-related innovative effort on the Caribbean island of Guadeloupe, which has generated widespread excitement in the French-speaking parts of the Caribbean and African world, more generally, is therefore of high relevance to our study as well. On 11 February 2021, the Caribbean pharmacist and doctor of pharmacognosy, Henry Joseph, announced that in collaboration with another Guadeloupean former NASA research chemist, Damien Bissesar, he had demonstrated that specific molecules from extracts of *'l'herbe à pic'* in French or *'zèb a pik'* in Guadeloupean Creole (Neurolaena lobata), an endemic plant on the island, could block the reproduction of RNA viruses in general, and the coronavirus in particular, in a living organism (Trésor, 2021).

Dr Joseph, an innovator and researcher of medicinal plants for 32 years, and director of Phytobôkaz Laboratories, already holds patented solutions that demonstrate the effectiveness of *l'herbe à pic* (Neurolaena lobata) for treating infections by RNA viruses such as the rhinovirus (responsible for head colds), myxoviruses, a group that includes influenza viruses, the Dengue virus, as well as several protozoan parasites (Joseph, 2006).

Of additional pertinence to us is Joseph's insistence that what he explicitly calls the clinical observations that were carried out by his ancestors, who had been 'legally' prohibited from practising medicine of any kind in 1799, are the basis for his contemporary research (AJ+, 2021; Trésor, 2021).

Expressing gratitude for the 'clandestine' transmission of this knowledge from generation to generation, Henry Joseph affirms an epistemic identity with his forebears. His world view is, therefore, consistent with the onto-triadic structure of being in Ubuntu philosophy (that is, the living, the living dead and the yet to be born) and conserves its core principles with respect to medical care (Ramose, 2005).

Empirical methodology: Mini case studies

In this section, we present a concise overview of the methodological approach that we employ to better ground our conceptual framework empirically. Our primary methods of data collection included in-depth semi-structured interviews, unstructured interviews in professional settings, questionnaires and relevant documentary evidence.

In total, we communicated in-depth with ten experts (five each from South Africa and Benin) with deep professional and experiential knowledge about the pandemic (see Table 1). This dialogical information was then triangulated using credible media reports, patents and results of laboratory trials.

The main findings of our investigations in both Benin and South Africa are now described in the illustrative rather than exhaustive mini case studies below. They primarily address the various dimensions of our conceptual framework but also highlight expressed perspectives that may depart from it.

Table 1: Key expert knowledge resource persons

	South Africa	Benin
1.	Pharmaceutical industry executive	Pharmacist and innovative entrepreneur
2.	Medical doctor and infectious diseases researcher	Immunologist and cellular biologist (Member – Ministry of Higher Education and Research Committee on COVID-19)
3.	Biotechnology research scientist	Research scientist in applied microbiology and pharmacology
4.	Culturally embedded phytomedicine practitioner	Sociologist, entrepreneur and phytomedicine manufacturer
5.	Medical doctor and occupational health specialist	Forensic doctor and public health specialist

Source: Authors' own.

South Africa

South Africa demonstrated its strong technological capabilities during the pandemic, particularly in terms of keeping abreast of international developments, adapting them to national conditions and contributing meaningfully to global research efforts in various health-related domains. For instance, the genomic sequencing capability that led to the identification of the 501Y.V2 variant by the genomics team based at the KwaZulu-Natal Research Innovation and Sequencing Platform (KRISP), which is part of South Africa's genomic surveillance network (KRISP, 2021), represents higher-order technological capabilities that are unusual in Africa. Initially reported in South Africa on 18 December 2020, this variant and others, according to Abdool Karim and de Oliveira (2021), had the ability to evade natural and vaccine immunity, thereby making it crucial to suppress the replication of viruses both through public health initiatives and through equitable vaccine distribution.

The innovative efforts described above can be thought of as preventive rather than curative interventions, but they are critical for strengthening the resilience of the healthcare system and can therefore be characterised as tertiary innovation. With respect to core pharmaceutical innovation, we also found evidence of good tertiary innovation capabilities, which implement the base technologies in the arena, such as testing, storage and dispensing vaccines and other globally available medicines. Vaccine distribution during the pandemic initially began slowly, partly due to rapidly changing variants in the virus, but subsequently picked up pace during the third and fourth 'waves' of the pandemic.

In terms of secondary innovation, however, we found that South Africa used to have strong domestic manufacturing and production capabilities, but only a few major ones have been left standing, including Aspen, Adcock Ingram and Novartis, which primarily manufacture generic medicines. The Biovac Institute, a biopharmaceutical company that was deliberately established in partnership with the South African government to develop domestic capabilities in vaccine manufacturing, was characterised as having lost its competitiveness over the years, despite its strong beginnings.

However, the political will to revive Biovac was reignited during the pandemic. On 2 March 2021, a partnership among the Wits/South African Medical Research Council (SAMRC) Antiviral Gene Therapy Research Unit (AGTRU), the Wits Commercial Enterprise and Biovac was announced. Its purpose was to build the skills required to manufacture viral vector-based vaccines, a highly specialised alternative to conventional vaccines, that could also be deployed against the pandemic in South Africa (Wits, 2021). The explicit strategic intent to spur a technological catch-up effort was also articulated in the communiqué by the CEO of Biovac, Dr Morena Makhoana, who expressed the view that it was important for South Africa to ultimately acquire the capability to manufacture vaccines across the entire value chain, based on its original, R&D-based innovation, as opposed to importing active pharmaceutical ingredients (API) (Wits, 2021). On 21 July 2021, Reuters reported that Biovac had signed a 'finish and fill' agreement with Pfizer and BioNTech to manufacture 100 million doses of their mRNA–based COVID-19 vaccine every year as of 2022 (Erman et al., 2021). And in February, 2022, the South African biotechnology firm, Afrigen Biologics and Vaccines, also reported its independent development and ability to manufacture an mRNA vaccine based on the publicly available genetic sequence that was used by Moderna (Maxmen, 2022).

With respect to phytomedicines, while our research interlocutors welcomed the favourable reference to 'indigenous knowledge systems' in the president's Heritage Day Speech, they differed on the level of expectation that they had of it. The culturally embedded medical practitioner, who acquired expertise in medicinal plants based on familial and lineage ties, as well as through well-structured training programmes in South Asia, was of the view that the proclamation was more nominal than substantive. This was based on the individual's professional experience, observation and considered judgement that the medical establishment generally 'looks down' on 'indigenous knowledge' practitioners and that the cost of getting various tests run by government laboratories are prohibitive for most fellow practitioners. On the other hand, a research scientist with expertise in phytomedicine thought that the president's announcement, in conjunction with analogous statements from the Ministry of Higher Education, Science and Innovation, clearly suggested that the initiative in favour of culturally embedded medicine would indeed rise to the top of the national agenda.

In relation to epistemic communities, despite the use of the more widespread terminology to refer to themselves and others, we did find a very close identification between the two sub-groups of the phytomedicinal epistemic community. They view themselves as allies, with the professional scientists providing a source of institutional support and legitimacy for the culturally embedded knowledge holders. Conversely, the culturally embedded practitioners give the research scientists a strong sense of connection with their common cultural roots, as well as an opportunity for the latter to contribute the contemporary scientific techniques acquired to improve upon age-old practices in a manner that could be beneficial to rural and grassroots communities.

Nonetheless, it is important to underscore a nuance that we did not originally anticipate in our framework. Our culturally embedded medical interlocutor actually holds a bachelor's degree in social sciences from an English-medium university. Thus, although unknown to each other, a hypothetical interaction between them would likely generate an even closer familiarity between them than our constructs might suggest if understood too rigidly. Both participants' views on the importance of intellectual property were also revealing. The practice among culturally embedded medical practitioners is to share information about the various herbal plants, although the specific preparation was generally only disclosed to close-knit family members and associates. However, once they reached out to research scientists with contemporary technological know-how, they were willing to divulge their preparation procedures in exchange for intellectual property protection in the form of trademarks and possibly, patents.

Our engagement with the synthetic medicine epistemic community yielded some valuable insights as well. A practising medical doctor and occupational health specialist informed us that during the first wave of the pandemic, the individual had used chloroquine as a prophylactic, which was well known from childhood, and later, the hydroxychloroquine/azithromycin/zinc combination. The individual speculated that pending further investigation, it seemed likely that infection was avoided by taking those drugs, especially given that all the other medical staff in the unit had been infected. A second interlocutor, a medical doctor and infectious diseases expert, nevertheless refuted this view. Citing the peer-reviewed scientific literature, the individual argued that a mere association between variables should never be mistaken for causality and that in the absence of evidence from the most rigorous clinical trials, there was still no known cure for the virus. Despite its experimental status and extreme costliness, monoclonal antibody therapy proved a promising treatment for COVID-19 symptoms at the time; a more affordable early treatment option based on inhaled budesonide also yielded encouraging results (Ramakrishnan et al., 2021).

An executive in the synthetic pharmaceutical industry expressed immense sympathy for 'common sense' prevention to strengthen immunity, including plant-based medicine that is embedded in cultural practices but rejected alleged associations between a given drug or genetic predisposition and resistance to COVID-19. In the final analysis, the individual stated, 'I am a science guy'. To further emphasise the value of phytomedicine, our participant drew our attention to the Svalbard Global Seed Vault, which was established by the Norwegian government in 2008, ostensibly to preserve the genetic diversity of plants, with the capacity to store more than four million seed samples in mountain caverns. Nevertheless, the industry executive pointed out that these kinds of genetic banks are of great interest to the pharmaceutical industry and that there may only be relatively few known medicinal plants that are yet to be mapped because of their potential to boost the profitability of the industry.

The transepistemic community that we conceptualised in our framework is therefore delicate to identify in practice. This is because, on the one hand, there is a common interest in medicinal plants between the synthetic medicine community and the phytomedicine community. But on the other hand, one subset of the synthetic community shares values with the latter regarding its potential for the collective good (whether on ecological or developmental grounds), while the other subset seeks to appropriate its potential rewards in an exclusive manner. It is only the subset with shared values that can be considered to be members of a transepistemic community.

Benin

Relative to South Africa and other hard-hit countries, Benin was less impacted by the pandemic, although its effects are still palpable. Some hypotheses that our research participants offered were the relative youth of the population and the notion that people in tropical regions of Africa are constantly exposed to various pathogens, which may have strengthened their immunity in the face of the pandemic. Others suggested that the better ventilated, somewhat claustrophobic housing preferences (e.g. fewer self-contained apartments), may have helped. All our participants agreed, however, that these were merely speculative and did not amount to controversies.

With respect to endogenous technological innovation, tertiary innovation on the basis of robust contact tracing and testing was characterised as being relatively low. Despite an agreement among the member states of the Economic Community of West African States (ECOWAS) to standardise the cost of a single test at the equivalent of USD 50 (roughly the same in South Africa) and to commit some of those revenues to a common vaccine fund, the cost in Benin ranged from USD 90 to USD 135 (Fraternité, 2021). Furthermore, the communication of data relating to the trajectory of the infection rate was erratic, and as such, there was a general lack of confidence in the reliability of data communicated by the state, despite the higher than average costs of testing for international entry and exit.

Conversely, however, the quarantine and treatment centres for those infected were reported to be more effective than those in the conventional health system. This was attributed to the efforts of dedicated medical personnel who rose to meet the new challenge. With respect to more central pharmaceutical considerations during the pandemic, our research participants in public health and in the pharmaceutical industry reported that hydroxychloroquine was the basis of the official protocol for treating patients in Benin, even after the drug had lost governmental endorsement in France and in the European Union, more generally. We would therefore characterise the state-driven tertiary innovation capabilities as weak, but the overall level in the country was medium due to its compensation by the conscientiousness of medical professionals.

In relation to plant-based medicines, a researcher on the biochemistry of natural bioactive substances reminded us that they have always been part of the popular, primary health system (i.e. outside the state) and confirmed that they were being relied upon during the pandemic, both as preventives and as treatments. The individual informed us that a plant known as Glycyrrhiza glabra L. (Fabaceae), typically known under the common name, liquorice, had been shown in a number of recent research publications to have strong anti-viral and immunoregulatory properties and to alleviate many symptoms of COVID-19. Our participant asserted that Benin's rich biodiversity boasted several medicinal plants with abundant secondary metabolites that have desirable anti-viral properties. Based on those, the individual's laboratory had produced three formulations that were tested during the pandemic, and others had been proposed by culturally embedded practitioners in its network. While these products were already used in society in a pragmatic manner, robust clinical evaluation on patients still needed to be undertaken. These efforts corresponded to attempts at original innovation in close collaboration with culturally embedded knowledge holders.

Another of our interlocutors, a professional pharmacist and co-founder of a pharmaceutical start-up company, described himself as straddling between culturally embedded medicine and synthetic medicine. In order to justify the positionality between these two, the individual quoted an African adage that may be translated in the following manner: 'it is from the end of an old rope that one knits a new one'. Along with the forensic doctor and public health specialist, both suggested that while culturally embedded medicine may help to identify effective medicinal plants, contemporary scientific techniques should help to further specify them with respect to dosage, efficacy and safety, and in alignment with the guidelines of international regulatory bodies. Based on this premise, the pharmacist and another researcher attested to having sufficient technical capability to scale up their pharmaceutical solutions (secondary innovation) but said that they were obliged to raise their own funding, which then undermined their ability to afford intellectual property protection and finance clinical trials.

An important debate relating to a phytomedicine named Apivirine in Benin, which was reported to have demonstrated anti-viral properties against the coronavirus, had implications for properly identifying epistemic communities. The medicine, which is based on the extract of the plant, Dichrostachys glomerata, often used in spices, had already been approved by the European Patent Office (EPO) (Agon and Kinnoudo, 2008). Apivirine was subsequently re-purposed for its potential efficacy in the context of the pandemic. It should be noted that one of its inventors, the pharmaceutical innovator and founder of the enterprise, Dr Valentin Agon, was the first place winner of the prestigious Innovation Prize for Africa in 2016 for his patented, low-cost, anti-malarial phytomedicine, Api-Palu, thereby demonstrating the possibility of this technological know-how being used for inclusive innovation (Soumonni, 2016).

However, Apivirine became the subject of some controversy in the context of the pandemic because of the lack of recognition in Benin and inconsistent support that the medicine received from authorities in Burkina Faso, where it was being tested against hydroxychloroquine. Two of our university-based research participants were sympathetic to phytomedicine but expressed the view that well-established national and international protocols for testing medicines should simply be the arbiter for this particular drug. On the other hand, a public health expert expressed some suspicion that larger interests were at play, which sought to undermine African-derived solutions. Likewise, another researcher perceived a reluctance from dominant international bodies to endorse more inclusive pharmaceutical solutions. Our pharmacist interlocutor thought that political will was ultimately necessary to promote such potentially innovative products until they were eligible for more rigorous testing. Thus, all of the participants were transepistemic in principle, but they each stated their perceived preconditions for a fruitful interaction among actors.

Solutions and recommendations

Based on our investigation of epistemological controversies and varied perspectives that came to the fore during the pandemic, we have proposed a conceptual framework that enables an improved understanding of the dynamics of endogenous pharmaceutical innovation. The framework can consequently highlight several potential pathways, and combinations thereof (corresponding to the nine pairs or boxes in Figure 1), for directing pharmaceutical innovation toward transformative change in Africa. Although we brought an etic (or outsider) perspective to pharmaceutical innovation, strictly speaking, the participation of the subject matter experts in our study helped us make much better sense of our own reading of the specialised literature that has a more outward orientation. We are therefore able to propose the following policy-relevant recommendations.

Semantic and terminological attention. The widespread terms 'indigenous' or 'traditional' knowledge in contradistinction with 'modern' knowledge are often used in a colloquial manner that roughly infers non-formal, ancestral and culturally embedded knowledge. However, they can also be used to give explicit attention to such knowledge, especially when marginalised, and the communities that hold them. The term phytomedicine (or plant-based medicine), on the other hand, covers a wide range of implications, from the use of botanical plants in an unprocessed form, to the extraction of pure molecules from them, to the formulation of medicines that can be subjected to controlled clinical trials. Similarly, synthetic medicine may range from very mature medicines (e.g. paracetamol and chloroquine) that are fairly easily manufactured locally, to frontier R&D solutions like viral vector vaccines. We, therefore, recommend that policy actors use, or at least, include such more precise categories, as 'precision herbal medicine' and 'endogenous pharmaceutical innovation' in order to underscore an ongoing effort to improve upon, or draw from socially inherited knowledge in light of contemporary challenges and with the benefit of novel approaches.

Substantive revision of existing policies. Beyond the terminological considerations above, there are also epistemological implications for the development and revision of broadly related policies. Our use of the concepts of endogenous knowledge and endogenous innovation is deliberately intended to emphasise a more critical, dialogical and interactive approach to knowledge generation across multiple grammars of science and across cultures but while being grounded in a given society's history. We, therefore, propose that if not terminologically, then substantively and more importantly, such concepts should be incorporated by researchers and policy-makers who are working to better shape pharmaceutical innovation dynamics in Africa, both during the pandemic, and continue to do so post-pandemic.

Platforms for communities of practice. More programmatically, epistemic communities with shared assumptions, commitments and overlapping subject matter expertise should be encouraged to deepen the knowledge possessed by their various members. For instance, the dearth of knowledge of medicinal plants in conventional textbooks used in Africa can be compensated for by a more intensive engagement with culturally embedded knowledge holders. Simultaneously, the latter would benefit from the availability of contemporary scientific techniques to investigate their efficacy in the face of emerging maladies. Such outcomes should be scrupulously documented and diffused with the support of policy actors. The same should be done for the synthetic epistemic community, as well as with respect to upgrading its average level of technological capabilities. Robust platforms for transepistemic interaction should also be promoted, especially in relation to challenges that are only partially addressed by one main community or the other. As such, a complementary and symbiotic relationship should be more deliberately nurtured and systematised in connection with the community of practice.

Political resources for weaker actors. We found that in South Africa, practitioners of phytomedicine benefit from a positive social construction by high-level policy-makers but may be seen as dependents because of their weak political influence. Their social construction in Benin may be seen as ambivalent, although phytomedicine, even if not necessarily valorised, is widespread in the country. In the two countries, the phytomedicine epistemic community should be more deliberate about mobilising valuable resources and gaining political recognition, both from state and non-state actors, such that their activities can achieve greater scale. One way to do that is to form advocacy coalitions to increase awareness about the scientific basis of phytomedicine as well as its cross-cutting social, cultural, economic and environmental benefits.

Boost pharmaceutical manufacturing capabilities. With respect to synthetic medicine, South Africa demonstrated strong technological capabilities (especially world-class scientific competencies) during the pandemic. Policy-relevant actors in this industry should revive the stagnating innovation capabilities and strive for global competitiveness in those areas in which it has notable expertise. South African pharmaceutical firms with manufacturing capabilities (secondary innovation) should therefore leverage the scientific know-how in the country (e.g. original innovation in vector viral vaccines) in the medium term, that is, beyond 'finish and fill' agreements with dominant multinational firms. They should also take advantage of the positive image that the country has achieved in the scientific community as a way to further boost their own credibility. The Beninese medical doctors who were tasked with managing the pandemic's patients also demonstrated a high level of competence and commitment in administering the existing solutions available to them. That cadre of professionals should seek stronger international linkages, particularly with other African countries such as South Africa, in order to deepen the endogenous capabilities in the continent. Both countries should further expand the manufacturing of generic medicines, but with a view to upgrading such capabilities with respect to producing novel medicines, whether synthetic or phytomedicinal.

Establish an inclusive and innovative division of labour. Our findings suggest that a transepistemic community exists in both countries, that is, actors in synthetic medicine who are sympathetic to phytomedicine and vice versa.

However, the inclusive dimension of the healthcare challenge should be elevated so that innovative activities in phytomedicine, for instance, are further incentivised, even if their products are temporarily classified as health foods, while more rigorous upgrading and testing are being done. This would be consistent with the more inclusive orientation of South Africa's 2019 White Paper on Science, Technology and Innovation. It would also prioritise collective human dignity over material wealth for a few, which is one of the core ethical tenets of Ubuntu philosophy that finds resonance across Africa and beyond. Furthermore, the notion of inclusion need not be limited to the distribution of benefits but should begin with the knowledge contribution to innovation itself.

In addition, a division of labour is desirable in which one epistemic community refers patients to the other based on a keen appreciation of the relative strengths and weaknesses of their knowledge bases. It would also apply within epistemic communities whereby some actors may have a deep knowledge of medicinal plants or preventive measures but may not have access to more contemporary techniques to improve their efficacy and vice versa. Innovation policy-makers and managers should therefore develop and work to implement policies that leverage these intersecting and complementary communities as a resource as opposed to reinforcing (even if inadvertently) silos that may be excessively rigid. Likewise, innovators, entrepreneurs, community groups, civil society organisations, researchers, linguistic and cultural communities, and public officials, both within and across borders, should be encouraged to elevate knowledge-based considerations in their various critical deliberations (see above for concrete examples). In this manner, numerous spaces, pathways and possibilities for constructive interaction can be identified (such as some of those suggested in our framework), which should contribute to the endogenous innovation imperative in the pharmaceutical industry.

Future directions

The ongoing debate at the World Trade Organization on whether intellectual property rules should be weakened to allow lower and middle-income countries to gain access to the know-how to manufacture vaccines underscores the imperative of strengthening innovation capabilities in Africa. As such, a follow-up to this study would be to look more closely at the intellectual property dimensions of both phytomedicine and synthetic medicine with respect to acceptable socio-economic and health outcomes, as well as inclusive catch-up with a desired standard of well-being. Another would be to identify and investigate in-depth case studies of unique and exemplary pharmaceutical organisations that can serve as models of endogenous pharmaceutical innovation for transformative innovation in Africa.

References

Abdool Karim, S. S., and de Oliveira, T. (2021). New SARS-CoV-2 variants – Clinical, public health, and vaccine implications. *New England Journal of Medicine*. https://doi.org/10.1056/NEJMc2100362

Adeloye, A. (1974). Some early Nigerian doctors and their contribution to modern medicine in West Africa. *Medical History*, 18(3), 275-293. https://doi.org/10.1017/S0025727300019621

Adjanohoun, E. (2010). Préface à l'édition anglaise. In: A. Sofowora (Ed.), *Plantes médicinales et médecine traditionnelle d'Afrique*. Nouvelle édition (5-7). Éditions Karthala.

AFP. (2020, 12 November). French professor faces disciplinary case over hydroxychloroquine claims. *Agence France-Presse*. https://www.theguardian.com/world/2020/nov/12/covid-professor-didier-raoult-hydroxychloroquine

Agon, A. V., and Kinnoudo, C. (2008). Propriétées antivirales des extraits de Dichrostachys glomerata (Europe) Patent No. W. 2004/052384.

AJ+. (2021, 22 February 22). *Et si la Guadeloupe avait le remède contre les virus à ARN?* AJ+ Français. https://twitter.com/ajplusfrancais/status/1363852040838012931

Augusto, G. (2005). Gambling on interaction: natural drug development through practitioners' eyes. *Indilinga African Journal of Indigenous Knowledge Systems*, 4(1), 184-209. https://doi.org/10.10520/EJC61478

Augusto, G. (2007). Knowledge free and 'unfree': Epistemic tensions in plant knowledge at the Cape in the 17th and 18th centuries. *International Journal of African Renaissance Studies: Multi-, Inter- and Transdisciplinarity*, 2(2), 136-182. https://doi.org/10.1080/18186870701751673

Augusto, G. (2017). Plants of bondage, limbo plants, liberation flora: Diasporic reflections for STS in Africa and Africa in STS. In: C. C. Mavhunga (Ed.), *What Do Science, Technology, and Innovation Mean from Africa?* (79-95). MIT Press.

Braithwaite, R. L., Akintobi, T. H., Blumenthal, D. S., Langley, W. M., and Rice, V. M. (2020). *The Morehouse Model: How one school of medicine revolutionized community engagement and health equity*. Johns Hopkins University Press.

Dhami, N. (2013). Trends in pharmacognosy: A modern science of natural medicines. *Journal of Herbal Medicine*, 3(4), 123-131. https://doi.org//10.1016/j.hermed.2013.06.001

Djellal, F., and Gallouj, F. (2005). Mapping innovation dynamics in hospitals. *Research Policy*, 34(6), 817-835. https://doi.org/10.1016/j.respol.2005.04.007

Erman, M., Roelf, W., Winning, A., Pullin, R., and Potter, M. (2021, 21 July). South African firm to help make Pfizer/BioNTech COVID vaccine. *Reuters*. https://www.reuters.com/business/healthcare-pharmaceuticals/pfizerbiontech-strike-south-africa-covid-19-manufacturing-deal-with-biovac-2021-07-21/

Essegbey, G. O., and Awuni, S. (2016). Herbal medicine in the informal sector in Ghana. In: E. Kraemer-Mbula and S. Wunsch-Vincent (Eds), *The Informal Economy in Developing Nations: Hidden engine of innovation?* (194-227). Cambridge University Press.

Feyerabend, P. (2010). *Against Method*. Verso.

Finch, C. S. (2007). The African background of medical science. In: I. Van Sertima (Ed.), *Blacks in Science: Ancient and modern* (140-156). Transaction.

Foster, L. A. (2017). *Reinventing Hoodia: Peoples, plants, and patents in South Africa*. University of Washington Press.

Fraternité. (2021, 27 January). *Covid-19: La CEDEAO impose une réduction des prix des tests aux frontières*. Fraternité: Quotidien béninois d'informations et d'analyses. https://www.fraternitebj.info/politique/article/covid-19-la-cedeao-impose-une-reduction-des-prix-des-tests-aux-frontieres

Gautret, P., Lagier, J.-C., Parola, P., Hoang, V. T., Meddeb, L., Mailhe, M., Doudier, B., Courjon, J., Giordanengo, V., Vieira, V. E., Tissot Dupont, H., Honoré, S., Colson, P., Chabrière, E., La Scola, B., Rolain, J.-M., Brouqui, P., and Raoult, D. (2020). Hydroxychloroquine and azithromycin as a treatment of COVID-19: Results of an open-label non-randomized clinical trial. *International Journal of Antimicrobial Agents*, 56(1), 105949. https://doi.org/10.1016/j.ijantimicag.2020.105949

Gbodossou, E. (1992). Une structure associative pour le développement endogène de la médecine de Fatick (Sénégal). In: J. Ki-Zerbo (Ed.), *La natte des autres: Pour un développement endogène en Afrique* (327-332). CODESRIA.

Gu, S., and Lundvall, B.-Å. (2006). Introduction: China's innovation system and the move towards harmonious growth and endogenous innovation. *Innovation*, 8(1-2), 1-26. https://doi.org/10.5172/impp.2006.8.1-2.1

Hodouto, K.-K. (1992). Nouvelle approche de l'étude chimique des plantes médicinales (Cas des alcaloïdes) In: J. Ki-Zerbo (Ed.), *La natte des autres: Pour un développement endogène en Afrique* (333-345). CODESRIA.

Hountondji, P. J. (1994). Introduction: Démarginaliser. In: P. J. Hountondji (Ed.), *Les savoirs endogènes: Pistes pour une recherche* (1-34). CODESRIA.

Hwang, S. (2020). Traditional medicine, modern science and the upgrading of the local pharmaceutical industry: Endogenous development of the phytomedicine innovation system in Korea. *Innovation and Development*, 10(3), 413-431. https://doi.org/10.1080/2157930X.2019.1679953

Ingram, H., Schneider, A. L., and deLeon, P. (2007). Social construction and policy design. In: P. Sabatier (Ed.), *Theories of the Policy Process* (93-126). Westview.

Iwu, M. M. (2002). Introduction: Therapeutic agents from ethnomedicine. In: M. M. Iwu and J. C. Wootton (Eds.), *Ethnomedicine and Drug Discovery* (1-22). Elsevier Science.

Joseph, H. (2006). Composition pour le traitement de pathologies provoquées par des refroidissements, et/ou par des infections virales (France) Patent No. FR2870457B1.

Ki-Zerbo, J. (1992). Le développement clés en tête. In: J. Ki-Zerbo (Ed.), *La natte des autres: Pour un développement endogène en Afrique* (1-71). CODESRIA.

Kouanda, S. (2020, 10 June (Updated)). Coronavirus : une réponse africaine, oui, mais une réponse sérieuse. *Jeune Afrique*. https://www.jeuneafrique.com/997354/societe/tribune-coronavirus-une-reponse-africaine-oui-mais-une-reponse-serieuse/

KRISP. (2021, 12 March). *What's unique about the body's response to the 501Y.V2 variant? Find out.* KwaZulu-Natal Research Innovation and Sequencing Platform (KRISP). https://www.krisp.org.za/news.php?id=488

Laleye, I. P. (1992). Transdisciplinarité et développement endogène. In: J. Ki-Zerbo (Ed.), *La natte des autres: Pour un développement endogène en Afrique* (307-323). CODESRIA.

Lee, K., Szapiro, M., and Mao, Z. (2018). From global value chains (GVC) to innovation systems for local value chains and knowledge creation. *The European Journal of Development Research*, 30(3), 424-441. https://doi.org/10.1057/s41287-017-0111-6

Livingston, J. (2007). Productive misunderstandings and the dynamism of plural medicine in mid-century Bechuanaland. *Journal of Southern African Studies*, 33(4), 801-810. https://doi.org/10.1080/03057070701646910

Löblová, O. (2018). Epistemic communities and experts in health policy-making. *European Journal of Public Health*, 28(suppl_3), 7-10. https://doi.org/10.1093/eurpub/cky156

Maxmen, A. (2022). South African scientists copy Moderna COVID vaccine. *Nature*, 602, 372-373. https://doi.org/10.1038/d41586-022-00293-2

Mayosi, B. M. (2015). The first black doctors and their influence in South Africa: Forum – Medical history. *South African Medical Journal*, 105(8), 635-636. https://doi.org/doi:10.7196/SAMJnew.7821

Mehra, M. R., Ruschitzka, F., and Patel, A. N. (2020). Retraction – Hydroxychloroquine or chloroquine with or without a macrolide for treatment of COVID-19: A multinational registry analysis. *The Lancet*, 395(10240), 1820. https://doi.org/10.1016/S0140-6736(20)31324-6

MSM. (2021). *MSM making a world of difference in health equity*. Morehouse School of Medicine. https://www.msm.edu/RSSFeedArticles/November2017/msmglobalhealthsenegal.php

Nabaloum, A. A. (2020, 6 April). Burkina et Bénin : Trois médicaments contre la COVID-19 à l'essai. *SciDev.Net*. https://www.scidev.net/afrique-sub-saharienne/news/covid-19-essais-cliniques-burkina-benin-06042020/

Nelson, R. R. (1974). Less developed countries technology transfer and adaptation: The role of the indigenous science community. *Economic Development and Cultural Change*, 23(1), 61. https://doi.org/10.1086/450770

Nelson, R. R., Buterbaugh, K., Perl, M., and Gelijns, A. (2011). How medical know-how progresses. *Research Policy*, 40(10), 1339-1344. https://doi.org/10.1016/j.respol.2011.06.014

Nelson, R. R., and Romer, P. M. (1996). Science, economic growth, and public policy. *Challenge*, 39(March-April), 9-21.

Newsome, F. (2007). Black contributions to the early history of Western medicine. In: I. Van Sertima (Ed.), *Blacks in Science: Ancient and modern* (127-139). Transaction.

Ogundiran, A. (2020). Managing epidemics in ancestral Yorùbá towns and cities: 'Sacred groves' as isolation sites. *African Archaeological Review*, 37(3), 497-502. https://doi.org/10.1007/s10437-020-09407-5

Ogungbemi, S. (2007). Traditional and orthodox medicine in Africa. In: S. Ogungbemi (Ed.), *Philosophy and Development* (71-84). Hope Publications.

Okigbo, R. N., and Mmeka, E. C. (2006). An appraisal of phytomedicine in Africa. *KMITL Science and Technology Journal*, 6(2), 83-92.

Osier, F., Ting, J. P. Y., Fraser, J., Lambrecht, B. N., Romano, M., Gazzinelli, R. T., Bortoluci, K. R., Zamboni, D. S., Akbar, A. N., Evans, J., Brown, D. E., Patel, K. D., Wu, Y., Perez, A. B., Pérez, O., Kamradt, T., Falk, C., Barda-Saad, M., Ariel, A., Santoni, A., Annunziato, F., Cassatella, M. A., Kiyono, H., Chereshnev, V., Dieye, A., Mbow, M., Mbengue, B., Niang, M. D. S., and Suchard, M. (2020). The global response to the COVID-19 pandemic: How have immunology societies contributed? *Nature Reviews Immunology*, 20(10), 594-602. https://doi.org/10.1038/s41577-020-00428-4

Paultre, A., and Sanon, R. (2020, 24 May). Haiti voodoo leaders prepare temples for coronavirus sufferers. *Reuters*. https://www.reuters.com/article/us-health-coronavirus-haiti-voodoo-featu-idUSKBN2300R9

Pollock, A. (2019). *Synthesizing Hope: Matter, knowledge, and place in South African drug discovery*. University of Chicago Press.

PROMETRA. (2021). *Prometra's preventive solutions for Covid-19 pandemic*. PROMETRA International. https://prometra.org/

Ramakrishnan, S., Nicolau, D. V., Langford, B., Mahdi, M., Jeffers, H., Mwasuku, C., Krassowska, K., Fox, R., Binnian, I., Glover, V., Bright, S., Butler, C., Cane, J. L., Halner, A., Matthews, P. C., Donnelly, L. E., Simpson, J. L., Baker, J. R., Fadai, N. T., Peterson, S., Bengtsson, T., Barnes, P. J., Russell, R. E. K., and Bafadhel, M. (2021). Inhaled budesonide in the treatment of early COVID-19 (STOIC): A phase 2, open-label, randomised controlled trial. *The Lancet Respiratory Medicine*, 9(7), 763-772. https://doi.org/https://doi.org/10.1016/S2213-2600(21)00160-0

Ramose, M. B. (2005). Medicine through Ubuntu. In: M. B. Ramose (Ed.), *African Philosophy through Ubuntu* (68-71). Mond Books.

Rosendaal, F. R. (2020). Review of: 'Hydroxychloroquine and azithromycin as a treatment of COVID-19: results of an open-label non-randomized clinical trial' Gautret et al 2010. *International Journal of Antimicrobial Agents*, 56(1), 106063. https://doi.org/10.1016/j.ijantimicag.2020.106063

RSA (2020, 24 September). *President Cyril Ramaphosa: Heritage Day 2020*. https://www.gov.za/speeches/address-president-cyril-ramaphosa-heritage-day-2020-24-sep-2020-0000#

Sawadogo, L. (1992). Étude de l'activité des plantes médicinales lactogènes. In: J. Ki-Zerbo (Ed.), *La natte des autres: Pour un développement endogène en Afrique* (347-354). CODESRIA.

Sayare, S. (2020, 21 May (Updated)). He was a science star. Then he promoted a questionable cure for Covid-19. *The New York Times Magazine*. https://www.nytimes.com/2020/05/12/magazine/didier-raoult-hydroxychloroquine.html

Scherer, F. M. (2010). Pharmaceutical innovation. In: B. H. Hall and N. Rosenberg (Eds), *Handbook of the Economics of Innovation* (539-574). Elsevier Science.

Sègla, A. (2015). Yoruba ethnoastronomy – 'Orisha/Vodun' or How people's conceptions of the sky constructed science. In: C. L. N. Ruggles (Ed.), *Handbook of Archaeoastronomy and Ethnoastronomy* (1051-1058). Springer.

Sina, K. N. (2020, 29 April). COVID-19: Archbishop Samuel Kleda proposes a herbal remedy. *Cameroon Radio Television* (CRTV). https://www.crtv.cm/2020/04/covid-19-archbishop-samuel-kleda-proposes-a-herbal-remedy/

Sofowora, A. (2010). *Plantes médicinales et médecine traditionnelle d'Afrique. Nouvelle édition*. Éditions Karthala.

Soumonni, E. (2012). Disease, religion and medicine: Smallpox in nineteenth-century Benin. *História, Ciências, Saúde – Manguinhos, Rio de Janeiro*, 19(supl., dez.), 35-45.

Soumonni, O. (2016). Innovation in emerging technologies and socio-economic transformation in Africa: Fallacy or foresight? *AfricaGrowth Agenda*, 13(4), 18-22.

Soumonni, O., and Ojah, K. (2022). Innovative and mission-oriented financing of renewable energy in Sub-Saharan Africa: A review and conceptual framework. *WIREs Energy and Environment*, 11(1), e416, 1-28. https://doi.org/10.1002/wene.416

Suleman, F., and Gray, A. (2017). Pharmaceutical policy in South Africa. In: Z. U. D. Babar (Ed.), *Pharmaceutical Policy in Countries with Developing Healthcare Systems*. Springer.

Tangwa, G. B. (2007). How not to compare Western scientific medicine with African traditional medicine. *Developing World Bioethics*, 7(1), 41-44. https://doi.org/10.1111/j.1471-8847.2006.00182.x

Tangwa, G. B., and Munung, N. S. (2020). COVID-19: Africa's relation with epidemics and some imperative ethics considerations of the moment. *Research Ethics*, 16(3-4), 1-11. https://doi.org/10.1177/1747016120937391

Trésor, J. (2021, 16 February). *[Covid-19] Le laboratoire PHYTOBOKAZ du Dr Henry Joseph réalise une découverte majeure dans la lutte contre la pandémie. Guadeloupe Actualités.* https://guadeloupe-actu.com/le-laboratoire-phytobokaz-du-dr-henry-joseph-realise-une-decouverte-majeure-dans-la-lutte-contre-la-pandemie/

Tu, Y. (2016). Artemisinin—a gift from traditional Chinese medicine to the world (Nobel lecture). *Angewandte Chemie International Edition*, 55(35), 10210-10226.

Verger, P. F. (1997). *Ewé: le verbe et le pouvoir des plantes chez les Yorùbá (Nigeria-Bénin)*. Maisonneuve et Larose.

Wilkerson, I. (2020). *Caste: The origins of our discontents*. Random House.

Wits. (2021, 8 March). *Wits and Biovac partner to develop skills to produce viral vectored vaccines in South Africa. Wits University.* https://www.wits.ac.za/news/latest-news/research-news/2021/2021-03/wits-and-biovac-partner-to-develop-skills-to-produce-viral-vectored-vaccines-in-south-africa.html

Woodson, C. G. (1941). Book Review of: *Native African Medicine With Special Reference to Its Practice in the Mano Tribe of Liberia* George Way Harley. *The Journal of Negro History*, 26(4), 539-540. https://doi.org/10.2307/2715019

Wu, X., and Li, J. (2015). Towards an innovation-driven nation: The 'Secondary Innovation' framework in China. *STI Policy Review*, 6(1), 36-53.

Yang, Y. (2020). Use of herbal drugs to treat COVID-19 should be with caution. *The Lancet*, 395(10238), 1689-1690. https://doi.org/10.1016/S0140-6736(20)31143-0

CHAPTER 9

A Pro-Poor Science–Policy Interface in Africa

Joanes Atela, Nora Ndege and Mark Pelling

Introduction

The pandemic presented a great global challenge with detrimental health and socio-economic impacts. At the onset of the outbreak, there were concerns from the World Health Organization (WHO) and other commentators that the pandemic could spread fastest in and cause the most damage to Africa, owing to the continent's weaker research/information systems as well as unstable socio-economic safety nets (OECD, 2020). This concern was severe for most informal settlements in Africa's cities, where the majority are poor and lack access to basic amenities such as water, sanitation and even information to support the required behavioural changes to control the spread of the pandemic (ARIN, 2020b).

Although the continent recorded relatively low infection rates and deaths than had been anticipated when the pandemic was declared, its experience revealed that there is a huge opportunity for the continent to boost its resilience to future pandemics through strengthening the science–policy interface across multiple levels. More particularly, resilience can be strengthened by supporting the most vulnerable groups in society who are at high risk of being negatively impacted by the outbreak of such pandemics. In the context of this chapter, the science–policy interface is defined as an intersection between science and policy where scientific knowledge is the main input for policy-making and where science is called upon to develop solutions for societal problems (Killen et al., 2020; van den Hove, 2007). Science is understood broadly as the application of knowledge through research, technology, various forms of innovation and types of knowledge (tacit, codified and indigenous) (Hanlin et al., 2021). We draw from earlier work by Martin (2019, 2012), who deciphers the development of science–policy work to reflect current development characterised by the terms 'innovation', 'technology', 'research and development'. We argue that the role of the science–policy interface is critical in driving both technological and innovation processes, including societal outcomes. Innovation in this chapter is understood as the technical, social and economic process that leads to the translation of ideas, new products and processes to create value and purpose (Fagerberg, 2004; Kraemer-Mbula and Wamae, 2010). We emphasise the need to pay attention to the science–policy interface dialogues between scientific, technological communities as well as policy processes. While scientific evidence[1] is one of the strategic inputs for policy-making (Gluckman, 2016, 969), it is not the only one, as diverse forms of knowledge and multiple actors (Caraça et al., 2009) exist. Therefore, science[2] provides useful evidence on what works and what does not work in a manner that informs decisions that align with the needs of society, and particularly the poor. Throughout Africa, the pandemic invoked various policy responses – both emergency and long-term policy priorities informed by different forms of evidence spanning across various knowledge sources.

Depending on the type of evidence and the way in which particular evidence is used, the resulting policy decisions could trigger different outcomes for various groups of people and particularly the local communities who already face multiple vulnerabilities from existing challenges such as poverty and poor access to quality health services. Yet insights from scientists and policy-makers during the 2020 ARIN International Conference that focused on the effects of the pandemic and lessons for research and policy indicate that the science–policy interface is not a straightforward process. It is complex and characterised by multiple negotiations, including

---

1 A wide variety of information at different stages of a decision-making process that incorporates both hard research and context-specific analysis, findings from systematic, replicable and objectively conducted observation, measurement and experimentation to support policy processes and ensure policy is based on 'what works'.
2 'All forms of knowledge across the science, technology, engineering and mathematics (STEM) fields as well as the equally important fields of the social sciences, arts and humanities' (Hanlin et al., 2021). The authors indicate that science covers all types of knowledge, including indigenous knowledge.

political interests, methodological preferences, regional and global politics and narratives, thus the need to better understand how this interface manifests to implicate decisions and actions, especially for the vulnerable and relatively voiceless groups in the society (ARIN, 2020a).

Across various African countries, the modalities of the science–policy interface vary, marked by both 'formal and ad hoc structures' (UNDESA, 2020). African countries witnessed various innovative pathways through which science was been deployed to respond to the pandemic, including rapid response and surveillance, diagnostic, clinical characterisation of cases, trend projection, variate detection and vaccine development. Similarly, solution-oriented innovations were witnessed in various contexts, especially at the grassroots, to support behavioural change (e.g. handwashing, social distancing, wearing of protective coverings, etc.) that have also informed public policy response strategies. More broadly, we witnessed the emergence of various forms of science–policy processes such as intra-African research collaboration and dialogues, which include transdisciplinary practices (e.g. constitutions of national committees across sectors to help in emergency response) and wider engagement to resolve divergent views to find collective solutions and to learn as well. The pandemic has also opened new consciousness around rethinking research agendas with societal solutions (Lambert et al., 2020) and ways in which African researchers can play a larger role in meeting the growing demand for evidence.

Despite the progress made during the pandemic, African countries post-pandemic still struggle with a lack of appropriate knowledge to trigger solutions, and efforts both at the national and at the international level remain challenging. In the African context, lack of evidence, data gaps, insufficient time and resources to test the evidence to establish what works, and lack of interactive evidence platforms are challenges that impede progress in strengthening the science–policy interface (Ruggeri et al., 2020). Even where systems exist and are established to support this interface (e.g. existence of science experts and science advisory systems), complexities still manifest in ways that necessitate learning and improvement (UNDESA, 2020). The lessons learnt from tackling the pandemic are critical and posit useful opportunities for the continent to pursue, query and invoke effective science–policy interfaces beneficial to the poor post-pandemic.

This chapter aims to use the experiences of the pandemic to identify some of the challenges and opportunities that African countries face in using science to inform policies that are beneficial to the poor based on case studies from four African countries. The case studies are part of the initiatives that the Africa Research and Impact Network Fellows documented from November 2020 to July 2021, focusing mainly on how scientific evidence was been used to respond to the pandemic; how this evidence inspired an evolution in the practice of science–policy activity; and how this evolution reflects innovations by actors in science–policy interfaces to inform effective future policies focusing on education, clean energy, health and agriculture/food systems sectors in the respective countries post-pandemic.

The chapter proceeds as follows: the next section provides a theoretical understanding of the science–policy interface based on literature review. Section 3 outlines the methodology employed in this study, while Section 4 applies the theoretical understanding to assess Africa's policy response based on case studies from four countries and the implications for the poor. In the last section, we build on stakeholder insights and discussion to identify opportunities and lessons for a more pro-poor science–policy interface. We conclude by identifying the gaps that this work has revealed and how it can be taken forward.

Models of science–policy interface

A number of models on science–policy interface are discussed in the literature. The science and power model identified where individual scientists are considered the voice of the scientific community (Doubleday and Wilsdon, 2013). Their role is that of brokerage (Unesco, 2011) and intermediary functions between science, technology and innovation, and the political side of decision-making (Wyborn et al., 2017). While they can be powerful actors in supporting and providing legitimacy to the various solutions, they could skew solutions and emancipate subjectivity, becoming bi-partisan (Stirling, 2014). This model is largely applied in experimental fields where scientific design and control experiments to develop solutions to particular societal challenges.

New schools of thought are also emerging, identifying the expert model, a delegation model where science comes up with answers and the politicians/decision-makers take the answers up (Gluckman et al., 2021; Koetz, 2011). Scientists carry out scientific research and applied science to come up with a menu of options, and the decision-makers choose the decisions to implement. Various international organisations and agencies employ such models and are usually the 'experts' providing solutions to be taken up by the political class, the decision-makers. What this model omits is multiple sources of evidence, including other types of knowledge such as indigenous knowledge (Diver, 2017). The assumption with this model is that the expert has experience and knowledge, thus a deeper understanding of the problem at hand.

Other models include the model of two worlds, where the scientists (also referred to as researchers) and decision-makers have divergent views (Wyborn et al., 2017). While they may be focused on solving similar sustainability challenges, their approaches, agendas and suggestions are completely different. Their approaches and evidence are often misaligned (Wyborn et al., 2017).

The pragmatic model has been developed following Habermasian theory and considers the nexus between science and politics, opening up to a diversity of views (Unesco, 2011). Policy-makers and scientists/experts are considered co-developers/joint owners of the solutions. Emerging schools of thought define this as a pluralistic model. Here, research and various forms of knowledge, including tacit and local knowledge, are included for decision-making (Soomai, 2017). In their study Turnheim et al. (2020) note that developing science–policy interfaces, which they termed science–policy interactions, require organisational adjustment towards knowledge types and partnerships to have wider engagement. Wesselink et al. (2013) make a clear distinction between the types of knowledge brought in by the experts and scientific knowledge. They prefer to use 'expertise' rather than 'scientific knowledge' as they argue that the source and character of knowledge used in policy-making varies. Their argument is that expert knowledge includes tacit and experiential knowledge that draws heavily from technical contextual knowledge 'to deal with the uncertainty of scientific knowledge' (Wesselink et al., 2013, 2).

While these models are well developed and support policy-making through a science–policy interface, none of these models explicitly emphasise the aspect of inclusivity or address the voices of marginalised and poor communities. Integrating the needs of the poor and marginalised in the science–policy interface is gaining recognition in emerging concepts such as the science–policy–society interface (Liberatore, 2001). Balvanera et al. (2020), Leach et al. (2020) and UNDESA (2020) have called for the inclusion of diverse views, diverse types of knowledge, and integration of the stakeholders and policy-makers to deliver both scientifically and socially relevant outcomes. Given the context-specific nature of challenges, co-construction of more sustainable pathways by the science–policy interface with the inclusion of diverse stakeholders is key (Balvanera et al., 2020). However, inclusion is broad and could imply inclusion in the processes, views and decision-making, including at the conceptualisation phase of the processes.

As Taylor and Dewsbury (2019, 2) outline, the process may mean engagement in the language, 'discussions around what engagement means and for whom, as well as what forms of engagement are needed to ensure that diverse voices are included, heard and served by these deliberations'. An engagement with marginalised voices through civic involvement and learning may support the transformative role of science and policy communications (Scheufele et al., 2021). This supports inclusion in two ways: science that gathers evidence from those it seeks to address; and developing targeted solutions to marginalised voices. Paying attention to local knowledge and cultural issues might open up new opportunities for policy processes to address (Leach and Scoones, 2013).

Methodology

Conceptualisation of the science–policy interface

The science–policy interface is understood as a social process that comprises relations between scientists and other actors in the policy process. It is an intersection between science and policy where scientific knowledge is the main input for policy-making – science is called upon to develop solutions for societal problems (Killen et al., 2020; van den Hove, 2007). Science and policy as two domains comprise different stakeholders often supporting co-evolution of knowledge and evidence for decision-making. These systems often have various missions, objectives and logics (Zondervan, 2006) that are divergent or convergent.

But more often than not, they interact to support decision-making and policy choices that address complex societal challenges. These interactions support collaborations between policy-makers and science for the purposes of informed, evidence-based decision-making (Killen et al., 2020). Zondervan (2006) argues to the contrary, postulating that the science–policy interface does not exist, and if it does, there is no clear-cut distinction between science and policy. Instead, the processes complement each other. Science needs to understand the perspective of those utilising the insight, that is, policy-makers, and, therefore, a more collaborative approach to evidence-based decision-making is required (Killen et al., 2020; Leach and Scoones, 2013; Ruggeri et al., 2020). Other scholars have observed that the interface is usually uni-directional but could potentially involve interactivity between and among scientists and experts (Daly, 2016; Killen et al., 2020). They argue that it is a linear model where policy-making is framed as a problem-solving challenge where knowledge is produced to contribute to use and is usually based on scientific knowledge. Wesselink et al. (2013) reinforce the nonlinearity of the science–policy interface by emphasising that science usually introduces new ideas and provides ammunition in political arguments.

In the early days of pandemic outbreak, urgent and robust inputs in scientific research in epidemiology, behavioural science, drugs and vaccines development, and prevention of spread were needed to support response and recovery strategies. The urgency of solutions was regarded as a basis for a linear model of the science–policy interface. In fact, Vallejo and Ong (2020) mention that in a crisis, research protocols and timescales differ from the usual practice of science, calling for various methodologies such as rapid evidence synthesis (see, for example, the Cochrane rapid review method). A trade-off between rapid response and a more holistic approach integrating politics, narratives and policy is needed (Leach and Scoones, 2013), broadening the focus to a diversity of experts and grassroots voices (Vallejo and Ong, 2020).

Therefore, the key question is how to move away from a linear model of science–policy such as the science and power model and the expert model towards a science–policy interface that fosters a plurality of models and dynamic interactions between processes of knowledge production and decision-making especially during emergencies such as the pandemic. There is a need for a science–policy interface that allows for knowledge exchange and co-production between researchers and decision-makers and consultations with the rural poor to ensure that the poor are central to providing the needed backstopping of policies (Scheufele et al., 2021; van den Hove, 2007). As such, co-production and inclusive dialogue supported models are central (Balvanera et al., 2020) to create awareness of the societal challenges and needs of the poor and most vulnerable to emergencies (Sarkki et al., 2019).

It is worth noting, however, that the approach of the science–policy interface is contextual and varies at different scales – and this determines the outcomes of particular science–policy interfacing. At the local level, the objective might be to inform local rules or relationships, and this could mean a relatively low scale of intersection and application, including negotiations and translations of scientific evidence. In many cases, the process of scoping scientific evidence relevant to the local context has meant intense knowledge deductions with the potential exclusion of some voices. At the national level, it may inform national legislation and policies where knowledge and decisions can be quite general with little differentiation of voices, while at the international level, it may relate more to various international commitments/agreements where knowledge and decisions can be infiltrated by international political and trade interests (von Maltitz, 2020). What this implies then is that at these different scales and contexts, the instruments and models for the science–policy interface and associated implications vary, although the goal is always to support decision-making in policy processes (von Maltitz, 2020). There is a need to explore the contextual nature of the science–policy interface, how the interactions of the local, national and international scales in decision-making occur, and the outcomes for various groups, especially the poor who require support most during emergencies like the pandemic. In this chapter, we attempt to provide a broader understanding of the models of the science–policy interface, expounding 'role of science, evidence and the expertise' (Leach et al., 2021, 9) and their applications at different scales.

In more detail, we have tried to understand and conceptualise the influence of science on policy and practice and how it is used to address pro-poor issues and challenges through various country's case studies. Pro-poor responses, in this chapter and in the context of the pandemic, are conceived of as processes of inculcating scientific temper (and policy) at grassroot level and going beyond inclusion to incorporate authentic local knowledge and belief systems and traditions, and supporting the involvement of targeted groups in the science–policy interface for collective decision-making.

Analytical framework

First, we reviewed the conceptual underpinnings of the various science–policy interface models. Through Google search using keywords such as 'science', 'policy evidence', 'science and policy', among others, we identified various typologies of science–policy interface and their applications, including strengths and weaknesses with respect to the African context. Additionally, this initial review enabled us to develop a framework for analysing the case studies. The literature demonstrates that the various science–policy (S-P) models chosen by the governments, whether explicitly or implicitly, are based on functional elements initially proposed by Lasswell 1956. These functional elements could include actors, processes and interactions in the science–policy realm and recognise the fact that policy outcomes are not just about scientific and technical expertise but also encompass other social elements. Weible et al. (2020) proposed ten categories that include: (1) national policy-making; (2) crisis response and management; (3) global policy-making; (4) transnational administration; (5) policy networks; (6) implementation and administration; (7) scientific and technical expertise; (8) emotions, narratives and messaging; (9) learning; and (10) policy success and failures. These perspectives, including emotions, narrative networks, crisis response and management, global policy-making and transnational administration, policy networks, as well as implementation and administration, contribute to policy success and failures. It is, however, worth noting that the scope of this chapter could not cover all the ten perspectives; instead, we focused on three main perspectives to analyse the case studies.

Figure 1: Science–policy interface framework used for comparative analysis of countries

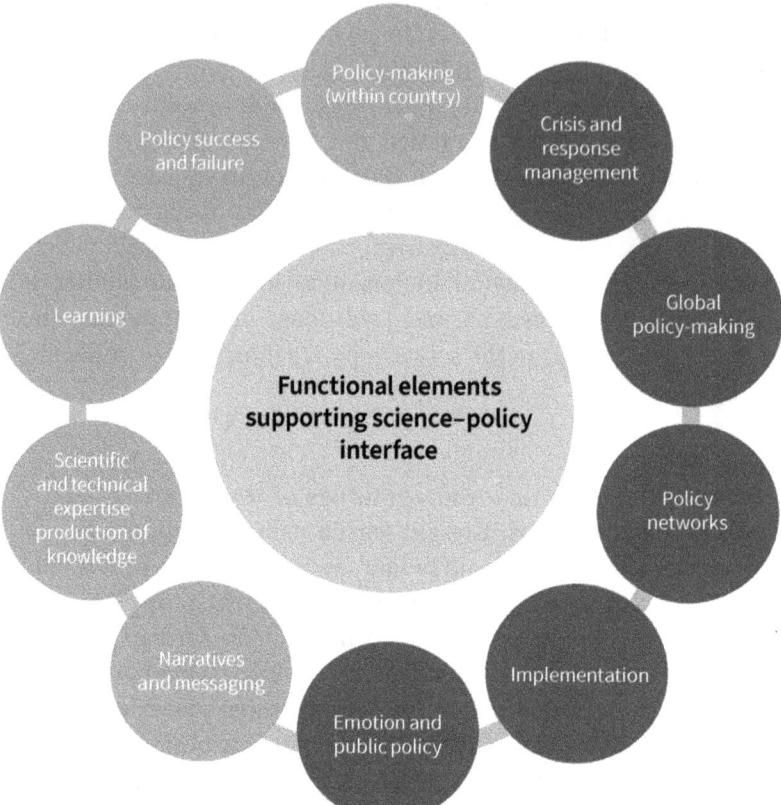

Source: Weible et al. (2020).

In other analyses (see Djalante et al., 2020), the ten perspectives have been segregated into three groupings: (a) policy and decision-making; (b) communication and perceptions; and (c) science and learning to assess the efficacy of governance responses to the pandemic. We, therefore, build on these three groupings borrowing from Lasswell's original framework that discusses policy orientation and outlines distinct stages of the policy cycle (with ten elements as key) directed towards policy processes. We focus on how policy processes in response to the pandemic in the case countries drew from scientific evidence to produce successes, failures and lessons. In this case, we integrate and select a set of perspectives (Figure 1 in green) to develop three key areas of assessment that are aligned to the study objectives (Table 1). For each of the areas, we generated a set of four indicator questions to aid the assessment, and these were informed by insights from panel discussions on the pandemic's science–policy interface at the 2020 ARIN International Conference on COVID-19. Similar desegregation has been applied by Djalante et al. (2020) to assess how governments responsed to the pandemic in the Association of Southeast Asian Nations (ASEAN).

Table 1: Science–policy interface – Perspectives and issues to consider

Science–policy perspective	Issues to consider/what this means
Policy-making and co-production with scientific and technical expertise	The process of COVID-19 policy decision-making and the role of scientific and technical experts in policy responses with the following indications: • How is research evidence ushered into decisions? • What platforms are applied to engage with evidence? • How do governments invoke scientific and technical expertise? • Is evidence used for decisions transparently available? • What roles have communities, especially poor communities, played in structuring decisions? • How are the poor affected by the resulting decisions? • How have the poor responded?
Implementation, narratives and messaging	This implies the way in which governments translate decisions into actions. The following questions were included: • How are policy decisions communicated? • What messaging is applied, that is. crisis, proactive, etc.? • How timely is the information provided? • Which actor implements what decision?
Policy success, failure and learning	Who is affected, and to what extent does influence frame success or failure? Success or failure judged as part of decisions, processes and politics. It is possible to conceive of a spectrum from success to failure and possible learnings. The following questions were included: • How is success defined and by whom?/Who is involved in determining success and at what stage in the policy process? How is learning built into the policy process? • Whose learning is considered? • Who is vulnerable, and who is excluded? • What lessons can be drawn from the process?

Source: Djalante et al. (2020).

Empirical case studies

We apply the conceptual framework discussed in the previous section to the empirical insights of science–policy engagements convened by ARIN from April to November 2020 that culminated in an International Conference themed 'Africa in the post-COVID World'.[3] ARIN is a science–policy convening and learning platform bringing together over 100 researchers and policy-makers across 36 African countries aimed at promoting research excellence and dialogue on best research and impact practices. The network also successfully convened one of the first science–policy engagements on the pandemic in Africa, which brought over 200 researchers and private sector players and innovators to discuss the lessons that the pandemic offers Africa's research and policy agendas.[4] The conference involved presentations, panel discussions, and case study presentations from various African countries. The case studies mainly focused on innovations, policy responses, and the role of knowledge in responding to the pandemic, and lessons from these experiences. Building on the conference, the network compiled over 25 case studies from different African countries, focusing on empirical experiences on how the pandemic interrupted various health, social, policy and economic systems in Africa.[5] From these 25 case studies we selected four from Ghana, Kenya, Nigeria and Malawi. The cases were selected based on their relevance to the aim of this chapter, that is, they shared a focus on these countries' decision-making processes. The selected case studies were further engaged through an in-depth online questionnaire to align details with the objectives of this study, especially: (i) the policy-interface strategies that have been adopted; (ii) how such focus has supported pro-poor responses and addressed concerns around inclusion; (iii) how the four countries have leveraged the science–policy interface to inform both emergency, medium- and long-term responses to the pandemic and planning post-pandemic; and (iv) the lessons thereof. A comparative matrix was applied to compare the various insights from the countries.

---

[3] https://www.arin-africa.org/the-africaresearch-and-impact-network-internationalconference-on-africa-in-the-post-covid-19-world-lessons-for-research-and-policy/

[4] The Africa Research and Impact Network International Conference on Africa in the Post COVID-19 World: Lessons for Research and Policy – Africa Research and Impact Network (arin-africa.org).

[5] Building Africa's Resilience in the Post-COVID-19 World: Lessons for Research and Development Priorities. Edited by Joanes Atela and Mark Pelling – Africa Research and Impact Network (arin-africa.org).

Results and discussions

Comparative analysis of country-specific responses

This section maps the divergent government responses taken by individual countries and discusses these in terms of policy-making and co-production with scientific and technical expertise and local communities, messaging and narratives, and policy success, failures and learnings. Generally, all the country analyses depended on border closures, travel restrictions, communication and behavioural changes, including working with science advisory systems to provide a more evidence-informed decision-making process given the high uncertainty of the virus. As such, both pre-existing models of consultations have been employed as well as newer ways of generating evidence. We now focus attention on the three areas identified and explore how the four countries responded to the pandemic, and reflect if and how the various models have been applied. Table 2 provides a summary of findings based on the S-P perspectives and indicators assessed in the four case study countries.

Table 2: Comparative summary of science–policy processes and implications in four case study countries

S-P perspectives considered	Kenya	Ghana	Nigeria	Malawi
Policy-making and co-production with scientific and technical expertise				
How is research evidence ushered into decisions?	Inter-agency communication. Expert consultative meetings	Existence of National Technical Coordinating Committee functioning as presidential advisors on health consisting of workers with prior experience working with the World Health Organization	Presidential Task Force (PTF) consisting of public health stakeholders such as virologists and infectious disease and diagnostic experts	Public health experts support government efforts, including scientists and researchers deemed as experts. This is cascaded down to district, area and village committees.
What platforms are applied to engage with evidence?	COVID-19 Expert Committees	National COVID-19 team led by the Ministry of Health	Presidential Task Force (PTF) on COVID-19	COVID-19 Expert Committees

S-P perspectives considered	Kenya	Ghana	Nigeria	Malawi
How do governments invoke scientific and technical expertise?	National Medical Research Centre (KEMRI) consolidates epidemiological data. Government appoints expert team to deliberate on data to provide expert opinion.	The Ministry of Health provides relevant research that is deliberated on by the National Technical Coordinating Committee.	Federal Ministry of Health (FMOH) and the Nigerian Center for Disease Control (NCDC) are responsible for the implementation of strategies to track the pandemic, and provision of trainings to local institutions.	Public health experts provide advice, and where possible public opinion informs decision-making. For example, Malawi uniquely conducted their elections even after experts warned against it. This was decided based on a survey carried out by the Institute of Public Opinion and Research (IPOR) which found that 77% of Malawians wanted elections to go ahead despite COVID-19.
Is evidence used for decisions transparently available to the public?	No – strictly managed by COVID-19 Secretariat at the Ministry of Health.	Public policy is top-down from the executive president and translated to the regional and local government levels for implementation.	Through local governments, although this is coordinated with the state government.	The current government has demonstrated public goodwill but yet to be determined once the government has been in office for a full year.

Implementation, narratives and messaging. This implies the way in which governments translate decisions into actions.

How are policy decisions communicated?	Daily briefing	Daily and later translated to weekly briefings	Weekly briefings	Daily and weekly briefings
What messaging is applied, that is, crisis, proactive, etc.?	Messages generally framed as caution, danger, warnings on the dangers and deaths. Infection rates and number of deaths and recoveries communicated daily. Socio-economic concerns communicated once in a while through presidential address.	Preventative measures, wearing of masks, social distancing, keeping safe. Infection rates, death rates, new developments of the virus.	Both crisis and more proactive through cash transfers raising funds, economic recovery plans lockdown orders, federal government plans.	Risk communication. Community engagement on the COVID-19 response. Countering spread of fake news on COVID-19. Encourage public to observe recommended measures for containing the pandemic. Fight stigma against suspected COVID-19 cases and promote solidarity among the general population.
How often is the information provided?	Daily briefs	Weekly through press releases	Weekly through media briefings	Weekly through media briefings

S-P perspectives considered	Kenya	Ghana	Nigeria	Malawi
Who implements what decisions?	Citizens implement and policy re-enforces.	Citizens, various ministries while decisions are subjected to parliamentary processes which may take long.	Citizens with both federal government and national government.	Citizens reinforced by key government actors: Public Communication Cluster led by Ministry of Information, Civic Education and Ministry of Communications Technology.
Policy success, failure and learning: Who is affected and to what extent influence frames successor failure. Success or failure judged as part of decisions, processes and politics. It is possible to conceive of a spectrum from success to failure and possible learnings.				
What roles have communities, especially poor communities, played in structuring decisions?	Implementing behavioural change directives, sources of information, local surveillance, innovating protective kits and sanitation equipment, reporting non-compliance.	Receive stimulus packages, support mapping of future scenarios and modelling to support projections of infection rates.	Come up with some frugal innovations to support response mechanisms, e.g. making masks, ventilators, etc. Local surveillance, support identification of the vulnerable.	Participated in public opinion surveys to echo their voices.
How are the poor affected by the resulting decisions?	Loss of jobs. Loss of businesses. Loss of social networks. Weakened representation in decision-making spaces. Gendered pressures and inequalities.	Increase in poverty and inequalities.	Increased hunger, starvation and malnutrition. Unemployment. Increased armed robbery. Gender-based violence. Mental health challenges.	Loss of jobs. Loss of businesses. Loss of social networks. Weakened representation in decision-making spaces. Gendered pressures and inequalities.
How have the communities responded?	Scoping for new social safety nets such as food aid. Handouts from well-wishers. Innovation and realigning enterprises to COVID opportunities.	Welcomed ideas of relief packages like free water, free electricity. Due to bad implementation of these packages and corruption, they have scouted for alternatives like borrowing, seeking support from family and friends, innovation with rudimentary activities.	Public disillusioned and not keeping to the government-issued guidelines and recommendations. Looking for social support and economic support from family and friends, religious institutions, etc.	Involved in various programmes and initiatives by the government. Are involved in community policing in collaboration with the Public Communication Cluster to report gender-based violence.

S-P perspectives considered	Kenya	Ghana	Nigeria	Malawi
What lessons can be drawn from the process?	Home-grown solutions critical for building resilience to global challenges with severe local socio-economic impacts.	Country's reliance on its human resources for solutions and consultations of experts to bring about solutions although country is still defined by top-down public policy.	Largest population in Africa but managed the pandemic through appropriate governance structures from national government to federal states.	Political landscape is a great influencer in terms of the decisions made, whether pro-poor or not.

Source: Authors' own.

The pandemic: Emergence, impacts and responses in the case study countries

The coronavirus disease emerged as a serious life-threatening health challenge that affected nearly all the countries in the world. The number of infections and deaths increased throughout 2020 and 2021. The outbreak greatly damaged global economic growth and caused a certain impact on the environment. Many African countries experienced a decline in economic activity and thus an impact on their revenues, particularly taxes (Ataguba, 2020), requiring divisive ways to manage the pandemic. These included investments in infrastructure to manage, treat and contain the pandemic.

Unprecedented measures were adopted to control the rapid spread of the pandemic in Africa and globally. When the first cases in Africa were identified in Egypt and in Kenya (13 March 2020), various governments began mandating the isolation of citizens who had come into contact either with the first cases or had been in the regions in which they were identified. As the spread continued, tougher lockdown measures were put in place. These measures included the closures of schools, places of work, borders, complete lockdowns, travel bans, bans on large gatherings, systematic quarantines, increased testing capacity and strict infection control measures (Lone and Ahmad, 2020). As such, governments were forced to provide stimulus packages to boost their economies, including coming up with measures to support the vulnerable and poor in society. Various governments employed income relief strategies and support to households affected by temporary workplace closures. Also, governments were forced to react due to the confounding nature of the disease and the urgency to provide response measures by providing quick evidence around this.

In all four countries, the emergence of the pandemic presented a crisis. While the world was informed of the dangers of the pandemic as it emerged from Wuhan, China, into Europe and North America, most countries were reluctant to put the appropriate preventative measures in place. The detection of initial cases in the four countries sounded the alarm and sent leaders, stakeholders and citizens in these countries into a confused flurry – arguably motivated by relatively reactive imaginations of potential consequences – and search for emergency management solutions. Consequently, these countries had no other managerial choices but to copy and implement what was happening elsewhere. These included emergency warnings widely informed by global trends and information from the WHO. The situation on the continent was worsened by an alarming warning from the WHO that Africa could be worse hit by the pandemic[6] given the continent's vulnerability to existing shocks such as climate change as well as poverty. Indeed in these initial stages, little science was involved in supporting decisions, thus creating a very weak S-P interface at the onset of the pandemic in the four countries. This trend already raises many questions about the effectiveness of the S-P interface in the context of crisis.

We discuss and compare the science–policy processes based on the three areas and implications from the case study countries below.

Policy-making and co-production with scientific and technical expertise. Although the initial management of the pandemic was largely reactionary (due to uncertainties), as mentioned by a number of interviewees in all four countries, the ways in which the responses to the pandemic interacted with science, policy and practice in the countries were numerous. Numerous aspects of policy planning were witnessed as the pandemic progressed.

As the pandemic continued to spread in the case countries, governments began to design policy measures focusing on managing the spread of the virus. As noted by Weible et al. (2020), during times of crisis, various policy pathways are tested, pursued and assessed in order to respond to the challenge. The emergence of the S-P interface became relatively clearer in the case study countries. Attempts to characterise the above responses reveal diversity around the interactions of the science–policy across countries locally (Table 2). These examples provide useful ways to reflect on the contextual nature of the S-P interface and how this was very different at the regional and international levels.

---

6   https://www.bbc.com/news/world-africa-52323375

An assessment of the policy planning and the roles of scientific knowledge indicates that the case countries applied a mix of expert and pluralistic policy models, especially through the establishment of expert committees and task forces under the leadership of health ministries. The expert committees, task forces and presidential advisories consisted mainly of government appointees from universities and national research organisations such as KEMRI in Kenya, the Noguchi Memorial Institute for Medical Research of the University of Ghana and Malawi Liverpool-Wellcome trust clinical research. Led by the ministries of health in the studied countries, the committees were widely composed of medical research experts who mainly provided epidemiological evidence around infection trends and recoveries.

In Kenya, for example, a COVID-19 management task force was put in place that included representatives of health, sub-national governments, education and other actors, and this task force spearheaded the response to the pandemic by supporting advisory to the president. In Nigeria, the Presidential Task Force (PTF) consisted of public health stakeholders such as virologists and infectious disease and diagnostic experts who studied, monitored and evaluated the coronavirus outbreak and the responses. Likewise in Ghana, where a national COVID-19 team was led by the Ministry of Health at the forefront of influencing the government in decision-making. Others included presidential advisors on health, professionals with prior experience working with the WHO, etc. In Malawi, a mix of expert committees comprising public health experts, including scientists and researchers deemed as experts, supported government efforts and, as a departure from the other countries, this cascaded down to district, area and village committees.

These committees studied the trends, especially from the testing laboratories, and applied their interpretations to provide expert opinions to the governments. The governments then made daily briefings and periodic adjustments of lockdowns and other decisions. In other words, the expert model of the S-P interface was predominantly applied to generate decisions that were largely harmonised with the public interest through a relatively vague pluralistic approach to managing any public uprising. It is worth noting that at the sectoral level, however, these S-P models were employed a bit more distinctively compared to the national level processes where public image is key. This practice demonstrated the potential of using a diversity of options and models where solutions are required. The options that were used complemented each other and strengthened policy science practice.

A major concern was related to how policy support had been mobilised through the science–policy interface to alleviate the negative impacts of the

Figure 2: Number of policies implemented as of December 2020 in selected countries

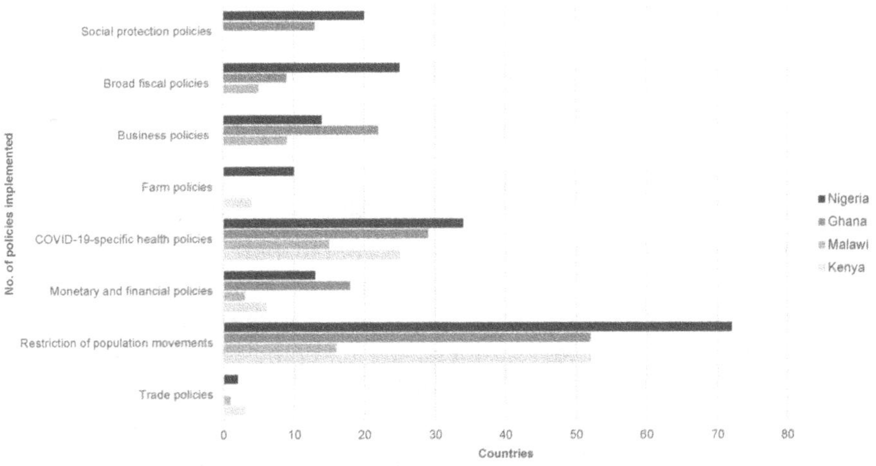

Source: Authors' own, compilation from https://www.ifpri.org/project/covid-19-policy-response-cpr-portal.

pandemic. In Figure 2 we provide a snippet of policies that were introduced in the four countries, including social protection policies. These policies were in line with the international responses and various policies that had a direct impact on households. The social protection policies introduced underscore the importance of supporting people's ability to respond to such crises and to enable them to adapt (Vogel et al., 2021).

Although marred by several limitations, the expert model of policy planning generated some progressive examples either directly or indirectly, and these could be built on further. Positive progress can mainly be seen in the increased investment in health research and health systems in all four countries. In Ghana, for example, the expert committees recommended additional investments in pharmaceutical industries[7] as well as local health institutions to help flatten the curve. As revealed, these examples of modalities were working, and at the time of the interview, Ghana recorded low infection rates attributed to these investments. In Kenya, the committees provided some expert analyses of the health systems that have led to the realisation of the need to invest in health research and systems. It was particularly noted that most of the 'developed hospitals' equipped with necessary facilities were out of reach to the local masses (Barasa et al., 2020).

---

7   https://oxfordbusinessgroup.com/news/covid-19-accelerates-ghanas-e-health-revolution

This meant that people had to travel to the cities to access 'better health' in an array of public and private hospitals. But during the lockdowns resulting from the pandemic, the local government put measures in place such as hiring more staff and equipping hospitals to serve previously marginalised members of local communities.[8] A similar approach in South Africa, through mobilisation of community health workers (Vogel et al., 2021), demonstrated positive progress generated by the S-P interface to the benefit of the marginalised, an opportunity to look at how development happens and support more pro-poor led development. Further, the interaction of science and the pandemic in policy planning in all of the four case study countries informed various stimulus packages, dedicated research grants to support cutting edge research, including mapping of future scenarios and modelling to support projections of infection rates. Such projections supported ideas around institutionalising measures aimed at curbing the spread of the virus, including advisory lockdowns and safe re-opening of schools and economies.

The S-P advisories have also spurred research and innovation speciality among non-state actors, including non-governmental organisations (NGOs) and local communities and entrepreneurs. In the case study countries, these actors have continuously developed new products such as protective kits, as witnessed in the Kenyan small business sectors. In Ghana, the efficacy of such products was approved by the Food and Drugs Board. In all four countries, S-P interfaces informed wider drug management, vaccine development and the generation of scientific data to guide sector-specific strategies.

While the S-P interface and resultant policies were widely focused on the health sector, there were some cases where this interfacing has produced broader socio-economic linkages, especially at the later phases of the pandemic. While indicators such as infection rates remained a key consideration in decisions, socio-economic considerations were widely advocated for by a range of studies (ARIN, 2020c) and civil society groups that exposed how the pandemic ravaged the socio-economic fabric of communities, especially the poor. Consequently, a number of social interventions were put in place, particularly the provision of food to the poor who could not afford meals in various countries (Akrofi and Antwi, 2020). In Kenya, for example, free meals were provided to the poor for a certain period of time, and the Kazi kwa Vijana (Swahili for 'jobs for the youth') initiative

---

8   https://www.businessdailyafrica.com/bd/news/covid-19-kenya-begins-hiring-of-6-000-more-health-workers-2285910

was also rolled out to help secure jobs for unemployed youth, but was on a number of occasions marred by unsustainability concerns. In Ghana, free water was offered during the lockdown period. While such measures were in place at crucial times, they could not be sustained (Amankwaa and Ampratwum, 2020), and as such, in some instances, countries were forced to re-open their economies, further exacerbating the effects of the pandemic on the poor. This situation implied that these socio-economic policy plans were not practical (and perhaps not backed up by appropriate evidence) but were necessary to support the vulnerable. As Weible et al. (2020) explain, uncertainties exist, and policy intents were terminated at the government's discretion. In other words, while some policies are terminated, others are carried forward and implemented.

Overall, while registering some achievements, the predominant expert models had multiple limitations with potentially negative implications. First, interviews revealed that these expert committees were not well known to the public and only seen alongside the ministers and/or presidents during the pandemic briefings. Second, interviews revealed that the public had little knowledge about the role of the experts and where they obtained the evidence to provide opinions to the ministers/presidents. Most of these policies were borrowed from already developed countries that had had relatively longer experience with the pandemic, while some were consultative and others applied top to bottom. Last, it was not clear who was consulted in the process of coming up with such policies and where there were consultations, these mainly happened between experts and government officials in the ministries of health. Some of the resultant policies were ultimately challenged. For example, in Malawi, when the president first announced lockdown measures, through the human rights commission, civil society immediately obtained a court injunction that temporarily lifted the lockdown.[9] The argument provided was that no consultations were carried out with the poorest and most vulnerable, implying that a more societal policy-driven effort was needed. The poor, for whom most of the policies were claimed to be designed, were often left out and, as a result, continue to be marginalised by the same policy agendas expected to protect them.

Additionally, the focus on epidemiological evidence meant that most of the resulting decisions were driven by epidemiological aspects such as infection rates. Resulting decisions such as lockdowns, closures and re-openings of schools, places of worship, markets and airports or easing the restrictions were purely based on the infection rates and the narrative around flattening the curve as defined by the WHO.

Consequently, the decisions appear to broadly exclude the social and economic implications of the pandemic especially for the poor who depend on daily wages, small business, or social safety nets. Indeed, consideration was given to social safety nets that were implemented to support the poor, but again, these were relatively out of media-driven advocacy[9] through which the plights of suffering youth, women and children were highlighted. At the same time, there was very little scientific evidence on what models of social protection would work for various groups. Instead, a plethora of impact assessment studies in local communities, including informal settlements in cities, emerged to build a case that the pandemic was not just a health challenge but a broader socio-economic challenge, especially for the poor.

Part of the challenge was that the expert model of S-P is often invoked during a crisis when quick solutions are sought (Balvanera et al., 2020). This means that the S-P process instigated during the pandemic was not adequately institutionalised to enable proactive planning and the generation of evidence from a wide range of stakeholders. As noted previously, the initial phases of the pandemic were marred by panic and outright replication of responses from elsewhere, given the lack of prior planning. In other words, without adequate institutionalisation of an S-P model, the S-P interface becomes weak and vague. Similar cases were observed in developed countries such as the United Kingdom, where the need to institutionalise science advice systems has been stressed (Vallejo and Ong, 2020). As an example, in one of the four case study countries, the STI Act of Kenya 2013 mentions that such advisory mechanisms will be established, but the implementation is still a challenge. This demonstrates that a number of countries were not implementing their policies to support scientific advisory mechanisms. Perhaps it is time to rethink and institutionalise such advisory mechanisms as they have proven to be effective and for science to provide solutions to current challenges.

Policy messaging and implementation. We also investigated how the resultant policies were implemented and what messaging was applied to get them through to the public. During times of crisis such as the pandemic, it is prudent to focus on key messages and narratives to

---

9   https://www.aljazeera.com/news/2020/4/17/malawi-high-court-blocks-coronavirus-lockdown 10https://blogs.worldbank.org/africacan/covid-19-africa-how-can-social-safety-nets-help-mitigate-social-and-economic-impacts

influence decision-makers or influence risk perceptions and risk reduction in the public (Weible et al., 2020).

In all four countries, frequent briefings were adopted. In Kenya, the Ministry of Health provided daily briefings, especially on the infection rates and new policy decisions. These daily briefs were coupled with presidential addresses after every cycle of the curfews. A similar approach was witnessed in Ghana, Nigeria and Malawi, where such daily briefings were translated to weekly briefings (Table 2). While this approach built confidence in the public by conveying that the government is taking the situation seriously and providing timely information (Weible et al., 2020), the messaging, accuracy and trust around relayed information was equally critical (ARIN, 2020a).

In all the countries, the prioritised messaging was generally framed in the context of caution, danger and clear warnings on the dangers and deaths caused by the pandemic. The crisis framing of messaging was also driven by global perspectives relayed by the WHO warning the World that African countries could be worse hit by the pandemic owing to the continent's weak socio-economic safety nets (OECD, 2020) – an indication of how the international policy process can influence national processes and perhaps create policy controversies. The crisis framing of messaging was often strengthened by predominant epidemiological information around rising or decreasing infection rates as well as death rates. The predominant crisis messaging was often followed by a passionate call for citizens to embrace behavioural change and avoid behaviours that could increase their chances of infection. In one famous phrase, Kenya's Minister of Health called for citizens to avoid behaving normally as, if infected, the disease would treat them abnormally:

> *Fellow Kenyans, this disease is not a joke [...] If you continue to behave normally, this disease will treat you abnormally. (Hon. Mutahi Kagwe, Kenyan Minister of Health)*[10]

According to stakeholders at the ARIN conference, the crisis framing and messaging of policy measures, while helpful in awareness creation, was also meant to whip emotions towards behavioural change. The citizens, including communities, especially those in urban areas (where

---

10   https://www.youtube.com/watch?v=tcJXU5z36zk; https://www.standardmedia.co.ke/ktnnews/video/2000186534/if-we-continue-to-behave-normally-this-disease-will-treat-us-abnormally-health-cs-mutahi-kagwe

the infection rates were reported), were expected to implement these measures through adhering to government restrictions and also embracing behavioural changes such as wearing masks, washing hands, avoiding crowded places, among others. In Malawi, the role of communities in implementing the policy measures was relatively enhanced through a differentiated Public Communication Cluster led by the Ministry of Information, Civic Education, and Ministry of Communications Technology. Compared to the other case study countries, the Malawi communication clusters usefully tailored messaging and communication to the needs and circumstances of various groups in the society.

According to Weible et al. (2020), effective implementation of policy during a crisis requires ideal communication targeted at relevant niches to catalyse differentiated actions with a common goal. Nonetheless, communication in most of the case study countries was largely broad with the underlying assumption that everyone within the countries had similar understandings of the expectations. This temporarily affected the effectiveness of the policies. The crisis framing worked well initially as it established a sense of alarm which led to the citizenry yearning to know more about the situation and embracing homogeneously relayed information about the pandemic. However, with time, most people became reluctant to observe behavioural change. As already highlighted in the policy planning section, the homogenous messaging around infection rates dominated the communication, and with time, most communities increasingly expected to hear about how to manage the socio-economic pressures imposed by the lockdowns. Coupled with cases of corruption and misappropriation of pandemic funds, the public trust around such policies significantly deteriorated, and resulted in relatively uncertain situations.

According to Weible et al. (2020), uncertainty in policy effectiveness can often result in termination or continuation of certain policies or even controversial measures to regain public control. The extent to which the governments in these cases applied controversial or non-factual information to regain control of the processes was not made clear. It is worth noting, however, that when reports emerged of new waves of infection and new variants of the virus, they were used to re-invigorate policy measures and to whip the public back into policy alignment.

Policy learning and outcomes for the poor. The study also assessed the various outcomes of the pandemic policies developed through the various S-P models. While a number of successes have been discussed above, here we provide some of the learning highlights and what implications these have had on the poor. Key among these is that the novelty of the virus allowed for experimentation, and as such, policy learning has brought to light the ability to understand, influence and address complex policy issues bringing about the needed innovation. Weible et al. (2020, 234) mention that stakeholder dialogue is one of the factors motivating learning as it contributes 'diverse forms of knowledge – whether scientific, experiential, or value-based – into policy decision-making'.

In Kenya, learnings included the awareness of the fact that home-grown solutions are critical for building resilience to global challenges with severe local socio-economic impacts. Similar learning was reported in Ghana, where the country's reliance on its human resources for solutions and consultations of experts to bring about solutions was critical. In Nigeria, in spite of the fact that the country has the largest population in Africa, which could be more vulnerable, through pandemic governance and effective communication and coordination at national and federal government levels as well as health system investment – largely informed by expertise – the country managed to contain the virus. In Malawi, the role of enabling the political landscape in influencing pro-poor actions was underscored. These country-specific learnings indicate the contextual opportunities for profiling pro-poor S-P interface, which could be strengthened by some of the universal learning insights provided by stakeholders during the ARIN International Conference and a side event on the impacts of STI indicators in policy uptake (ARIN, 2020a)

S-P dialogues and convenings were also been enhanced, both at domestic and international levels. A number of policy convenings through webinars, highlighted in the section on empirical case studies, were witnessed across the countries. These convenings were not only sector-specific but engaged and targeted a wide variety of stakeholders, including diverse voices, in a bid to find collective solutions. These convenings informed the diagnosis of the policy context and aired various policy messages. As to whether these were taken into account in decision-making processes is another question altogether but what we can highlight is the new sense of consciousness around dialogue and collective efforts. This has created a new sense of policy learning within countries, regionally and continentally.

The sharing of experiences on how different countries were tackling the pandemic in its various waves, variants and forms was inspiring, the outcomes of these learnings notwithstanding. Such learning further ushered in useful collaborations in research and the resultant success in vaccine development and its administration. For example, Kenya launched their vaccination strategy to counter the pandemic in 2021 which mirrored that of the UK in prioritising frontline health workers and security personnel during the first phase, while the second phase, up to July 2022, targeted the vulnerable, the elderly and adults (above 18 years) with comorbidities (Kyobutungi, 2021). This reflected a relatively high level of policy learning where learning/information was passed from high-level scientific experts but modified by countries to their contexts and informed responses. The case studies also show that stakeholders stressed the significance of domestic systems given the pandemic's impact and limitation on imports and exports, especially when travel bans were executed. The experience in all four countries showed that various communities and innovators emerged to profile solutions that were locally driven and aligned to local needs and abilities. The potential for building such local systems required a broader narrative change and a shift from viewing innovations through broader conceptual lenses and framing around global competitiveness to intentional support of these local systems through science and policy (ARIN, 2020a).

Overall, these country-specific and universal learnings were critical. They should, however, ideally have gone beyond superficial learning and be more reflective of past crises to bring about policy choices while being more aware of different political ideologies and on-the-ground conditions, etc.

Science–policy interface and the role of the poor

Reflecting on the outcomes of the S-P interface with respect to the poor, several points have been made. Figure 3 illustrates the key implications of S-P experiences in the case study countries: old poverty, new poverty, weak urgency and on a more positive note, grassroots innovations.

The case studies demonstrate that some of the policies that were aimed at containing infection rates severely affected the socio-economic well-being of the poor who already suffered low-income levels and other vulnerabilities, thereby reinforcing existing poverty. The countries reported massive losses in jobs and businesses. More broadly, the World Bank global economic prospect predicted a 5% gross domestic product (GDP) contraction resulting in a significant economic recession (World Bank, 2020) which could push more than 80–100 million people into extreme poverty. While the governments initiated a number of relatively pro-poor social protection measures (Figure 2), including measures such as Kazi kwa Vijana in Kenya, free food and water in Nigeria and Ghana, as well as income subsidies in Malawi, sustainability concerns hampered their effectiveness in cushioning the poor.

Other than impacting the existing poor, the policy measures further created a new cadre of poor people. In all the case study countries, the

Figure 3: Key implications that S-P experiences in the case study countries

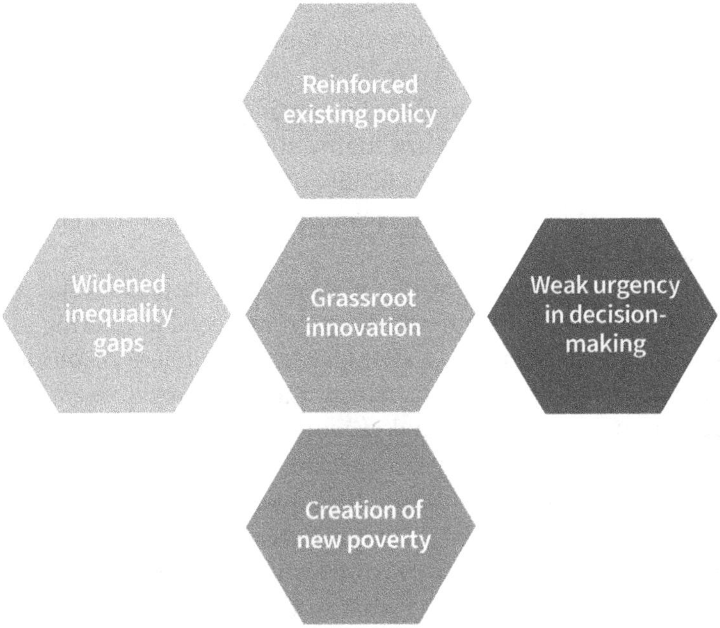

- Reinforced existing policy
- Widened inequality gaps
- Grassroot innovation
- Weak urgency in decision-making
- Creation of new poverty

Source: Authors' own.

resultant job and business losses meant that some people who, prior to the pandemic, were relatively above the poverty line were pushed into poverty, creating a new cadre of poor people. This phenomenon is illuminated by the World Bank, which calls for policy options that recognise the changing profiles of poverty and vulnerability (World Bank, 2020). According to the World Bank, these people are mainly found in middle-income countries, but from our study, evidence shows that there is an increasing number of people, even in low-income countries, who slid back into poverty. For most stakeholders, this is largely a result of a lack of consideration of the socio-economic dimension of the pandemic from its onset (ARIN, 2020a).

Other implications for the poor include increased inequality, which has been witnessed across income clusters, gender and other social classes (ARIN 2021b). Emergency policy directives and lockdowns have widely disrupted value chains of feminised sectors such as food services and home-based care, with 19% more women affected than men (UN Women, 2020). In most African countries, the pandemic cut off income for over 50% of women-led micro, small and medium enterprises (MSMEs) compared to 22% of men-led ventures (Kaberia and Muathe, 2020). In sub-Saharan Africa, the pandemic has exacerbated women's economic vulnerability, which was already characterised by systemic gender inequality, including poor access to credits and factors of production due to informality, culture and market constraints (Ferrant and Thim, 2019). More broadly, a recent OECD survey shows that 75% of women, globally, participate in MSMEs, including unpaid care work, most of which are highly susceptible to shocks such as that caused by the pandemic (ARIN, 2020d) and climate change (Atela et al., 2018) and with a 5.9% higher risk of closure than male-owned enterprises (World Bank, 2020).

Finally, the S-P model applied in the case study countries has widely resulted in the exclusion of voices of the poor in decision-making spaces. While this has been a traditional challenge, the experiences resulting from the pandemic have reinforced that, indeed, the circumstances of the poor were excluded in policy planning and execution. The challenge here might not necessarily be about the exclusion but perhaps involves wider concerns around the fact that these local communities were affected the most by the impacts of the pandemic and were also expected to implement the emergency directive measures. Lack of people-centred consultations with these groups, especially on what they wanted and what worked for them, and a broader lack of transparency in information and resources regarding the pandemic significantly weakened the voices of the poor. This was exacerbated by the fast-changing nature of the pandemic, which did not allow adequate time for civil society organisations to advocate for the rights of the poor.

On a more positive note, however, the pandemic-related experiences in the case study countries triggered a new wave of grassroots innovations and locally driven solutions. Some cases of such innovations were addressed in one of the ARIN blog series (Mbeva et al., 2020). Dubbed 'the last mile networks' and 'last mile innovations', the 'last mile' networks of actors, entrepreneurs and innovators emerge to develop solutions towards the pressing needs of the vulnerable. In the context of the pandemic, these actors innovated COVID-19 kits, created awareness and enhanced pro-poor communication and interpretation of broader policy issues in the local context. A number of these 'last mile' innovations to tackle the pandemic across the continent were profiled.[11] In Kenya, for example, some of the actors worked with communities in the informal settlements of Kawangware, Mathare and Majengo, to identify risk families and provided targeted assistance through direct cash transfers and food parcels. These

---

11   https://africacenter.org/spotlight/african-adaptations-to-the-covid-19-response/

actors also created community champions who promoted behaviour change through effective communities and packaging and dissemination of relevant pandeic-related information through arts. Similarly, a number of technical innovations emerged, including new models of local hand washing machines and small mask manufacturing factories, amongst others. While most of these locally driven innovations were not new, the fact that they have emerged and were profiled as critical in providing solutions to a global challenge is a critical outcome of the pandemic-related experience. In the context of the S-P interface, they present new frontiers for rethinking the S-P interface and producing pro-poor policies in the face of shocks. These frontiers could be better supported through enhanced linkage to research evidence as a promising pro-poor pathway. However, the extent to which efforts will be made post-pandemic to ensure that national policy and regulatory frameworks facilitate long-term upscaling of marketing of the innovations and indeed domestic innovation capacity remains unclear (Atela and Ndege, 2020).

Summary and conclusion

This chapter analyses the importance of the science–policy interface where research, technology and innovation can support the advancement of policies that respond to societal needs. The pandemic revealed how science and policy are intertwined, requiring scientific evidence that encompasses technology and innovations to inform policy responses. With this growing momentum for science to inform policy, two clear trends have been elucidated; first, the role of scientific experts in realigning scientific evidence to be useful for policy-makers; and second, the wider stakeholder engagement, including pro-poor responses as important in influencing policy development.

The chapter explored the S-P interface and implications for the poor in four African countries using the case of the pandemic. While this is a work in progress, we highlighted the fact that the virus propelled the science–policy relationship into the public arena, exposing a number of opportunities and challenges. It resulted in innovations in the science–policy interface and merged understanding of scientists and local people supporting a people's/ citizen driven response. The pandemic supported the rapid evolution of the S-P interface by relying on the expert models, the pluralistic models to support response. This emphasised a need to promote innovation in the science–policy interface by fostering a plurality of models, co-production and consultations with the poor to ensure that they provide the 'technical' backstopping of policies. The establishment of science–policy committees, to some extent, supported evidence-based policy actions but then again were faced with many challenges such as lack of trust and general exclusion of certain important voices and needs, especially of the poor. Further, the narrow focus on health-related evidence, policies and messages encouraged siloed ways of tackling global challenges and led to negative outcomes and loss of opportunities (expertise, evidence, income, etc.) that could have been offered by other sectors. Additionally, the initial stages of the pandemic created panic among policy-makers, scientists and citizens resulting in copy-paste policy measures that were not aligned to the country circumstances and indicated that S-P requires proactive planning and institutionalisation to enhance the effectiveness of decisions in times of crisis.

The S-P models employed subsequently nonetheless registered some achievements, especially in enhancing a better understanding of the health systems and priority health research. These include increased investments in health facilities, personnel, capacity and research that resulted in some milestones in dealing with the pandemic. This success was, however, marred by systemic challenges that need to be unlocked to ensure that such gains are sustained and upscaled. First, the need to enhance transparency to the public, especially about the expert committees and their sources of evidence, remains a major bottleneck in the S-P pursuit. In the four case study countries, these committees were not well-known to the public and were only seen alongside the ministers and/or presidents during the pandemic's media briefings. The citizens had little knowledge of their roles or the sources of the evidence they relied on to provide opinions to the ministers/presidents. Second, the need to adopt a multi-sectoral approach to the S-P interface was crucial to enable effective communication with the various audiences. The sector-based approach in addressing the pandemic led to a huge part of the public losing interest and trust in the information shared by policy-makers. For more poor communities, maintaining a livelihood was just as critical as lowering the infection rates. Several implications on the poor have been reported ranging from loss of jobs, businesses and income, but one outstanding outcome was the proliferation of grassroots innovations that steered new frontiers for bottom-up and pro-poor policy planning towards global challenges.

Finally, it is also worth noting that this study has largely explored the S-P interface in Africa using the pandemic as a case. It has provided a framework that can be used to provide a more in-depth analysis of country experiences and consolidate this further to inform the science–policy debate and create space for stakeholders and knowledge producers to reflect how their work can sustain science–policy cooperation beyond the pandemic. The following lessons can help inform such further work:

1. New frontiers for rethinking the S-P interface: Despite the implications on the poor caused by the policy directives, the case studies also reveal new forms of science–policy governance, especially at the local community levels. Multiple locally driven solutions that emerged outside the policy process have helped salvage many lives and livelihoods. These experiences present new frontiers for rethinking S-P and producing pro-poor policies in the face of shocks. These frontiers could be better supported through enhanced linkage to research evidence as a promising path to pro-poor S-P interfacing. However, the extent to which efforts will be made to ensure that national policy and regulatory frameworks facilitate long-term upscaling of marketing of the innovations and indeed domestic innovation capacity post-pandemic remains unclear (Atela and Ndege, 2020).
2. Institutionalised science advisory systems: The pandemic demonstrated that reactionary, crisis-oriented and ad hoc science advisories are bound to be less effective in addressing global challenges. Countries need to institutionalise such advisories to offer long-term science–policy engagements and planning that accounts for the needs of all, especially the poor.
3. Sustained S-P dialogue platforms: There is a need for sustainable forums for science–policy dialogues so as to continuously enhance the co-creation of solutions. The ARIN International Conference stressed the need for supporting such dialogues with evidence and data platforms that can enhance the understanding of trends and uncertainties of pandemics through continuous research, generation of evidence, and management to help predict and inform foresight policies post-pandemic (Atela, 2021).
4. Leveraging the role of non-state actors to complement state capacity in addressing emergencies such as the pandemic: The state-centric approach to defining the S-P interface provides useful direct policy entry but certainly excludes useful evidence, expertise and voices from important decisions. Drawing on the stakeholder perspectives at the 2020 ARIN International Conference, stakeholders specifically dubbed some of these efforts as 'last mile initiatives' that are critical for steering policy implementation, especially by providing information to the poor living in vulnerable localities where government systems

developed community champions to promote surveillance and feedback (Mbeva et al., 2020).
5. Calling on policy processes to pay attention to locally driven innovations: In most of the innovations, calls for these to be locally led have been accentuated by the pandemic, which otherwise would not be a key focus of the current policies. This highlighted the need to pay attention to locally driven innovations and solutions. It also indicated that most innovations and breakthroughs come from a more bottom-up approach, were locally driven and thus had the potential to provide solutions to global challenges. Therefore, science and policy need to interface at the local levels as well as the national levels to ensure that bottom-up innovations are supported.

References

Akrofi, M. M., and Antwi, S. H. (2020). COVID-19 energy sector responses in Africa: A review of preliminary government interventions. *Energy Research and Social Science,* 68. DOI: 10.1016/j.erss.2020.101681.

Amankwaa, G., and Ampratwum, E. F. (2020). COVID-19 'free water' initiatives in the Global South: What does the Ghanaian case mean for equitable and sustainable water services? *Water International,* 45(7-8), 722-729. DOI: 10.1080/02508060.2020.1845076.

ARIN. (2020a). COVID-19 implications on Africa's research and policy. Insights from ARIN International Conference 2020. In: J. Atela, K. Mbeva, K., and J. Onyango (Eds), *Technical Report* No. 004. Africa Research and Impact Network.

ARIN. (2020b). Seminar discussions on low carbon development and resilience in the post COVID-19 world. In: V. Chengo, K. Mbeva and J. Atela (Eds), *Technical Report* No. 003. Africa Research and Impact Network.

ARIN. (2020c). Seminar discussions on harnessing the applications of science technology and innovation in the fight against COVID-19: Lessons for science policy. In: N. Ndege and J. Atela (Eds), *Technical Report* No. 002. Africa Research and Impact Network.

ARIN. (2020d). Conference session discussions on a gender lens in disaster risk reduction in the context of COVID-19. In: A. Maobe and J. Atela (Eds), *Technical Report* No. 005. Africa Research and Impact Network.

Ataguba, J. E. (2020). COVID-19 pandemic, a war to be won: Understanding its economic implications for Africa. *Applied Health Economics and Health Policy,* 18(3), 325-328. DOI: 10.1007/s40258-020-00580-x.

Atela, J. (2021). COVID-19 Lessons for Africa's public policy. *ARIN Policy Brief* no. 001/2021. https://www.arin-africa.org/wp-content/uploads/2021/03/ARIN-Policy-Brief-_-COVID-19.pdf

Atela, J., and Ndege, N. (2020). What lessons can Africa learn from COVID-19 to improve its knowledge systems? https://www.arin-africa.org/2020/08/05/covid-19-is-re-shaping-our-perspectives-of-africas-knowledge-systems/

Atela, J., Gannon, K. E., and Crick, F. (2018). Climate change adaptation among female-led micro, small, and medium enterprises in semi-arid areas: A case study from Kenya. In: W. Leal Filho (Ed.), *Handbook of Climate Change Resilience*. Springer (pp.). https://idl-bnc-idrc.dspacedirect.org/bitstream/handle/10625/59287/IDL-59287.pdf

Balvanera, P., Jacobs, S., Nagendra, H., O'farrell, P., Bridgewater, P., Crouzat, E., Dendoncker, N., Goodwin, S., Gustafsson, K. M., Kadykalo, A. N., Krug, C. B., Matuk, F. A., Pandit, R., Sala, J. E., Schröter, M., and Washbourne, C.-L. (2020). The science–policy interface on ecosystems and people: Challenges and opportunities. *Ecosystems and People*, 16(1), 345-353. https://doi.org/10.1080/26395916.2020.1819426

Barasa, E. W., Ouma, P. O., and Okiro, E. A. (2020). Assessing the hospital surge capacity of the Kenyan health system in the face of the COVID-19 pandemic. *PLoS ONE*, 15, 1-13. DOI: 10.1371/journal.pone.0236308.

Caraça, J., Lundvall, B. Å., and Mendonça, S. (2009). The changing role of science in the innovation process: From queen to Cinderella? *Technological Forecasting and Social Change*, 76(6), 861-867. DOI: 10.1016/j.techfore.2008.08.003.

Daly, M. E. (2016). Co-production and the politics of usable knowledge for climate adaptation in Tanzania. University of Colorado. https://scholar.colorado.edu/downloads/cj82k734s

Diver, S. (2017). Negotiating indigenous knowledge at the science policy-interface: Insights from the Xáxli'p Community forest. *Environmental Science and Policy*, 73, 1-11. https://doi.org/10.1016/j.envsci.2017.03.001

Djalante, R., Nurhidayah, L., Van Minh, H., Phuong, N. T. N., Mahendradhata, Y., Trias, A., Lassa, J., and Miller, M. A. (2020). COVID-19 and ASEAN responses: Comparative policy analysis. *Progress in Disaster Science*, 8, 100129. https://doi.org/10.1016/j.pdisas.2020.100129

Doubleday, R., and Wilsdon, J. (2013). *Future Directions for Scientific Advice in Whitehall*. http://www.csap.cam.ac.uk/media/uploads/files/1/fdsaw.pdf

Fagerberg, J. (2004). Innovation. A guide to the literature. In: *The Oxford Handbook of Innovation* (1-26). Oxford University Press.

Ferrant, G., and Thim, A. (2019). Measuring women's economic empowerment: Time use data and gender inequality. *OECD Development Policy Papers*, no. 16. https://doi.org/10.1787/02e538fc-en.

Gluckman, P. (2016). The science–policy interface. *Science*, 353(6303), 969. http://science.sciencemag.org/content/sci/353/6303/969.full.pdf

Gluckman, P. D., Bardsley, A., and Kaiser, M. (2021). Brokerage at the science–policy interface: From conceptual framework to practical guidance. *Humanities and Social Sciences Communications*, 8(1), 1-10. https://doi.org/10.1057/s41599-021-00756-3

Hanlin, R., Tigabu, A. D., and Sheikheldin, G. (2021). Introduction: The role of science councils in building African science systems. In: R. Hanlin, A. D. Tigabu and G. Sheikheldin (Eds), *Building Science Systems in Africa. Conceptual foundations and empirical considerations* (pp.). Mkuki na Nyota and African Centre for Technology Studies.

Kaberia, S. K. and Muathe, S. (2020). Effect of Covid-19 pandemic on performance of women owned micro, small and medium enterprises in Kenya. *International Journal of Social Science Studies*, 9(1), 7. DOI: 10.11114/ijsss.v9i1.5089.

Killen, L., Castro, C., Woodwrad, O., and Manning, I. (2020). Leadership at the science policy interface: A case study of the policy challenges collaboration between Cambridgeshire County Council and Cambridge University Science and Policy Exchange. *Cambridge Journal of Science and Policy*, 1(1), 63-72.

Koetz, T. (2011). Institutional dynamics of science-policy interfaces in international biodiversity governance. PhD thesis, Universitat Autònoma de Barcelona.

Kraemer-Mbula, E., and Wamae, W. (Eds). (2010). *Innovation and the Development Agenda*. OECD/IDRC. https://doi.org/10.1787/9789264088924-en

Kyobutungi, C. (2021). (2021, 4 March). The ins and outs of Kenya's COVID-19 vaccine rollout plan. *The Conversation Africa*. https://theconversation.com/the-ins-and-outs-of-kenyas-covid-19-vaccine-rollout-plan-156310

Lambert, H. Gupte, J., Fletcher, H., Hammond, L., Lowe, N., Pelling, M., Raina, N., Shahid, T., and Shanks, K. (2020). COVID-19 as a global challenge: Towards an inclusive and sustainable future. *The Lancet Planetary Health*, 4(8), e312-e314. DOI: 10.1016/S2542-5196(20)30168-6.

Lasswell, H. D. (1956). *The Decision Process: Seven categories of functional analysis*. Bureau of Governmental Research, College of Business and Public Administration, University of Maryland.

Leach, M., and Scoones, I. (2013). The social and political lives of zoonotic disease models: Narratives, science and policy. *Social Science and Medicine,* 88, 10-17. DOI: 10.1016/j.socscimed.2013.03.017.

Leach, M., MacGregor, H., Scoones, I., and Wilkinson, A. (2020). Post-pandemic transformations: How and why COVID-19 requires us to rethink development. *World Development*, 138, 105233. https://doi.org/10.1016/j.worlddev.2020.105233.

Liberatore, A. (2001). From science/policy interface to science/policy/society dialogue. In: R. A. Roehrl, W. Liu and S. Mukherjee (Eds), *Social Sciences for Knowledge and Decision Making* (pp.). OECD Publishing. https://read.oecd-ilibrary.org/science-and-technology/social-sciences-for-knowledge-and-decision-making_9789264189812-en#page112

Lone, S. A., and Ahmad, A. (2020). COVID-19 pandemic – An African perspective. *Emerging Microbes and Infections*, 9(1), 1300-1308. DOI: 10.1080/22221751.2020.1775132.

Martin, B. R. (2019). The future of science policy and innovation studies: Some challenges and the factors underlying them. In: *Handbook on Science and Public Policy* (523-542). https://doi.org/10.4337/9781784715946.00039

Martin, B. R. (2012). The evolution of science policy and innovation studies. *Research Policy*, 41(7), 1219-1239. https://doi.org/10.1016/j.respol.2012.03.012

Mbeva, K., Chengo, V., and Atela, J. (2020, 5 August). Building community networks to respond to the COVID-19 pandemic in Africa through 'last mile' initiatives. *ARIN COVID-19 Blog Series*. https://www.arin-africa.org/2020/08/05/building-community-networks-to-respond-to-the-covid-19-pandemic-in-africa-through-last-mile-initiatives-authors-kennedy-mbeva-victoria-chengo-and-joanes-atela/

Organisation for Economic Co-operation and Development (OECD). (2020). COVID-19 in Africa: Regional socio-economic implications and policy priorities. OECD.

Ruggeri, K., Linden, S., Wang, C., Papa, F., Riesch, J., and Green, J. (2020). Standards for evidence in policy decision-making. PsyArXiv Preprints. https://psyarxiv.com/fjwvk/

Sarkki, S., Balian, E., Heink, U., Keune, H., Nesshöver, C., Niemelä, J., Tinch, R., Van den Hove, S., Watt, A., Waylen, K. A., and Young, J. C. (2019). Managing science-policy interfaces for impact: Interactions within the environmental governance meshwork. *Environmental Science and Policy*, 113, 21-30. https://doi.org/10.1016/j.envsci.2019.05.011

Scheufele, D. A., Hoffman, A. J., Neeley, L., and Reid, C. M. (2021). Misinformation about science in the public sphere. *Proceedings of the National Academy of Sciences of the United States of America*, 118(15), 15-17. DOI: 10.1073/pnas.2104068118.

Soomai, S. S. (2017). The science-policy interface in fisheries management: Insights about the influence of organizational structure and culture on information pathways. *Marine Policy*, 81, 53-63. DOI: 10.1016/j.marpol.2017.03.016.

Stirling, A. (2014). Transforming power: Social science and the politics of energy choices. *Energy Research and Social Science*, 1, 83-95. DOI: 10.1016/j.erss.2014.02.001.

Taylor, C., and Dewsbury, B. (2019). Barriers to inclusive deliberation and democratic governance of genetic technologies at the science-policy interface. *Journal of Science Communication*, 18(3), 1689-1699.

Turnheim, B., Asquith, M., and Geels, F. W. (2020). Making sustainability transitions research policy-relevant: Challenges at the science-policy interface. *Environmental Innovation and Societal Transitions*, 34, 116-120. DOI: 10.1016/j.eist.2019.12.009.

United Nations Department of Economic and Social Affairs (UNDESA). (2020). The COVID-19 pandemic: A wake-up call for better cooperation at the science–policy–society interface. United Nations. https://www.un.org/development/desa/dpad/publication/un-desa-policy-brief-62-the-covid-19-pandemic-a-wake-up-call-for-better-cooperation-at-the-science-policy-society-interface/

Unesco. (2011). *Mapping out the Research Policy Matrix. Highlights from the First International Forum on the Social Science-Policy Nexus*. Unesco.

UN Women. (2020). From insights to action: Gender equality in the wake of COVID-19. 80% of whom are women, have lost their jobs as a result of COVID-19. https://www.unwomen.org/en/news/stories/2020/9/feature-covid-19-economic-impacts-on-women

Vallejo, B. M., and Ong, R. A. C. (2020). Policy responses and government science advice for the COVID 19 pandemic in the Philippines: January to April 2020, *Progress in Disaster Science*, 7(June 2020), 100115. DOI: 10.1016/j.pdisas.2020.100115.

van den Hove, S. (2007). A rationale for science-policy interfaces. *Futures*, 39(7), 807-826. DOI: 10.1016/j.futures.2006.12.004.

Vogel, C., Maree, G., Köhler, T., Stanwix, B., Bhorat, H., Sodi, T., Ubomba-Jaswa, Drimie, S., Mbhenyane, X., Symington, E., Adebayo, P., and Ndinda, C. (2021). Impact on vulnerable groups: South Africa Covid-19 Country Report [Interim draft]. Department of Planning, Monitoring and Evaluation, Government Technical Advisory Centre and National Research Foundation.

von Maltitz, G. P. (2020). Harnessing science-policy interface processes for tackling sustainability challenges in sub-Saharan Africa. In: A. Gasparatos et al. (Eds), *Sustainability Challenges in Sub-Saharan Africa II: Insights from Eastern and Southern Africa* (217-243). Springer. DOI: 10.1007/978-981-15-5358-5_9.

Weible, C. M., Nohrstedt, D., Cairney, P., Carter, D. P., Crow, D. A., Durnová, A. P., Heikkila, T., Ingold, K., McConnell, A., and Stone, D. (2020). COVID-19 and the policy sciences: Initial reactions and perspectives. *Policy Sciences*, 53(2), 225-241. DOI: 10.1007/s11077-020-09381-4.

Wesselink, A., Buchanan, K. S., Georgiadou, Y., and Turnhout, E. (2013). Technical knowledge, discursive spaces and politics at the science-policy interface, *Environmental Science and Policy*, 30, 1-9. DOI: 10.1016/j.envsci.2012.12.008.

World Bank. (2020). *Supporting Women Throughout the Coronavirus (COVID-19) Emergency Response and Economic Recovery*. World Bank. https://openknowledge.worldbank.org/handle/10986/33612

Wyborn, C., Leith, P., Hutton, J., Ryan, M., Montana, J., and Gallagher, L. (2017). The science, policy and practice interface. https://luchoffmanninstitute.org/wp-content/uploads/2017/11/Science-policy-practice-interface.pdf.

Zondervan, R. (2006). Science-policy. *Journal of Chemical Information and Modeling*, 53(9), 1689-1699.

SECTION III

CROSS-CUTTING ISSUES

CHAPTER 10

Different Strokes of the Fourth Industrial Revolution

Lessons from the pandemic on technological change and prospects for Africa

Julius Gatune, Geci Karuri-Sebina, Ann Kingiri, Edward Lorenz and Diederik de Boer

Introduction

Technological progress has been a crucial driver of how value is created and thus of the nature of work. For Schumpeter, while development is first and foremost a process of technological change, the latter ultimately takes place through innovations carried out by entrepreneurs (Lima, 1996). Technological breakthroughs, which have seen human capacity multiplied, largely drive economic development as technology has augmented human productive capacity, giving more output for the same input (Rifkin, 2013). The world is currently considered to be at the cusp of a technological revolution that is being referred to as the 4IR (WEF, 2017). This is driven by monumental breakthroughs in the use of information and communication technologies (ICTs) that are unleashing new capabilities and fundamentally changing the nature of work through new forms of automation and digitalisation (see appendix for definitions of 4IR technologies).

The 4IR is seen as presenting unprecedented opportunities. For instance, the McKinsey Global Institute (MGI) (2016) argues that systems enabled by machine learning are general purpose in nature and can provide value across the economy and generate productivity gains and improved quality of life. At a macroeconomic level, automation could raise productivity growth on a global basis by as much as 0.8 to 1.4% annually (MGI, 2017a). Businesses everywhere will have an opportunity to capture benefits and achieve a competitive advantage from automation technologies, not just from labour cost reductions but also from performance benefits. The 4IR technologies are also connecting many devices and allowing the development of new business models through the clever use of generated data.

In a study of 12 African countries, ACET (2018) found that Africans are generally positive about AI, with 55% seeing a positive impact on jobs and only 16% expressing a negative view, however, many stakeholders found that Africa was largely unprepared for 4IR. The 4IR, therefore, presents clear opportunities, but the current wave of disruptive technologies is causing great anxiety[1] as they have the potential for automating many tasks that were formerly thought to be out of reach for machines. Some authors have raised the possibility that new digital technologies, including AI, are the harbinger of a singularity that will progressively eliminate all or most human labour in industrial production (Brynjolfsson and McAfee, 2014).[2] The impact is not fully understood, however, and the very high estimates of job losses made in earlier studies have been revised downwards, possibly suggesting that the risk was exaggerated.[3]

The shift to the 4IR has been further accelerated by the pandemic, which has seen firms and people rapidly adopt new ways of working and doing business. Business and social activities have significantly moved online (Soto-Acosta, 2020). What is less clear is what the 4IR could practically mean for Africa with its huge informal economies and how the pandemic's impact may provide some insights in this regard, which this chapter seeks to explore. The chapter aims to clarify what the 4IR means for African economies and

---

1 Anxiety about new technologies is not new; the rise of the First Industrial Revolution saw resistance by Luddites, who violently opposed new machines and went on destruction rampages. Similar anxiety was seen as computing ushered in the Third Industrial Revolution (Autor, 2015; Juma, 2016).
2 For a critical discussion of the singularity hypothesis, see Nordhaus (2015).
3 Early estimates by Frey and Osborne (2013) put jobs at high risk of automation at 47% in the United States. Estimates by Arntz et al. (2016), however, found that only 5-10% of jobs are susceptible to automation. A 2017 MGI report estimated that for 60% of the jobs, at least 30% of the tasks could be automated (MGI, 2017a). McKinsey's latest estimate puts global job losses due to automation at 15% through to 2030 (MGI, 2017b).

to identify how opportunities for equitable African development can be leveraged with a focus on lessons that can be derived from the experience of the pandemic. It contributes to the sparse academic literature on 4IR in Africa while also commenting on African policy initiatives such as the African Union's *Digital Transformation Strategy for Africa 2020–2030* (2020) and the digital policies of various African nations (including Nigeria, South Africa, Ethiopia, Tanzania and Kenya). These policies articulate what policy-makers consider to be their challenges, opportunities and expectations.

The chapter is structured as follows: the next section will look at the impact of the pandemic on 4IR developments in Africa. Section 3 explores the impact and potential of 4IR for the largely informal African economies, while Section 4 considers the potential for 4IR to help Africa leapfrog. Section 5 concludes with a discussion of the regulatory challenges facing African countries, specifically the risks due to the potential of the emerging digital platforms to establish monopoly positions.

The pandemic and 4IR developments: A global overview

The pandemic provides insights into how the 4IR is likely to unfold. As summarised by Marr (2020), the transformative effects of the pandemic were immense. The reality of everything being conducted remotely saw 4IR technologies being deployed to support a range of activities in distance work, entertainment, education, and as well as connecting with friends. Indeed, the pandemic accelerated the adoption of many 4IR technologies[4] and pushed them to new levels as they were applied to mitigate the health impact and assure business continuity. Marr (2020) and UNIDO (2020) point to some key developments that are worth noting:[5]

- *Artificial intelligence (AI)* was a key technology in the pandemic response. Public health officials relied on AI to better understand infection patterns and to try to predict surges in COVID-19. Bots were put into use for contactless deliveries, cleaning and administering medication. This experience resulted in a learning process leading to improvements in the use of AI over time. The surge in reliance on AI

---

[4] As the Microsoft CEO has commented, 'We've seen two years' worth of digital transformation in two months.' The pandemic accelerated the adoption of 4IR technologies as people and companies relied on cloud computing, artificial intelligence, the speed of the 5G network, big data and more (Marr, 2020).

[5] See Appendix A for definitions of these technologies.

will result in artificial intelligence becoming more advanced (Marr, 2020).
- *Cloud computing* moved mainstream. As workforces moved home to slow down the spread of coronavirus, cloud computing helped companies continue with day-to-day operations. Now that more companies have experienced the flexibility of cloud computing, they can be more strategic about how they will use it.
- The shift to the *5th generation mobile network (5G)* with enhanced connectivity based on a faster data transfer speed will promote the greater use of the *Internet-of-Things (IoT)*. The demand to handle a varied stream of data from interconnected devices at a quick speed makes the 5G network crucial to the advance of the 4IR. The pandemic created new use cases and business demands for stable wireless networking.
- *Big data* and *big data analytics* were relied upon by health officials to understand the pandemic. They tracked the number of cases, traced infections and modelled spread throughout various cities, regions, and countries. Several tracking tools were created throughout the course of the pandemic.
- *Robotics* was used to transport essential medical supplies in heavy transmission areas of some countries.[6]
- *3D printing* filled the gap in order to provide much-needed personal protective equipment for medical professionals.[7]

UNIDO (2020) sees the emergence of a 'new normal' in the post-pandemic world that will increasingly be driven by advanced technologies and their applications for inclusive and sustainable industrial development. However, there is potential for a few big winners and many small losers, underscoring the need for policies to steer the revolution and to mitigate the potential entrenching of inequalities. In the wake of the pandemic, new 4IR-powered giants have emerged, for example, Zoom, which saw meeting participants grow from 10 million in December 2019 to 300 million by April 2020, as many people transitioned to working and socialising from home. In May 2020,

---

[6] For the case of Nuro, an autonomous vehicle startup, see https://www.theverge.com/2020/4/22/21231466/nuro-delivery-robot-health-care-workers-food-supplies-california

[7] See, for example, https://www.nihlibrary.nih.gov/services/3d-printing-service/3d-printing-medical-equipment-response-covid-19-pandemic

Zoom was valued higher than the seven biggest airlines (Ghosh, 2020). More crucially, the pandemic has exposed deep structural inequalities in Western societies (Pazzanese, 2020). This has revealed a huge chasm between the owners and employees of the big tech companies thriving in the wake of the pandemic, while those with low skills often line up for food aid. In 2020, Eurostat reported that low-income workers were more likely to lose their jobs and that the hardest hit were young and low-skilled workers.

4IR and African economies

The potential for 4IR to help transform African economies and unleash new opportunities is substantial. For Africa, 4IR technologies are showing considerable dynamism, with significant potential to support various transformation strategies proposed for Africa (see notably ACET, 2018; AfDB, 2013; AU 2020). Drones, for example, can be deployed to monitor agriculture, supply blood and lifesaving medicines, among other services (Sylvester, 2018). Blockchain technologies can help in automating land registries (see Appendix B). Arguably, mobile money can transform financial inclusion. The transformational impact of 4IR needs to be given more attention through the generation of evidence for policy and practice.

Much of the trepidation about 4IR depends on new technology's automation potential, with the impact on employment likely to be the greatest in the manufacturing sectors due to the potential for industrial robots to replace human workers (Chandy, 2017). While the extent to which this is occurring is debated,[8] in considering the potential impact of automation technologies on employment in the African context, it is important to consider that what may be technically feasible is not necessarily economically feasible. Even though the cost of robots is falling, they are unlikely to offer a viable alternative to more traditional methods for several decades in most African countries.[9]

---

[8] Empirical research on the impact of robots in European countries, including Germany, shows that after taking into account the compensating effects, the impact of robot adoption on employment is neutral or positive. See, for example, Graetz and Michaels (2018). A recent study by Lorenz and Kraemer-Mbula (2020) in reference to the auto sector in South Africa found that employment levels did not fall with investments in robots because output increased substantially. Further, one component supplier interviewed stated that he had refrained from investing in automation technologies so as to avoid reductions in employment for the unskilled.

[9] For example, Banga and te Velde (2018) point out that given the wage rate of a high-end robot (costing USD 28 per hour) that can be used to make furniture and assuming an annual decline in the cost of robots of 6.5%, it will take until 2032 for robots to be economically viable in the sector in Kenya.

More crucially, manufacturing accounts on average for only 7% of national products in Africa, and even though the sector might be more susceptible to automation, the impact on employment in the short to medium term is likely to be small. The most important impact is the loss of what can be termed 'could have been jobs' as Africa's low-cost labour advantage becomes less of a factor in determining patterns of international production and trade (Hallward-Driemeier and Nayyar, 2017). For Africa, the more significant impacts will arguably be in the application of 4IR technologies to public and private services.

In the West, computerisation has resulted in labour market polarisation, with the share of mid-level jobs declining relative to those of the low and upper skilled groups (Autor et al., 2003; Goos and Manning, 2007). The evidence is much more uncertain for developing countries (World Bank, 2016). Digitalisation has ushered in the 'gig economy', with digital platforms being used for commissioning tasks leading to the challenges that come with an increase in informal work, including low pay and lack of social security (Schmid and Wagner, 2017). However, informality has been the dominant way for the majority of people in Africa, and the advent of the 4IR may provide the potential to increase employment through the development of digital platforms that can offer jobs and other services. Further, to the extent that 4IR is spurring new occupations in services and construction, it can lead to an increase in middle-wage occupations (MGI, 2017b).

Some potential innovations leveraging 4IR technologies in the wake of the pandemic have been explored in the last section. These examples may seem limited in application or scope given the long-standing challenges that Africa has had in leveraging technology-based transformations at scale (Adesida et al., 2016). However, there is emerging research distinguishing between which of these pandemic-inspired innovations could reflect systemic and lasting innovation ecosystem shifts, compared to those which might be rightly considered to be just incidental and transient (Adesida et al., n.d.). Indeed, the crisis stimulated innovations, especially in food security and health across Africa. We saw the leveraging of technologies and also innovation in business models to address the challenges induced by the pandemic. Some initiatives included:

- Use of drones: Drones were deployed in Ghana to send blood samples to testing laboratories (Reuters, 2020), and the country also planned to use drones to distribute vaccines (Prabhu, 2021).
- Deployment of robots: In Rwanda, robots were deployed in hospitals to help in screening, including performing temperature checks and

reading other vitals, detecting lack of masks and cautioning people to wear them (WHO, 2020).
- Leveraging ICTs for food aid collection and delivery: In Kenya, mobile apps were developed to collect food packages at designated collection points. Potential donors went to the application's dashboard and generated the list of individuals they had identified as people in need and assigned collection points, whether large-scale supermarkets or small-scale kiosks.[10]
- Automated border checks: The East Africa Community developed the EAC COVID-19 Test Certificate for truck drivers and crew members. The system was developed to facilitate a common approach to certifying results of those tested for COVID-19, by using the system to generate a COVID-19 test certificate for drivers and crew members. Consequently, the generated COVID-19 certificate for drivers and crew members who had undergone tests would be shared with all respective stakeholders both at accredited designated testing points and border crossing points in the region. This certificate, that was recognised in the EAC, was expected to be valid for 14 days and allowed the holder to travel in the region without being subjected to re-testing unless he or she was found to show symptoms of the virus on screening at checkpoints using the screening tool.[11]
- Financial innovations: In response to the pandemic, Nigerian consumers migrated to digital transactions for their financial services, and most consumers surveyed said that they expected to increase their use of digital and mobile banking services post-crisis.[12] The banking sector also saw a significant rise in agent banking, which is dramatically opened up the unbanked and underbanked segments. Agent transactions surged by 859% between March and April 2020, with agents being able to provide money – including government aid – and perform various transactions (Kola-Oyeneyin et al., 2020).
- Business model innovations: Many businesses were forced to re-invent their business models in the wake of disruptions. Some examples included:

---

10 https://www.capitalfm.co.ke/business/2020/04/centum-subsidiary-develops-zero-contact-covid-19-food-distribution-app/
11 https://eac.int/press-releases/147-health/1736-eac-partner-states-adopt-the-eac-regional-electronic-cargo-and-drivers-tracking-system
12 This situation may change; following intense lobbying, the central bank has set the capital requirements for payment banks very high, which may slow the pace of progress in financial inclusion.

- In South Africa, Bottles, which had traditionally been an online platform operating in the sale and distribution of alcohol, could no longer operate due to government restrictions on liquor trade and entered into an agreement with retailer Pick n Pay to leverage its last-mile delivery network to deliver essential groceries to consumers during lockdown (Johnson et al., 2020).
- In Nigeria, e-commerce and payments startup Jumia partnered with vendors to use its ePayment and last-mile delivery capabilities to offer contactless delivery of food and other necessities to all areas, including remote and rural locations (Johnson et al., 2020).
- GetBoda, a logistics/courier platform, reported a 150% increase in demand for delivery services during one week in April 2020, which they expected to rise further (Johnson et al., 2020). Indeed, the motorcycle delivery man was a key part of the supply chain as home deliveries increased, and continues to do so post-pandemic.

The success of the above innovations can be attributed to the old adages that necessity is the mother of invention on the one hand, and opportunity meets preparedness on the other. Confronted by closure and lockdown, businesses were forced to think of new business models, and these innovations were ready to meet new demands. In addition, some governments provided requisite support accordingly. In Kenya, for instance, the government put up a COVID-19 ICT advisory committee and equipped it to fund ICT innovations to mitigate the effects of the pandemic (Abuya, 2020). Arguably, the policy support and ability of the technologies to adapt to the pandemic can be attributed to the notable success, which is important for progressive policies and regulations as well as potential scaling up towards sustainability.

The potential of new deeper innovations building on the new business models which emerged in the wake of the pandemic was also huge, as shown by a study by the Maastricht School of Management (MSM). Examples cited by the study include:

- Peer-to-Peer Humanitarian Aid in Ethiopia, a local home to home (peer-to-peer) food supplier that has emerged during the closure period. This approach can be further leveraged using technology developed to create peer-to-peer food supply programmes (MSM, 2020b).
- Rethinking School Feeding and Tying to Online learning: The School feeding programme had important social support tools and stimulus packages. This called for a rethinking of innovative ways of ensuring a sustained delivery of the support (MSM, 2020a).

The impact of innovations was, however, mixed. The impact of the pandemic on the informal economy was mixed, as was experienced through food distribution systems. In some sectors, especially in prepared foods value chains, innovation in new business models saw greater integration of the informal sector to the formal sector. For example, increased online orders have seen the motorcycle become the key last-mile connector. This type of business increased considerably. On the other hand, some pandemic-driven innovations saw the removal of some informal players from the fresh foods value chain. For example, in Kenya, one development of note was the collaboration between Twiga Foods, which distributes foods for many small farmers (17,000) directly to informal food retailers (mama mboga), and Jumia, which is the biggest e-commerce platform in Africa. Under the arrangement, Jumia sold bundles of Twiga's fresh produce on its e-commerce website. Jumia's delivery fleet picked up orders from Twiga's sorting and distribution centres and then completed last mile, contactless delivery.[13] This innovation essentially cut out the 'mama mboga', the retailer, and thus her livelihood.

This implies that policy interventions are needed, and this will vary across value chains if the benefits of innovation are to be distributed more widely. UNIDO (2020) proposes a proactive intervention utilising 4IR technologies in several areas, notably for institutional transformation; strengthening innovation clusters and ecosystems; upgrading the capacities of medium and small-medium enterprises (MSMEs); technology upskilling and learning; enhancing investment promotion agencies; and fortifying quality infrastructure in order to boost business resilience and competitiveness; as well as fostering smart production and effective partnerships.

Leveraging 4IR to leapfrog: Exploring the potential

Freeman and Perez (1988) argue that if society and economies could adapt gradually and easily to the new products and means of transport and communication associated with a technological revolution, the whole process could be described simply as normal 'progress' and technological change could be treated as an exogenous variable. They provide evidence that such changes are far from smooth as societies are profoundly shaken and shaped by each technological revolution, and, in turn, their technological

---

13   https://techcrunch.com/2020/04/28/goldman-backed-ventures-jumia-and-twiga-partner-on-produce-in-kenya/

potential is shaped and steered as a result of intense social, political and ideological confrontations and compromises. As such, a technological revolution ushers in a new economic and social order depending on the intensity of the confrontations and compromises reached. More developed, stable economies might experience disruption, while relatively less developed economies that make the necessary investments in skills and the new infrastructure might actually get a chance to leapfrog to a new order.

The proposition being made in the last section is that 4IR may have to be considered differently from the perspective of Africa. In addition, the idea that this may provide a window of opportunity for Africa to catch up needs to be put into focus. This requires thinking about how to both mitigate the negative impacts and take advantage of the opportunities of 4IR, as well as to assess these in a context-specific manner. The pandemic opened new perspectives on the application of 4IR, and potential paradigm shifts. Potential pathways to leapfrogging are discussed below.

Infrastructure provision

The internet is a key enabler of the 4IR, especially for Africa. Banga and te Velde (2018) find that a doubling of the internet penetration rate increases labour productivity by about 11% on average, underscoring the crucial role of infrastructure. However, internet penetration growth has been tepid overall, and Africa lags behind other regions. In addition to suffering lower access to the internet, African countries also suffer from poorer performance, with average download and upload speeds significantly lower than in Asian economies. African internet users also face longer delays in processing network data and pay much higher prices relative to their incomes (Banga and te Velde, 2018).

Debatably, there is an opportunity for Africa to change this. The mobile cellular phone probably gives the best illustration for leapfrogging where many countries leapfrogged the fixed landline infrastructure and went straight to mobile phones. Furthermore, leapfrogging is happening in African countries as mobile phones have become the dominant means of accessing the internet (Ngunjiri, 2018).

The leading e-commerce platform in Africa, Jumia, has an increasing share of its sales coming from the mobile platforms. Some 70% of Nigerian buyers use mobile platforms, while 60% of buyers in Kenya and Egypt also buy using mobile platforms (Kariuki, 2018).

Figure 1: Proportion of internet traffic coming from mobile telecommunications platforms

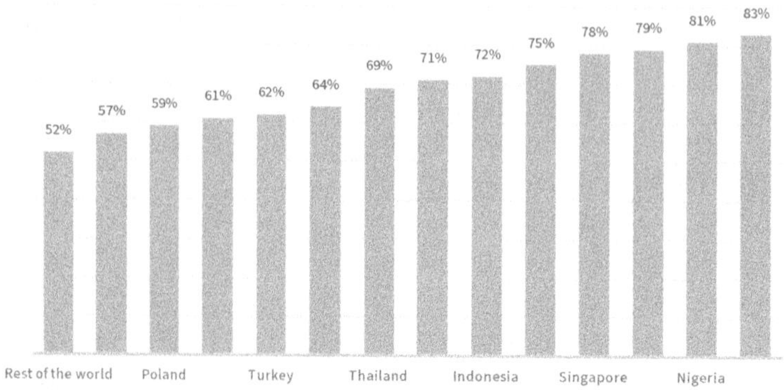

Rest of the world	Poland		Turkey		Thailand	Indonesia		Singapore		Nigeria
52%	57%	59%	61%	62%	64%	69%	71%	72%	75%	78% 79% 81% 83%

Source: Ngunjiri (2018).

Financial inclusion

Africa has a huge proportion of people who are not included in the banking system, a consequence of the informal nature of the economies. For example, Global Findex data show that as of 2017, 60% of Nigeria's population remained unbanked, yet Nigeria is the biggest economy in Africa.

4IR has the potential to bank many of the unbanked through financial technology (fintech) innovation, especially mobile money. The exemplar of this is the M-Pesa platform in Kenya. In this regard, fintech has provided another opportunity to leapfrog. Mobile banking works to support the further development of the digital platform economy as transactions through a digital platform require access to a bank or a non-bank mobile money service.

While lagging behind China,14 African countries, and especially Nigeria and Kenya, have emerged as fintech hotbeds. Nigeria is now home to over 200 fintech standalone companies, and between 2014 and 2019, Nigeria's fintech sector raised more than USD 600 million in funding, attracting 25% (USD 122 million) of the USD 491.6 million raised by African tech start-ups in 2019 alone, second only to Kenya, which attracted USD 149 million (Kola-Oyeneyin et al., 2020). The key to the success of fintech innovation in Africa is using inexpensive, accessible tech to mobilise consumers in ways never seen before (Chitavi et al., 2018). Today the M-Pesa platform has

---

14 In 2018, China's USD 25.5 billion fintech market accounted for 46% of all fintech investments globally, making it the largest such market in the world (Chitavi et al., 2018).

110,000 agents spread throughout the country, ensuring anyone can access e-money. Banks are also innovating to fend off competition from mobile phone companies. In Kenya, Equitel, owned by Equity Bank, is pushing boundaries for financial inclusion even further by offering a full suite of banking services on mobile devices. Equitel is a new type of hybrid firm: a telecommunications company born of a bank. The impact of the innovation has been immense. While financial inclusion in Kenya was at just 26% in 2006, this has risen to 83% of the population (Chitavi et al., 2018). Many countries in Africa are following Kenya's model, and this is promoting a rapid rise in financial inclusion.

Technology innovation is, however, only one requirement. Countries need to change laws on banking, and social adjustments are also needed to make mobile banking work. A strong preference for cash can hinder the adoption of mobile money.[15] The explosive growth of mobile money in Kenya and in other East African countries, including Tanzania and Rwanda, points to the importance of having a supportive regulatory environment. On the other hand, growth sputtered in Nigeria, where, until recently, mobile network operators (MNOs) were prohibited by law from issuing mobile money (Evans and Pirchio, 2015).[16]

The rise of indigenous platforms

Although global platforms like Uber and Airbnb have already settled in Africa, a rapidly growing and vibrant indigenous platform economy is growing alongside and with huge potential to foster inclusive growth based on local entrepreneurship. One such example is the Lynk platform (www.lynk.co.ke) which connects households and businesses with verified domestic workers, artisans and blue-collar professionals in Nairobi. As of September 2018, the platform had successfully 'Lynked' 20,000 jobs. The insight2impact facility in South Africa has been tracking the number of platforms in Africa. They identify 365 platforms, of which 301 are indigenous platforms.[17] Kenya's digital entrepreneurship ecosystem has spawned a large number of digital startups providing services to agriculture ranging from information on market pricing, finance, data analytics and connections along the value

---

15 See GMSA (2019), which identifies the preference for cash as being one of the main reasons that mobile money has not been adopted in Senegal and Mozambique.
16 Regulatory reform in Nigeria in 2018 allowed non-financial companies, including MNOs such as MTN, to issue e-money. However, the decision in 2020 to raise the minimum capital base requirements to USD 13 million has hindered the development of mobile money service providers. See: https://weetracker.com/2020/09/01/nigeria-mobile-money-license/
17 See: http://researchictafrica.net/wp/wp-content/uploads/2018/12/DInfo_V11.pdf

chain (World Bank, 2019b). Johnson et al. (2020) estimate that in 2018, indigenous digital platforms created income-generating opportunities to 4.8 million workers across seven African countries. However, many of the workers lack social protection, underscoring the need to further build these platforms beyond being just places for jobs and adding other services.

Despite the potential of leveraging 4IR for leapfrogging, the impact of 4IR will hinge significantly on the readiness of countries. Readiness may be considered in relation to four key pillars: infrastructure, skills, innovation systems and regulatory capacity. Recent studies suggest that Africa is quite unprepared in all four pillars, which is a matter of grave concern (ACET, 2018). The education systems are not able to provide the needed skills, the internet infrastructure is generally poor and expensive to access, the innovation systems are still nascent, and the regulatory capacity is weak (ACET, 2018). Significant work is needed to improve readiness. ACET (2018) pointed to the following actions:

- *Policies to improve infrastructure*: Incentives for private sector investment in infrastructure, especially for the rollout of 4G and 5G networks. Public investment, especially in key backbone infrastructure such as transport and energy in remote areas.
- *Policies to improve education systems*: The focus on lower education should be to learn good foundational skills and Technical and Vocational Education and Training (TVET) skills. Upper secondary should focus on increasing the uptake of science, technology, engineering and mathematics (STEM) skills. Life-long learning to ensure worker skills match the needs of a rapidly changing labour market. Policies should focus on market failure, for instance, limited information on potential returns to investing in skills and imperfections in credit markets.
- *Policies to improve innovation systems*: Investment by government in science and technology parks (for instance, Kigali Innovation City). Strengthening the institutional frameworks for innovation by ensuring all elements are there.
- *Policies to improve regulatory capacity*: Adopting a sandbox environment that will allow experimentation with technologies before devising an appropriate regulatory regime is recommended. This requires a balance between fostering innovation and safeguarding the public interest. An example in Africa is the out-manoeuvring by ride-hailing companies and the government responses. In response to the Nigerian authorities banning smaller engine motorcycle taxis from

some cities, ride-hailing companies entered the market and invested heavily in larger engine motorcycles, only to see the government later ban any motorcycle (Odunsi, 2020). Uganda has also gone for regulatory overkill with the potential to kill a nascent motorcycle ride-hailing industry. The regulation seeks to classify the motorcycle riders as couriers, which carries a licence fee of USD 1,000 that is out of reach for many young motorcycle riders (Ojakol, 2020).

Discussion and recommendation

The process of revolutionary technological change provides a window for leapfrogging for Africa. The 4IR is already disrupting developed economies with fears of huge job losses and growing inequalities. The trend so far has been that those few who control the emerging high-tech platforms powered by 4IR capture the lion's share of the value created. Africa is not being spared either, as demonstrated in this chapter. Like mobile telephony, emerging 5G technologies promise to help Africa leapfrog yet again and bypass broadband technology, potentially contributing to levelling the playing field in terms of digital infrastructure.

Paradoxically, 4IR platforms, which have the potential to organise the informal sector at the same time, are breaking up the formal sectors in the developed countries and creating gig economies that are more akin to the character of economies in Africa. In this way, 4IR may be enabling a paradoxical type of convergence as the Western job landscape starts to look more like Africa.

As Africa attempts to leapfrog, however, there are clear dangers ahead. While a vibrant innovation system is emerging and creating applications that have the potential to contribute to solving many of the developmental challenges faced by countries on the continent, the weak capacity to execute and regulate, coupled with limited resources, means that the innovations emerging can be easily harvested by well-resourced and more experienced international venture capitalists. Furthermore, the new platforms emerging to organise the economies can easily morph into monopolies that can be very adept at evading regulations while capturing much of the value created.

The fact that the 4IR provides a window to leapfrog does not necessarily mean that the opportunity will automatically yield the expected benefits. The rapidly increased shift to digital transformation as a result of the pandemic has had both positive and negative impacts on social inclusion. The areas of concern include: widened financial and digital gap, security, data privacy, market monopolisation, transparency and predatory lending

(Benni, 2021). In addition, the first-mover advantages mean that network effects can give one big player an unassailable lead. For example, the M-Pesa platform has given Safaricom a dominant position in mobile money transfer in Kenya. This has been parlayed into other businesses, making Safaricom a key player in many sectors where apps are being developed to digitise services, including banking, agriculture and media. The potential to abuse this monopoly is huge. Governments should look into how digital money could be leveraged to foster integration and interoperability of payment systems (Davidovic et al., 2020). There may also be a possibility to impose fines, although these may seem insignificant given that many of the tech companies have accumulated huge reserves of cash with which they can easily pay. This underscores the challenge of indiscriminate regulation. Considering that the 4IR and digital tech multinationals are global in nature, governments may consider regional or international cooperation, which may help in addressing some of the regulatory challenges.[18]

Beyond the ability to regulate, African countries need to develop stronger innovation systems that can enable the development of platforms to solve the many pressing development challenges they are faced with (Adesida et al., n.d.). Already Africa has begun to form the basis for potentially robust innovation systems with over 442 active technology hubs in Africa and more than $1 billion in venture capital investment on the continent (Bright, 2017). Thus, there is ample potential for the emergence of many innovations that could build versatile platforms to support leapfrogging ambitions. While inventiveness is key, innovation resulting in impact depends on execution and marketing. The success of Silicon Valley firms is partly due to their huge marketing budgets and ability to execute. International venture capitalists are behind many of the innovations happening in Africa. In fact, it has been pointed out that the motivation behind their support is really to harvest ideas and take the best out of Africa to Silicon Valley or elsewhere for upscaling and execution (ACET, 2018). Thus, the innovations for leapfrogging may not be owned by African entities, and indeed even the most celebrated innovator, M-Pesa, is owned by Vodafone, a UK company. There is a clear and real potential for emerging digital platform enterprises to fall under the ownership of international investors, creating new forms of extraction from the continent with limited local benefits.

---

18 https://ettg.eu/2020/10/26/strengthening-the-digital-partnership-between-africa-and-europe/; https://ettg.eu/wp-content/uploads/2020/10/ETTG-Publication-Strengthening-the-digital-partnership-between-Africa-and-Europe.pdf

While we may celebrate the innovative, upgrading and upskilling potential of the informal sector, there is potential for one or a few international investors to control significant sections of the informal sector and essentially extract all of the value created. This is further enabled by an international political economy that increasingly requires the opening up of all sectors, including services, and an international dispute regime that tends to favour international investors over countries (Viñuales, 2015).

The emergence of 4IR platforms raises the risk that significant sectors of developing economies are controlled by international investors with little domestic leverage over their development. The key mitigating factor here is that there are also indigenous platforms that can counter the monopolistic tendencies of well-resourced global platforms. While it is unlikely that indigenous firms will have the marketing resources of Silicon Valley platforms, they have contextual knowledge, and their sheer number shows that entrepreneurial spirit is thriving.

The big challenge for Africa is how to strike a balance so that regulation nurtures innovations and ushers new business models while also ensuring that there is a level of self-determination and equity in the value captured. Russo and Stasi (2016) argue for the need to define the markets covered by the share economy platforms and their relationship to existing markets in order to effectively regulate their new services within current legislative frameworks. They argue that where network effects play a key role, competition law becomes particularly pertinent. However, this does not make it easier because definitions are fluid. For example, is Uber a technology company or a taxi company? Uber has effectively argued that it is a technology company and thus not subject to the regulations that apply to taxi companies. There are no easy answers on how to manage this.

In conclusion, the 4IR is far from being a single story – it may truly be a case of different strokes for different folks.

References

Abuya, K. (2020, 22 July). COVID-19 ICT Advisory Committee invites innovations that address the effects of the pandemic. *Techweez*. https://techweez.com/2020/07/22/covid-19-advisory-committee-invitations/

ACET. (2018). *The Future of Work in Africa: The impact of the fourth industrial revolution on job creation and skill development in Africa; Report for Africa Development Bank (AfDB)*. African Centre for Economic Transformation (ACET).

Adesida, O., Karuri-Sebina, G., and Resende-Santos, J. (Eds). (2016). *Innovation Africa: Emerging hubs of excellence*. Emerald.

Adesida, O., Karuri-Sebina, G., and Thaver, K. (n.d.). Strengthening innovation ecosystems in Africa: Harnessing old and new lessons in the wake of COVID-19.

AfDB. (2013). *At the Centre of Africa's Transformation: Strategy for 2013-2022*. African Development Bank Group.

Arntz, M., Gregory, T., and Zierahn, U. (2016). The risk of automation for jobs in OECD countries: A comparative analysis. *OECD Social, Employment, and Migration Working Papers*, no. 189.

African Union (AU). (2020). *The Digital Transformation Strategy for Africa 2020-2030*. The African Union.

Autor, D. H. (2015). Why are there still so many jobs? The history and future of workplace automation. *Journal of Economic Perspectives*, 29(3), 3-30.

Autor, D. H., Levy, F., and Murnane, R. J. (2003). The skill content of recent technological change: An empirical exploration. *The Quarterly Journal of Economics*, 118(4), 1279-1333.

Autor, D., and Salomons, A. (2017). Does productivity growth threaten employment? *Working paper prepared for ECB Forum on Central Banking*, June.

Banga, K., and te Velde, D. W. (2018). Digitalisation and the future of manufacturing in Africa. Draft report, February. ODI SET Programme.

BBC (2012, 28 February). Cryptocurrencies: Why Nigeria is a global leader in Bitcoin trade. https://www.bbc.com/news/world-africa-56169917

Benjamin, N., and Mbaye, A. A. (2014). Informality, growth, and development in Africa. WIDER Working Paper 2014/052. UNU-WIDER.

Benni, N. (2021). *Digital Finance and Inclusion in the Time of COVID-19: Lessons, experiences and proposals*. FAO. DOI: 10.4060/cb2109en.

Bright, J. (2016, 5 May). A brief overview of Africa's tech industry and 7 predictions for its future. *World Economic Forum*. https://www.weforum.org/agenda/2016/05/a-brief-history-of-africa-s-tech-industry-and-7-predictions-for-its-future/

Brynjolfsson, E., and McAfee, A. (2014). *The Second Machine Age: Work, progress, and prosperity in a time of brilliant technologies*. W. W. Norton.

Chandy, L. (2017). *The Future of Work in the Developing World*. Brookings Institution. https://www.brookings.edu/research/the-future-of-work-in-the-developing-world/

Chitavi, M., Cohen, L., and Hagist, S. C. N. (2018, February). Kenya is becoming a global hub of fintech innovation. *Harvard Business Review*.

Davidovic, S., Prady, D., and Tourpe, H. (2020). You've got money: Mobile payments help people during the pandemic. IMF Blog. https://blogs.imf.org/2020/06/22youve-got-money-mobile-payments-help-people-during-the-pandemic/

Eurostat. (2020). *Statistics Explained: Covid-19 labour effects across the income distribution*. https://ec.europa.eu/eurostat/statistics-explained/index.php?title=Covid-19_labour_effects_across_the_income_distribution#A_EU_level_overview

Evans, D. S., and Pirchio, A. (2015). An empirical examination of why mobile money schemes ignite in some developing countries but flounder in most. *Review of Network Economics*, 13(4), 397-451. DOI: 10.1515/rne-2015-0020.

Freeman, C., and Pérez, C. (1988). Structural crises of adjustment: Business cycles and investment behaviour. In: G. Dosi, C. Freeman, R. Nelson, G. Silverberg and L. Soete (Eds), *Technical Change and Economic Theory* (3rd edn). Pinter.

Frey, C., and Osborne, M. (2013). *The Future of Employment: How susceptible are jobs to computerisation?* Oxford Martin School Programme on the Impacts of Future Technology.

Gatune, J. (2018). The 4th Industrial Revolution and future of work. *Working Paper.* African Centre for Economic Transformation.

Ghosh, I. (2020, 15 May). Zoom is now worth more than the world's 7 biggest airlines. *Visual Capitalist.* https://www.visualcapitalist.com/zoom-boom-biggest-airlines/

Gillespie, P. (2017). Intuit: Gig economy is 34% of US workforce. *CNN Money.* http://money.cnn.com/2017/05/24/news/economy/gig-economy-intuit/

GMSA. (2020). *State of the Industry Report on Mobile Money 2019.* GSM Association.

Goos, M., and Manning, A. (2007). Lousy and lovely jobs: The rising polarization of work in Britain. *Review of Economics and Statistics,* 89(1), 118-133.

Graetz, G., and Michaels, G. (2018). Robots at work. *Review of Economics and Statistics,* 100(5), 753-768.

Hallward-Driemeier, M., and Nayyar, G. (2017). *Trouble in the Making? The future of manufacturing-led development.* World Bank.

Hatzakis, E. D. (2016). *The Fourth Industrial Revolution.* CIO Reports. Merrill Lynch.

IRENA. (2019). *Innovation Landscape Brief: Artificial intelligence and big data.* International Renewable Energy Agency.

Johnson, C., Dunn, M., and Van Vuuren P. J. (2020). Digital platforms' role in African digitisation and gig work on the back of Covid-19. *FinMark Trust.* https://finmark.org.za/knowledge-hub/blog/digital-platforms-role-in-african-digitisation-and-gig-work-on-the-back-of-covid-19

Juma, C. (2016). *Innovation and its Enemies: Why people resist new technologies.* Oxford University Press.

Kariuki, J. (2018, 20 March). Drones firm in plea to reduce fees for would be owners. *Business Daily.* https://www.businessdailyafrica.com/corporate/tech/Drones-firm-in-plea-to-reduce-fees-for-would/4258474-4349910-35uwp8/index.html

Kola-Oyeneyin, E., Kuyoro, M., and Olanrewaju, T. (2020). *Harnessing Nigeria's Fintech Potential.* McKinsey & Company. https://www.mckinsey.com/featured-insights/middle-east-and-africa/harnessing-nigerias-fintech-potentiale

Lima, G. (1996). Development, technological change and innovation: Schumpeter and the neo-Schumpeterians. *Revista Brasiliera de Economia,* 50(2), 179-204.

Lorenz, E., and Kraemer-Mbula, E. (2020). The impacts of adopting 4IR-related technologies on employment and skills: The case of the automotive and mining equipment manufacturers in South Africa. In: Z. Mazibuko-Makena and E. Kraemer-Mbula (Eds), *Leap 4.A: African perspectives on the Fourth Industrial Revolution.* MISTRA.

Mann, K., and Püttmann, L. (2017). Benign effects of automation: New evidence from patent texts. *SSRN.* https://ssrn.com/abstract=2959584 or http://dx.doi.org/10.2139/ssrn.2959584

Marr, B. (2020, 21 December). What's been the impact of Covid-19 on the 4th Industrial Revolution? *Forbes*. https://www.forbes.com/sites/bernardmarr/2020/12/21/whats-been-the-impact-of-covid-19-on-the-4th-industrial-revolution/?sh=557f20615c0d

Medina, L., Jonelis, A., and Cangul, M. (2017). The informal economy in sub-Saharan Africa: Size and determinants. *IMF Working Paper*, WP/17/156. IMF.

McKinsey Global Institute (MGI). (2016). *The Age of Analytics: Competing in a data-driven world*. McKinsey Global Institute.

MGI. (2017a). *A Future that Works: Automation, employment, and productivity*. McKinsey Global Institute.

MGI. (2017b). *Jobs Lost, Jobs Gained: Workforce transitions in a time of automation*. McKinsey Global Institute.

Maastricht School of Management (MSM). (2020a, 20 May). Covid-19 updates: Food security initiative: Why do school closures have impact on food security? *MSM*. https://www.msm.nl/news-events-and-blogs/covid-19-updates/the-impact-of-school-closures-on-food-security

MSM. (2020b, 18 June). Covid-19 updates: Food security initiative: Emergency food flows. *MSM*. https://www.msm.nl/news-events-and-blogs/covid-19-updates/emergency-food-flows

Ngunjiri, J. (2018, 20 March). Kenya tops in phone internet traffic globally. *Business Daily*. https://www.businessdailyafrica.com/corporate/tech/Kenya-tops-in-phone-internet-traffic-/4258474-4349966-3m4lrez/index.html

Nordhaus, W. (2015). Are we approaching an economic singularity? *Information Technology and the Future of Economic Growth,* no. 2021. Cowles Foundation for Research in Economics, Yale University.

Odunsi, W. (2020, 12 August). Lagos regulations on Bolt, Uber, taxis effective August 20. *Daily Post*. https://dailypost.ng/2020/08/12/lagos-regulations-on-bolt-uber-taxis-effective-august-20-full-details/

Organisation for Economic Co-operation and Development (OECD). (2019). *Economic Outlook*. OECD Publishers.

Ojakol, I. A. (2020, 9 September). Why government should go slow on regulation of the gig economy. *Nile Post*.

Patel, M. (2018, 27 February). Fintech in Africa: Kenya. *Fintech Times*.

Pazzanese, C. (2020). How political ideas keep economic inequality going. *The Harvard Gazette*. https://news.harvard.edu/gazette/story/2020/03/pikettys-new-book-explores-how-economic-inequality-is-perpetuated/

Perez, C. (n.d.). The social shaping of technological revolutions. http://www.carlotaperez.org/downloads/pubs/PEREZ_TRFC_Ch%203.pdf

Prabhu, M. (2021, 26 February). COVAX vaccines take to the air by drone. *GAVI*. https://www.gavi.org/vaccineswork/covax-vaccines-take-air-drone

Pratap, S., and Quintin, E. (2006) The informal sector in developing countries: Output, assets and employment. *Research Paper* 2006/130. UNU-WIDER.

Reuters. (2020, 20 April). Ghana turns to drones to enable faster coronavirus testing. https://www.reuters.com/article/us-health-coronavirus-ghana-drones-idUSKBN2220H7

Rifkin, J. (2013). *The Third Industrial Revolution*. Palgrave Macmillan

Russo, F., and Stasi, M. L. (2016). Defining the relevant market in the sharing economy. *Internet Policy Review*, 5(2). DOI: 10.14763/2016.2.418.

Schmid, G., and Wagner, J. (2017). Managing social risks of non-standard employment in Europe. *ILO Working Paper: Conditions of Work and Employment Series*, 91.

Simbanegavi, W., Patel, A., Senbet, L. W., Mouelhi, R. B. A., Gatune, J., Amaoko, K. Y., Mutanga, S., Altenburg, T., Coulibaly, B., and Prakash, A. (2018). World of work in the 4th Industrial Revolution: Inclusive and structural transformation for a better Africa. *T20 Agentina Policy Brief*. African Institute of South Africa.

Soto-Acosta, P. (2020). COVID-19 pandemic: Shifting digital transformation to a high-speed gear. *Information Systems Management*, 37, 260-266.

Susskind, R., and Susskind, D. (2015). *The Future of Professions: How technology will transform the work of human experts*. Oxford University Press.

Sylvester, G. (Ed.). (2018). *E-Agriculture in Action: Drones for agriculture*. FAO & ITU. https://www.fao.org/3/I8494EN/i8494en.pdf

UNCTAD. (2017). Robots and inclusive growth. In: *Trade and Development Report*.

UNCTAD. (2021). *Technology and Innovation Report, Catching Technological Waves, Innovation with Equity*.

United Nations Industrial Development Organisation (UNIDO). (2019). *Industrial Development Report 2020. Industrializing in the digital age*. UNIDO.

UNIDO. (2020). *Covid-19 Implications and Responses: Digital transformation and industrial recovery*. United Nations Industrial Development Organisation (UNIDO).

Viñuales, J. E. (2015). Strengthening the global trade and investment system for sustainable development – International investment law and natural resource governance. E15 Expert Group on Trade and Investment in Extractive Industries. September. International Centre for Trade and Sustainable Development (ICTSD). http://e15initiative.org/wp-content/uploads/2015/07/Extractive-Vinuales-FINAL1.pdf

Wallach, O. (2021, 3 March). Which streaming service has the most subscriptions? *Visual Capitalist*. https://www.visualcapitalist.com/which-streaming-service-has-the-most-subscriptions/

World Economic Forum (WEF). (2016). *Mastering the Fourth Industrial Revolution*. Annual Meeting 2016 Davos-Klosters, Switzerland 20-23 January.

WEF. (2017, May). *The Future of Jobs and Skills in Africa: Preparing the region for the Fourth Industrial Revolution*. World Economic Forum.

WHO. (2020, 31 July). Robots use in Rwanda to fight against Covid-19. https://www.afro.who.int/news/robots-use-rwanda-fight-against-covid-19

World Bank. (2016). *Digital Dividends, World Bank Development Report*.World Bank.

World Bank. (2019a). *The Changing Nature of Work, World Bank Development Report*. World Bank.

World Bank. (2019b). Securing future growth, policies to Kenya's digital transformation. *Economic Update*, no. 20. World Bank.

Appendices

Appendix A: Fourth Industrial Revolution (4IR) technologies definitions

Technology	Definition
Cloud computing	This is a computing business model where users buy computing services (including processing power, storage, and applications) rather than owning the infrastructure. The cloud services providers develop the infrastructure and offer the services. The key advantage of this model is that firms can avoid the upfront cost and complexity of owning and maintaining their own infrastructure. In turn, providers of cloud computing services can benefit from significant economies of scale by delivering the same services to a wide range of customers.
Machine learning/AI and robotics	This is the aspect of technology that perhaps most defines the 4IR. AI is enabling machines to be trained to undertake tasks that previously were the domain of humans. Much like humans, machines are now being enabled to learn and adapt, thus increasing their capability. Significant milestones in this area include the first computer to beat a human in the game of Go, an abstract strategy board game. More recently, a machine has outperformed a human expert at lip-reading. Autonomous (self-driving cars) are also being piloted.
Internet of things (IoT)	Computing and communication power are increasingly being embedded in all kinds of hardware and devices, including white goods such as washing machines and refrigerators. As more and more of these devices are linked together, they form what is now known as the 'Internet of Things' (IoT) – a giant network of connected 'things' (which also includes people). The IoT allows for virtually endless opportunities and connections to take place, many of which cannot be fathomed or fully understood yet. Rwanda, for example, has deployed drones (autonomous aerial vehicles) to deliver blood.
Data mining technologies /Data science	The proliferation of mobile devices, online sensors, and other means of collecting information digitally is a key driver of 4IR. The capture of vast amounts of data, when combined with powerful computing capabilities and AI algorithms, generate unprecedented amounts of insights. New businesses are emerging from these digital platforms and disrupting established industries. Shared economy apps (such as Uber, a shared taxi service) and supply and demand matching services (such as Airbnb, an accommodation rental facilitation service) allow for instant interaction, information exchange, and closer and broader collaboration.
3D Printing	3D printing refers to a manufacturing process which additively builds or forms 3D parts in layers from Computer-Aided Design (CAD) data, and the design is printed in a printer. The technology is significant because it offers direct manufacturing, meaning a design goes directly from the designer to the physical product. Other advantages are: the digital design can be tweaked with a few mouse clicks; the 3D printer can run unattended; and the printer can make many things that are too complex for a traditional factory to handle. Thus 3D printing combines the customisation of the cottage industry and also cost efficiencies that can beat the mass-production model. This technology is changing the manufacturing landscape, and as costs fall and technology improves, this technology will completely disrupt the manufacturing industry.
Blockchain	As new technologies connect disparate peoples and disrupt existing models, trust systems developed over a long period of time are being eroded. Specifically, the blockchain lets people who may have no confidence in each other collaborate without having to go through a neutral central authority. Blockchain is an open, distributed ledger that can record transactions between two parties efficiently and in a verifiable and permanent way. As a result, intermediaries such as lawyers, brokers, bankers and even government bureaucracies may no longer be necessary. Simply put, it is a machine for creating trust. More crucially, blockchain technologies can cut the time of transactions drastically, from weeks or months to days, hours, or minutes. With blockchain-based sources of influence and control emerging, economies are poised to undergo a radical shift.
5G	The fifth generation of cellular data technology. It succeeds 4G and related technologies. The benefits of 5G include faster speeds, low latency (the time to establish a connection), and greater capacity. The theoretical maximum data transfer rate of 5G is 20 Gbps (2.5 gigabytes per second). That is 20x faster than LTE-Advanced, which has a peak download speed of 1,000 Mbps. 5G latency is estimated to be 10 to 20 milliseconds, compared to 4G's average latency of 40 milliseconds. The maximum traffic capacity of 5G is roughly 100x greater than a typical 4G network.

Appendix B: Potential applications of 4IR in driving transformation

Transformation strategy	4IR technology					
	AI/machine learning	Internet of things (IoT)	Big data/Data science	3D printing	Blockchain technologies	Net impact on competitiveness
Agricultural transformation	• Application in breeding to speed varietal selection • Intelligent robots are reducing inputs applications by over 90%	• Use of drones for crop monitoring • Internet-enabled irrigation systems	• Telephone farming • E-extension • Inputs-as-service business models • Big Data for credit scoring	• Locally fabricated agricultural machines	• Food traceability system for international trade	• Very high • Agriculture has potentially many entry points and few downsides in terms of job losses
Modernised services	• Driverless cars will kill jobs in transportation • Potentially very many applications, e.g. credit scoring using non-standard data	• M-Kopa selling solar power as utility/service through internet-enabled cookers and solar panels	• Shared economy e.g. Airbnb • Financial inclusion e.g. Micro-insurance • E-commerce e.g. Jumia, iRoko	• Toll/contract manufacturing • Community workshops	• Numerous trust-based applications (land registries, contracting) • Crypto-currency based transactions	• Very high • This sector is already very dynamic. An e-commerce company, M-Pesa, valued at $1 billion, is the biggest money transfer service in the world
Local content	• Potential for development of sophisticated machine-learning algorithms for interpretation and/or exploration data	• Drone-based services, e.g. facilities inspection, mapping etc.	• Geological data mining may create new opportunities	• Locally manufactured parts • Scope for small scale, flexible production		• High to Moderate • Much potential here but will require much support to build new capability, especially in AI, data science and 3D printing
Export-led manufacturing	• Advanced robots will kill cheap labour advantage		• Will enable fine-grained market segmentation and kill mass markets	• Will kill the factory manufacturing model		• Very low • This will not be a viable strategy in the 4IR world
Infrastructure	• Smart metering and smart grid technologies	• Alternative infrastructure e.g. drones	• Smart cities and other tools to help optimise infrastructure	• On site manufacture of parts		
Creative industries	• New tools		• Platforms for distribution	• Ability to convert designs to products		• Very high • Products highly amenable to digitalisation
Tourism	• New tools to showcase e.g. virtual reality		• Better targeting of marketing efforts • New platforms e.g. Airbnb expanding potential tourist pool			• High • 4IR can help create new experiences and improve service delivery
Overall impact of 4IR technology	• Will kill traditional paths to industrialisation		• The most dynamic of 4IR technology for Africa • Potential to create many jobs	• Presents great opportunity for leapfrogging into manufacturing	• Potential to formalise the huge informal sector	

Sources: Compiled by authors from different sources (ACET, 2018; OECD Economic Outlook, 2019, Ch. 2; World Bank, 2016; 2019a; MGI, 2016; 2017a; 2017b; UNCTAD, 2017; 2021; Hallward-Driemeier and Nayyar, 2017).

CHAPTER 11

Sustainable Development Finance and Investments

Theoretical and policy implications for Africa

Jacob Park

Introduction: Framing the problem

Kafue National Park[1] in Zambia might be a good starting point to understand how Africa and the issues of the pandemic and sustainable development intersected in the year 2021. As one of the largest protected areas in Africa, Kafue National Park is a collection of rivers, woodlands, teak forests and open plains, home to hundreds of rare bird species and mammals, including lions, cheetahs and leopards. Despite such problems as poaching, habitat fragmentation and the loss of connectivity to other nearby ecosystems, wildlife tourism efforts in recent years have encouraged the local communities around the national park to see animals as an economic asset rather than as a threat to their well-being, while philanthropic grants from the US and Europe

---

1 Kafue National Park, https://www.zambiatourism.com/destinations/national-parks/kafue-national-park

provided funding to protect conservation zones. When the pandemic reached Zambia, however, the economic impact was immediate. The tourist economy just vanished overnight, and poachers were able to enter the Kafue National Park without worrying about detection. Bushmeat poaching problems exploded within Kafue's conservation zones, with the amount of bushmeat seized by rangers increasing from about 100 pounds (45 kg) in 2019 to more than 3,300 pounds (1,497 kg) in 2020 (Nuwer, 2020).

The global tourism sector accounts for more than USD 8 trillion worldwide and about 10% of the global jobs, while wildlife tourism generates more than USD 29 billion and employs 3.6 million people in the case of Africa. With the advent of the pandemic, it was estimated that 90% of African tour operators experienced a 75% or greater decline in their bookings, and some experienced almost a 100% drop in their revenue (Lindsey et al., 2020). Beyond the economic impact on local communities and the budgets of national governments, such a dramatic decline in tourism revenue poses a critical threat to Africa's conservation and environmental sustainability efforts since tourism revenue, along with donations and development aid, account for nearly all the funding resources for the continent's 7,800 terrestrial protected areas. Even before the pandemic crisis, tourism revenue and development aid did not adequately finance the conservation needs of African parks and reserves, with 90% of the nearly 300 protected savannah ecosystems in Africa facing a collective deficit of at least USD 1 billion and representing more or less 'paper parks' or areas designated for conservation in name only (Lindsey et al., 2018).

Wildlife tourism represents an important economic sector for many African countries, but it is not the only African industry that has been negatively impacted by the pandemic. According to the UN Initiative on Financing for Development in the Era of COVID-19 and Beyond (2020), as the result of the global pandemic crisis, the world's gross domestic product was estimated to decline by 4.9%, 40% in foreign direct investment, and 20% in remittances respectively in 2020, and as a result, African governments were likely to confront a short-term financing gap of at least USD 44 billion that year (Selassie, 2020). Looking beyond the short-term economy and at the sustainable development goals (SDG) financing gap within the context of sub-Saharan Africa, the region's annual additional spending requirements are estimated to amount to 24% of the continent's GDP or about USD 420 billion.[2] What

---

2   According to UN (2014), the pre-pandemic annualised global SDG financing gap was estimated to be USD 2.5 trillion.

makes this financing gap such an economic challenge for many African countries is that over 20 of the 54 African countries are in or at high risk of debt distress (Gaspar et al., 2019).

Although more than a third of the required financing for African SDG needs was expected to come from the private sector, the actual contributions from the private sector have so far been significantly smaller, at only 4–8% (Brookings Institution, 2020a). The task African countries face in trying to strike a balance between their short-term governmental budgetary needs along with their long-term SDG funding priorities proved even more challenging amidst a global pandemic. This chapter explores new and emerging models of SDG investment and finance and then examines how these models might be applicable to the African context. By reviewing the academic literature and analysing three mini case studies, the following two questions are examined:

> *1. What types of policy and business mechanisms can most effectively catalyse and accelerate the financing, particularly private sector-support, of SDG priorities?*

There is a key emphasis in this chapter on the concept of 'blended finance', which can be defined as 'catalytic capital from public or philanthropic sources to increase private sector investment in sustainable development' (Convergence, 2020). According to the OECD, blended finance is the 'strategic use of development finance for the mobilisation of additional finance towards sustainable development in developing countries' by mobilising 'commercial capital towards projects that contribute to sustainable development, while providing financial returns to investors'.[3] Blended finance encompasses a range of approaches that mix private and public sources to achieve a specific social and environmental impact (e.g. development impact bonds) while achieving market returns for investors and risk mitigation for investments in developing countries.

> *2. Which financial mechanisms have the best potential for Africa in terms of applicability and suitability?*

Goal 17 of the United Nations Sustainable Development Goals (SDGs) states that 'a successful sustainable development agenda requires partnerships

---

3   See OECD: https://www.oecd.org/dac/financing-sustainable-development/blended-finance-principles/

between governments, the private sector and civil society'. This chapter examines how Africa as a region can best utilise blended finance mechanisms to 'mobilize, redirect and unlock the transformative power of trillions of dollars of private resources to deliver on sustainable development objectives' (UN 2017) as well as to serve potentially as market-based financial solutions to the health crisis resulting from the pandemic.

Background

Theory and practice of finance, innovation and market development

The global capital market, which consists of USD 95 trillion in equities and USD 105 trillion in fixed income or bonds, among others, is one of, if not the largest economic sectors in the world (SIFMA, 2020). While modern financial instruments such as mortgage-backed securities, pension funds and mutual funds can be traced back to 18th-century Netherlands (Rouwenhorst, 2016), the actual theoretical framework of finance and innovation did not materialise until Joseph Schumpeter placed finance at the centre of his theory of innovation in 1939. Modigliani and Miller elaborated on the relationship between finance and innovation in 1959, while Hall and Lerner (2009) highlighted the roles of the public governmental sector and private venture capital markets in fostering innovation (Mazzucato and Semieniuk, 2018).

Recent literature on finance, innovation and market development has a more explicit focus on social norms and community development. According to Flora and Flora (1993), the finance, innovation and market development nexus contains three important community dimensions: (1) symbolic diversity, that is, to the degree that community-level orientation turns toward inclusiveness; (2) resource mobilisation, that is, communities need to localise their resources (e.g. local food production); and (3) quality of linkages (particularly information) in formal and informal community networks. Sharp and Flora (1999) and Fortunato and Clevenger (2017) argue that community embeddedness and collective action play an important role in economic development, while Klinenberg (2018) underscores the importance of 'social infrastructure', which he defines as the physical spaces and organisations that shape the way people interact (e.g. libraries, playgrounds, churches, cafés, community gardens), in building community social capital and economic development.

Given the centrality of the role the financial market plays in business sustainability, there has also been active academic scholarship on the role the financial market plays in both undermining and enhancing sustainable business practices. Pressure from financial markets can undermine business sustainability efforts (Bansal and DesJardine, 2014) by shrinking the investment horizons of managers (DesJardine and Bansal, 2019) and discouraging firms from investing in long-term corporate social responsibility practices (David et al., 2007). However, the rapid increase in capital flows into sustainable investing on the global level has led to the exploration of how investment firms integrate environmental, social, governance (ESG) data (Arjaliès and Bansal, 2018), how key considerations in sustainable investing evolve over time (Dumas and Louche, 2016), and how the rise of sustainable investing varies between countries (Yan et al., 2019).

Over the past decade, the most influential voice in connecting finance, innovation and market development, particularly in terms of integrating public sector and private capital to accelerate an innovation ecosystem, may be Mariana Mazzucato, professor in Economics of Innovation and Public Value at University College London, with her analysis of 'innovation-led smart growth [...] that requires long-run strategic investments and public policies that aim to create and shape markets, rather than just 'fixing' failed markets' and 'not only 'de-risk' the private sector, but also to the creation of new technological opportunities and market landscapes' (Mazzucato, 2016, 140). As Mazzucato (2013, 1) observes: 'Never before than today is it necessary to question the role of the State in the economy – a burning issue since Adam Smith's *An Inquiry into the Nature and Cause of the Wealth of Nations*. Business is accepted as the innovative force, while the State is cast as the inertial one – necessary for the 'basics', but too large and heavy to be the 'dynamic engine'.

Enabling future finance, innovation and sustainable development research to be less WEIRD

In his book, *The Bottom Billion: Why the Poorest Countries are Failing and What Can Be Done About It* (2007), Paul Collier explores how one billion people in 60 different countries (most of which are concentrated in sub-Saharan Africa) are caught in what he describes as 'development traps,' most visibly in countries with extensive oil and gas, mining and other resources, and links the resource curse and institutional corruption dilemmas to these traps. I highlight the Bottom Billion book because it represents a rare scholarship that does not fall into the trap of trying to make reductionist conclusions in terms of international development across diverse socio-economic and institutional settings packaged together as 'frontier economies' or something similar. The one thing these frontier economies arguments often share is that they are countries located outside of North America and the European Union, even though one argument can be generalising from a country as small in terms of population as Singapore (5.6 million) or as large as China (1.4 billion). Due to the complex panoply of diverse cultural and institutional contexts, trying to provide an analytically dense frame from which to examine Africa remains a challenge.

In an article published in the Behavioral and Brain Sciences Journal, Henrich et al. (2010a, 61) argue that 'behavioral scientists routinely publish broad claims about human psychology and behavior in the world's top journals based on samples drawn entirely from Western, Educated, Industrialised, Rich and Democratic (WEIRD) societies. Researchers – often implicitly – assume that either there is little variation across human populations, or that these 'standard subjects' are as representative of the species as any other population [...] The findings suggest that members of WEIRD societies, including young children, are among the least representative populations one could find for generalising about humans.' A 2008 survey of the top psychology journals, for instance, found that 96% of the subjects were from Western industrialised countries, which only account for 12% of the world's population (Henrich et al., 2010b). Of course, this is not something unique to the fields of behavioural sciences, international management, or development economics. Enabling research to be less WEIRD is and remains a critical scientific methodological problem in many management, legal, and social and behavioural sciences disciplines.

Finance, innovation and market development: Implications for Africa

In their book, *Theory from the South: Or, How Euro-America is Evolving Toward Africa* (2012, 1), Comaroff and Comaroff observed that 'Western enlightenment thought has, from the first, posited itself as the wellspring of universal learning, of Science and Philosophy, uppercase; concomitantly, it has regarded the non-West – variously known as the ancient world, the orient, the primitive world, the third world, the underdeveloped world, developing world and now the global south – primarily as a place of parochial wisdom, of antiquarian traditions, of exotic ways and means.' Furthermore, 'what if [...] we invert that order of things? What if we subvert the epistemic scaffolding on which it is erected? What if we posit that, in the present moment, it is the global south that affords privileged insight into the workings of the world at large?'

In terms of the academic management literature, however, there remains a major gap in terms of Africa-based management research (George et al.,

2016). *Theory from the South* and other Africa-based scholarly research have not yet fulfilled its potential to contribute to the innovation and broader business management literature (Kolk and Rivera-Santos, 2016). Although there is an emerging management and social sciences scholarship on inclusive market development (Mair et al., 2012), frugal innovation (Numminen and Lund, 2017; Weyrauch and Herstatt, 2016), sustainable business model development (Bocken et al., 2014) and grassroots innovation (Seyfang and Smith, 2007), management research on innovation, finance and market development in the context of Africa continues to be underdeveloped.

Main focus

Blended financing approaches to sustainable development priorities
Institutional failure to provide adequate financial support for global climate change or some other sustainable development priority is a long-standing tradition of the United Nations and other international organisations. At the 1992 UN Conference on Environment and Development (UNCED), more popularly known as the Earth Summit, the late Maurice Strong, the UNCED secretary-general, defined one of the 'success' markers at the international environmental conference 'as a minimum of an extra $10 billion a year of 'new money' from Western countries to finance summit commitments in the Third World' (Pearce, 1992, 4).

While mechanisms for additional funding were announced at UNCED, including the launch of a new financing mechanism (e.g. the Global Environment Facility), only about USD 2 billion in 'additional' funding were allocated, far short of the USD 125 billion extra funding (beyond existing development assistance funding levels) that was needed (Davidson, 1992). Although there has always been a gap between what the international community needs and what the international community has available in terms of resources, there is an unsustainable disconnect in the international community's financial commitment to meet the goals of the Paris Climate Agreement (USD 12 trillion over the next 25 years) and SDGs – an estimated gap of USD 2.5 trillion in financing in annual terms between 2015 and 2030 (UN, 2014).

Gaps between the international community's needs and resources have brought much attention to the issue of 'blended finance' or what InterAction, a Washington-based international development network, describes as innovative finance for development (IF4D). According to InterAction, IF4D represents 'any mechanisms beyond a traditional grant that mobilizes new capital and/or improves the efficiency or effectiveness of existing capital to tackle social and environmental problems' (Mandaville and Cordoba, 2019, 17). Although there are small conceptual differences, blended finance and IFAD are used interchangeably in this chapter.

Typology of blended finance mechanisms

In Table 1 some of the commonly used blended finance mechanisms are described. In relation to the list of blended finance mechanisms (Mandaville and Cordoba, 2019), three mini case studies focusing on (1) climate change investment and finance; (2) the conservation investment fund; and (3) the development impact bond will be analysed in terms of how blended finance mechanisms can be operationalised to finance sustainable development and the health solutions required post-pandemic in the context of Africa.

Table 1: Select list of blended finance mechanisms

Mechanisms	Description	Examples
Awards and prizes	A type of results-based approach which provides a financial reward for the delivery of a development solution in a competitive selection process.	• The Keeling Curve Prize • Nestle Prize
Concessionary loans	Loans extended on terms substantially more generous than market loans. The concessionality is achieved either through interest rates below those available on the market or by grace periods, or a combination of these.	• MyC4.com
Crowdfunding	The practice of funding a project or venture by raising monetary contributions from a large number of people and leveraging their networks for greater reach and exposure.	• Kiva • Kickstarter
Debt swaps/ Buy-downs	The process normally involves a foreign non-governmental organisation (NGO) that purchases the debt from the original creditor at a substantial discount using its own foreign currency resources and then resells it to the debtor country government.	• Debt2Health • World Bank's IDA buy-down
Development/ Social impact bonds	Impact bonds provide upfront funding for social programmes by private investors, who are remunerated by donors or host-country governments and earn a return if evidence shows that programmes achieve pre-agreed outcomes.	• Educate Girls development impact bond
Direct equity	Generally refers to a situation whereby a company/ organisation takes an ownership interest or stake in a socially driven business or social enterprise.	• Mercy Corp's Social Venture Fund
Advance market commitments	Donors commit funds to guarantee the price of a product once it has been developed, providing manufacturers with the incentive to invest in product research and development.	• AgResults • Various COVID-19 vaccine development efforts

Mechanisms	Description	Examples
Bonds (to fund development projects)	A debt investment in which an investor loans money to an entity (typically corporate or governmental) that borrows the funds for a defined period of time at a variable or fixed interest rate. Bonds can be used by companies, municipalities, states and sovereign governments to raise money and finance a variety of projects and activities.	• World Bank Green Bonds
Insurance	The insurance transaction involves the insured assuming a guaranteed and known relatively small loss in the form of payment to the insurer in exchange for the insurer's promise to compensate the insured in the event of a covered loss.	• Index-based weather insurance for smallholder farmers
Microfinance investment funds	These take on various legal forms but serve the same main purpose of channelling an increasing source of funding to micro-entrepreneurs via microfinance institutions (MFIs) established in developing countries.	• Triodos Microfinance Fund • Accion Venture Lab
Performance-based contracts	Results-oriented contracts that tie at least a portion of a contractor's payment to the achievement of specific, measurable indicators linked to outputs, quality, or outcomes.	• Health Results Innovation Trust Fund • Global Partnership on Output-Based Aid
Impact investment	Impact Investment Funds are investment vehicles that are structured and funded to target a specific sustainability challenge, often blending investors with different risk and return profiles.	• Acumen Fund

Source: Adapted from InterAction (2019).

Mini case study: Climate change investment and finance. Climate change finance can be categorised into two major types: adaptation or mitigation. Adaptation describes 'actions that countries will need to take to respond to the impacts of climate change that are already happening […] (as well as future actions) […] that can reduce our vulnerability to climate change impacts (e.g. investing in flood prevention practices)' (UNFCCC, 2018a). Mitigation refers to actions that directly decrease 'the amount of emissions released into the atmosphere' and indirectly reduce 'the current concentration of greenhouse gas emissions by enhancing sinks (e.g. increasing the area of forests)' (UNFCCC, 2018b).

While both of these climate change finance types are important, there is an important difference in terms of flows, geography and impacts of climate change mitigation versus adaptation finance. In 2016, 93% of the total climate finance flows of USD 383 billion went to fund climate change mitigation activities, with 74% of the mitigation investments going to renewable energy generation projects. By comparison, only 7% of the USD 383 billion in 2016 climate finance flows went to adaptation activities (Oliver et al., 2018).

According to the UN Environment Adaptation Gap Report (2016), the costs of adapting to climate change in developing countries could rise to USD 280–500 billion per year by 2050, a figure that is four to five times greater than previous estimates in 2010. Due in part to the worsening effects of climate change in the developing world, the cost of adapting to climate change may range between USD 140 and USD 300 billion per year in 2030, and between USD 280 and USD 500 billion per year in 2050.

Looking at the implications for African adoption and scaling, Baarsch et al. (2020) conclude that the majority of African countries have already experienced average annual losses induced by climate variability of between -15–10% in GDP per capita growth over the 1986 to 2015 period. There is growing consensus that Africa's economic priorities will not be achieved without greater investments in deepening climate change and sustainability actions (FSD Africa, 2020).

While there are many current and emerging regional African green finance platforms and initiatives led by Financial Sector Deepening (FSD) Africa,[4] the African Development Bank,[5] and other development finance institutions, there is a major shortage of Africa-focused climate change blended finance instruments, as well as a particularly large gap in terms of such blended finance instruments (e.g. insurance and risk management) that address adaptation issues in economically insecure rural communities in African countries. Even within the context of the climate-vulnerable developing world, African countries remain the most vulnerable to the impacts of climate change as well as most in need of financial support to strengthen local resilience to climate change (Soanes et al., 2017).

Mini case study: Conservation impact investment fund. Over the past decade, scientists have concluded that an unprecedented extinction and loss of biodiversity is underway, and there is a real danger that the planet will lose critical ecosystems and their services such as pollination, and pest and disease control (IPBES, 2019). Ceballos et al. (2015) conclude that the extinction rate among terrestrial vertebrate species is significantly higher than prior estimates, and that scientists know of 543 species lost in the last 100 years, a tally that is estimated to normally take 10,000 years to amass without human intervention. Consequently, many scientists

---

4   FSD Network Green Finance Strategy Development, https://www.fsdafrica.org/jobs-opportunities/fsd-network-green-finance-strategy-development
5   African Development Bank Green Climate Fund, https://www.afdb.org/en/topics-and-sectors/initiatives-partnerships/green-climate-fund

and policy-makers are arguing for a different type of approach to global conservation: 'transformative conservation', which can be defined as 'conserving biodiversity while justly transitioning to net negative emissions economies and securing the sustainable and regenerative use of natural resources' (Fougères et al., 2020, 2).

To help fund this new concept of transformative conservation, there are current and emerging models of conservation and blended finance mechanisms, including forest resilience bonds (a pay-for-performance mechanism for private investors to invest in forest restoration and increase water outputs in drought-prone areas) and land degradation investment funds (financial mechanisms that invest in profit-generating sustainable land management and land restoration projects).

A good recent example of a conservation investment fund model is the IUCN (International Union for Conservation of Nature and Natural Resources) Nature+ Accelerator Fund, a conservation impact fund launched in November 2020 that seeks to provide conservation and social benefits while delivering financial returns for investors. With USD 8 million in financing from the Global Environment Facility, the Nature+ Accelerator Fund[6] is aiming to eventually grow to a USD 200 investment portfolio with early-stage investments in marine conservation and coastal resilience, sustainable marine agriculture, and ecosystem conservation and restoration.

While the launch of the Nature+ Accelerator Fund and other conservation investment funds is good news, at least in the short term, very little of this conservation and biodiversity financial capital is likely to be invested in a country in Africa or some other developing country regions. Although the social and environmental benefits are likely to be equal, if not higher, than projects based in North America and Europe, the investment returns in typical African conservation and biodiversity projects are not likely to be high enough to offset the investment risks.

There is already a significant annual global conservation and biodiversity financing gap (estimated to be USD 711 billion by the Paulson Institute), even though the current financial flows into global biodiversity conservation in 2019 (estimated to be between USD 124 and USD 143 billion is a near-tripling of the financial flows in 2012) (Paulson Institute, 2020). The international community would need to design and develop 50 to 100 times the number of

---

[6] Additional information about the IUCN Nature+ Accelerator Fund can be found here: https://www.iucn.org/theme/nature-based-solutions/initiatives/nature-accelerator-fund

Nature+ Accelerator Funds every year over the next ten years to effectively meet the annual USD 598 billion to USD 824 billion global conservation and biodiversity investment capital gap.

Mini case study: Development impact bond. To more effectively address the socio-economic problems confronted by marginalised tribal women in India, ChildFund India, a Bangalore, India-based non-governmental organisation, designed, developed and launched the WHEEL (Women Holistic Enhancement and Empowerment Livelihood) development impact bond[7] to provide financial and organisational support to 1,000 women and their families in the Indian states of Maharashtra and Madhya Pradesh.

The WHEEL impact bond is designed to help the most marginalised tribal women in these two Indian states to become self-reliant and empowered by training them to become poultry farmers and micro-entrepreneurs. The WHEEL development impact bond is designed to enable 1,000 female poultry micro-entrepreneurs to attain an average annual income of INR 30,000 (or USD 406 as of 24 November 2020) and to create an impetus towards achieving sustainable development goal number 5 (achieve gender equality and empower all women and girls) (ChildFund India, 2020).

The need to help and support female economic empowerment in India represents one of the most critical sustainable development priorities since the country has one of the lowest female labour force participation rates in the world, with social norms and the lack of education/vocational skills continuing to constrain women from accessing livelihood opportunities. As a result, women in India, particularly in rural communities and those living in tribal communities, lack the necessary agency and voice to positively influence their own and their families' livelihoods (ChildFund India, 2020)

The pandemic also put a spotlight on migrant workers' precarious working conditions when a sudden pandemic lockdown in March 2020 left many workers jobless and forced workers and their families to walk hundreds of kilometres to their native villages. Migrant labourers in India have traditionally been vulnerable to unfair labour practices, which represents a critical socio-economic and systemic poverty concern in India, since an estimated 450 million internal migrant workers make up 92% of the country's workforce (Roy, 2020).

---

7   I served as an innovative finance advisor for ChildFund International and its subdivision in India on the design of this development impact bond project from 2018 to 2019.

Similar to what is often described as a social impact bond in the UK, US and Australia, the WHEEL financial instrument is a development impact bond (see appendices, Figures 1 and 2) that uses an outcome-based financing model in which an investor (e.g. government agency, private investors, foundation) agrees to provide the necessary investment capital for a specific social/market intervention and the outcome funder (e.g. government agency, private investor) agrees to repay the investor only if agreed-upon outcomes are achieved (Brookings Institution, 2020b). Unlike grants and other forms of traditional development assistance, the development impact bond is designed, in theory, to incentivise the process to better link financial transfer to a specific impact or outcome.

Under the best of circumstances, designing and implementing a development impact bond project like WHEEL represents a very difficult project management process since the payment is tied to a specific impact or an outcome to be achieved at some future point. There is some preliminary evidence that development impact bonds and other forms of blended finance instruments can have a positive impact on poverty reduction and sustainable livelihood issues in the developing world context (Development Initiatives, 2019). However, it is difficult to say anything about the overall impacts of developing impact bonds on sectors outside of education due to the limited number of impact evaluations and peer-review research carried out on their long-term outcomes.

Moreover, as in many developing countries, the global pandemic has had a devastating impact on India's economy and socio-economic development of the country's self-employed, casual labourers and working poor. India's economy declined 24% from April to June 2020, the worst decline among the world's largest economies (Agarwal and Bellman, 2020), while 140 million people lost jobs, pushing the unemployment rate up to 26% from 8% before the crisis (Kazmin and Singh, 2020). Unless these pandemic socio-economic circumstances change, it is doubtful that there will be a receptive market for a development impact bond experiment in Africa or anywhere in the developing world.

Improving understanding of the role blended finance plays in Africa's post-pandemic transformational future

To fully understand what role blended finance and other sustainable development finance mechanisms are likely to have in Africa's post-pandemic transformational future, we need to better understand three issues and questions: (1) the nexus of finance, innovation and sustainable development in a non-WEIRD context; (2) what constitutes systematic and transformative (versus transient and incremental) innovation; and (3) the context for scalable triple nexus financing solutions.

Understanding the nexus of finance, innovation and sustainable development in a non-WEIRD context

Ravi Gurumurthy, chief executive officer of Nesta, a London-based foundation that focuses on innovation issues, posed a question in a blog post that is often asked, but one that is rarely explored with any depth: what makes a good innovation? According to Gurumurthy, we need to be able to demonstrate that a certain solution adds true value to what already exists within a given field. Second, we need to ask if the solution has been reviewed through a proven, rigorous evaluation process. Third, we need to know if the solution has a credible route to large-scale adoption. Finally, and most importantly, we need to know if the solution focuses on outcomes that will substantially benefit society and address the real needs of people (Gurumurthy, 2020).

It is Gurumurthy's fourth observation about improving the understanding of innovation that benefits society and people within non-WEIRD societies that represents the truly most pertinent point in the context of this chapter. Many social, environmental and cross-sector innovation models are well-known (e.g. microfinance, clean cookstoves). However, what is less known is how finance and investment instruments can be catalysed to replicate and scale these models in a wide range of non-WEIRD societal contexts. We understand the important role that investment and finance have played in accelerating SDG innovation and market development in the US, Canada, Denmark and other OECD countries. We just need to have a better understanding of how investment and finance can replicate and scale SDG innovation and market development in Nigeria, Liberia, Gambia and other African countries.

Understanding what constitutes systematic and transformative innovation

Understanding the process of innovation has been a core concern among economists and management scholars (arguably) for centuries, but there are still many aspects of the innovation process academics still do not fully understand. Traditional academic framing of 'cutting-edge' innovation research tends to de-emphasise what Dove and Kammen (2015) describe as 'mundane science', which they define as the study of policies that have the 'greatest impact on the environment of everyday life' (Kammen and Dove, 1997, 10). Traffic congestion, for instance, might not be improved by 'chasing the newest shiny smart-city technology' (Saxe, 2019, A31) like autonomous vehicles.

Another understanding gap centres on what Rebecca Henderson describes as the challenge of 'systematic' innovation. As suggested by Henderson (2021), deploying renewable energy at scale, for instance, requires expertise on specific renewable energy like solar power. Doing this also requires additional knowledge of the power distribution grid itself, 'a task that is both highly technical [...] and simultaneously deeply political since it requires rethinking the nature of regulation'.

A case in point are the 'innovative' components of the Nature+ Accelerator Fund and other conservation investment funds which are likely to lead to the accelerated financing of and investments in ecological conservation efforts in Africa. However, in viewing the Nature+ Accelerator Fund example on a system level, it is important to reflect on how many new and additional Nature+ Accelerator Fund-type instruments need to be designed and launched every year over the next ten years to meet the USD 598 billion to USD 824 billion annual gap in anticipated global conservation and biodiversity investment capital requirements.

Understanding the context for scalable triple nexus financing solutions

According to Jessica Alexander (2020), the total spending in the global humanitarian sector has increased more than twelve-fold to USD 24 billion between 2010 and 2019. Despite this sharp increase in funding, in 2020, the humanitarian sector did not have a good sense of 'the impact that they had on people, and what change they brought really meaningfully to people's lives' even as outputs ('how many tents we delivered, how much water we provided, how many trainings we've offered') have been carefully documented (Alexander, 2020). Simply calling for more investments in economic and social development is unlikely to change the current situation in which short-term crisis responses continue to be prioritised over long-term investments in humanitarian operational infrastructure (Moreira da Silva and Rosand, 2019).

To address this policy gap in the humanitarian sector and to foster a more integrated international response from governments, civil society and the private sector, Tanner et al. (2016) argue that a new approach is needed to enhance the business case for investments in building resilience by unlocking development potential by stimulating economic activity and reducing disaster-related investment risks. Moreover, there is an increasing call for a new model of a humanitarian-development-peace nexus or the 'triple nexus', which envisions stronger collaboration among actors from the fields of development cooperation, humanitarian action and peacebuilding (Zamore, 2019).

Whereas the 'triple nexus' problem may be well established, the challenge of how best to finance and accelerate funding to address the triple nexus problem continues to be an international development dilemma. Fortunately, there is growing evidence that development impact bonds (e.g. the WHEEL bond) and other forms of blended finance instruments might have a positive impact (Development Initiatives, 2019) on a wide range of 'triple nexus'-related sustainable livelihood issues in the developing world. In the case of the African community health sector, development impact bonds might be used to scale the efforts and accelerate the impact of a social venture like Last Mile Health[8] and initiatives like the African Collaborative for Health Financing Solutions.[9]

Conclusion: Africa's post-pandemic sustainable development finance and investment narrative

If the Kafue National Park in Zambia represents a good starting point to understand how Africa and the issues of the pandemic and sustainable development intersected in the year 2021, COVAX, which is an abbreviation of COVID-19 Vaccines Global Access, might be one of the best examples to understand how Africa and the issues of the pandemic, sustainable development and blended finance are linked in the present and beyond. COVAX, which was established as an institutional partnership between the World Health Organization (WHO), the Coalition for Epidemic Preparedness Innovation (CEPI) and the Global Alliance for Vaccines and Immunization (GAVI), sought to accelerate the development and manufacture of vaccines to assauge the pandemic and to provide 'fair and equitable' access for every country in the world.[10]

Of course, the critical question might be: who and how do we define 'fair and equitable' access? COVID-19 vaccine purchasing agreements outside of the COVAX framework show that a number of high-income countries (most notably, the US, Canada and the European Union) pre-ordered billions of doses, placing themselves in a position to vaccinate their entire populations by the summer of 2021. By contrast, even vulnerable healthcare professionals

---

8 https://lastmilehealth.org
9 https://acs.r4d.org
10 A brief background on COVAX can be found here: https://www.who.int/initiatives/act-accelerator/covax

in poorer countries in Africa seem likely to remain unvaccinated until 2023 or 2024. In 2020, Ethiopia, Africa's second-largest country, was counting on COVAX for enough vaccines to cover 20% of its population, lacking the resources to secure additional doses (Hodges, 2020).

It should be noted, however, that COVAX relied on a blended finance instrument called advanced market commitment (see Table 1) to accelerate the development and distribution to 92 low- and middle-income countries[11] around the world, encompassing virtually all countries on the African continent. As of 30 March 2021, COVAX had shipped 32.9 million vaccine doses to 70 mostly low- and middle-income countries and was on track to deliver 2 billion doses on or by the end of 2021. Most of those shipments were donations to lower-income countries. At the same time, the 32.9 million vaccine doses delivered to low- and middle-income countries represented just 6% of the 564 million doses that had been administered worldwide at the time. Moreover, 86% of the shots that had then been administered worldwide had taken place in high- and upper-middle-income countries. Only 0.1% of the doses had been administered in low-income countries (Collins and Holder, 2021).

By the time COVAX was able to deliver its initial batch of vaccines to the first group of countries in Africa (Ghana and Côte d'Ivoire) in the first week of March 2021, the US and other high-income countries used the advanced market commitment instrument to secure sufficient vaccine supplies for their respective citizens. As highlighted in the three mini case studies, if properly designed and implemented, there is strong evidence that blended finance instruments could help accelerate the financial resources towards SDG priorities in the developing world as well as scale the required vaccine distribution to low- and middle-income African countries. What blended finance cannot do is magically undo centuries of unjust and unequal business practices of a global finance and investment system whose default setting reinforces OECD countries' economic advantages over African countries' health and sustainable development needs.

References

Agarwal, V., and Bellman, E. (2020, 1 September). Indian economy shrank record 23.9% last quarter. *Wall Street Journal*. https://www.wsj.com/articles/indian-economy-shrank-record-23-9-last-quarter-11598878379

---

[11] The complete list of the 92 low- and middle-income countries can be found via: https://www.gavi.org/news/media-room/92-low-middle-income-economies-eligible-access-covid-19-vaccines-gavi-covax-amc

Alexander, J. (2020). Jeremy Konyndyk and Heba Aly. Humanitarianism: Making Of. Rethinking Humanitarianism, Episode 2. Center for Global Development. Alexander's comment in the paper retrieved from p. 7 of the podcast transcript: https://www.cgdev.org/sites/default/files/RethinkingHumanitarianismE02Transcript.pdf

Arjaliès, D. L., and Bansal, P. (2018). Beyond numbers: How investment managers accommodate societal issues in financial decisions. *Organization Studies*, 39(5-6), 691-719.

Baarsch, F. et al. (2020). The impact of climate change on incomes and convergence in Africa. *World Development*, 126. https://doi.org/10.1016/j.worlddev.2019.104699

Bansal, P., and DesJardine, M. R. (2014). Business sustainability: It is about time. *Strategic Organization*, 12(1), 70-78.

Bocken, N. W. P., Short, S. W., Rana, P., and Evans, S. (2014). A literature and practice review to develop sustainable business model archetypes. *Journal of Cleaner Production*, 65(15), 42-56.

Brookings Institution. (2020a). *Foresight Africa: Top priorities for the continent 2020-2030*. Brookings Institute.

Brookings Institution. (2020b). Social and development impact bonds by the numbers November 2020 Snapshot. https://www.brookings.edu/research/social-and-development-impact-bonds-by-the-numbers

Ceballos, G., Ehrlich, P. R., Barnoskly, A. D., Garcia, A., Pringle, R. M., and Palmer, T. M. (2015). Accelerated modern human–induced species losses: Entering the sixth mass extinction. *Science Advances*, 1(5).

ChildFund India. (2020). *WHEEL Bond Internal Assessment*. January. ChildFund International.

Collier, P. (2007). *The Bottom Billion: Why the poorest countries are failing and what can be done about it*. Oxford University Press.

Collins, K., and Holder, J. (2021, 1 April). How rich countries got to the front of the vaccine line. *New York Times*. https://www.nytimes.com/interactive/2021/03/31/world/global-vaccine-supply-inequity.html

Comaroff, J., and Comaroff, J. L. (2012). *Theory from the South or How Euro-America Is Evolving Toward Africa*. Paradigm.

Convergence. (2020). Blended finance primer. https://www.convergence.finance/blended-finance.

David, P., Bloom, M., and Hillman, A. J. (2007). Investor activism, managerial responsiveness, and corporate social performance. *Strategic Management Journal*, 28(1), 91-100.

Davidson, J. (1992). The Earth summit. *Development in Practice*, 2(3), 201-203. http://www.jstor.org/stable/4029044

DesJardine, M. R., and Bansal, P. (2019). One step forward, two steps back: How negative external evaluations can shorten organizational time horizons. *Organization Science*, 30(4), 647-867.

Development Initiatives. (2019). How blended finance reaches the poorest people development initiatives. https://www.convergence.finance/resource/yGlGgOlyvIcsfPzcWKbMw/view

Dove, M., and Kammen, D. (2015). *Science, Society, and the Environment*. Routledge

Dumas, C., and Louche, C. (2016). Collective beliefs on responsible investment. *Business and Society*, 55(3), 427-457.

Flora, C. B., and Flora, J. L. (1993). Entrepreneurial social infrastructure: A necessary ingredient. *Annals of the American Academy of Political and Social Science*, 529, 48-45.

Fortunato, M., and Clevenger, M. (2017). *Toward Entrepreneurial Community Development Leaping Cultural and Leadership Boundaries.* Routledge.

Fougères, D., Andrade, A., Jones, M., and McElwee, P. (2020) Transformative conservation in social-ecological systems. *Discussion paper for the 2021 World Conservation Congress.* April. IUCN.

FSD Africa. (2020). Climate change options paper. *FSD Africa.* https://www.fsdafrica.org/wp-content/uploads/2020/08/20-02-18-FSD-Climate-change-options-paper.pdf

Gaspar, V., Amaglobeli, D., Garcia-Escribano, M., Prady, D., and Soto, M. (2019). Fiscal policy and development: Human, social, and physical investments for the SDGs. *IMF Staff Discussion Notes,* 19/03.

George, G., Corbishley, C., Khayesi, J., Haas, M., and Tihanyi, L. (2016). Bringing Africa in: Promising directions for management research. *Academy of Management Journal*, 59(2), 377-393.

Gurumurthy, R. (2020). Defining success: Four tests of good innovation. *Nesta.* https://www.nesta.org.uk/blog/defining-success-four-tests-good-innovation

Hall, B. H., and Lerner, J. (2009). The financing of R&D and innovation. *NBER Working Paper* no. w15325. https://ssrn.com/abstract=1469119

Henderson, R. (2021). Innovation in the 21st century: Architectural change, purpose, and the challenges of our time. *Management Science*, 67(9), 5479-5488.

Henrich, J., Heine, S., and Norenzayan, A. (2010a). The weirdest people in the world? *Behavioral and Brain Sciences*, 33(2-3), 61-83.

Henrich, J., Heine, S., and Norenzayan, A. (2010b). Most people are not WEIRD. *Nature*, 466(7302), 29.

Hodges, E. U. (2020). Will low-income countries be left behind when COVID-19 vaccines arrive? *Duke Global Health Innovation Center.* https://globalhealth.duke.edu/news/will-low-income-countries-be-left-behind-when-covid-19-vaccines-arrive

InterAction. (2019). *Innovative finance for development: A snapshot of InterAction members' IF4D activities.*

IPBES. (2019). *Global Assessment Report on Biodiversity and Ecosystem Services of the Intergovernmental Science-Policy Platform on Biodiversity and Ecosystem Services.* IPBES secretariat.

Kammen, D. M, and Dove, M. R. (1997). The virtues of mundane science. *Environment*, 39(6), 10-15.

Kazmin, A., and Singh, J. (2020, 30 April). India: the millions of working poor exposed by pandemic. *Financial Times.* https://www.ft.com/content/dec12470-894b-11ea-9dcb-fe6871f4145a

Klinenberg, E. (2018). *Palaces for the People: How social infrastructure can help fight inequality, polarization, and the decline of civic life.* Penguin Random House.

Kolk, A., and Rivera-Santos, M. (2016). The state of research on Africa in business and management: Insights from a systematic review of key international journals. *Business and Society*, 56(7), 1-22.

Lindsey, P. A., Miller, J. R. B., Petracca, L. S., Coad, L., Dickman, A. J., Fitzgerald, K. H., Flyman, M. V., Funston, P. J., Henschel, P., Kasiki, S., Knights, K., Loveridge, A. J., Macdonald, D. W., Mandisodza-Chikerema, R. L., Nazerali, S., Plumptre, A. J.,

Stevens, R., Van Zyl, H. W., and Hunter, L. T. B. (2018). More than $1 billion needed annually to secure Africa's protected areas with lions. *Proceedings of the National Academies of Sciences*, 115(45), E10788-E10796.

Lindsey, P., Allan, J., Brehony, P., Dickman, A., Robson, A., Begg, C., Bhammar, H., Blanken, L., Breuer, T., Fitzgerald, K., Flyman, M., Gandiwa, P., Giva, N., Kaelo, D., Nampindo, S., Nyambe, N., Steiner, K., Parker, A., Roe, D., Thomson, P., Trimble, M., Caron, A., and Tyrrell, P. (2020). Conserving Africa's wildlife and wildlands through the COVID-19 crisis and beyond. *Nature Ecology Evolution*, 4, 1300-1310.

Mair, J., Martí, I., and Ventresca, M. J. (2012). Building inclusive markets in rural Bangladesh: How intermediaries work institutional voids. *Academy of Management Journal*, 55(4), 819-850.

Mandaville, A., and Cordoba, L. (2019). *Innovative Finance for Development (IF4D): A snapshot of InterAction members' IF4D activities*. InterAction.

Mazzucato, M. (2013). *The Entrepreneurial State: Debunking public vs private sector myths*. Anthem.

Mazzucato, M. (2016). From market fixing to market-creating: A new framework for innovation policy. *Industry and Innovation*, 23(2), 140-156.

Mazzucato, M., and Semieniuk, G. (2018). Financing renewable energy: Who is financing what and why it matters. *Technological Forecasting and Social Change*, 127, 8-22

Moreira da Silva, J., and Rosand, E. (2019). Prevention calls for strengthening development, humanitarian, peace 'triple nexus'. *Global Observatory*. International Peace Institute.

Numminen, S., and Lund, P. (2017). Frugal energy innovations for developing countries – a framework. *Global Challenges*, 1(1), 9-19.

Nuwer, R. (2020, 17 November). Africa's pandemic-fueled conservation crisis. *bioGraphic*. https://www.biographic.com/africas-pandemic-fueled-conservation-crisis

Organisation for Economic Co-operation and Development (OECD). (2018). *Making Blended Finance Work for the Sustainable Development Goals*. OECD. https://doi.org/10.1787/9789264288768-en

Oliver, P., Tonkonogy, B., Wang, D., and Wang, X. (2018). *Supporting the Momentum of Paris: A systems approach to accelerating climate finance*. Climate Policy Institute.

Paulson Institute (2020). *Financing Nature: Closing the global biodiversity financing gap*. University of Chicago.

Pearce, F. (1992, 20 June). Earth at the mercy of national interests. *New Scientist*, 20, 4.

Rouwenhorst, K. G. (2016). Structured finance and the origins of mutual funds in 18th-century Netherlands. In: D. Chambers and E. Dimson (Eds), *Financial Market History: Reflections on the past for investors today* (207-226). CFA Research Foundation.

Roy, R. (2020, 29 March). Exodus of workers reveals the limits of India's coronavirus lockdown. *Wall Street Journal*. https://www.wsj.com/articles/exodus-of-workers-reveals-the-limits-of-indias-coronavirus-lockdown-11585431270

Saxe, S. (2019, 19 July). What we really need are good 'dumb' cities. *New York Times*.

Selassie, A. A. (2020, 24 May). Africa needs an economic lifeline to help it fight COVID-19: Here's why it's a solid investment. *World Economic Forum*. https://www.

weforum.org/agenda/2020/05/africa-desperately-needs-external-financing-as-it-wrestles-with-the-covid-19-economic-fallout-heres-why-its-a-solid-investment

Seyfang, G., and Smith, A. (2007). Grassroots innovations for sustainable development: Towards a new research and policy agenda. *Environmental Politics*, 16(4), 584-603.

Sharp, J. S., and Flora, J. L. (1999). Entrepreneurial social infrastructure and growth machine characteristics associated with industrial-recruitment and self-development strategies in nonmetropolitan communities. *Journal of the Community Development Society*, 30(2), 131-153.

Securities Industry and Financial Markets Association (SIFMA). (2020). *Capital Markets Factbook*. https://www.sifma.org/wp-content/uploads/2020/09/US-Fact-Book-2020-SIFMA.pdf

Soanes, M., Rai, N., Steele, P., Shakya, C., and Macgregor, J. (2017). *Delivering Real Change: Getting international climate finance to the local level*. IIED.

Tanner, T., Surminski, S., Wilkinson, E., Reid, R., Rentschler, J., Rajput, S., and Lovell, E. (2016). The triple dividend of resilience – A new narrative for disaster risk management and development. In: S. Surminski and T. Tanner (Eds), *Realising the 'Triple Dividend of Resilience': A new business case for disaster risk management*. Springer.

United Nations (UN). (2014). *Report of the Intergovernmental Committee of Experts on Sustainable Development Financing*. United Nations.

UN. (2017). Sustainable development knowledge platform. https://sustainabledevelopment.un.org/sdg17

UN. (2020). *Financing for the Development in the era of COVID-19 and Beyond Initiative* (FFDI). https://www.un.org/en/coronavirus/financing-development

UN Environment. (2016). *Adaptation Gap Report*. UN Environment. https://www.unenvironment.org/resources/emissions-gap-report-2016

UNFCCC. (2018a). *e-Handbook: Adaptation*. UNFCCC. https://bigpicture.unfccc.int/content/adaptation.html#content-adaptation

UNFCCC. (2018b). *e-Handbook: Mitigation*. UNFCCC. https://bigpicture.unfccc.int/content/adaptation.html#content-mitigation

Weyrauch, T., and Herstatt, C. (2016). What is frugal innovation? Three defining criteria. *Journal of Frugal Innovation*, 2(1). DOI: 10.1186/s40669-016-0005-y.

Yan, S., Ferraro, F., and Almandoz, J. (2019). The rise of socially responsible investment funds: The paradoxical role of the financial logic. *Administrative Science Quarterly*, 64(2), 466-501.

Zamore, L. et al. (2019). *The Triple Nexus in Practice: Toward a new way of working in protracted and repeated crises*. Center on International Cooperation.

Appendices

Figure 1

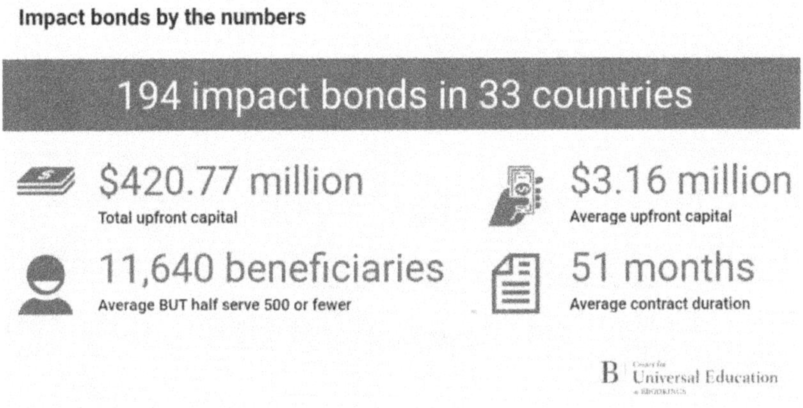

Impact bonds by the numbers
194 impact bonds in 33 countries
$420.77 million
Total upfront capital
$3.16 million
Average upfront capital
11,640 beneficiaries
Average BUT half serve 500 or fewer
51 months
Average contract duration
Universal Education

Source: Brookings Institution (June 2020).

Figure 2

The majority of impact bonds are in high income countries with the U.S. and the U.K. in the lead.
0
1-2
3-15
16+
Universal Education

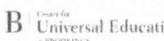

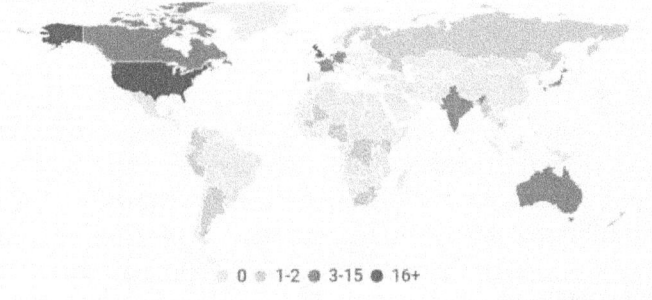

Source: Brookings Institution (June 2020).

CHAPTER 12

Industrial Recovery in Post-Pandemic Sub-Saharan Africa

Massoud Hedeshi

Introduction

Recent decades have clearly demonstrated a need for greater stability and resilience in the global economy. Booms, busts, environmental degradation, widening inequality, natural and human-made disasters, conflicts and an unprecedented global refugee crisis have been the hallmarks of a world otherwise apparently committed in recent years to Agenda 21, halving absolute poverty first through the Millennium Development Goals followed by the Sustainable Development Goals. With the global impact of the pandemic added, it is increasingly apparent that current production, trade and consumption practices and relations are destabilising the world, both socially and environmentally. From January to October 2020, GDP contractions ranged from 2% to 20% (IMF, 2020, 67) among several countries across the world with alarming levels of rising unemployment and social instability.

The pandemic revealed the critical role that a strong, indigenous and sustainable manufacturing sector plays in the resilience and stability of countries. The capacity to produce goods needed for the smooth functioning, maintenance and operations of various economic sectors (such as agribusiness, health, energy, education, utilities, telecommunications, transportation infrastructure and machinery), and the capability and the central role of states to cater for the basic needs and protection of their people in times of crises is largely dependent on a well-developed industrial sector that is oriented toward social inclusion and economic justice over and above the private profit motive without necessarily negating or dismissing the role or desirability of the latter.

It has, in addition, further exposed the risks and vulnerabilities involved in a country's over-dependence on services, tourism, foreign aid/investment and loans, and imports of know-how, basic goods and machinery. Furthermore, the presentation of 'export orientation' and/or 'private sector-led free trade' as a panacea versus centrally planned import-substitution for newly industrialising countries has been exposed as a false dichotomy.[1] Ideologies and geopolitical agendas aside, there is no logical reason for pitting the state and the private sector against each other under the guise of economic/political 'science'. This assertion is evidenced by the rise of 'economic nationalism' and heavily state-centred, anti-market pandemic response strategies adopted by several OECD countries. It is also important to note that OECD countries' highly interventionist responses to the pandemic crisis were similar to how the 2008 Financial Crisis (caused, one could argue, by an entirely deregulated, corrupt and private financial sector) was responded to by the same. Both crises have demonstrated that the 'private sector' and 'the market' are fragile and unable to handle crises without state intervention.

Among sub-Saharan African (SSA) countries, the pandemic's infection rates were on the rise throughout 2020 with the appearance of new and more infectious virus mutations, but the recorded incidence and fatality rates remained comparatively low. As of 4 November 2020, the pandemic's mortality rate per million of population in SSA stood at 18, while the global average stood at 154. Moreover, the rate for Africa as a whole was 25, while the figures for Asia, Europe, Southern America and Northern America stood at 60, 386, 690 and 926, respectively (see Table 1). Since then, the rates around the world fluctuated as COVID-19 infections flared up and then stabilised, but Africa's share of cases remained significantly lower than in other parts of the world.

Despite lower incidence rates and with relatively underfunded health systems,[2] and the experience and prevalence of other endemic diseases

---

1   In the sense that import substitution is a logical prerequisite for successful export performance.
2   Standing at USD 200 per capita PPP for SSA as compared to a global average of USD 1,409 in 2017 (World Bank, https://data.worldbank.org/indicator/SH.XPD.CHEX.PP.CD).

such as HIV[3] and malaria,[4] virtually all countries in SSA began introducing containment measures early in 2020.[5]

Table 1: Comparative population data, crude death rates and COVID-19 mortality rates

	World	Africa	Sub-Saharan Africa	Asia	Oceania	South America	Central America	North America	Europe
Total population (millions)	7,795	1,351	1,094	4,641	43	431	180	369	748
Population density (per km²)	60	45	51	150	5	33	33	20	34
Life expectancy (WHO, 2016)	73	63	62	73	78	75	75	79	78
Median age	30	20	19	31	36	31	31	38	43
Crude death rate (annual, per million, all causes combined)	7,500	8,200	7,300	6,900	6,800	6,300	6,300	8,600	11,000
Total CV-19 fatalities, as of 4 Nov. 2020	1,204,028	34,404	20,000	276,246	940	297,388	14,903	341,513	289,052
CV-19 fatality rate (per million)	154	25	18	60	22	690	83	926	386

Sources: Author's own calculations based on: https://www.brookings.edu/blog/brookings-now/2019/01/18/charts-of-the-week-africas-changing-demographics/; UN Population Data, https://population.un.org/; WHO data, https://COVID-19.who.int/; World Bank, https://data.worldbank.org/indicator/EN.POP.DNST; (all accessed December 2020).
Notes: Population density for Oceania is skewed by Australia's low score. Big variation exists across the Oceania region from 3 up to 600 (see https://who.maps.arcgis.com/). Around 66% of deaths by November 2020 occurred in South Africa.

Furthermore, it is widely recognised that younger people were more resilient to the pandemic and the fact that sub-Saharan Africa has the youngest population in the world, with a median age of 19 as compared to a global median age of 31 (see Table 1), boded well for the region's continued resilience against the virus. Moreover, Africa had much experience and know-how in fighting and containing the spread of infectious diseases such as HIV and Ebola despite a relative shortage of resources.

---

3   Two-thirds of all people living with HIV – 25.7 million out of a global total of 33 million – were recorded in Africa in 2019 (WHO HIV Factsheet, July 2020, https://www.who.int/news-room/fact-sheets/detail/hiv-aids).
4   In 2018, 93% of all global cases of malaria occurred in Africa while 'six Sub-Saharan countries accounted for more than half of all malaria cases worldwide: Nigeria (25%), the Democratic Republic of the Congo (12%), Uganda (5%) and Côte d'Ivoire, Mozambique and Niger (4% each)' (WHO, World malaria report 2019. https://www.who.int/news-room/feature-stories/detail/world-malaria-report-2019).
5   See ICNL, African Government Responses to COVID-19. https://www.icnl.org/post/analysis/african-government-response-to-covid-19

Expected impact on SSA economies

Against the above background, the most negative impact of the global pandemic for the SSA region was in the economic realm, particularly for informal sector micro and small business traders and producers who lost out on business during lockdowns, lost remittances from their families abroad and whose lowered income likely further reduced local demand for manufacturing, as described in Figure 1.

Figure 1: Effects of the pandemic on SSA industries and households

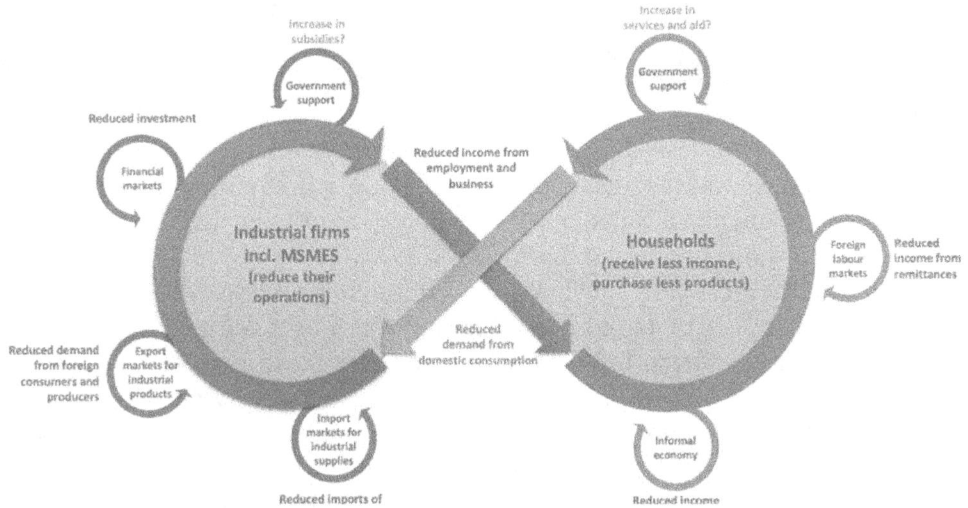

Source: Hartwich and Hedeshi, 2020.

In 2020, the impact of the pandemic on global trade in goods, in fact, appeared to be lower than feared: 'Overall, UNCTAD expects a drop of 7–9% in world trade for 2020, depending on the severity of the pandemic' (UNCTAD, 2020). In fact, global trade in goods fell by a larger margin (around 12%) over 2018–2019 (UNCTAD, 2020). Interestingly, trade among developing countries was more resilient for both imports and exports and South–South trade was more resilient than among other country groupings. UNCTAD data showed a record-breaking, Global South-led trade recovery in 2021, particularly in the goods sector.[6]

---

6   See https://unctad.org/news/global-trades-recovery-covid-19-crisis-hits-record-high

The severity of the pandemic's impact on the SSA region's industrial development, therefore, was not as severe as initial concerns, in large part due to the relative inelasticity of demand for essential and comparatively cheap primary commodities, the production practices of which were often mechanised (particularly in extractive industries and industrial farms) and therefore 'socially distanced'.

As has been the case with most global recessions, the hardest hit sectors were luxury goods and services, particularly tourism. Conversely, the economic crises tended to favour low-cost, affordable goods and services due to the general population's lower purchasing power. The pandemic may, in fact, has served as a boost in demand for cheaper local produce and greater diversification in SSA's industrial production (e.g. in economic restructuring, prioritising industry above services, the local production of medical supplies and vaccines,[7] infrastructure, and general, global recognition of the desirability of local and regional manufacturing and trade within shorter value chains, inter alia in relation to both climate change and emerging geopolitical shifts) once the initial shock of lower global trade was absorbed, as will be discussed below.

Due to their considerably lower rates of infection, the pandemic did not affect economic activity quite as much in most of Asia and Africa, and had little impact on the transportation of goods for most of these countries. According to UNIDO,[8] Rwanda and South Africa had largely recovered their production level losses by July 2020, while Senegal's production remained under par. Moreover, the pandemic presented a forced opportunity for increasing African intra-trade, South–South trade and diversification in local production.

On the other hand, for SSA countries that depended heavily on the export of crude oil/gas (e.g. Nigeria and Angola) and diamonds (Botswana, DR of Congo and, to a lesser extent, South Africa), the picture was quite different. Countries most dependent on the export of crude oil and tourism were hit the hardest by the pandemic. UNECA estimated that Nigeria's pandemic-related losses would amount to USD 19 billion and that the crisis would also hit certain African sectors hard in the short term, including the automotive industry (-44%), airlines (-42%) and energy and basic materials industries (-13%) (UNECA, 2020). However, the 2021 UNECA report on East African

---

7   See for example https://www.nature.com/articles/d41586-021-01048-1
8   UNIDO's index of industrial production (IIP) measures the growth of the volume of industrial production in real terms, free from price fluctuations on a monthly or quarterly basis.

Trade attested to ab early and strong recovery in the subregion, stating: 'Aggregate exports from the region declined sharply in April 2020 but picked up again in the ensuing months. By the third quarter, most of the EAC Partner States' exports surpassed their 2019 levels' (UNECA, 2021, ix)

However, SSA's industrial development faces far stronger and longer-term structural impediments than the recent pandemic.

Economic vulnerability

The foregoing discussion has emphasised the temporary nature of the pandemic's impact on industrial development and trade globally and for Africa. This is particularly demonstrated by a strong commodities boom and record-breaking rise in global trade in goods in the first quarter of 2021 mentioned above. However, this is far from 'good news' for Africa's industrial development if long-term structural impediments are allowed to persist in a post-pandemic world.

While successive waves of infections may yet cause further acute damage to SSA's economies, pandemics are nevertheless by nature transient. And the severity of their impact is directly linked to the level of pre-existing vulnerability embedded in the region's industrial infrastructure.

African economies remain among the most vulnerable globally, traversing a difficult, uphill transition path from an agrarian base to an industrial one within a unconducive, interventionist geopolitical and economic world order. Whether by design or not, intricate global value chains – long-established by often exploitative multinational corporations (MNCs) and backed up today by their countries of origin's multilateral and bilateral agencies as well as their coercive/military forces – encourage trade and investment in SSA primary commodities such as minerals and precious stones, crude oil and gas, coffee, uranium, tobacco and cocoa rather than in locally manufactured goods.

This trend emanated from centuries of unequal trade with Europe, the Americas and Asia (see Box 1 for a brief introduction), which sought to open African (and other) markets for their value-added goods in exchange for minerals, labour and agricultural commodities with minimal local processing content.

Detrimental terms of trade in primary goods in exchange for the importation of secondary goods over a prolonged period of time have hindered SSA's ability to invest in industry due to the simple fact that value-added goods are more expensive than primary goods, and thus it is not possible for primary goods exporters to accumulate the requisite level of capital for

> **Box 1: Corporations as pioneers of colonialism**
>
> From the mid-16th through the 17th century, there was an explosion in the number of joint-stock companies, particularly in the English Atlantic: the Guinea Company (1618) and later the Royal African Company (1672) in West Africa; the Somers Island (Bermuda) Company (1615) and the Providence Island Company (1630) in the West Indies*; and the Newfoundland Company (1610), the Virginia Company (1606)#, the Plymouth (1606) and later Massachusetts Bay Company (1629)+ in North America&. A good number of these companies lasted only decades, but they laid the foundations for the English slave trade, Atlantic commerce, and 'foreign plantations' in the Americas.
>
> * https://www.encyclopedia.com/places/latin-america-and-caribbean/caribbean-political-geography/west-indies
> # https://www.encyclopedia.com/history/united-states-and-canada/us-history/virginia-company
> + https://www.encyclopedia.com/history/united-states-and-canada/us-history/massachusetts-bay-company
> & https://www.encyclopedia.com/places/oceans- continents-and-polar-regions/oceans-and-continents/north-america
>
> Source: https://www.encyclopedia.com/history/encyclopedias-almanacs-transcripts-and-maps/colonization- and-companies

reinvestment in local value addition and value chain development, as has also been the case in other regions, such as the Middle East and South Asia.

Consequently, agriculture remains the predominant sector in terms of employment and household incomes in SSA[9] while primary goods exports are the main source of government income and foreign exchange, and Africa's existing trade and transportation infrastructure today makes it 'cheaper' and faster for the region's countries to trade with or through non-African countries rather than with many of their neighbours.[10]

It has also resulted in overt dependence on imports of non-African production tools, inputs, intermediate goods, technologies and innovation, much in line with other predominantly agrarian economies of the world. As such, Africa's record of industrialisation over the past half a century has been one of deindustrialisation, often with MNCs at the helm, as will be outlined below.

---

9   According to the ILO, employment in agriculture as a percentage of total employment in SSA remained at 52% in 2020, representing a 10% fall over three decades since 1991. See ILO: https://data.worldbank.org/indicator/SL.AGR.EMPL.ZS?locations=ZG

10 For example: 'When I import raw materials like leather from Hamburg in Germany to Lagos in Nigeria, I pay 850 Euro [USD 986] for a 40-foot container. But the same container transporting our products from Lagos to Tema Port in Ghana costs 1,350 Euro [USD 1,566].' https://www.un.org/africarenewal/magazine/august-november-2018/infrastructure-key-intra-african-trade

Structural challenges for Africa: Multi-national corporations as a deindustrialising factor

The global pandemic may have temporarily caused mayhem with the livelihoods of a large section of the population due in large part to social distancing imperatives, which were adapted relatively quickly with soft cultural adjustments in terms of social contact and gatherings, and the development of a vaccine.

But the debilitating impact of structural challenges to countries on the African continent has a much longer history which will remain long after the end of the pandemic. A case in point is the impacts of structural inequality, often created by MNCs, on African livelihoods and the global ecosystem which is likely to continue for decades unless their threat is confronted head-on, with a hard jab.

Conglomerates and corporations that were the main drivers behind European colonial projects from the 17th century onwards[11] became even more prominent in the 20th century as they grew into multinational corporations once Europe was decimated by war and their centre of economic gravity shifted to North America. Often hailed as 'enterprising entrepreneurs' or 'champions of free trade' or 'agents of technology transfer', and usually in an overt or covert public-private partnership with various states and their military forces, corporations have a long history in global resource extortion and deindustrialisation,[12] surplus extraction, and market penetration and monopolisation in predominantly agrarian economies.

This was done usually at the direct expense of a majority of local traders and industries, driving them out of their traditional modes of production and trade and into the status of 'service providers' who might be lucky enough to link at some lower point to 'global value chains'.[13] To a lesser (slower) extent, this trend has also held true for industrialised countries that have seen a steady shift towards services, as manufacturing small and medium enterprises (SMEs) have gradually given way to privately owned

---

11 See for example https://www.encyclopedia.com/history/encyclopedias-almanacs-transcripts-and-maps/colonization-and-companies
12 The deliberate destruction of India's textile industry by Britain's East India Company is a classic case in point.
13 It should also be noted that this statement is in no way intended to support the implied, pessimistic conclusions of the Dependency or World Systems schools of thought. On the contrary, the heterogeneous and non-linear experiences of Asian and Latin American 'Tigers' or Emerging Economies and a rapidly changing world economic order today clearly dispel such deterministic, ahistorical approaches.

corporate monopolies whose reach extended into public utilities (natural monopolies) in many countries, much as was the case with the privatisation drive forced on heavily indebted African countries in the 1980s and the 1990s by the Bretton Woods Institutions and various think tanks with equally poor results and similarly 'trickling-up', destabilising and impoverishing effects.

Perhaps the most poignantly debilitating impact of MNCs was their astounding level of licit and illicit wealth transfer from developing countries – SSA countries included – to offshore and onshore tax havens mostly established in European countries or their (ex-)colonies.[14] In effect, MNC practices have ensured that Africa cannot accumulate adequate indigenous capital for reinvestment and independent industrial development.

According to Global Financial Integrity reports, for the period 1980–2012, 'developing countries lost USD 16.3 trillion dollars through broad leakages in the balance of payments, trade misinvoicing and recorded financial transfers' (GFI, 2016). Figure 2, published in the organisation's 2016 report, provides a graphic representation of this accelerating trend since 1980 (GFI, 2016). The report does not mince its words on the main culprit in this trend:

> *At the center of this most unfortunate development sit the offshore centers facilitating criminal, corrupt, and commercially tax evading financial flows, having their most damaging impact on the poor of the world. (GFI, 2016, iv)*

Furthermore, the report identifies sub-Saharan Africa as having the fastest growth rate (at 20% a year) of assets held in offshore tax havens over the period 2005–2011 and declares:

> *There is perhaps no greater driver of inequality within developing countries than the combination of illicit financial flows and offshore tax havens. (GFI, 2016, iv)*[15]

MNC practices, at times effected using bribes and 'divide-and-rule' tactics, had already been highlighted in the African Union and UN Economic Commission for Africa's (ECA) 2015 report on illicit financial flows:

---

14 See, for example, *The Guardian*'s reports on the *Panama Papers*: https://www.theguardian.com/world/panama-papers
15 http://www.gfintegrity.org/wp-content/uploads/2016/12/Financial_Flows-final.pdf

Figure 2: Net resource transfers from developing countries to high-income countries (1980–2012). Total: USD 16.3 trillion

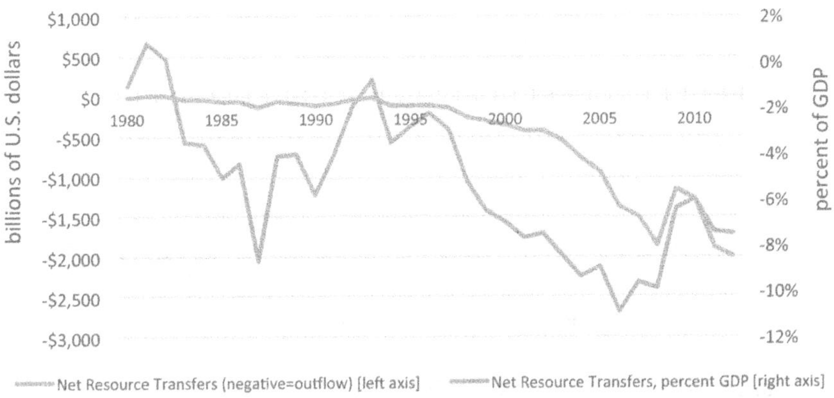

Source: Global Financial Integrity; https://gfintegrity.org/

> *Despite the challenges of information gathering about illicit activities, the information available to us has convinced our Panel that large commercial corporations are by far the biggest culprits of illicit outflows, followed by organized crime. We are also convinced that corrupt practices in Africa are facilitating these outflows, apart from and in addition to the related problem of weak governance capacity. (AU/ECA, 2015, 3)*

The same report refers to 65% of all illicit financial flows (IFFs) as being linked to 'commercial activities' (i.e. MNCs), with the remainder being related to criminal (30%) and corrupt (5%) activities. The report also highlights several case studies, including a Danish Government-funded study covering five of its priority countries (Ghana, Kenya, Mozambique, Tanzania and Uganda), showing that 'Kenya's tax loss from trade misinvoicing by multinational corporations and other parties could be as high as 8.3% of government revenue' (AU/ECA, 2015, 17).

Estimating IFFs (rather conservatively) at around USD 50–80 billion a year in 2019, the African Union makes a link between the predominance of such flows and the activities of extractive industry MNCs:

From the evidence in the recent past, East and Central Africa have the lowest levels of IFFs, while the southern and West African region have the highest amounts of IFFs. Oil-exporting countries have a prominent share of IFFs, while higher levels of IFFs are linked to the size of economic activity in countries and regions. There is even a 'top ten' of countries in Africa, all of which are implicated in approximately 75% of total IFFs. Dominant on this list are several resource-rich countries. (African Union, 2019, 2)[16]

The 2015 AU/ECA report refers to estimated annual illicit flows ranging from USD 50 billion to USD 148 billion (which in the 21st century alone so far would amount to a range of between USD 1 trillion and almost USD 3 trillion):

These cross-border transfers of illicit money have a considerable detrimental impact on Africa's development and governance, especially in the transnational context. Among other things, illicit financial flows stifle Africa's socioeconomic progress by draining scarce foreign exchange resources, reducing government tax revenues, deepening corruption, aggravating foreign debt problems and impeding private sector development. (AU/ECA, 2015, 2)

One of the starkest examples of exploitative practices by some MNCs in SSA is in Nigeria's petroleum sector,[17] which has consistently accounted for over 90% of the country's export earnings but has failed to help diversify its economy, despite several decades of foreign investment and trade in the sector since the late 1950s. In fact, much of the conflict and poverty in the oil-rich Niger Delta region has been directly attributed to the industry's repeated oil spills and resultant environmental degradation for decades (Babatunde, 2020).

In terms of the opportunity cost to the continent, the above-mentioned African Union report states:

Some authors have shown that Africa's capital stock would have increased by over 60% if funds leaving Africa illegally had remained

---

16 https://au.int/sites/default/files/documents/37326-doc-k-15353_au_advocacy_brief_brochure_devv3.pdf
17 See, for example, a recent report on a USD 1.3 billion corruption scandal involving Shell and Eni oil conglomerates and a former Nigerian oil minister: http://north-africa.com/2020/01/africa-corruption-in-nigerias-oil-sector/

in the continent, while GDP per capita would have increased by 15% (Boyce and Ndikumana, 2012). The ratio of domestic investment to GDP in Africa would have increased from 19% to 30% if the capital stock leaving Africa remained available for investment within the continent. (African Economic Outlook, 2012; African Union, 2019, 20)[18]

The opportunity cost of such capital flight to the continent's manufacturing performance is reflected in around four decades of deindustrialisation, as described below.

Characteristics of four decades of deindustrialisation

Manufacturing value added (MVA) as a percentage of GDP for the SSA region has been falling constantly over the past four decades, save for a slight improvement since 2012, as seen in Figure 3. Measured as industry's share of GDP against services and agriculture, Africa has been deindustrialising for decades.

Disaggregated by subregion, covering the entire continent for the period since 1990, Southern and Western Africa have seen the largest falls in their MVA shares of GDP (by around 9 and 7 percentage points, respectively) (UNIDO, 2020), while Middle Africa has uniquely seen a slight net growth (at around 1 percentage point) over the period.[19] Southern and Western Africa have also been identified in the above-mentioned African Union report as resource-rich regions with the highest levels of illicit financial flows out of the continent (as detailed under Section 4 above). Other things being equal, the debilitating effect of MNCs on their industrial development, therefore, cannot be overstated.

Closer examination of the MVA graphs also reveals the dominant impact of these two subregions' performance on the picture for the continent as a whole, which fairly closely correlates with their trends, while Middle Africa's MVA/GDP trends appear to have fluctuated rather independently of the rest. Furthermore, 2012 marked a positive turning point for the continent as a whole, except for Eastern Africa.

The relative strength in African manufacturing measured as MVA growth per capita in the period since the year 2012 (as compared to the previous two

---

18 African Union (2019). Domestic resource mobilisation: Fighting against corruption and illicit financial flows. https://au.int/sites/default/files/documents/37326-doc-k-15353_au_illicit_financial_flows_devv10_electronic.pdf
19 Largely due to a more recent oil boom in Angola taking off around 2005.

Figure 3: Sub-Saharan Africa manufacturing value added as a percentage of GDP 1980–2020

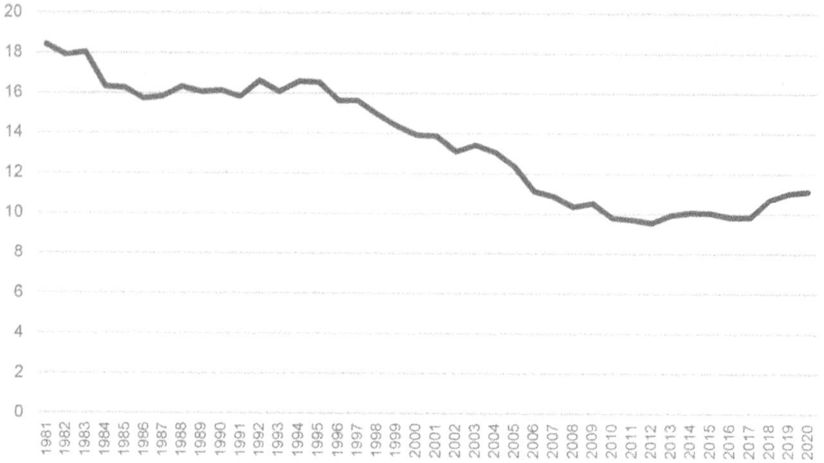

Source: World Bank Development Indicators.https://databank.worldbank.org

decades) is most likely due to a significant and steady shift in Africa's trade partnerships in favour of South–South trade and foreign direct investment in the continent.

This trend has gradually overtaken North–South investments in Africa since the turn of the century, with a focus on infrastructure development, banking services, digitalisation and retail as against extractive industries alone and with a significant role by investors from China, India, Kenya and South Africa. Despite these positive trends, foreign direct investments (FDI) in Africa have averaged at 2.8% of the global total since the 1970s and stood at only 3.1% in the 2010s, while developing economies and Asia have averaged over 33% and 26% of the total, respectively, over the period 1970–2019, as outlined in Table 2.

Given the fact that Africa accounts for 17% of the global population, the continent's 50-year long deindustrialisation and comparatively low FDI trends clearly demonstrate that external sources alone are highly unlikely to meet the financing needs of Africa's industrial development. On the contrary, Africa's FDI balance sheet is strongly negative with enormous capital flight (much of which is directly linked to MNCs), a deteriorating share of manufacturing, rising environmental degradation and conflict in some areas, as described above. Put differently: not only has FDI failed to support Africa's industrialisation, but it has also led to the loss of local capital

Table 2: Foreign direct investment: Inward flows and stock, annual (USD millions current prices)

	1970s			1980s			1990s			2000s			2010s			1970-2019		
	Average Annual FDI for period (mil. $)	Share of Global FDI	Share of Total FDI for Africa	Average Annual FDI for period (mil. $)	Share of Global FDI	Share of Total FDI for Africa	Average Annual FDI for period (mil. $)	Share of Global FDI	Share of Total FDI for Africa	Average Annual FDI for period (mil. $)	Share of Global FDI	Share of Total FDI for Africa	Average Annual FDI for period (mil. $)	Share of Global FDI	Share of Total FDI for Africa	Average Annual FDI for period (mil. $)	Share of Global FDI	Share of Total FDI for Africa
World	23 800			92 931			397 497			1 093 156						631 838		
Africa	1 124	4,7%	100,0%	2 202	2,4%	100,0%	6 636	1,7%	100,0%	30 986	2,8%	100,0%	49 457	3,1%	100,0%	17 749	2,8%	100,0%
Northern Africa	184	0,8%	16,4%	895	1,0%	40,6%	2 014	0,5%	30,3%	12 084	1,1%	39,0%	13 209	0,8%	26,7%	5 569	0,9%	31,4%
Sub-Saharan Africa	940	4,0%	83,6%	1 307	1,4%	59,4%	4 622	1,2%	69,7%	18 903	1,7%	61,0%	36 248	2,2%	73,3%	12 179	1,9%	68,6%
Eastern Africa	126	0,5%	11,2%	151	0,2%	6,8%	749	0,2%	11,3%	3 556	0,3%	11,5%	12 926	0,8%	26,1%	3 435	0,5%	19,4%
Middle Africa	174	0,7%	15,5%	337	0,4%	15,3%	704	0,2%	10,6%	3 909	0,4%	12,6%	4 769	0,3%	9,6%	1 943	0,3%	10,9%
Southern Africa	120	0,5%	10,7%	114	0,1%	5,2%	1 041	0,3%	15,7%	4 939	0,5%	15,9%	5 179	0,3%	10,5%	2 236	0,4%	12,6%
Western Africa	520	2,2%	46,3%	705	0,8%	32,0%	2 127	0,5%	32,1%	6 499	0,6%	21,0%	13 374	0,8%	27,0%	4 564	0,7%	25,7%
Developing economies	5 941	25,0%		18 892	20,3%		125 450	31,6%		345 920	31,6%		653 367	40,5%		209 553	33,2%	
Northern America	6 354	26,7%		37 463	40,3%		99 692	25,1%		215 732	19,7%		318 620	19,8%		133 038	21,1%	
Latin America & Carib.	2 654	11,2%		6 363	6,8%		37 631	9,5%		81 568	7,5%		167 075	10,4%		57 952	9,2%	
Asia	2 094	8,8%		12 077	13,0%		75 525	19,0%		247 540	22,6%		493 656	30,6%		162 961	25,8%	
Europe	10 259	43,1%		30 518	32,8%		169 808	42,7%		494 993	45,3%		529 742	32,8%		242 421	38,4%	

Source: UNCTAD Trade Statistics https://unctadstat.unctad.org/

needed for reinvestments and turned the continent into a net exporter of capital to other regions.

Lessons from old and newly industrialised countries

Having identified MNCs as central players in wealth extraction in many African countries with poor industrialisation results, it is also important to highlight and acknowledge their positive potential for industrial development, as has been the case in a number of old and newly industrialising countries. Accelerated industrial recovery and growth in the post-pandemic context could be aided by the know-how and technology that MNCs may be able to bring to the table for local decision-makers, investors and entrepreneurs.

However, and contrary to the dominant discourse by various agencies and think tanks, the success of newly industrialised countries in leveraging this particular potential has not been achieved merely through technical refinements such as technology transfer, productivity improvements, management practices, free trade, special economic zones, laissez faireism, tax incentives, private property rights, or similar policy prescriptions however useful some of them may be.[20]

Rather, their success has been primarily due to their treatment of foreign MNCs in the same manner that they would treat their geopolitical rivals, namely, in identifying and protecting their national interests and security concerns, maintaining local ownership, establishing red lines and collaborating in areas of shared interest while being ready to use their coercive/punitive tools in defence of their rights and against MNC infringements. This is highlighted by the quote from the UNCTAD 2019 World Investment Report in Box 2.

Beyond these ownership and security concerns, the experience and policies of newly industrialising countries with corporations have been diverse and heterogeneous. At the same time, the presentation of success stories and their factors of success as reflected in the policy prescriptions of various development agencies have been less than fully in line with reality and have proven insufficient for countries that have prioritised such policy impositions in Africa (Kirkpatrick et al., 2019; Power, 2019).

---

20   See, for example, the IMF, 2019, on 'industrial policy': https://www.imf.org/-/media/Files/Publications/WP/2019/WPIEA2019074.ashx. The IMF has finally admitted the 'Leading hand of the State' as a key factor in planning but remains analytically oblivious to any mention of geopolitical imperatives, focusing solely on internal challenges – an approach that effectively favours big powers.

> **Box 2: Recent approaches to FDI inflows**
>
> 'New national investment policy measures show a more critical stance towards foreign investment. In 2018, some 55 economies introduced at least 112 measures affecting foreign investment. More than one third of these measures introduced new restrictions or regulations – the highest number for two decades. They mainly reflected national security concerns about foreign ownership of critical infrastructure, core technologies and other sensitive business assets. Furthermore, at least 22 large MandA deals were withdrawn or blocked for regulatory or political reasons – twice as many as in 2017.'
>
> Source: UNCTAD, 2019 World Investment Report

Put differently: one would have to look very hard to find an example of an industrialised country anywhere in the world that has followed Washington Consensus' policy prescriptions in its transition from an agrarian economy to a technologically advanced industrial one with success. In fact, a majority of (if not all) high-income, industrialised nations today have followed interventionist, anti-market, state-led paths that sought to create comparative advantages, often through surplus-extracting colonialism and war in close collaboration with (and often led by) mega-corporations. In the past, this was usually also accompanied by the mass emigration of European 'surplus labour' out to other regions of the world during the entire period of the Industrial Revolution, which fully coincided with European colonial projects in the 1700s and beyond – a 'luxury' that is not available to other countries today.

From this perspective, industrial development and other economic policy prescriptions espousing a 'free market' approach designed by Western institutions and aimed at 'guiding' other countries could be fairly described as irrelevant or even counterintuitive due to their contextual and experiential inappropriateness.

A common feature of the most successful newly industrialising countries in the world (such as China, India, Iran, Malaysia, Mexico, Thailand, Turkey and Vietnam) in recent decades is in the fact that they have had relatively few interactions with international financial or 'aid' entities in their national planning processes or their policy space, choosing instead to handpick specific elements (e.g. land reform, development banks, investments in power plants and other infrastructure, special economic zones, industrial parks, value chain development action plans for specific sectors, technology, acquisition strategies, vocational training and selective, time-bound tax incentives) that suit their contextual needs.

By a combination of maintaining control over the management and ownership of their means of production – particularly vis-a-vis MNCs – and keeping the 'free market' or 'Washington Consensus' gurus[21] at bay, they were not only successful at industrialisation, but they were also the only countries that met their 50% target in poverty reduction set out in the Millennium Development Goals (United Nations, 2015).

As the UN chart shows, the most successful developing regions in the world were the ones furthest away from the influence of the UN and other multilateral and bilateral aid agencies, Bretton Woods Institutions and international NGOs. These include Eastern Asia (94% poverty reduction rate); South-Eastern Asia (84%), Northern Africa (81%), Caucasus and Central Asia (77%) and Southern Asia excluding India (73%).

In contrast, the region with the highest concentration of aid agencies and NGOs for decades, namely SSA, was also the least successful in poverty reduction (28%), together with Western Asia (46%) with the latter having been mired in long-term 'resource curse' conflicts despite being among the richest regions in the world in terms of per capita export earnings. It is important to also note that both of these regions have also been deindustrialising for some decades.

The most striking feature of the large group of countries with high industrial development and poverty reduction rates is its political, social and economic heterogeneity. Hong Kong could be argued to have benefitted from an authoritarian British colonial regime that safeguarded private property rights and has continued to flourish since it was handed back to China, which itself has emerged strongly through pragmatic central planning and with less regard for private ownership of the means of production.

Chinese Taipei and South Korea, on the other hand, could be argued to have flourished under US tutelage with enormous levels of geopolitically driven foreign investment, starting with land reform under military rule and transitioning to democracy over time. Malaysia and Thailand also show contrasting paths to industrial development, with Malaysia being a foreign protectorate with a multicultural population for much of its modern history before transitioning to an independent democracy, while Thailand was never colonised and retains a more homogenous culture that also transitioned to democracy.

---

21 See for example the case of Malaysia's Prime Minister famously railing against the IMF during the 1997 Asian Financial Crisis, from which Malaysia was also the first country to recover with strength: https://www.wsj.com/articles/SB883586713304528000

This heterogeneity attests to the fact that successful industrialisation and poverty reduction have no specific political or policy characteristics other than what is made imperative by the local and regional geographic, political and cultural contexts. It is, therefore, logical, if this line of argument is continued, to also infer that externally imposed policies and conditionalities are likely to do more harm than good.

It is clear that the policies imposed on and/or adopted by sub-Saharan Africa since the early 1980s coupled with the foreign aid agencies' expensive social services, human rights and human development agendas (comprising over 90% of all 'aid' for Africa) did not only fail to alleviate poverty but have also indirectly helped to deindustrialise the region by ensuring that the most basic elements needed for industrialisation (such as savings for long-term local investments) and indigenous wealth generation (such as the construction of industrial production units) were largely removed from the list of funding priorities for donors. There are signs that this is changing on a rhetorical level (as Goal 9 of the SDGs attests a focus on infrastructure and industrialisation), but FDI (as discussed above) and/or aid for Africa's industrial and infrastructure development remain far below the requisite levels. In relation to aid, this is demonstrated by the OECD/DAC's 2019 report on donor aid to Africa (OECD/DAC, 2019). Of all donor aid in 2017, including bilateral and multilateral assistance, the 'industry, mines and construction' sector's share ranged between 1.7 and 4.1% of the total, while social sector support's share ranged between 37% to 49% across various types of aid modality.

Geopolitics, threats and control over essential factors of production

The global pandemic did not only highlight the need for indigenous production and know-how for human security in every country, it also presented pandemics as another potential external threat – and one that exacerbated geopolitical rivalries and trade disputes – to Africa's sustainable industrial development.

More soberingly, and in the final analysis, a technologically advanced, industrialised and competitive Africa is likely to be viewed as a threat to the dominant economic and political position of existing powers. The currently growing Western antagonism towards China, the intense sanctions regimes (re-)exacted against energy resource-rich countries such as Venezuela and Iran during the global pandemic, which should have been a time of global collaboration, and the halting of exports of vaccines by some countries in

2021, all impact the ability of the affected countries to industrialise; as well as have a knock-on impact for other countries.

In addition to material inputs, a key determinant of successful long-term industrialisation is, therefore, political in nature. From this perspective, the critical role of the African Union and the newly operationalised (January 2021) African Continental Free Trade Area (AfCFTA) in building and strengthening Africa's political and industrial power should be apparent. The Economic Commission for Africa estimates that AfCFTA could increase intra-African trade by 52% within a year.[22]

The African Union can also play a central role in enhancing the terms of trade for its member states. The dynamism and evolving nature of the world economic order since the turn of the century have led some countries to tear up old trade agreements and alliances in order to establish new ones. In the same manner, and given the region's accelerating capital flight and slow economic performance overall for the past half a century, SSA countries should not feel beholden to the limitations of existing trade agreements and regimes with the rest of the world and treat all such bilateral and multilateral 'obligations' as fully and justifiably negotiable. Indeed, such a step in revising or revisiting all existing trade agreements may be long overdue, and the recently launched AfCFTA provides the opportunity for their comprehensive review.

One area where these issues can be highlighted relates to energy production and its relationship with industrial development in Africa. The next section of the chapter discusses this in more detail.

Energy poverty and the dilemma of CO_2 emissions vs industrialisation

What good is a highly sophisticated hospital ward with the latest high-tech equipment, ventilators, diagnostic tools and plentiful supplies of vaccines against the spread of the pandemic if there is no reliable power source to run its machines and refrigerators?

---

22   'The new agreement that comes into effect today will take some time to be fully operational but has the potential to be transformative for Africa, breaking our dependence on a neo-colonial pattern of trade that characterised trade' (South Africa's Trade and Industry Minister Ebrahim Patel).
Source: https://www.vanguardngr.com/2021/01/south-africa-urges-manufacturers-farmers-to-expand-exports-through-afcfta/

A dearth of access to electricity is commonly perceived as a consequence of a country's relative poverty,[23] whereas the reverse is perhaps closer to the truth: poverty is caused by a lack of access to abundant and affordable electricity. Africa's energy poverty is the main cause of its economic poverty.

This seeming contradiction is exemplified by the record of Nigeria, whose citizens and manufacturers remain highly dependent on imported diesel for the operation of imported electricity generators due to the lack of a functional national power grid.[24] The lack of affordable electric power undermines the country's production capacity as well as its balance of payments, causing major opportunity costs in terms of productivity and investments.

Africa's energy output and carbon emissions are negligible as compared to the rest of the world. Measured in terms of millions of tonnes of oil equivalent (Mtoe), the International Energy Agency (IEA) describes the global energy production and consumption levels in 2018 as follows:

> *World energy production was 14,421 Mtoe in 2018 – a 3.2% increase compared to 2017. It was mostly driven by fossil fuels: natural gas (+5.0%), coal (+3.3%) and oil (+2.0%), increasing together by more than 370 Mtoe in 2018. All renewables and nuclear also increased, by 60 Mtoe and 19 Mtoe respectively. Fossil fuels ultimately accounted for more than 81% of production in 2018, as was the case in 2017. (International Energy Agency, 2020, 4)*[25]

It is important to note that the increase in global energy production alone (449 Mtoe) represented close to 40% of Africa's total energy output, which stood at 1,169 Mtoe in 2018 (International Energy Agency, 2020, 2). Furthermore, and despite all the climate change warnings, fossil fuels continue to dominate energy production globally, with coal remaining as the leading global fuel for electricity generation. The increase in renewable energy production in 2018 as compared to a year earlier amounted to 60 Mtoe, accounting for a mere 13% of new energy production or 0.4% of total energy use.

In 2019, global CO_2 emissions stood at 4.93 tonnes on a per capita basis. Only two African countries (South Africa with 8.52 tonnes and Libya with 7.92 tonnes) exceeded this average while the EU's average stood at 6.47 tonnes, China's at 8.12 tonnes and the USA's at 15.52 tonnes. The great majority of

---

23 See, for example, G. Nzobadila, African Energy Commission, 'Energy Poverty in Africa'.
24 See, for example, https://guardian.ng/opinion/incessant-collapse-of-national-power-grid/
25 International Energy Agency 2020 Statistics Report, World Energy Balances Overview.

SSA countries produced between 0.1% and 10% of the global average in CO_2 emissions (i.e. ranging from 0.03 to 0.5 tonnes per capita per year).[26]

On average, one US citizen emits as much CO_2 into the atmosphere as 517 citizens of the Democratic Republic of Congo. Canada, with a population of 38 million people, currently emits around 580 million metric tonnes of CO_2 into the Earth's atmosphere every year from fossil fuel and cement production alone, up from 495 in 1995,[27] while Africa's total CO_2 emissions in 2008 were estimated at 311 million tonnes for a population of over 1 billion.[28]

Within the above context, it is rather surprising to note the extent to which the climate change debate has skewed the current discourse on Africa's current and future energy production. There appears to be an unrealistic demand, particularly among development/aid agencies, for renewable resources to take centre stage for Africa when no other country or region in the world is anywhere near such a target. In fact, the share of global fossil fuels versus renewables in energy production has hardly changed over the past five decades while overall energy production has increased 2.6 times over the period, as IEA's comparative graphs for 1971 and 2018 demonstrate (Figure 4).

Figure 4: Total global energy supply by fuel in 1971 and 2018

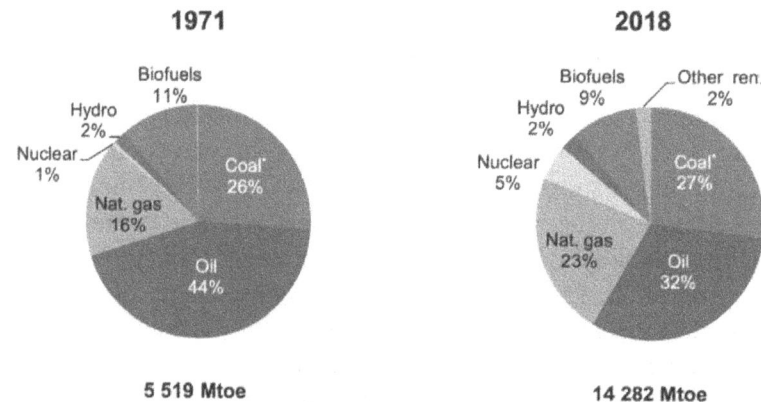

Source: IEA World Energy Balances, 2020.

---

26   European Commission's Emissions Database for Global Atmospheric Research, https://edgar.jrc.ec.europa.eu/
27   https://www.statista.com/statistics/209619/canadian-co2-emissions/
28   https://cdiac.ess-dive.lbl.gov/trends/emis/tre_afr.html

IEA figures indicate that the shares of renewables and coal (which includes peat and shale oil in Figure 4) in total global energy production have remained stagnant at 13% and 26–27%, respectively, over the period, while the shares of natural gas (up by 7%) and nuclear energy (4% increase) have increased at the expense of oil with concomitant greenhouse gas benefits.

The share of renewable biofuels (such as corn-based bioethanol and fuelwood) has fallen by 2%, as they have proven more harmful than fossil fuels both environmentally and health-wise,[29] and can threaten food security.[30] It is, therefore, ironic to note that this renewable source of energy, which in its fuelwood form is also the cheapest and most common source of energy in Africa, is also the least 'green' and most harmful among major energy sources.

Between 1971 and 2018, the share of biofuels in Africa's total energy supply fell by 16%, though its total volume rose from 115 Mtoe in 1971 to 376 Mtoe in 2018 – a rise of over 320%, which is directly proportional to the continent's population increase (340%) over the same period (Figure 5).

Figure 5: Total African energy supply by fuel in 1971 and 2018

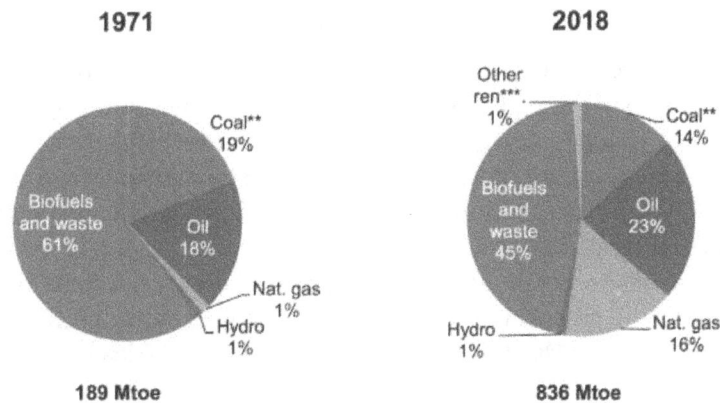

Excluding electricity trade.
** In this graph, peat and oil shale are aggregated with coal. Source: IEA World Energy Balances, 2020.

---

29   See, for example, https://www.theguardian.com/environment/2017/dec/31/biomass-burning-misguided-say-climate-experts
30   UN Economic Commission for Africa, 2016, Policy Brief 9, 'Bio-Energy for Africa: Opportunities, Constraints and Trade-Offs'. See also: International Economics, December 2019 'The impact of biofuels on food security'.

The IEA report cited above describes recent (though modest and not necessarily sustainable) reductions in CO_2 emissions by OECD countries as a consequence of (a) improved efficiencies in industry (cleaner, more efficient production), (b) greater use of natural gas, solar, wind and nuclear energy at the expense of oil and coal, and (c) milder weather (lower demand for electricity generation) (International Energy Agency, 2020). One can also safely propose improved construction and insulation materials together with increased use of electric and hybrid engines in transportation as other positive factors. In other words, a large share of recent reductions in OECD's CO_2 emissions has come from the use of more advanced technologies associated with higher stages of industrialisation.

This suggests that, given time, science and technology hold the key to industry's polluting practices. Other things being equal, the solution to industrial pollution is embedded in more advanced technologies and efficiencies that evolve in tandem with greater mechanisation, digitalisation, automation and artificial intelligence.

Current lessons from 'learning by doing' and trials of various alternative energy approaches indicate that some of the most effective actions for reducing CO_2 emissions may be reforestation (likely the most effective and cheapest remedy of all [Bastin et al., 2019]), cleaner and more efficient production, waste reduction and management (including rationalising consumerism), and switching as far as possible away from biofuels, coal, and oil to natural gas, geothermal, hydro and nuclear energy, etc. In the case of SSA countries, as with most countries, cutting energy and water loss in distribution systems can go a long way toward cutting current and future emissions and saving scarce resources at the same time.[31]

SSA has tremendous potential for leveraging its resources for its own energy production and prosperity. According to the African Natural Resource Centre, and with around 17% of the total global population, Africa is:

> *home to the world's largest arable landmass; second largest and longest rivers (the Nile and the Congo); and its second largest tropical forest [...] its fisheries and aquaculture sector alone is estimated at*

---

31   The prevalence of regularly inaccessible, expensive, low-quality and highly privatised infrastructure in the USA today should be a warning sign for African countries implementing major infrastructure projects in partnership with or through the private sector. The profit motive does not always encourage the use of high quality, durable materials in immediate construction, or long-term maintenance work. Nor does it include incentives for saving lives and protecting the health of citizens.

USD 24 billion. In addition, about 30% of all global mineral reserves are found in Africa. The continent's proven oil reserves constitute 8% of the world's stock and those of natural gas amount to 7%. Minerals account for an average of 70% of total African exports and about 28% of gross domestic product. (African Development Bank, 2016)

Given this natural resource endowment, the continent is well placed to harness technology and scientific advance – if the geopolitical and governance issues can be successfully navigated – to reverse or at least halt the effects of climate change while still industrialising. In fact, such technological advances in the energy field are essential for accelerated industrial development. In the author's opinion, some sources such as solar, geothermal and hydro are particularly suited for decentralised electricity generation for both domestic and small-scale business and manufacturing while others such as coal, oil, gas and nuclear (as well as large-scale hydro and geothermal) are essential for accelerated industrial development and can help power whole cities and regions on the scale needed.[32]

Conclusions and policy recommendations

The global pandemic has not only highlighted the need for indigenous production and know-how for human security in every country, but it has also presented pandemics as another potential external threat to sustainable industrial development. In Africa, the pandemic has had an acute impact on market demand and informal micro-enterprises and traders in several countries of the region, but in terms of industrial production and/or development, it is unlikely to have a major negative impact due to (a) pre-existing and more serious economic vulnerabilities and (b) its economic diversification effect (see below).

While successive waves of infections may yet cause further acute damage to SSA's economies, pandemics are nevertheless by nature transient. And the severity of their impact is directly linked to the level of pre-existing vulnerability embedded in the region's industrial infrastructure. The greater threat to SSA's industrial development emanates from longer standing structural inequalities created by inadequate investment and the domination and exploitation of Africa's natural resources by MNCs, which in turn

---

32   For a review of the utility of various energy sources, see Dincer and Abu-Rayesh (2020).

siphon the continent's wealth off to their offshore and onshore tax havens at staggering levels that dwarf the continent's total external debt.

Given the fact that African countries are among the youngest nation-states in the world, it is perhaps of no surprise that their 'mobilisation' has come somewhat later than in other regions. However, all the ingredients are in place, and some strong moves have been made in the expected direction already for there to be plenty of optimism for the region's future as a powerhouse.

Key among these are the fledgling regional Free Trade Area (AfCFTA), electricity power pools, and major intra-African transportation infrastructure development efforts, which, despite their challenges, are precisely what would be needed as the next steps to augment already existing regional economic commissions.

The fact that SSA's energy resources are spread all across the region is in itself a potentially unifying force for greater regional integration and the pooling of resources. Moreover, and given the violent, anti-market behaviour of major powers and some oil producers in the Middle East keeping oil prices artificially high, there is no reason why Africa's oil producers should not manage their own oil and gas reserves and set their own prices for Africans alone even if this results in technological and inevitable geopolitical issues in the initial phase.

With so much 'financial terrorism', sanctions and outright bullying by global powers with their control over global financial transactions, bartering or trading in local currencies (or a single African currency) could also foster major economic security and stability benefits.

The single most common hindrance to such large investment needs that one hears about is 'budgetary constraints'. A UNIDO Working Paper based on a survey of African policy-makers lists this constraint as the biggest one for the region's governments and manufacturing companies alike (Hartwich and Isaksson, 2020). And the pandemic's recovery solution that was most commonly applied by African governments to help affected firms boils down to tax relief and debt relief. Companies needed to be relieved of their external debts and taxes to be able to function during the crisis. In the same vein, highly indebted countries' governments cannot fulfil their basic industrialisation goals without debt relief.

In fact, given the ever-worsening problem of debt for so many Least Developed Countries, it is suggested that they should have simply demanded debt forgiveness with immediate effect during the pandemic (and post-pandemic) under the leadership of the African Union. Without such a move, there is little scope for capital accumulation, independent growth, political stability and industrialisation.

If SSA countries can achieve an adequate level of political alignment and coherence, they may be able to relieve many existing industrialisation bottlenecks in the region through:

- Devising a region-wide energy strategy that leverages all existing energy potentials from wind and solar to fossil fuels, geothermal and nuclear energy.
- Formulating a strong technology acquisition and management strategy through pooling of resources.
- Establishing a common, region-wide policy front vis-a-vis MNCs with standardised conditionalities and oversight, their management, taxation, technology and know-how transfer, waste management, environmental practices, etc.
- Securing local food supplies through effective land reform/redistribution favouring small-medium farmers in order to halt food imports from outside the region and to help accumulate savings and surplus capital for investment.
- Securing water access and distribution for the entire population and for industrial and agricultural production.
- Diversifying the region's economy through intra-African trade, import-substitution and use of shorter value chains in the post-pandemic era.
- Strengthening regional institutions that aim to promote regional solidarity.
- Expanding regional transportation infrastructure (already underway).
- Favouring intra-regional trade with discrimination against imports (European Union-style), focusing on the consumption of local and regional products (per the AfCFTA).
- Renegotiating and signing new trade regimes with the rest of the world without feeling beholden to current, disadvantageous and externally imposed terms of trade.
- Increasing local and regional tax revenues.
- Incorporating social distancing, digitalisation and automation in industrial design.
- Taking greater ownership control over the information technology industry in order to avoid a repetition of past 'technology (non)leaping' and ownership mistakes made with the minerals and energy sectors.

In conclusion, while taking into account the devastation that the pandemic has wrought on the continent, the key to sustainable industrialisation for SSA countries is first and foremost in taking full ownership of their means/factors of production and distribution in a collective manner. In short: the alleviation of longer-term structural inequalities in industrialisation efforts.

Success in such an ambitious endeavour would hinge on a political mobilisation strategy that focuses on leveraging the energy and dedication of young people with local and regional cultural characteristics. SSA's young population is perhaps the strongest and most under-utilised asset that the region possesses. The role of the African Union and regional economic commissions is crucial in this regard.

References

African Development Bank. (2016). *Catalyzing Growth and Development Through Effective Natural Resources Management*. African Development Bank.

African Union (AU). (2019). *Domestic Resource Mobilisation: Fighting against corruption and illicit financial flows*. AU. https://au.int/sites/default/files/documents/37326-doc-k-15353_au_illicit_financial_flows_devv10_electronic.pdf

AU/ECA. (2015). *Illicit Financial Flows: Track it, stop it, get it. Report of the High Level Panel on Illicit Financial Flows from Africa*. Commissioned by AU/ECA Conference of Ministers of Finance, Planning and Economic Development. https://repository.uneca.org/bitstream/handle/10855/22695/b11524868.pdf?sequence=3andisAllowed=y

Babatunde, A. O. (2020). Oil pollution and water conflicts in the riverine communities in Nigeria's Niger Delta region: Challenges for and elements of problem-solving strategies. *Journal of Contemporary African Studies*, 38(2), 274-293. https://doi.org/10.1080/02589001.2020.1730310

Babatunde, A. O. (2020, 21 April). How oil and water create a complex conflict in the Niger Delta. *The Conversation*. https://theconversation.com/how-oil-and-water-create-a-complex-conflict-in-the-niger-delta-135105

Bastin, J.-F., Finegold, Y., Garcia, C., Mollicone, D., Rezende, M., Routh, D., Zohner, C. M., and Crowther, T. W. (2019). The global tree restoration potential. *Science*, 365(6448), 76-79. https://doi.org/10.1126/science.aax0848

Dincer, I., and Abu-Rayesh, A. (2020). Energy sources. In: I. Dincer and A. Abu-Rayash, *Energy Sustainability* (eds). Elsevier. https://doi.org/10.1016/B978-0-12-819556-7.00002-4.

GFI. (2016, 5 December). New report on unrecorded capital flight finds developing countries are net-creditors to the rest of the world. *Global Financial Integrity*. https://gfintegrity.org/press-release/new-report-on-unrecorded-capital-flight-finds-developing-countries-are-net-creditors-to-the-rest-of-the-world/

GFI. (2016). *Financial Flows and Tax Havens: Combining to limit the lives of billions of people*. Global Financial Integrity. https://secureservercdn.net/45.40.149.159/34n.8bd.myftpupload.com/wp-content/uploads/2016/12/Financial_Flows-final.pdf

Hartwich, F., and Hedeshi, M. (2020). COVID-19 effects in sub-Saharan Africa and what local industry and government can do. UNIDO's Department of Policy Research and Statistics. https://www.unido.org/news/covid-19-effects-sub-saharan-africa-and-what-local-industry-and-governments-can-do

Hartwich, F., and Isaksson, A. (2020). Policy response to COVID-19 – Supporting African industry through the pandemic. Based on a survey among policymakers in Africa. *Inclusive and Sustainable Industrial Development Working Paper Series 12/2020*. UNIDO.

International Energy Agency. (2020). *Statistics Report, World Energy Balances Overview*. https://stats2.digitalresources.jisc.ac.uk/metadata/IEA/WEB/World_Energy_Balances_2020_Overview.pdf

International Monetary Fund (IMF). (2020). *World Economic Outlook, October 2020: A long and difficult ascent*. IMF. https://www.imf.org/en/Publications/WEO/Issues/2020/09/30/world-economic-outlook-october-2020

Kirkpatrick, C., Lee, N., and Nixson, F. (2012). *Industrial Structure and Policy in Less Developed Countries*. Routledge.

OECD/DAC. (2019). *Development Aid at a Glance, Statistics by Region*. Africa edition. https://www.oecd.org/dac/financing-sustainable-development/development-finance-data/Africa-Development-Aid-at-a-Glance-2019.pdf

Power, M. (2019). *Geopolitics and Development*. Routledge.

UNCTAD. (2020). *Global Trade Update, October 2020*. https://unctad.org/system/files/official-document/ditcinf2020d4_en.pdf

UNECA. (2020). *Economic Impact of the COVID-19 on Africa*. Economic Commission for Africa.

UNECA. (2021). *Waving or Drowning? The impact of Covid-19 pandemic on East African trade*. UNECA. https://repository.uneca.org/handle/10855/43923

UNIDO. (2020). INDSTAT 2 2020, ISIC Revision 3. https://stat.unido.org/database/INDSTAT%202%202021,%20ISIC%20Revision%203

CHAPTER 13

Sectoral Reflections

Energy transitions and mobile money

Introduction

Drawing this book to a close, the editors were keen to address two areas where the pandemic has had a significant impact but which have not been addressed by dedicated chapters, namely, the energy sector in sub-Saharan Africa and mobile technologies. There are in fact many other areas where the pandemic has impacted the lives of African communities and which have not been addressed in this book so far. These include the implications on the innovation in the informal sector, the implications of the pandemic, innovation and issues of gender or disability and, at a sectoral level, innovation in the agricultural space. We are unable to cover all areas in this edited book but as a result we have included two reflection pieces to help address a couple of the discrepancies. At the same time, we have included these to start a narrative – that is continued in the conclusion chapter – of the science, technology and innovation policy implications of the pandemic.

These two reflection pieces raise key policy questions around the role of the state in preparing for and navigating any future crisis; of the importance of building up resilience (a concept we come back to in the concluding chapter). They also raise questions – as many of the earlier chapters do about capabilities building and ensuring systems are put in place to enable greater capability building. The reflections by Rob Byrne asks us to think about the ability to transform innovation policy. The disruptive opportunity that the pandemic has created for governments across the continent to review and revise their innovation policy so as to change the narrative or, the meta-rules to use Byrne's terminology, by which change occurs.

Reflection 1:
The energy sector in sub-Saharan Africa in light of pandemic responses

Rob Byrne

The pandemic and energy: Headline impacts

The response to the pandemic had various impacts on, and implications for, energy systems across the world, and the regionally differentiated state of energy systems has had a range of impacts on the pandemic experience and outcomes for populations and groups within them. At the global level, the impact of lockdowns has been felt in reduced overall economic activity, with global GDP contracting during 2020 by 3.1% (IMF, 2022, 7), electricity demand falling by about 1% and CO_2 emissions by 3.5% (IEA, 2021, 3). For sub-Saharan Africa (SSA), the economic contraction during 2020 was estimated at 1.6% (with South Africa hit especially hard at 6.3%) (IMF, 2022, 7) and Africa as a whole experienced a drop in electricity demand of about 3% (IEA, 2021, 76). The situation was significantly different in 2021. For SSA, GDP grew by 4.6% (South Africa by 4.8%) (IMF, 2022, 7) and electricity demand across the whole of Africa grew by about 7% (IEA, 2022, 14). In terms of sustainable universal energy access, it was forecast that the pandemic response would slow the already insufficient progress towards meeting the 2030 targets of the Sustainable Development Goal for energy (SDG 7) and SSA remains the region with the most significant energy access challenges (IEA et al., 2021). According to 2020 data – the most recent available – 568 million people in SSA do not have access to electricity and 923 million do not have access to clean cooking fuels and technologies (IEA et al., 2022, 25, 57).

Key issues

Energy for healthcare facilities

On the frontline of managing the pandemic were healthcare facilities, which needed energy to provide their services. Reliable electricity supply was crucial in this regard – for lighting, powering medical instruments and devices, cold storage and more (Castán Broto and Kirshner, 2020; WHO and World Bank, 2015) – but there are many healthcare facilities without reliable electricity access across SSA. There is no up to date information available on the extent of electricity access in SSA health facilities but past studies suggest there are widespread problems: Adair-Rohani et al. (2013, 253), in their systematic review, found on average that only 28% of SSA health facilities with electricity had reliable access; Chawla et al. (2018, 138) found that Africa as a whole has hospitals with an average of 39.1% access to reliable electricity.

Apart from the lack of reliable power intensifying the challenges of providing the usual health services, the difficulties of dealing with a health crisis such as the pandemic are especially acute. Effective testing, diagnosis, treatment and the rollout of vaccinations – notwithstanding the challenges of vaccine availability and coverage in SSA[1] – were all put in jeopardy by a lack of reliable electricity access (Castán Broto and Kirshner, 2020). There were some attempts to address the lack of reliable electricity in African health facilities. For example, in September 2020 Power Africa announced grants for health facility electrification totalling USD 2.6 million to companies in nine countries[2] and, together with other donors, in March 2021 announced USD 1 million to provide technical support and data to African governments

---

1 According to the Africa Centres for Disease Control and Prevention Vaccine Dashboard, as of 12 September 2022, about 945 million COVID-19 vaccine doses had been supplied to African countries and 21.3% of the African population had been fully vaccinated: https://africacdc.org/covid-19-vaccination/

2 The countries are Ghana, Lesotho, Madagascar, Malawi, Mozambique, Nigeria, Rwanda, Togo and Zambia. See https://powerafrica.medium.com/usaid-power-africa-announces-2-6-c003fa75f004

and decision-makers[3] to help in their health facility electrification efforts. Although apparently spurred by the pandemic, this level of funding, number of projects and timescale were clearly inadequate to respond to the immediate pandemic-related needs of most health facilities across Africa.

Energy access at the household level

At the household level, many people across Africa were directly impacted by lockdown measures in particular as so many derive their incomes from day-labour and/or informal sector activities involving face-to-face interactions (Kiaga et al., 2020; Ohnsorge and Yu, 2021). The resulting reduction or loss of income has meant an inability to pay for modern energy services and a consequential turn to using lower quality energy carriers, whether for lighting, cooking or other household needs (Shupler et al., 2021; UN Energy, 2021). Reduced access to electrical services such as clean lighting and communications (e.g. with mobile phones) impacted on needs such as children studying at home and access to information (e.g. on pandemic response measures) (Castán Broto and Kirshner, 2020). Increased reliance on lower quality energy carriers for cooking meant increased indoor air pollution, potentially exacerbating co-morbidity conditions that put poorer people at greater risk of serious outcomes from the pandemic.

There were various responses across Africa to address or mitigate the negative consequences of reduced ability to pay for modern energy services (Akrofi and Antwi, 2020). Some governments imposed moratoria on disconnections for those using grid-based electricity who could not pay their bills. In the private sector, some companies selling off-grid energy services loosened payment conditions and introduced other kinds of flexibility[4] in order to enable their customers to continue to use their systems. But these kinds of measures were uneven across the continent and either short-lived or ad hoc.

Energy supply chain issues

The pandemic response impacted on energy projects and energy-related supply chains. A decline in demand for electricity saw the cancellation

---

[3] Power Africa, SE4All and others announced the initiative on 31 March 2021. See https://www.seforall.org/news/health-facility-electrification-in-sub-saharan-africa

[4] For an overview of some of the responses from off-grid energy companies, see the blog by Koen Peters, Daniel Waldron and Jacob Winiecki: 'Keeping the Lights On: How PAYGo Solar Can Offer Customer Relief During COVID-19' at https://nextbillion.net/paygo-solar-customer-relief-covid19/

of coal-fired power projects across the African continent (e.g. in Egypt, Ghana and Kenya), uncertainties over the future of some coal projects (e.g. in South Africa and Zimbabwe) and delays in the installation of others (e.g. in Botswana, Mozambique and Tanzania) (IEA, 2021, 38). In terms of energy exports, China's early lockdown caused reductions in demand for oil from African countries, with Chinese importers cancelling orders (Akrofi and Antwi, 2020). For renewable energy technology imports, especially for solar home systems (SHSs) and components, disruptions to supplies[5] delayed progress on SDG 7 (Zaman et al., 2021) and, in combination with households' energy payment difficulties, severely stressed off-grid energy companies, many of whom, according to the Global Off-Grid Lighting Association[6] (GOGLA), had less than two months' operating funds.

Policy responses to these project and supply chain issues across the African continent were varied. Countries in North Africa acted to safeguard their oil and gas sectors, as did Burundi for its strategic oil reserves, while Nigeria was to use falling oil prices to remove fuel subsidies[7] (Akrofi and Antwi, 2020). In the off-grid energy sector, Burkina Faso reduced the cost of solar PV systems by 50% for vulnerable households, and several relief funds were made available by other countries to support off-grid energy companies experiencing difficulties (see Akrofi and Antwi, 2020, 5–6; and Zaman et al., 2021, 3): in Nigeria, USD 500,000 supported four renewable energy companies; in Kenya, the Swedish Government provided USD 2 million for relief for off-grid energy companies. Beyond specific national government funds, GOGLA provided information and links to a range of other relief sources but, at the time of writing the article, none of the 13 sources applicable to African countries[8] (including the above-mentioned Kenya fund) was accepting applications. It is unclear the extent to which these short-term efforts to

---

5   For a summary of a small June 2021 survey of primarily SHS manufacturers, see https://www.gogla.org/about-us/blogs/off-grid-solar-supply-chain-disruption-87-of-manufacturers-expect-increased-prices

6   A GOGLA survey cited in an International Energy Agency comment: 'Africa and Covid-19: Economic recovery and electricity access go hand in hand', 2 June 2020, available at https://www.iea.org/commentaries/africa-and-covid-19-economic-recovery-and-electricity-access-go-hand-in-hand

7   Although Nigeria had announced it would remove fuel subsidies (see https://www.reuters.com/world/africa/nigerias-renewed-use-fuel-subsidies-concern-imf-says-2021-06-17/) they were either reintroduced or maintained and they are set to continue for some time yet (https://www.reuters.com/world/africa/nigeria-petrol-subsidy-could-cost-162-billion-2023-finmin-2022-07-21/).

8   The GOGLA search result can be found at https://www.gogla.org/advanced-search?combine=covid

provide relief were successful but, according to GOGLA,[9] investment in off-grid solar companies remained robust throughout 2020, although the investment levels were considered much lower than is required to meet SDG 7 targets. Since these efforts in 2020, GOGLA et al. (2022, 8–9) reported that the global off-grid solar market continued a slow recovery during 2021, but this was highly uneven across regions and across off-grid solar companies.

Policy reflections

Looking across these impacts and responses, a range of lessons and questions relevant to policy are immediately apparent. They arise substantially from the slow progress on energy access across SSA and the even slower pace of developing related national level industrial production systems. But the impacts and responses also demonstrate, at all levels and across different social categories, how structural inequalities condition grotesquely unjust outcomes that not only affect those at the 'bottom' but also threaten what we could consider are our collective interests. For example, the highly unequal access to healthcare – in part because of the inadequate levels of access to reliable electricity – meant that the poor, who were more likely to contract the virus but needed to maintain some kind of income were less able to isolate and so were more likely to transmit the virus to others, and were at greater risk of severe illness or worse. The most direct effect could have been personal tragedy, with further tragic impacts on the person's family. At a collective level, the continued circulation of the virus provides opportunities for new variants to emerge that could have prolonged the pandemic, (unequally) affecting us all. The now familiar slogan 'no one is safe until everyone is safe' distils this tragedy of inequality and reflects the argument meticulously evidenced in Wilkinson and Pickett (2010) that equality is better for everyone.

Understanding the reasons for the slow pace of energy access could help us in formulating more effective responses. We might examine, for example, the extent to which the liberalisation and privatisation of power sectors has hampered the electrification of community services, which may not offer profitable sources of revenue. One example of direct government intervention countering this neoliberal approach is Kenya's publicly funded (approximately USD 100 million) drive to electrify schools and other

---

9   For a summary of GOGLA's investment database see https://www.gogla.org/about-us/blogs/2020-off-grid-solar-investment-remains-robust-during-covid-19-pandemic

institutions, which achieved upwards of 1,500 solar PV installations during the period 2009 to 2017 (Byrne et al., 2018) or perhaps the push for universal household energy access has focused (inadequate) resources on one aspect of the electrification challenge, compounded by a siloed approach to strengthening health and energy systems (Porcaro et al., 2017). Nevertheless, it is somewhat surprising that more progress has not been made, given that, in the off-grid space at least, experiments in SSA with solar PV systems to power vaccine storage and health centres were being conducted in the early 1980s (Byrne, 2011). Perhaps the impact of the pandemic has opened up a crisis will open up political space in which it is now possible to seriously question the assumption that private sector led development is the only option.

We could ask similar questions about the achievements in household energy access. Considerable progress has been made globally over the past decade but the record is not so encouraging in SSA, where expanding electricity access marginally outpaced population growth pre-pandemic but has fallen back since and access to clean cooking fuels and technologies has continued to worsen (IEA et al., 2022). For off-grid household energy access, the introduction of the pay-as-you-go (PAYGo) model in the early 2010s, which enabled customers to pay for electricity from their SHSs in a similar pattern of expenditure to their kerosene purchases, raised hopes that the private sector had found a way to achieve electrification that would at long last reach the poorest (e.g. see Rolffs et al., 2015). More recently, the PAYGo business model is being applied to liquified petroleum gas (LPG) systems to expand clean cooking (ENEA Consulting and Global LPG Partnership, 2019). Progress on electrification has been impressive, with an estimated 184 million people worldwide now benefitting from solar powered Tier 1 electricity access[10] (Vivid Economics and Open Capital Advisors, 2020) and PAYGo sales for all off-grid solar systems accounted for 1.53 million of the 3.97 million units globally during the second half of 2021 (GOGLA et al., 2022, 11). However, there are signs that PAYGo solar companies may be shifting their target market to higher income groups (Harrison et al., 2020). If this is indeed happening then we need to understand why and address the issue urgently, otherwise the already inadequate progress on household electrification overall could reverse the minor reductions achieved to date in energy inequality.

---

10   Tier 1 electricity access refers to a person being able to get electric light and mobile phone charging for at least four hours per day.

On disrupted supply chains, the issue of local manufacture of energy technologies is an obvious point of discussion. We do not know the precise extent to which supply chain disruptions affected the availability of technologies in SSA and thus opportunities to further innovate, but we do know that it had some effect on the progress of SDG 7. As has been widely debated regarding vaccine production, reliance on technology manufacturing elsewhere and the smooth running of international supply chains proved to be problematic. This is not necessarily an argument for the complete manufacturing of energy technologies within the national borders of SSA countries, but it is a policy issue that needs strategic deliberation. It also aligns with the industrialisation visions of many SSA countries. The ways in which renewable energy technologies can be exploited to achieve industrialisation goals is highly relevant, partly because of the supply chain issues the pandemic response revealed but also because strengthening renewable energy innovation systems can help SSA countries set more sustainable development pathways while avoiding the unsustainable ones associated with fossil fuels (Lema et al., 2021; Ockwell and Byrne, 2017). It would be useful to know, for example, the extent to which the assembly of solar modules and products in Kenya, which has a successful assembly plant (Ockwell and Byrne, 2017), lessened the impact of the otherwise disrupted supply chains. If this local assembly did indeed provide some supply chain resilience then lessons for similar localisation may be available from studying various attempts to do so elsewhere in Africa (e.g. see Hansen et al., 2019). But neoliberal policy prescriptions may stand in the way of such efforts by creating conditions that ultimately favour production in whichever countries happen to have the most suitable capabilities at present (Reinert, 2007).

Looking to the future

Reflecting on the experience of the pandemic and what we can learn from it, it is clear that we need to question the resilience of the systems of energy supply and use as they are currently constituted. The first question is what do we mean by resilience? Answering this, it must surely not mean returning to the systems as they were pre-pandemic; rather, it must mean transforming the systems to be resilient for people, especially for the livelihoods and aspirations of those currently in poverty, but resilient also for the environments upon which we all depend, with economies working in support of both people and environments.

To do so, it can be helpful to think of the social and technical (and environmental) elements as working together, for better or worse, as socio-technical systems and to analyse the extent to which they help or hinder sustainability (Schot and Steinmueller, 2018). In general, the pandemic experience has shown us that our socio-technical systems – whether constituted around energy or other societal needs – hinder sustainability, and it has shown us that innovations as understood in the traditional sense will not be enough to transform these systems. For example, in the energy socio-technical systems, the use of solar PV will not address the structural inequalities that perpetuate and create new deeply unjust outcomes. Universal access to sufficient energy services may, in time, enable the erosion of some structural inequalities but this will not happen without other kinds of work and other kinds of change. Lying at the heart of a socio-technical system are 'rules' (semi-coherent guides for actor behaviours) or 'meta-rules' (rules that influence multiple socio-technical systems) (Schot and Kanger, 2018). It is these rules or meta-rules that must change if we are to achieve transformation, and these will need political, cultural and/or social work – perhaps enabled by technological innovations – if they are to change.

We could consider the neoliberal development model as a meta-rule (or meta-rules) as it has profoundly conditioned public policy choices across multiple socio-technical systems for the past four decades. Whether the various state interventions we have seen in response to the pandemic signal a retreat of neoliberal development (Tooze, 2021) or the neoliberal state bearing its authoritarian teeth (Šumonja, 2020), transformation will need new models or meta-rules. In the conceptual language of socio-technical transitions theory, to find, develop and stabilise these new meta-rules, we will need to experiment in niches. But we will also need to do the political work noted above, articulating the effects of the pandemic in terms that help to destabilise the dominant socio-technical systems so as to open windows of opportunity for emerging meta-rules to take hold (Schot, 2020). In the energy domain, we have places from which to start. For example, we can look to ideas of energy sovereignty, defined as '[l]ocal people determining their energy systems in ways that are culturally relevant and ecologically sustainable' (Laldjebaev et al., 2016, 98), or to more general ideas about social organisation currently being explored under the 'degrowth' banner (D'Alisa et al., 2014). Some or all of these and other approaches can be the focus of experimentation. The question is whether the pandemic experience has opened up the political space in which debate and development of these new rules is now possible.

Reflection 2:
Mobile money, the pandemic and policy

Ann Numi, Josephat Okemwa and Ann Kingiri

Background

The pandemic's disruptions in the global economy with lasting implications for consumers and corporates necessitated a change in traditional ways of managing financial transactions during lockdowns while maintaining minimal physical interaction by both individuals and institutions. In response to the pandemic, traditional financial institutions heavily invested in digital channels to adjust their delivery mechanisms and business models to cater for their consumers during the pandemic. In parallel, various governments, businesses and individuals increasingly relied on disruptive technologies, especially the digital platforms to carry out various activities including financial transactions (IFC, 2020).

It has been noted that during the pandemic, the fintech industry demonstrated resilience and an ability to handle financial difficulties despite the shocks. The industry played a pivotal role by offering insights to policymakers and regulators seeking to promote digitalised innovation and services. The major objective for the industry was to leapfrog its benefits at the same time managing risks to consumers, investors, financial stability and integrity. In many emerging markets and developing economies, characterised by strong growth in all types of digital services, the fintech market continued to help expand and access financial services. This being the case, the fintech industry has showed its potential to close gaps in the delivery of financial services to both households and firms (CCAF, World Bank and World Economic Forum, 2020).

During the pandemic, the financial services industry recorded increased transaction through peer-to-peer (P2P) transfers, government-to-persons (G2P), credit, salaries, deposits and cashflow among others. The utilisation of digital financial services especially mobile money was promoted as a secure, alternative and efficient choice of cash payments. Many governments in developing countries in Africa found it possible to reach vulnerable groups quickly and more efficiently during the pandemic, especially in 2020 and early 2021. In West Africa for example, where mobile money was not popular compared to other regions within the continent, a change was noticeable (World Economic Forum, 2020).

Mobile money and the pandemic: Lessons from Kenya

Sub-Saharan Africa (SSA) has been at the forefront of the mobile money industry for over a decade and, in 2020, it continued to account for the majority of growth at 43% of all new accounts (Baah et al., 2021). The pandemic has disrupted economic, health and social fronts. However, out of necessity and in response to the pandemic, there was widespread shift in the adoption of digital tools at government and individual levels. The increased use of mobile money to substitute in-person cash transactions and as a tool through which governments provide social assistance to citizens is notable (Davidovic et al., 2020). Arguably, the digitisation of financial services significantly revolutionised the financial innovation system (Benni, 2021). However, despite the increased digital transactions on mobile money platforms, the benefits associated with the embedded innovation have not translated into commercial benefits for mobile money providers (Baah et al., 2021).

The numerous development and socio-economic challenges witnessed during the pandemic necessitated the use of mobile money platforms. Arguably, with over 5.2 billion registered users across the world, the mobile industry has the capacity to address financial exclusion and inequality on a vast scale (Baah et al., 2021). Under an appropriate regulatory framework, digital financial inclusion has the potential to contribute towards reduced income inequalities and poverty and increased economic development (Cihak and Sahay, 2020), and inclusion (access to and use of financial services by individuals and firms). Prior to the pandemic, mobile money had already had a track record as a crucial enabler of financial inclusion in both emerging and developing economies.

The introduction of mobile money led to changes in user practices, social networks, market shares and regulatory frameworks across different regimes. As witnessed in Kenya's digital innovation ecosystem, mobile money was at the core of socio-technical transformation in the financial services sector. The Kenyan case witnessed a mobile money revolution which took only 15 years, compared to the normal duration of most socio-technical transitions which can take approximately 50 years. This is linked to the tremendous success observed in the financial inclusion of marginalised people (Onsongo and Schot, 2017).

The most famous mobile money service in Kenya, and perhaps in Africa, is the mobile money platform, M-Pesa. It was launched in 2007 by the telecommunication company, Safaricom, the largest telecom provider in Kenya. M-Pesa had tremendous success and contributed to the wide and rapid acceptance of mobile money in SSA (Onsongo and Schot, 2017). It is the largest mobile money payment platform in Africa with approximately 40 million users and over 1 billion transactions on a monthly basis. M-Pesa has a vast coverage within the continent with users and agents in various countries, for example, Kenya, Tanzania, Mozambique, Egypt and Congo. This coverage is anticipated to expand throughout the continent (Mwita, 2021).

M-Pesa was used in several ways to minimise physical contact, necessitated by the pandemic. This mobile money innovation has enabled users to engage in online financial transactions with zero to no contact or travel thus mitigating the spread of the virus. The adoption of M-Pesa has provided opportunities for financial inclusion.[11] For instance, the number of M-Pesa customers has tremendously grown since 2019 and in Kenya, Safaricom recorded a 13.5% increase in M-Pesa customers hitting 26.8 million with over 70% of all Safaricom users using M-Pesa. Furthermore, the M-Pesa transactions in Kenya increased by 32.9% to KES 9.04 trillion (~USD 80 billion), while the volume of M-Pesa transactions increased by 14.9%, to 5.12 billion transactions.[12]

With other forms of mobile money, external shocks like the pandemic deepened the social and financial circumstances that low-income people are exposed to. And M-Pesa-enabled services were also affected. A case in point is M-Kopa, which is an innovation that aims at digitising saving groups in Tanzania (Muhura, 2020).

It is argued that during the pandemic's lockdown, the value of M-Kopa contributions to saving accounts declined. This was due to the fact that saving group members could not quickly adapt to digital transactions as they were used to remitting their contributions during physical meetings.

Digital credit facilities were also severely affected by the pandemic in Kenya. Although the value of credit products offered by banks, microfinance institutions (MFIs), and saving and credit cooperatives (SACCOs) increased in 2020, regulatory measures were introduced to cushion the impacts of the pandemic on digital lenders and consumers. For instance, optional or

---

11 https://cytonn.com/topicals/fintech-amid-covid-19
12 http://www.connectingafrica.com/author.asp?section_id=761anddoc_id=765686and

mandated debt relief measures were introduced to provide for suspension of payments temporarily or stagger loan repayments (Zetterli, 2020). The M-Shwari product developed by Safaricom and Kenya's National Commercial Bank of Africa (NCBA), allowed their customers to take more time to repay their loans during the lockdown. Further, there was a reprieve for borrowers after a decision not to list loan defaulters on Kenya's credit reference bureau enabled them to maintain their credit scores (Zetterli, 2020).

These measures improved access to digital credit via mobile money, albeit for a short period. A private school operator in Kenya who was affected by the closure of schools and could not honour the required digital loan remittance had the following to say:

> *The short-term measures by government to cushion small businesses is not enough because the SACCOs are just deferring the payment period without reducing the interest rates. People should be supported to repay the loans through an inclusive government fund targeted at needy SMEs. (Zetterli, 2020)*

This exposes the vulnerability of the digital financial innovation system to external shocks. It, however, also offers opportunities for building a more resilient, inclusive and functional system using the lessons learnt during the pandemic (Zetterli, 2020).

Policy reflections

The rapidly increased shift to digital transformation as a result of the pandemic had both positive and negative impacts on pro-innovation and inclusive efforts.

Enhancing digital innovation for inclusion

Mobile money innovation is considered a promising tool by both policy-makers and international organisations for addressing financial inclusion among the poor in the Global South (Onsongo and Schot, 2017). On the downside, the rapid digital transformation led to a widened and deepened digital divide within and between countries – magnifying inequalities and further marginalising those who are not connected digitally (UNDESA, 2021). Marginalised groups who experienced severe socio-economic consequences due to the pandemic included those living in poverty, the elderly, rural people, illiterate people, women, migrants and refugees, among others (Benni, 2021). Arguably, digital financial services, including mobile money, proved crucial during the pandemic as a tool for families to manage economic emergencies thus reducing the risk of financial despair. The services enhanced inclusivity by providing mechanisms through which families could save, borrow and make payments through digital platforms (Machasio, 2020). The impact of the pandemic therefore points towards the need for more resilient and stable financial inclusion strategies.

Digital inequality remains a major issue especially in the rural areas and expansion of mobile network coverage and acquiring of smartphones is often considered the remedy. However, the way networks amplify these inequalities is rarely addressed. For some marginalised groups and people in rural areas, the necessity of obtaining basic survival items like food, housing, healthcare, among other basic needs, far outweighs the need of maintaining a phone, buying airtime and paying money transfer fees. This further magnifies the digital divide in regard to access to mobile technology based on social class, disability or gender.

Mobile money users in rural settings sometimes have to borrow handsets in order to access their accounts, something which is common amongst women, which brings with it security implications (Tarantola, 2021). For inclusive transition to digital transfers and payments, due to external shocks like the pandemic, national governments and financial institutions need to ensure that the process does not widen the gap between those with access to mobile money and those without. This gap can be reduced through improved financial and digital literacy. Other interventions could include provision of adequate information and communications technology (ICT) infrastructure, mobile ownership for everyone, including the marginalised, and support from sector regulations among others. The lack of these measures risks an increased gap in financial and digital inclusion for the marginalised groups, especially women, youth and people in rural areas (Benni, 2021). Sadly, most countries in Africa have not made sufficient effort to enhance inclusive innovation, but there is hope that lessons learnt during the pandemic will inform policy reviews accordingly.

Despite the enhanced efforts to promote the use of mobile money, the majority of low- and middle-income countries, remain excluded due to complex socio-demographic factors, unfavorable market or regulatory conditions, or mere lack of awareness of mobile money services. In low- and middle-income countries, women are still 33% less likely to own a mobile money account across these markets due to lack of awareness and literacy, among other reasons (SMA, 2021). In the context of the pandemic, the socio-economic cost of financial exclusion was projected to worsen[13] as argued by Baah et al. (2021).

It is important therefore for policy-makers in the post-pandemic era to build requisite capabilities to strengthen sustainability of social protection and payment systems that are effective and inclusive in addressing challenges faced by the digitally disadvantaged members of their societies.

Policy-makers find themselves in a regulatory dilemma in finding a balance between enabling fintech and safeguarding financial systems. It is therefore crucial for stakeholders to engage in policy measures that can enable innovation and efficiency, reduce financial and economic vulnerability while keeping risks in check.[14] Governments need to prioritise financial expansion channels through ICT infrastructure and network deployment in marginal and rural regions (Machasio, 2020). This includes access to safe and affordable internet for sustainable digital payment strategy in order to fully exploit the benefits of digital technologies like mobile money (Adrian and Mancini-Griffoli, 2021). Collective efforts should be made towards addressing the digital divide and promotion of digital inclusion given the high correlation between digital divide and socio-economic inequality (UNDESA, 2021).

The lack of both digital and financial literacy remains a major obstacle to digital inclusion. It is therefore necessary to invest in digital financial education, literacy and skills (UNDESA, 2021). Other measures to increase literacy in digital finance include media platforms to promote financial inclusion for the less educated and elderly. Through these platforms, people can access videos, articles or podcasts that they could use to recuperate to recuperate post-pandemic and/or prepare for future crises (Machasio, 2020).

In an effort to shield the vulnerable user segment during the pandemic, governments and a number of mobile money providers and their regulators responded with specific temporary and permanent inclusive mitigation measures through a number of policies, regulatory and provider-led measures.[15] The examples provided below provide useful learning for stakeholders towards sustained inclusive policy strategies in the post-pandemic period.

---

13 https://www.gsma.com/mobilefordevelopment/blog/assessing-mobile-money-consumer-trends-in-the-wake-of-the-covid-19-pandemic/
14 https://blogs.worldbank.org/psd/fintech-can-help-response-covid-19-where-should-policymakers-start
15 https://www.gsma.com/mobilefordevelopment/resources/mobile-money-recommendations-to-central-banks-in-response-to-covid-19/

- The reduced/waived digital transaction fees (AFI, 2020; Miriri, 2020; Safaricom, 2020).
- Increased transaction and balance limits: This limits the use of hard currency by mobile money users on a daily basis while making payments of both essential and non-essential products/services even after surpassing the threshold. In Kenya, for instance, the Central Bank of Kenya (CBK) increased the daily transaction limit of M-Pesa from KES 70,000 (≈ USD 626) to KES 150,000 (≈ USD 1,340) while the M-Pesa wallet capacity was increased from KES 140,000 (≈ USD 1,251) to KES 300,000 (≈ USD 2,681).
- Decreased minimum amount required for transaction: This measure encouraged users to make small and everyday payments through mobile money.
- Promoting digital innovation for enhanced service delivery: Most developing countries have a deeply rooted cash-on-delivery (COD) culture which is a major hindrance to the acceptance of mobile money. However, since the onset of the pandemic, COD payments have drastically decreased as a result of restrictions by various agencies and fear of contracting the virus through the handling of hard currency. To promote and sustain this innovative behaviour and motivate customers to continue avoiding COD during the post-pandemic period will require policy and promotion of culture change interventions. In Kenya for instance, county governments promoted M-Pesa revenue collection systems as one of the mitigation measures towards curbing the spread of the virus. By June 2021, 25 counties had fully integrated M-Pesa payment systems and there was a unanimous decision to accept cash payments through M-Pesa among all the counties.
- Mutually beneficial partnerships between mobile money operators (MMOs) and e-commerce firms: Creation of public-private working groups is essential to foster mutual collaborations in order to promote business as well as dialogue and address regulatory and logistical barriers (Benni, 2021). One example of this in Kenya is Safaricom's partnership with the National Social Security Fund (NSSF) to facilitate service fee payments and rent payments through the NSSF Tenant Purchase Scheme (TPS) via M-Pesa (NSSF, 2020). During the pandemic, payment organisations formed partnerships with other industry players to increase the use of mobile money payments and minimise human contact and movement (Kanali, 2020).

Despite these learning experiences, for mobile money and other digital innovations to be clear, simple, culturally relevant and meet the users' needs, innovation developers need to involve these marginalised groups in the development of these applications. Campaigns to promote awareness of these digital tools are therefore key for their increased and widespread adoption.

Promoting security for technological innovation

An increased number of people switched to digital payment methods out of necessity due to pandemic restrictions. This practice is likely to be sustained in the post-pandemic era. This has implications for security given that mobile money attracts higher cybersecurity risk and increases avenues for digital fraud, scams and theft (Benni, 2021). Cybersecurity is one of the major challenges that plagues mobile money platforms like M-Pesa, and other digital financial institutions like banks. The risk might be higher in developing countries where there are low levels of financial and digital literacy thus increasing vulnerability. To enhance security, the different stakeholders in the digital finance ecosystem have a role to play. Governments can enforce several measures, for instance strengthening ICT related security, regulations, supervision of financial institutions and targeted capacity building for developers and users of technology (Benni, 2021).

Further, to maintain the dynamism of digital innovations requires constant innovation through relevant upgrading, something that tele-communication companies should invest in. Safaricom in Kenya, for instance, updated the M-Pesa application through the introduction of a verification process called 'Tuwaanike' which means 'expose' to minimise fraud risk in M-Pesa. This update allows unsuspecting users to receive SMS notifications if scammers try to register a new SIM card using their ID number. The users are prompted to either authorise or reject the transaction (Jackson, 2020). Safaricom also initiated campaigns on mainstream and social media to protect users from fraudsters (Mwita, 2021). This suggests the need for sustained innovation by mobile money service providers. For instance, provision of multifactor authentication schemes and continuous upgrading of security features to keep ahead of fraudsters who are also innovative. Mobile money customers should be made aware of the unscrupulous activities of fraudsters through educational campaigns on strategies on how to avoid falling into fraudulent traps and how to remain vigilant. MMOs need to develop a comprehensive consumer protection framework in order to promote common standards for transparency and enforcement and ensure protection of their customers (CAK, 2020).

Learning lessons and looking into the future

It is noted that the contribution of financial digital innovation to the overall growth during the pandemic was positive, especially for effective functioning of the banks.[16] To maintain and sustain the learning that has occurred since the onset of pandemic, a holistic and systemic approach to innovation and policy is proposed.

Governments have a role in fintech growth through pro-innovation policies
Governments have a crucial role to play in promoting digital technologies and financial inclusion. Pro-innovation frameworks and services should have the capacity to incentivise the scaling up and shift of transactions across border and digital channels. In Kenya for instance, a task force to look into how the country can leverage on blockchain and internet of things (IOT) technology was established through the Ministry of ICT. The government also partnered with Master Card Foundation in developing an M-Pesa-enabled digital payment platform for government services. The remittance providers needed government support to mitigate against the impact of the pandemic. Benni (2021) provides policy recommendations in this regard, which included innovation support for enhanced institutional and product digitisation processes.

Expansion of financial access for inclusive digital systems
Countries that have established strong digital financial services like Kenya were able to disburse funds during the pandemic. The Kenyan government estimated that 1.36 billion Kenya Shillings (~USD 12,152,829) per month was transferred to beneficiaries spread out across low-income, urban informal settlements using mobile money at the height of the pandemic in 2020. Further, studies in Kenya have shown that a large proportion of M-Pesa mobile money users comprise small and medium enterprises (SMEs) (Rotich, 2021). This calls for evidence-based research that would support development of strategies to scale up digital systems in these informal sectors and expand financial access across low-income consumers.

---

16   https://cytonn.com/topicals/fintech-amid-covid-19

Conclusion

The pandemic has demonstrated that innovations in fintech were instrumental in bridging the gap for marginalised groups in the region through provision of essential services. This diversification of services on mobile money platforms included services like purchase of goods and services, savings and loans, payment of utility bills and transport fees, among others. This enabled low income individuals to access various financial services at affordable rates (Mulumba and Schmidt, 2021) and thus increased economic growth. Nevertheless, the number of financially excluded populations in developing countries continues to be very high. This reflection has explored the role of financial technology (fintech). Mobile money service, the M-Pesa platform for instance, has proved to be a fundamental tool in the achievement of financial inclusion in Kenya.

The role of mobile money in bridging the gap for the financially excluded in the event of external shocks like the pandemic needs policy support through (a) promotion of digital technologies and financial inclusion, (b) promoting security for technological innovation and (c) expansion of financial access for inclusive digital systems.

References

Adair-Rohani, H., Zukor, K., Bonjour, S., Wilburn, S., Kuesel, A. C., Hebert, R., and Fletcher, E. R. (2013). Limited electricity access in health facilities of sub-Saharan Africa: A systematic review of data on electricity access, sources, and reliability. *Global Health: Science and Practice*, 1(2), 249-261. https://doi.org/10.9745/GHSP-D-13-00037

Adrian, T., and Mancini-Griffoli, T. (2021). A new era of digital money. *IMF*. https://www.imf.org/external/pubs/ft/fandd/2021/06/online/digital-money-new-era-adrian-mancini-griffoli.htm

AFI. (2020). Alliance for Financial Inclusion—COVID-19. *Alliance for Financial Inclusion – COVID-19*. https://www.afi-global.org/covid-19/

Akrofi, M. M., and Antwi, S. H. (2020). COVID-19 energy sector responses in Africa: A review of preliminary government interventions. *Energy Research and Social Science*, 68, 101681. https://doi.org/10.1016/j.erss.2020.101681

Baah, B., Kipkemboi, K., Lindsey, D., Muthiora, B., Nautiyal, A., Pathy, V., Pors, B.-J., Tricarico, D., and White, Z. (2021). *State of the Industry Report on Mobile Money 2021*. GSMA. https://www.gsma.com/mobilefordevelopment/wp-content/uploads/2021/03/GSMA_State-of-the-Industry-Report-on-Mobile-Money-2021_Full-report.pdf

Benni, N. (2021). *Digital Finance and Inclusion in the Time of COVID-19*. FAO. https://doi.org/10.4060/cb2109en

Byrne, R. (2011). Learning drivers: Rural electrification regime building in Kenya and Tanzania. University of Sussex. http://sro.sussex.ac.uk/id/eprint/6963/

Byrne, R., Mbeva, K., and Ockwell, D. (2018). A political economy of niche-building: Neoliberal-developmental encounters in photovoltaic electrification in Kenya. *Energy Research and Social Science*, 44, 6-16. https://doi.org/10.1016/j.erss.2018.03.028

CAK. (2020). *Digital Lenders Market Inquiry Consumer Survey Report 2020*. https://www.cak.go.ke/sites/default/files/Digital%20Lenders%20Market%20Inquiry%20Consumer%20Survey%20Report%202020.pdf

Castán Broto, V., and Kirshner, J. (2020). Energy access is needed to maintain health during pandemics. *Nature Energy*, 5(6), 419-421. https://doi.org/10.1038/s41560-020-0625-6

CCAF, World Bank, and World Economic Forum. (2020). *The Global Covid-19 FinTech Market Rapid Assessment Study 2020*. https://www3.weforum.org/docs/WEF_The_Global_Covid19_FinTech_Market_Rapid_Assessment_Study_2020.pdf

Chawla, S., Kurani, S., Wren, S. M., Stewart, B., Burnham, G., Kushner, A., and McIntyre, T. (2018). Electricity and generator availability in LMIC hospitals: Improving access to safe surgery. *Journal of Surgical Research*, 223, 136-141. https://doi.org/10.1016/j.jss.2017.10.016

Cihak, M., and Sahay, R. (2020). Finance and inequality. *Staff Discussion Notes*, 20(1). https://doi.org/10.5089/9781513526546.006

D'Alisa, G., Demaria, F., and Kallis, G. (Eds). (2014). *Degrowth: A vocabulary for a new era*. Routledge. https://doi.org/10.4324/9780203796146

Davidovic, S., Prady, D., and Tourpe, H. (2020, 22 June). You've got money: Mobile payments help people during the pandemic. *IMF Blog*. https://blogs.imf.org/2020/06/22/youve-got-money-mobile-payments-help-people-during-the-pandemic/

ENEA Consulting, and Global LPG Partnership. (2019). *Scaling LPG for Cooking in Developing Markets: Insights from Tanzania*. Clean Cooking Alliance. https://www.enea-consulting.com/en/publication/scaling-lpg-for-cooking-in-developing-markets/

GOGLA, Lighting Global, Efficiency for Access Coalition, Energy Saving Trust, CLASP, and Berenschot. (2021). *Global Off-Grid Solar Market Report: Semi-annual sales and impact data, July–December 2020*. Global Off-Grid Lighting Association. https://www.gogla.org/sites/default/files/resource_docs/global_off-grid_solar_market_report_h2_2020.pdf

GOGLA, Lighting Global, ESMAP, World Bank, Efficiency for Access Coalition, Energy Saving Trust, CLASP, and Berenschot. (2022). *Global Off-Grid Solar Markets Report: Semi-annual sales and impact data, July–December 2021*. Global Off-Grid Lighting Association. https://www.gogla.org/sites/default/files/resource_docs/gogla_sales-and-impact-reporth2-2021_def2.pdf

Hansen, U. E., Nygaard, I., Davy, E., Larsen, T. H., and Wabuge, C. W. (2019). *Challenges to Establishing and Sustaining Local Production of Renewable Energy Technologies in Sub-Saharan Africa*. UNEP-DTU Partnership. https://orbit.dtu.dk/files/200567400/challenges_and_opportunities_final_layout_for_upload.pdf

Harrison, K., Khan, S., Adams, T., and Dichter, S. (2020). *Why Off-grid Energy Matters: An impact performance report*. 60_decibels. https://60decibels.com/energy-report

International Energy Agency (IEA). (2021). *Electricity Market Report July 2021*. IEA. https://www.iea.org/reports/electricity-market-report-july-2021

IEA. (2022). *Electricity Market Report July 2022*. IEA. https://www.iea.org/reports/electricity-market-report-july-2022

IEA, IRENA, UNSD, World Bank, and WHO. (2021). *Tracking SDG 7: The energy progress report*. World Bank. https://www.iea.org/reports/tracking-sdg7-the-energy-progress-report-2021

IEA, IRENA, UNSD, World Bank, and WHO. (2022). *Tracking SDG7: The energy progress report*. World Bank. https://trackingsdg7.esmap.org/data/files/download-documents/sdg7-report2022-full_report.pdf

IFC. (2020). *The Impact of COVID-19 on Disruptive Technology Adoption in Emerging Markets*. https://www.ifc.org/wps/wcm/connect/537b9b66-a35c-40cf-bed8-6f618c4f63d8/202009-COVID-19-Impact-Disruptive-Tech-EM.pdf?MOD=AJPERESandCVID=njn5xG9

International Monetary Fund (IMF). (2022). *World Economic Outlook Update: Gloomy and more uncertain*. IMF. https://www.imf.org/-/media/Files/Publications/WEO/2022/Update/July/English/text-en.ashx

Jackson, E. (2020). Safaricom tackles fraud in latest M-Pesa update. *Kenyan Wallstreet*. https://kenyanwallstreet.com/safaricom-tackles-fraud-in-latest-mpesa-update/

Kanali, N. (2020, 27 January). Mobile money and mobile banking transaction rates in Kenya (24Bit Podcast Episode 18). *TechTrendsKE*. https://techtrendske.co.ke/24bit-podcast-episode-18-mobile-money-mobile-banking-transactions-rates-in-kenya/

Kiaga, A. K., Lapeyre, F., and Marcadent, P. (2020). *The Impact of the COVID-19 on the Informal Economy in Africa and the Related Policy Responses*. International Labour Organization. https://www.ilo.org/africa/information-resources/publications/WCMS_741864/lang--en/index.htm

Laldjebaev, M., Sovacool, B. K., and Kassam, K.-A. S. (2016). Energy security, poverty, and sovereignty: Complex interlinkages and compelling implications. In: L. Guruswamy (Ed.), *International Energy and Poverty: The emerging contours* (97-112). Routledge. https://doi.org/10.4324/9781315762203

Lema, R., Andersen, M. H., Hanlin, R., and Nzila, C. (Eds). (2021). *Building Innovation Capabilities for Sustainable Industrialisation: Renewable electrification in developing economies*. Routledge. https://doi.org/10.4324/9781003054665

Machasio, I. N. (2020). *COVID-19 and Digital Financial Inclusion in Africa: How to leverage digital technologies during the pandemic*. 7. World Bank.

Miriri, D. (2020). Kenya's central bank extends mobile payments relief by six months. https://Kyc360.Riskscreen.Com/. https://kyc360.riskscreen.com/news/kenyas-central-bank-extends-mobile-payments-relief-by-six-months/

Muhura, A. (2020, 23 March). M-Koba: Vodacom Tanzania's innovation to digitise savings groups. *Mobile for Development*. https://www.gsma.com/mobilefordevelopment/blog/m-koba-vodacom-tanzanias-innovation-to-digitise-savings-groups/

Mulumba, Y., and Schmidt, K. (2021). Financial technology: The key to achieving financial inclusion in developing countries post COVID-19 from an East African perspective. *International Journal of Economics and Management Engineering*, 15(3), 5.

Mwita, M. (2021). Safaricom enhances measures to curb M-Pesa fraud. *The Star.* https://www.the-star.co.ke/business/kenya/2021-06-07-safaricom-enhances-measures-to-curb-mpesa-fraud/

NSSF. (2020). NSSF partners with Safaricom on Tenant purchase.

Ockwell, D., and Byrne, R. (2017). *Sustainable Energy for All: Innovation, technology and pro-poor green transformations.* Routledge. https://doi.org/10.4324/9781315621623

Ohnsorge, F., and Yu, S. (Eds). (2021). *The Long Shadow of Informality: Challenges and policies.* World Bank. https://www.worldbank.org/en/news/press-release/2021/05/11/widespread-informality-likely-to-slow-recovery-from-covid-19-in-developing-economies

Onsongo, E. K., and Schot, J. (2017). Inclusive innovation and rapid sociotechnical transitions: The case of mobile money in Kenya. *SSRN Electronic Journal.* https://doi.org/10.2139/ssrn.2940184

Porcaro, J., Mehta, S., Shupler, M., Kissel, S., Pfeiffer, M., Dora, C. F. C., and Adair-Rohani, H. (2017). *Modern Energy Access and Health: State of electricity access report.* World Bank. http://hdl.handle.net/10986/26648

Reinert, E. (2007). *How Rich Countries Got Rich ... and Why Poor Countries Stay Poor.* Constable and Robinson.

Rolffs, P., Ockwell, D., and Byrne, R. (2015). Beyond technology and finance: Pay-as-you-go sustainable energy access and theories of social change. *Environment and Planning A,* 47(12), 2609-2627. https://doi.org/10.1177/0308518x15615368

Rotich, K. (2021, 31 May). Nine in 10 SMEs use M-Pesa for payments. *Business Daily.* https://www.businessdailyafrica.com/bd/corporate/enterprise/nine-in-10-smes-use-m-pesa-for-payments-3420674

Safaricom. (2020). Safaricom news and latest press releases. https://www.safaricom.co.ke/about/media-center/publications/press-releases/release/911

Scheme (T.P.S) Payments. *NSSF Kenya.* https://www.nssf.or.ke/nssf-partners-with-safaricom-on-tenant-purchase-scheme-t-p-s-payments

Schot, J. (2020). Interpreting COVID-19 through the lens of the second deep transition. *Ökologisches Wirtschaften-Fachzeitschrift,* 35(3), 19-21. https://doi.org/10.14512/OEW350319

Schot, J., and Kanger, L. (2018). Deep transitions: Emergence, acceleration, stabilization and directionality. *Research Policy,* 47(6), 1045-1059. https://doi.org/10.1016/j.respol.2018.03.009

Schot, J., and Steinmueller, W. E. (2018). Three frames for innovation policy: R&D, systems of innovation and transformative change. *Research Policy,* 47(9), 1554-1567. https://doi.org/10.1016/j.respol.2018.08.011

Shupler, M., Mwitari, J., Gohole, A., Anderson de Cuevas, R., Puzzolo, E., Čukić, I., Nix, E., and Pope, D. (2021). COVID-19 impacts on household energy and food security in a Kenyan informal settlement: The need for integrated approaches to the SDGs. *Renewable and Sustainable Energy Reviews,* 144, 111018. https://doi.org/10.1016/j.rser.2021.111018

Šumonja, M. (2020). Neoliberalism is not dead – On political implications of Covid-19. *Capital and Class,* 45(2), 215-227. https://doi.org/10.1177/0309816820982381

Tarantola, A. (2021, 6 February). Hitting the books: Kenya's digital divide is hampering its mobile money revolution. *Engadget.* https://www.engadget.com/

hitting-the-books-reimagining-money-sibel-kusimba-stanford-university-press-163058129.html

Tooze, A. (2021, 2 September). Has Covid ended the neoliberal era? *The Guardian*. https://www.theguardian.com/news/2021/sep/02/covid-and-the-crisis-of-neoliberalism

UNDESA. (2021). *Leveraging Digital Technologies for Social Inclusion*. UN. https://www.un.org/development/desa/dspd/wp-content/uploads/sites/22/2021/02/PB_92-1.pdf

UN Energy. (2021). *Theme Report on Energy Access: Towards the achievement of SDG 7 and net-zero emissions*. United Nations. https://www.un.org/sites/un2.un.org/files/2021-twg_1-062321.pdf

Vivid Economics, and Open Capital Advisors. (2020). *Off-Grid Solar: Market trends report 2020*. International Finance Corporation. https://www.gogla.org/resources/2020-off-grid-solar-market-trends-report

Wilkinson, R., and Pickett, K. (2010). *The Spirit Level: Why equality is better for everyone*. Penguin.

World Economic Forum. (2020). West Africans are switching from cash to mobile money because of COVID-19. https://www.weforum.org/agenda/2020/04/coronavirus-set-to-spur-mobile-money-growth-in-w-africa/

World Health Organization (WHO), and World Bank. (2015). *Access to Modern Energy Services for Health Facilities in Resource-Constrained Settings: A review of status, significance, challenges and measurement*. WHO. https://www.who.int/publications/i/item/9789241507646

Zaman, R., van Vliet, O., and Posch, A. (2021). Energy access and pandemic-resilient livelihoods: The role of solar energy safety nets. *Energy Research and Social Science*, 71, 101805. https://doi.org/10.1016/j.erss.2020.101805

Zetterli, P. (2020). Four ways microfinance institutions are responding to COVID-19. *CGAP Blog Series: Microfinance and COVID-19: Insights from CGAP's Global Pulse Survey*. https://www.cgap.org/blog/four-ways-microfinance-institutions-are-responding-covid-19

CHAPTER 14

Conclusion

*Rebecca Hanlin, Erika-Kraemer Mbula, Rob Byrne,
Chux Daniels and Ann Kingiri*

The pandemic revealed the fragility of the systems upon which we rely for the continued functioning of our societies. Moreover, it exposed how those living in poverty and those who are marginalised or powerless experienced this fragility as vulnerability, not just in terms of risks to their health but also as risks to their livelihoods. All the contributions to this volume provided examples – to a greater or lesser degree – of the ways in which fragility and vulnerability manifested during the pandemic. Even though they can only touch on some of the ways in which fragility is played out, the range of examples provided in this book strongly suggests that fragility and vulnerability are inherent features of our societal – or socio-technical – systems, which are thus unsustainable and so in need of thorough transformation. The pervasiveness of the disruption induced by the pandemic is perhaps one reason why it has revealed the unsustainability of our socio-technical systems in a way that many other crises and moments of instability in recent years did not, whether these be earthquakes, hurricanes, flooding, diseases such as Ebola, or wars[1] and political unrest. The fact that this infectious and dangerous disease

---

[1] One exception is the Russian military aggression in Ukraine, which is still unfolding as we write this and is creating hugely disruptive consequences well beyond its horrifying impacts in Ukraine itself.

spread rapidly to all parts of the world is perhaps another reason, having directly touched most people's lives in some form.

The pandemic's pervasive reach is one consequence of trajectories of economic and social development that, accelerated through the related process of globalisation, have increased our interconnectedness across territorial boundaries and intensified our interdependencies. Such processes are in part the result of innovation or the invention and subsequent introduction and use of new products, processes, or ways of working and organising. As outlined in the introductory chapter, innovation has increasingly been acknowledged as essential for a country's economic development and – as is well understood in the academic literature – the processes of innovating can be enhanced, and the innovations that emerge can be spread more widely, by increased interconnectedness and intensified interdependencies.

On the face of it, the idea that the pandemic's global reach and consequent devastating disruptions were in part facilitated by greater interconnectedness and interdependencies – both of which tend to be 'good' for innovation – suggests we might be better closing our borders, retreating permanently to our homes, and seeking to become inward-looking and self-sufficient in as many ways as possible. But many of the contributions to this volume, as well as providing a variety of examples of the fragility and vulnerability exposed by the pandemic, have described, analysed and discussed a variety of ways in which different kinds of actors have responded – innovated, we could say – to alleviate or even overcome the pandemic's impacts on their lives. And other contributions have examined how the pandemic offered new impetus to rethink broader changes to the way we nurture economic and social development trajectories. In other words, the book contains a set of examples that can contribute to discussions on what addressing fragility and vulnerability with resilience and sustainability might look like: Which parts of our fragile, vulnerable and unsustainable systems need transforming? Who needs to be included in these transformations and why? How can they best be included? What opportunities and existing practices can be harnessed to enhance resilience and sustainability, especially to the benefit not only of our environments but also to communities and those suffering poverty and marginalisation of different kinds? There is also increasing recognition of the need for those involved in promoting and conducting innovation to consider not just its economic effects, but also its environmental and social effects, especially on issues of inclusion and equity. Specifically, there has been a call for innovation to be focused on 'transformation'.

In the first section of this concluding chapter, we make some general observations about the definition of innovation as traditionally understood, how preceding chapters in the book expand this definition in various ways, and why this is relevant to the concept of transformative innovation. Section 2 goes deeper into the insights in the chapters, synthesising the thread of the discussions on the interconnectedness between change, innovation, and the building and affirmation of resilience. Section 3 focuses on the theoretical areas and concepts that have been discussed across multiple chapters, and what this means for building theoretical responses to understanding innovation and change. And the chapter ends with a discussion of possible policy-related responses to enable African countries to be better equipped to build and affirm resilience through transformative innovation in times of change.

Transformative innovation

As noted in the introduction, this book aims to highlight the multiple types of innovation that exist and to move the dialogue beyond innovation considered purely in terms of changes in products and processes that generate profitable returns to privately owned firms in the formal sector. Various chapters have highlighted the existence of different forms of innovation that work outside of these traditional definitions, notably:

- Social innovation – Wandji and Allouche, in Chapter 2, highlighted how this form of innovation is focused on both social effects and social interactions that realise those effects. They also highlighted that social innovation is not, by their definition, focused predominately on hard scientific or technological solutions, although these – especially information technology – may be used in 'innovative social practices' that are often vernacular or locally produced.
- Inclusive innovation – Mentioned briefly in Soumonni and Sègla in Chapter 8, this approach was made popular by Richard Heeks and colleagues (Foster and Heeks, 2013; Heeks et al., 2014) and refers – at its simplest – to innovation that includes marginalised groups. Heeks and colleagues, however, also developed a taxonomic ladder of inclusive innovation that goes from innovation that addresses the needs of the most marginalised to that which occurs as a result of inclusion being embedded in the structure and discourse of society.
- Endogenous or indigenous innovation – Several chapters in this volume focused on the need for innovation to be grounded in the use of local

knowledge and natural ingredients (Soumonni and Sègla, Chapter 8), the importance of locally produced innovations and manufacturing (Adesida et al., Chapter 3; Chakravarty and Knorringa, Chapter 7; Hedeshi, Chapter 12), and innovation in the informal sector (Petersen et al., Chapter 6). These arguments arise from the ethical imperative to ensure that innovation is inclusive and builds long-term capabilities. The concept of endogenous innovation (Soumonni and Sègla, Chapter 8) goes one step further to argue that local or informal knowledge is not discounted; that it is not seen as either inferior or considered less 'useful' to society.

- Frugal innovation – This is the idea of being able to 'do more with less' (Chakravarty and Knorringa, Chapter 7), and builds on the proverb 'necessity is the mother of invention' and the resulting innovation (Gatune et al., Chapter 10). It is dependent on the skills and capabilities within society, but again focuses – like the concept of social innovation used by Wandji and Allouche in this volume – on recognising that the skills and capabilities needed for innovation are not always those that are formally promoted.

As many of the chapters in this volume have articulated, these approaches to innovation are not suggesting an 'either/or' dichotomy; rather, they are seen as being important and necessary complements to more traditional approaches to innovation. They also often look similar to the way formal innovation occurs in the setting of the firm – in products, processes, business models or organisational change. And, similarly to formal innovation, these 'non-traditional' forms of innovation vary in terms of the degree to which they are incremental, are existing innovations adopted in, or adapted for, new environments, or are radical and original innovations that have never before been developed.

But there are potentially other kinds of innovation not captured by the four described above. One of these other types might be called policy or governance innovation, with examples discussed in the contributions by Lee (Chapter 5), Atela et al. (Chapter 9) and Hedeshi (Chapter 12). Lee argued in his chapter for the adoption by African governments of resource-based industrialisation policy, and Atela et al. analysed the consequences of the adoption by several African governments of different models of scientific advice meant to help guide pandemic responses. Hedeshi's argument could be understood (perhaps only crudely) as attributing the frailties revealed in African economies to historically conditioned global political economic forces, the response to which should be a return to greater autonomy in industrial and trade policy alongside several other actions in the vein of the developmental state. All three of these discussions can be seen as focused on a form of policy or governance innovation that might be classed as adoptive: that is, they are about using, and perhaps adapting, policy approaches from other places and/or other times.

Despite these similarities, there are significant differences in their underlying epistemological approaches, even if we constrain ourselves only to considering firm-level innovation. This brings us back to the distinction made in the introductory chapter between 'traditional' views of innovation – those informing what have been termed the 'first' and 'second' frames of innovation policy (Schot and Steinmueller, 2018) – focused on economic growth and competitiveness, and a need for a third frame of innovation policy focused on 'transformative change'. This third frame represents the aspiration to make innovation efforts supportive of social justice and environmental integrity from the outset, whether such efforts be towards ending poverty, reducing inequality, or addressing climate change and broader sustainability imperatives.

Many of these innovations, as exemplified in various chapters, are enabled by digital technologies. These can be seen in the broader context of digital transformation in Africa (e.g. the *Digital Transformation Strategy for Africa*, 2020). The response to the pandemic has accelerated digital dynamics and presents the continent with challenges and opportunities for digitally enabled versions of the types of innovation described above.

All the chapters in this book have highlighted the need to think differently about innovation when considering how to realise societal development that moves us in sustainable directions, and a key reason for this is the need for African countries to build and strengthen resilience to detrimental change, especially in the context of crises and their impacts on the lives of those living in poverty and/or experiencing various injustices. All the chapters have also highlighted that changing (or, at the very least, expanding) the focus to other rationales for the promotion of innovation beyond economic growth – moving towards transformative innovation – is necessary.

Innovation, systems, transformative change and resilience

Innovation and transformative change are both possible through either directed or undirected means. In other words, innovation and economic or social change can be promoted and conducted deliberately by governments, firms or communities, or can emerge more organically out of circumstance, chance, or learning by doing. Several chapters in the book have provided examples of 'undirected' innovation and reflected on what these mean for our understanding of what counts as innovation, and of how innovation relates to transformative change and strengthened resilience. The insights provided by these various chapters, and the arguments the various authors develop, have implications for enabling innovation processes, who should be supported as innovators, what innovation goals should be prioritised (especially at the policy level), and what changes are needed to address the various systemic and structural challenges to innovation that exist. Arising from these insights and arguments, explicitly or implicitly, are questions about what transformation means, what transformative change that supports sustainability and resilience should be – especially in favour of those who are powerless or marginalised – and how the various insights on innovation can help to foster such transformative change.

Innovation rooted in local knowledge

At the micro level of specific innovations and firms (including in the informal sector), and the level of communities, cases discussed in the book show that crises of various kinds, including those such as the pandemic, can be powerful stimulants to (sometimes rapid) innovation processes giving rise to a diversity of innovation outcomes. However, much of this diversity falls within the spectrum of incremental or adoptive innovation. Few of the innovations discussed in the book could be considered radical – new to the world – innovations. Nevertheless, many of them can be seen as important for the firms (formal or informal), communities, and the local and national economies in which they have been developed or adopted. Amongst those innovations discussed in the book that could be classified as radical are medical devices that Chakravarty and Knorringa (Chapter 7) characterise as having frugal innovation qualities (and meet some aspects of inclusive innovation). But even these 'radical' innovations tend to be based on the existing knowledge base and so the innovation process is akin to incremental technological change rather than science-intensive R&D.

More clearly incremental or adoptive innovations are those Petersen et al. (Chapter 6) discussed in relation to informal sector food enterprises in South Africa. In these cases, innovations tended to be adoption of more formal financial and business management systems triggered by either financial peril or significant personal events. This suggests that simple business survival is an important stimulant of informal sector innovation but even this kind of innovation activity has, according to the analysis by Petersen et al., deeper and wider benefits. For informal enterprises, such innovation activity drives business evolution with implications for better business survival and increasing prosperity. For the local economy, with its interdependent network of informal enterprises, the evolution of its businesses has the potential to increase employment and strengthen its resilience. And, for the national economy, such business evolution means realising greater degrees of formality that can contribute to more economic stability and increased tax revenue.

At the community level, the contribution from Wandji and Allouche (Chapter 2) raises some interesting points about social innovation and its relationship with resilience. The first interesting point is that the authors' notion of social innovation goes well beyond something that provides a product-like or process solution to a narrowly defined (by an entrepreneur or policy-maker, for example) social challenge, and so their definition is not directly analogous to the traditional understanding of innovation. Instead, they offer an interpretation of social innovation that is novel on perhaps two levels. At the level of the 'solution', it is about innovation that can address multiple interacting local crises. At a deeper level, it is about communities innovating by using their intuitive knowledge of the multiple crises they experience in their local contexts. The second interesting point is the implication of this form of social innovation: the authors argue that it is more promising for strengthening local resilience than social innovation understood as a version of the traditional kinds of product and process innovation. Strengthened resilience arises from the idea that such a response takes account of multiple crises – their causes and consequences – as opposed to tackling only part of the problem, and so reduces the risk that a piecemeal solution may create new problems. And resilience is further enhanced in the community by building the social innovation capabilities to respond to future multiple crises.

Finally, in respect of specific innovations, in their analysis of the ways in which different models of scientific advice were taken up quickly by several African governments during the pandemic, Atela et al. (Chapter 9) provide a cautionary case for how innovations adopted unreflexively or uncritically can be detrimental to communities and especially marginalised groups. The authors acknowledge that some of the actions emerging from the top-down models of scientific advice – the science–policy interface – had beneficial impacts, but many actions have hit the poor, women and others hard. This may have been a consequence – in part, at least – of the fact that the science–policy interface model adopted was a narrow 'hard' science expert form, neglecting other kinds of expertise and, crucially, any connection with affected communities. In response to the adverse effects felt by communities, 'grassroots' actions emerged that to some extent underscore the argument made in the Wandji and Allouche contribution about the importance and form of social innovation for building and strengthening resilience at the community level.

Systemic and structural challenges to innovation

Several chapters in the book have considered the systemic and structural aspects of innovation in the context of the pandemic. Manyuchi and Ouma-Mugabe (Chapter 4) discussed how the pandemic provided opportunities for both short-term and long-term innovations in the African health sector, but they also argue that the efforts to innovate have revealed systemic and structural barriers to innovation. As a result, many of the inventions emerging out of the pandemic response will remain 'stunted'; they will not be realised as innovations. Furthermore, the barriers to innovation exist because of weaknesses in other interdependent sectors and in systems other than health provision: for example, amongst others, in the energy systems that do not provide reliable and affordable or universal electricity; in the communications systems that do not provide reliable and affordable internet connectivity (weakened also by inadequate energy systems); in the education and training systems that result in poor literacy levels (including the digital literacy needed for using what internet connectivity does exist).

To some extent resonant with Manyuchi and Ouma-Mugabe's argument concerning systemic and structural barriers to innovation in African health systems, Adesida et al. (Chapter 3) investigated the role of crises in creating opportunities for systemic change more generally across African innovation ecosystems. Their comparison of the results of an innovation survey conducted pre-pandemic with one conducted during the pandemic enabled them to distinguish between systemic and non-systemic changes. Virtualisation and e-commerce appear to be two of the most likely systemic changes, although virtualisation appears to be only a transient response when it comes to education and medical practices. This, the authors argue, highlights that there are limits to the degree to which crises such as the pandemic can create opportunities for systemic change in African innovation ecosystems. Among the reasons for these limits is the existence of long-standing weaknesses in these systems (similarly to Manyuchi and Ouma-Mugabe) that cannot be addressed quickly during a crisis response. This points to fundamental qualities of such systems, and whose responses count and are supported. In this vein, Wandji and Allouche (Chapter 2) referred to the importance of conceptualising crises as integral parts of the innovation ecosystem but that the system is one that should include those who have intuitive knowledge of the social complexities of their local spaces. Indeed, the contribution from

Soumonni and Sègla (Chapter 8) resonates with this last point about intuitive knowledge when they discuss the structural biases in the health sector against traditional knowledge of the medicinal use of plants.

Even when innovations do emerge, weak innovation ecosystems may result in the economic benefits being appropriated by a small number of corporations and/or investors outside Africa. Gatune et al. (Chapter 10), for example, make this argument in respect to 4IR technologies. The urgency of the pandemic response has included businesses moving to digital platforms – the virtualisation discussed by Adesida et al. in Chapter 3 – which means that, in the absence of strong innovation ecosystems and appropriate regulations, successful innovations related to this process emerging from within Africa were relatively easily bought up by a few larger companies. In this case, the trajectory of development of the 4IR is to monopolisation and concentrated economic (and political) power. This suggests a development path resembling what Hedeshi (Chapter 12) criticises as now long-standing in Africa, where global corporations, assisted by powerful geopolitical forces, have been exploiting African countries.

Transformation and transformative change

Each chapter in this book has provided insights and developed arguments that speak in different ways to the notions of transformation and transformative change. Perhaps unsurprisingly, given the diversity of studies contained in the book and the range of authors' perspectives, there is no simple agreement on what transformation means and thus what transformative change should be. Neither do we, as editors, propose any single definition of these ideas. Rather, one of the aims of the book was to open up discussion on these concepts to progress theoretical development of the notion of transformative innovation and to inform approaches to transformative innovation policy in African contexts. But, as we observed at the beginning of this chapter, across all the book's contributions, there is a clear recognition that the systems upon which African populations rely are unsustainable in terms of realising social justice, economic prosperity and environmental integrity. While much the same could be said about the rest of the world, inequality, poverty and environmental degradation are arguably especially severe across the African continent. Moreover, the historical injustices associated with imperialism and colonialism, which have shaped and conditioned the systems Africans rely upon, continue to position African countries at the global margins. The contributions to the book thus all share the goal of transformation; that systems from the local to the international need to be transformed if the ambitions such as those articulated in the SDGs, for example, are to be realised. With such deep and wide-ranging challenges to address, no single study or piece of analysis can hope to provide definitive solutions; rather, each contribution can highlight something important that warrants action and from which we can begin to identify what transformative innovation (and policy) could look like as a response, as well as understand its limitations. Following this last point, we highlight several observations relevant to transformative change that have emerged from the work discussed in this book by pointing to the insights and arguments provided in some of the chapters and reflect on what these could mean for our understanding of transformative innovation in African contexts.

Returning to the micro level of specific innovations, and formal and informal enterprises, as well as the level of communities, we could deduce that transformation does not necessarily materialise through radical (new to the world) innovation, as that term would be understood in the traditional innovation studies literature and in innovation policy circles. Petersen et al. and in some ways Chakravarty and Knorringa (Chapters 6 and 7, respectively) show that incremental innovations can have transformative impacts for the enterprises involved as well as for the customers of their innovations, assuming we accept that the frugal innovations analysed by Chakravarty and Knorringa are incremental in the sense that they largely rely on the existing knowledge base. And the offering from Wandji and Allouche (Chapter 2) shows how incremental innovations adopted (and perhaps adapted) through community-driven processes can have transformative impacts on the resilience of those communities. At this micro level, then, transformative innovation relates to the changes in daily practice that, resonating with Sen's notion of capabilities (e.g. Sen, 2005), empower people to achieve what they hold to be of value to them, whether or not this involves technologies.

At systemic and structural levels, the variety of insights provided by the contributing authors is perhaps wider than at the micro level just discussed. Working from the more traditional innovation (eco)systems perspective, the arguments presented by Adesida et al. (Chapter 3) on systemic and non-systemic innovations, and Manyuchi and Ouma-Mugabe (Chapter 4) on systemic barriers to innovation, suggest the need to transform African innovation systems from their currently weak conditions into systems that better support innovation processes and better embed the value of innovation outcomes in African economies. But embedding value in African economies needs to avoid establishing trajectories of monopolisation and power concentration, as Gatune et al. (Chapter 10) caution in the case of the 4IR. And, as Manyuchi and Ouma-Mugabe argue, the fragmentation of policy action across different innovation systems (around, for example, energy, communications, education and so on) needs to be transformed into something much more coherent and coordinated. Thus, based on these discussions, transformative innovation at the system and multi-system level would relate to the changes that facilitate valuable innovation processes to empower African economies to construct more resilient, sustainable and equitable development pathways.

Innovation and resilience

Along with 'innovation', a term that has been raised frequently in this book is 'resilience'. We should, therefore, say something more specific about what we mean by the term and how the concept may be related to innovation. In the introduction, we referred to resilience as the ability of society to understand, recover and re-orient in response to external disruption or internal system failures. The contributions to this book suggest that innovation provides opportunities to build and enhance resilience: it is an important part of achieving the necessary speed of effective responses and of achieving the changes to development pathways required in any rebuilding efforts.

Figure 1 depicts one way of understanding the relationships between innovation, change and resilience. This is drawn from the experiences shared in this book. The framework is centred on change, whether it is directed or undirected. This can be equated to the debate in international development theory between intentional development and unintentional or organic development (Hanlin and Brown, 2013). It recognises the role of policy in shaping and promoting directed change and, with this, also directed innovation efforts. This framework also recognises the embedding of much undirected change and innovation in practice, and the important place of 'learning by doing, using and interacting' (Jensen et al., 2007). It also understands that policy and practice are only two parts of a larger innovation ecosystem that is made up of numerous different stakeholders. In fact, we interchangeably refer in the diagram to the innovation system and the innovation ecosystem. The former refers to the body of literature from which most of the chapters in the book draw and that builds on innovation systems thinking at the national level (c.f. Lundvall, 1992) or at the sectoral level (cf. Breschi and Malerba, 1997). Adesida et al. (Chapter 3) use the term 'innovation ecosystem', which recognises the evolutionary innovation processes, notably the competition and substitution practices of species (Granstrand and Holgerssen, 2020). This acknowledgement of the living nature of innovation processes is important, given the evidence provided in this book on the adaptability and resilience of those actors involved in innovation activities.

In Figure 1, we indicate the ability of directed innovation to create spaces and opportunities for building resilience. This recognises that innovation can be used strategically to enhance resilience in society, and to strengthen a country's ability to withstand external shocks and internal system failures. In recognising the learning that occurs through innovation, we note that the chapters in this book highlight examples where the pandemic has provided opportunities for undirected change and innovation – innovation from necessity or in response to the shocks – and, through this, the system's resilience is strengthened. This recognises that policy should focus on more than promoting intentional and directed innovative activity to meet predetermined development or 'good change' goals (Chambers, 1997). Policy must recognise that innovation and change occur all of the time, and therefore the (eco)system must be strengthened to ensure unintentional and undirected (spontaneous) innovation can be promoted to enable the continued affirmation of resilience within the innovation system, and within society more generally. This is particularly necessary in many African countries, where not only social security nets, but also economic systems, are weak. Certain chapters have discussed this in terms of a number of approaches, from high-level policy support to encourage local manufacturing through to recognising degrees of informality. We address these policy issues in the final section. First, we discuss how these different ways of thinking about innovation, change and resilience provide learnings for our academic study and theory building. We start this with a call to build resilience concepts into innovation systems thinking.

Figure 1: Interrelationships between innovation, change and resilience

Source: Editors

Lessons for theory from the pandemic

Developing resilience concepts within innovation systems thinking

As noted above, a key theme of this book has been resilience and, more importantly, the interrelationship between resilience and innovation. A burgeoning set of literature has focused on innovation resilience at the project level (Oeij et al., 2017; Todt et al., 2018), while another set of literature looks at organisational resilience in relation to the robustness of firms, as well as their focus on sustainability issues (and the triple bottom line of people, planet and profit) (Carayannis et al., 2017). Carayannis et al. (2017) discuss innovation as a resilience enabler, especially at the organisational level, and the importance of firms being open to resilience considerations and building these into their systems. There is also literature on resilience and regional innovation efforts (Cooke et al., 2012; Pinto and Pereira, 2018). There is, however, a lack of focus on these issues in African contexts, save a small amount of work – predominately in Nigeria – on organisational resilience and its relationship with innovation efforts in firms (e.g. Ikechukwu, 2016; Olaleye, 2021). Where there is a larger focus by African scholars is in the area of agriculture, and also the environment and broader issues of resilience in the context of environmental sustainability.

This is largely informed by what has become known as the sustainability transitions literature (Markard et al., 2012). A practical example of those putting this into action can be found in the Resilience Africa Network,[2] a group of academics focused on strengthening the resilience of households and communities across 13 countries on the continent through the use of innovative technologies and solutions.

There is, however, a distinct lack of interest in the national innovation systems approach to issues of resilience. At the time of writing, Scopus showed only two papers containing the phrase 'national systems of innovation' and the term 'resilience' in their abstracts. One document that does refer to resilience in the context of national innovation systems is a 2002 OECD report entitled 'Dynamizing National Innovation Systems' (OECD, 2002). Specifically, it refers to the role of complex interactions between system actors and their importance in determining the extent to which the system is resilient, dynamic and adaptive.

The pandemic highlighted the importance of building resilience concepts into innovation systems thinking, both as an output of innovation efforts

---

2   See https://www.ranlab.org/

and also as a much-needed input into the system to ensure that innovation can occur in times of change. This is important given, as articulated by Hedeshi in Chapter 12, that systems have a set of pre-existing vulnerabilities and longer-term challenges that they have to address. Lee, in Chapter 5, highlights the importance of looking at the past experiences of other countries.

Therefore, any consideration of resilience in innovation systems (at any scale – national, regional or local) needs to be reviewed with respect to both the past and the present.

Endogenous, local and appropriate (contextual) innovation theory
Soumonni and Sègla (Chapter 8) discussed the need to strengthen endogenous innovation and, by extension, innovation theory. Other contributors highlighted the importance of locally focused innovation efforts. For example, Petersen et al. (Chapter 6) suggested the need to frame innovation within local innovation and production systems (or LIPS). This focus on local and endogenous innovation is rarely conceptualised in theory on innovation in African contexts. As noted above, however, there are other ways in which innovation takes place in African contexts and, therefore, a broader definition of innovation is warranted. To move this forward, academic and theoretical discussions of what innovation is must also be considered. Unfortunately – as outlined in the introduction – in relation to the African continent, thinking about innovation, and ways of measuring it, has been deeply influenced by theory from elsewhere. As such, much of the theory that is currently considered may be said to be inappropriate to the context in which it is applied.

This book presents several cases of innovation with different characteristics to those innovations encountered in many European and American settings. There is, in fact, a burgeoning empirical literature highlighting how and why African innovation happens (e.g. Adesida et al., 2016; Fu, 2020; Kraemer-Mbula and Wunsch-Vincent, 2016). At the same time, it has been argued that innovation activities in some Asian and Oceanic settings may have more similarities to those in Africa due to the ecosystem similarities across these contexts (Hanlin and Kaplinsky, 2016). As an alternative approach, Park (Chapter 11) refers to the need to consider the constellation of 'non-WEIRD' countries (i.e. those that are not Western, educated, industrialised, rich and democratic).

There is a significant need for Africanised innovation systems thinking. The LIPS approach is one effort to redress this, as the idea is to re-purpose the concept of 'emerging innovation systems' (Jacobsson and Bergek, 2006) to specific African contexts (Djeflat, 2015). Several authors have written on the challenges and opportunities of developing an innovation systems perspective built on pan-Africanism (Muchie, 2004, 2016), African histories and regional integration (Scerri, 2012, 2016). More such efforts are needed.

Through the focus areas of this book, we see two ways in which innovation systems thinking can be made more appropriate to the African context: (a) by strengthening interdisciplinarity and transdisciplinarity and (b) by recognising the uneven distribution of innovation and policy effects (both negative and positive).

Strengthening interdisciplinarity and transdisciplinarity. The various contributors to this book come from a range of fields spanning economics, development studies and policy studies, and include not just academics. Some have been innovation practitioners, and some remain active policy-makers. The inclusion of authors from multiple fields – many of which are interdisciplinary, and the combination of which achieves a degree of transdisciplinarity – was deliberate and provides a rich and diverse set of views and focus areas. Just as triangulation in research methods provides opportunities to strengthen the validity of findings, so too does the inclusion of chapters by authors from a range of diverse backgrounds in helping establish key areas for new theory to consider. Themes that have resonated across the book include resilience and the need for locally appropriate solutions, despite the authors approaching the issues from a range of different world views and theoretical and academic standpoints.

Recognising the uneven distribution of innovation and policy effects. Several of the chapters have focused on the need to learn from what has gone wrong: that is, to learn from mistakes rather than seeing negative outcomes as things to forget. Atela et al. (Chapter 9) highlight the importance of learning from situations where innovation policy has had a negative effect on populations. Gatune et al. (Chapter 10) recognise that many innovations that were pushed during the pandemic have helped some in the population, but at the expense of others. Wandji and Allouche (Chapter 2) refer to the 'dark side of innovation'. More research is needed that focuses on these issues of learning from mistakes and learning from failure: that is, to see failure as a fundamental part of long-term learning. We also need more research (and policy recognition – see below) on the inequalities and inequities that arise from innovation efforts.

Possible policy learnings from the pandemic

While all the chapters in this book include discussions related to innovation policy, several focus specifically on policy (chapters by Atela et al.; Chakravarthy and Knorringa; Manyuchi and Ouma-Mugabe). The innovation responses that have occurred as a result of the pandemic were hindered and facilitated by policy. As a result – and as stressed in the introductory chapter – recognising what policy should look like and how it should best be implemented are essential to ensuring that innovation can be used to bring about change and adapt to changes and, through this, build and enhance resilience within innovation ecosystems.

The introduction highlighted the need for the recognition of new forms of knowledge, and also of policy mixes. We look at these, first, through a broader discussion of the importance of policy that acknowledges and builds resilience against the negative effects of power and politics, and creates spaces for agency, especially that of excluded groups and different kinds of knowledge. We then discuss policy mixes and the need for innovation in policy (as opposed to just policy for the promotion of innovation) to resist the tendency of policy being made in silos. As part of this discussion, we also come back to challenge-based approaches to innovation policy.

Agency, power and politics

The lens of innovation systems that is used in a number of chapters in the book recognises that there are multiple actors and interactions within the system. The ability of policy to facilitate these interactions is important. However, innovation systems theory has often been criticised for being insufficiently focused on the power and politics that exist within these interactions. By extension, policy to promote innovation systems often does not adequately give agency to the excluded voices within innovation processes. The chapters by Petersen et al., Wandji and Allouche, and Soumonni and Sègla focus on the need to encourage more actors who are traditionally marginalised to enter the innovation process, especially those at the community level and in the informal sector, who are often seen as passive recipients of innovation by others.

The chapters by Hedeshi (Chapter 12) and Lee (Chapter 5) focus on the need for innovation policy to recognise the global nature of innovation processes and the role of external actors in national-level innovation activities. Atela et al. (Chapter 9) focus on the need to include more stakeholders in the policy process to ensure that the real-world context informs policy.

Linked to this discussion in the current volume are the more general barriers to innovation discussed by Adesida et al. and Manyuchi and Ouma-Mugabe, which include issues of infrastructure, education, finance, resources, access to skills and capabilities. Both of these chapters focus on the need for systemic measures to remove these barriers and, in doing so, to enable positive transient change to become more systemic. A crucial factor towards realising innovation is that of finance and we therefore have a dedicated discussion (Park, Chapter 11) on financial mechanisms and instruments to promote and support innovation. However, as noted by Gatune et al. and Hedeshi in their chapters, the issue is not only access to finance, but also how finance is given and the degree of local ownership (especially for private firms) this enables.

A special mention in relation to agency in innovation policy needs to be made of the role of the state. African governments are responsible for drawing up formal STI policy. They hold the potential to promote innovation through the use of public procurement (Chakravarthy and Knorringa, Chapter 7). This has been gained traction since the pandemic in relation to governments' promotion of innovation through advanced market commitments, as outlined by Park in Chapter 11. A similar discussion arose on the promotion of local pharmaceutical manufacturing in Africa. For example, the African Union developed its Pharmaceutical Manufacturing Plan for Africa in 2007, and the pandemic revived such discussions (Nwaka, 2021). This was allied to broader discussions on the importance of local manufacturing capabilities being built and strengthened more generally, as discussed in chapters here by Adesida et al., by Lee, and by Hedeshi.

Much of the discussion on the state supporting the development of local manufacturing capabilities is from a top-down perspective, especially in the case of public procurement. However, as noted in the introduction and in Atela et al. (Chapter 9), this needs to be balanced with a bottom-up approach to policy that supports and enables innovation to occur more organically. This is where the idea of governments facilitating the development of innovation building blocks that make up the system and enable its functioning becomes especially useful.

Policy mixes and challenge-based approaches to policy

A key obstacle to effective innovation policy, even when a state promotes bottom-up and organic processes of innovation, is the silos in which policy is made. There is a burgeoning body of literature that looks at the delineation or 'siloing' of health policy and industrial policy, and the negative implications this has for both health and economic outcomes (e.g. Mackintosh et al., 2016; Srinivas, 2012), and with a specific focus on the pandemic's implications (Banda et al., 2021). However, as these authors – and many in our book – also argue, when thinking about policy development there is a need for a move towards policy mixing and the breakdown of silos across government departments.

One way to move away from siloed policy-making is through a movement towards challenge-based policy-making. An early consideration of this approach was in 2012, when Daimer and colleagues called for innovation policy to have a specific normative framing and focus on the grand challenges. Practically, we see that some African governments are now reviewing their STI policies in line with the SDGs (UNDESA, 2021). In addition, many governments are now taking the idea of 'mission-oriented innovation policy' (Mazzucato, 2018) seriously. Mission-oriented innovation policy similarly takes as its starting point the focus of innovation policy on specific problems that need solving. Both challenge-based and mission-oriented innovation policy stress the need to work across sectoral boundaries (and therefore the traditional departmental boundaries of ministries) and ensure a bottom-up process that includes stakeholders. We prefer the term challenge-based approaches because it keeps at the forefront the notion that there is a problem that needs solving around which stakeholders can coalesce (as opposed to the term 'mission', which is focused on the process to reach the intended outcome).

Concluding remarks

To conclude, this book has provided a review of a range of different examples of innovation processes that have been taken up by and enable African countries to be better equipped to build and strengthen resilience through transformative innovation in times of change. It offers learning for theory and policy, which has been the focus of this final chapter. Such learning needs to be continuous and contextual. It also needs to be documented consistently. Therefore, we hope this book can add to the growing literature on the lessons learnt from the pandemic, but also provide an impetus for continued work during the post-pandemic era in the areas outlined in this final chapter. This is necessary because change occurs at various scales – from micro to macro – and occurs all the time. We should not wait for the next big crisis to occur to ensure that the world, and Africa in particular, has the innovation systems and policy in place to be ready for it.

References

Adesida, O., Karuri-Sebina, G., and Resende-Santos, J. (Eds). (2016). *Innovation Africa: Emerging hubs of excellence*. Emerald.

Banda, G., Mugwagwa, J., Wanjala, C., Mackintosh, M., and Kale, D. (2021). Local manufacturing, local supply chains and health security in Africa: Lessons from COVID-19. *BMJ Global Health*, 6(6), e006362.

Breschi, S., and Malerba, F. (1997). Sectoral innovation systems: Technological regimes, Schumpeterian dynamics, and spatial boundaries. In: C. Edquist (Ed.), *Systems of Innovation: Technologies, institutions and organizations*. Pinter.

Carayannis, E. G., Grigoroudis, E., Sindakis, S., and Walter, C. (2014). Business model innovation as antecedent of sustainable enterprise excellence and resilience. *Journal of the Knowledge Economy*, 5(3), 440-463.

Chambers, R. (1997). Responsible well-being – A personal agenda for development. *World Development*, 25(11), 1743-1754.

Cooke, P., Parrilli, M. D., and Curbelo, J. L. (Eds). (2012). *Innovation, Global Change and Territorial Resilience*. Edward Elgar.

Daimer, S., Hufnagl, M., and Warnke, P. (2012). Challenge-oriented policy-making and innovation systems theory: Reconsidering systemic instruments. In: ISI Fraunhofer (Ed.), *Innovation System Revisited: Experiences from 40 years of Fraunhofer ISI research* (217-234). Fraunhofer Verlag.

Djeflat, A. (2015). Emerging innovation systems (EIS): A new conceptual framework for analysing GCC and Maghreb countries policies. *International Journal of Innovation and Knowledge Management in the Middle East and North Africa*, 4(2), 75-85.

Foster, C., and Heeks, R. (2013). Conceptualising inclusive innovation: Modifying systems of innovation frameworks to understand diffusion of new technology to low-income consumers. *The European Journal of Development Research*, 25(3), 333-355.

Fu, X. (2020). *Innovation Under the Radar: The nature and sources of innovation in Africa*. Cambridge University Press.

Granstrand, O., and Holgersson, M. (2020). Innovation ecosystems: A conceptual review and a new definition. *Technovation*, 90, 102098.

Hanlin, R., and Brown, W. (2013). Contesting development in theory and practice. In: T. Papaioannou and M. Butcher (Eds), *International Development in a Changing World* (31-48). Bloomsbury Academic.

Hanlin, R., and Kaplinsky, R. (2016). South–South trade in capital goods: The market-driven diffusion of appropriate technology. *The European Journal of Development Research*, 28(3), 361-378.

Heeks, R., Foster, C., and Nugroho, Y. (Eds). (2014). *New Models of Inclusive Innovation for Development*. Routledge.

Ikechukwu, E.U. (2016). Innovation and organizational resilience in selected manufacturing firms in Enugu State, Nigeria. Doctoral dissertation.

Jacobsson, S., and Bergek, A. (2006). A framework for guiding policy-makers intervening in emerging innovation systems in 'catching-up' countries. *The European Journal of Development Research*, 18(4), 687-707.

Jensen, M. B., Johnson, B., Lorenz, E., and Lundvall, B. Å. (2007). Forms of knowledge and modes of innovation. *Research Policy*, 5(36), 680-693.

Kraemer-Mbula, E., and Wunsch-Vincent, S. (Eds). (2016). *The Informal Economy in Developing Nations*. Cambridge University Press.

Lundvall, B. Å. (1992). *National Systems of Innovation: Towards a theory of innovation and interactive learning*. Pinter.

Mackintosh, M., Mugwagwa, J., Banda, G., Tibandebage, P., Tunguhole, J., Wangwe, S., and Karimi Njeru, M. (2018). Health-industry linkages for local health: Reframing policies for African health system strengthening. *Health Policy and Planning*, 33(4), 602-610.

Markard, J., Raven, R., and Truffer, B. (2012). Sustainability transitions: An emerging field of research and its prospects. *Research Policy*, 41(6), 955-967.

Mazzucato, M. (2018). Mission-oriented innovation policies: Challenges and opportunities. *Industrial and Corporate Change*, 27(5), 803-815.

Muchie, M. (2004). Resisting the deficit model of development in Africa: Re-thinking through the making of an African national innovation system. *Social Epistemology*, 18(4), 315-332. DOI: 10.1080/0269172052000343321.

Muchie, M. (2016). Towards a unified theory of pan-African innovation systems and integrated development. In: O. Adesida, G. Karuri-Sebina, and J. Resende-Santos (Eds), *Innovation Africa: Emerging hubs of innovation* (13-35). Emerald. https://doi.org/10.1108/978-1-78560-311-220151002

Nwaka, S. (2021). *Social and Technological Innovation in Africa*. Springer.

Organisation for Economic Co-operation and Development (OECD). (2002). *Dynamising National Innovation Systems*. https://doi.org/10.1787/9789264194465-en

Oeij, P. R. A., Dhondt, S., Gaspersz, J. B. R., and Van Vuuren, T. (2017). Innovation resilience behavior and critical incidents: Validating the innovation resilience behavior-scale with qualitative data. *Project Management Journal*, 48(5), 49-63.

Olaleye, B., Anifowose, O., Efuntade, A., and Arije, B. (2021). The role of innovation and strategic agility on firms' resilience: A case study of tertiary institutions in Nigeria. *Management Science Letters*, 11(1), 297-304.

Pinto, H., and Pereira, T. S. (2018). The resilience of innovation systems under economic turbulence. In: T. Baycan and H. Pinto (Eds), *Resilience, Crisis and Innovation Dynamics* (47-67). Edward Elgar.

Scerri, M. (2012). Economic integration in Africa – The systems of innovation approach. In: S. Osha, M. Muchie and P. M. Matlotleng (Eds), *The Africana World: From fragmentation to unity and renaissance*. Africa Institute of South Africa.

Scerri, M. (Ed.). (2016). *The Emergence of Innovation in South(ern) Africa: Long histories and contemporary debates*. Real African Publishers.

Schot, J., and Steinmueller, W. E. (2018). Three frames for innovation policy: R&D, systems of innovation and transformative change. *Research Policy*, 47(9), 1554-1567.

Sen, A. (2005). Human rights and capabilities. *Journal of Human Development*, 6(2), 151-166.

Srinivas, S. (2012). *Market Menagerie: Health and development in late industrial states*. Stanford University Press.

Todt, G., Weiss, M., and Hoegl, M. (2018). Mitigating negative side effects of innovation project terminations: The role of resilience and social support. *Journal of Product Innovation Management,* 35(4), 518-542.

UNDESA. (2021). *Assessment of STI roadmaps.* IATT Issues Brief. https://www.uneca.org/sites/default/files/TCND/AFSTIF2021/Assessment_of_STI_Roadmaps_27012021.pdf

About the authors

Olugbenga Adesida, *The Africa Innovation Summit & Bonako*
Dr Adesida is the co-founder of Bonako and of The Africa Innovation Summit (AIS). He consults widely across the African continent on foresight, innovation and strategy issues for governments, international organisations and companies. Dr Adesida has published many articles and co-edited special issues of major journals such as the *Africa Development Review, Futures, Foresight* and *Africa Journal of Science, Technology, Innovation and Development,* and co-edited books such as *Innovation Africa* and *African Voices, African Visions.* He holds an MA in economics from The City College of New York (USA) and a PhD from the London School of Economics (UK).

Jeremy Allouche, *Institute of Development Studies*
Prof. Jeremy Allouche is a co-director of the Humanitarian Learning Centre and principal investigator of the GCRF-funded project Islands of Innovation in Protracted Crisis and the AHRC/DFID-funded project New Community-Informed Approaches to Humanitarian Protection and Restraint.

Joanes Atela, *Africa Research and Impact Network*
Dr Joanes Atela is an interdisciplinary scholar with more than five years of research experience in the area of environment, climate change, agriculture and development. Joanes obtained a PhD in environment and development from the University of Leeds, an MSc in agriculture and resource management from the University of Bonn, and a BSc in environmental sciences from Maseno University, Kenya. His PhD research provided one of the first multilevel analyses of climate change policies from the global design process down to national and local level implementation in an African setting.

Rob Byrne, *Science Policy Research Unit (SPRU), University of Sussex*
Dr Rob Byrne is now a Senior Lecturer whose research focuses on energy and climate change, specifically sustainable energy access, sustainability, poverty reduction, social justice. His life before academia in East Africa and the UK working in the low carbon energy field provides a strong backdrop for Rob's work as a policy researcher and educator. Rob has a PhD in Science and Technology Policy Studies from University of Sussex.

Sanghamitra Chakravarty, *International Institute of Social Studies, Erasmus University Rotterdam and International Centre for Frugal Innovation*
Sanghamitra Chakravarty has been working at the interface of innovation and development with government agencies in India and Oman for several years. Initially

trained as a chemical engineer, a need to better understand the theories behind practice led her to the doctoral programme in development studies at the International Institute of Social Studies, The Hague. Her PhD research explored resource-constrained innovation and inclusive technological change with fieldwork data from the medical device sector in South Africa and was embedded in the Leiden-Delft-Erasmus International Centre for Frugal Innovation. She is currently a researcher at the Faculty of Technology, Policy, and Management, Delft University of Technology, where she is exploring issues of governance in a project on electrochemical conversion of CO_2 for sustainable energy transitions.

Chux Daniels, *Science Policy Research Unit (SPRU), University of Sussex*
Dr Daniels holds a doctorate in science and technology policy studies from SPRU, University of Sussex. His research connects ST&I and public policies in ways that contribute to addressing development challenges and fostering transformative change across sectors, systems and societies. His areas of research interest include ST&I, public policies and policy processes, capabilities, policy-making (formulation, implementation, evaluation and governance), research excellence, inclusion in ST&I, entrepreneurship, ST&I indicators and metrics, and technology management. He leads the Transformative Innovation Policy (TIP) Africa hub research project, which involves Ghana, Kenya, Senegal and South Africa.

Diederik de Boer, *Maastricht School of Management*
Dr Diederik de Boer is an assistant professor in sustainable business development at Maastricht School of Management (MSM). He holds a PhD from the Erasmus University (the Netherlands), an MPA from Leiden/Rotterdam University (the Netherlands), an MBA from Bradford/Tilburg University (UK/ The Netherlands) and a minor in small and micro credit schemes from Harvard University (USA). He worked for seven years for the United Nations and the Dutch Ministry for Development Cooperation in Cambodia, Mongolia, Korea and Palestine. His research focuses on partnerships and cluster competitiveness in developing countries in Asia and Africa.

Nicole Dunn-van Rheede, *Centre for Science, Technology and Innovation Indicators (CeSTII), Human Sciences Research Council*
Ms Nicole Dunn-van Rheede is a chief researcher in the Centre for Science, Technology and Innovation Indicators (CeSTII) of the Human Sciences Research Council (HSRC) in South Africa. She holds a master's degree in development studies from Nelson Mandela University (2018). Dunn-van Rheede specialises in organisation studies, development studies and informal business innovation, as well as science, technology and innovation policy for inclusive development and transformative innovation policy. She is currently pursuing a PhD in business administration from the University of Cape Town's Graduate School of Business.

Julius Gatune, *Maastricht School of Management*
Dr Julius Gatune is a senior project consultant with the Maastricht School of Management (MSM). He is also the Unesco Chair of Futures at the Dedan Kimathi University of Science and Technology (DeKUT) and a senior fellow with the African

Centre for Economic Transformation. He has previously worked for McKinsey. He holds a PhD in policy analysis from the Pardee RAND Graduate School, and a master's degree in computer science from the University of Cambridge, UK. He also holds a BSc in civil engineering and an MBA from the University of Nairobi.

Rebecca Hanlin, *DSI/NRF/Newton Fund Trilateral Research Chair in Transformative Innovation, the 4th Industrial Revolution and Sustainable Development, University of Johannesburg*
Prof. Hanlin is a Professor of Innovation and Sustainable Development. She has a PhD from the University of Edinburgh in science and technology studies. She is a science, technology, and innovation (STI) policy expert who has worked in many African countries with senior government officials to improve the policy environment for research and innovation. Her research focuses on capabilities and capacity building in STI systems especially in the renewable energy and health fields.

Massoud Hedeshi, *Independent policy analyst*
Massoud holds a master's degree in development economics from Manchester University with specialisation in industrial policy and the political economy of development. He has over 20 years of development policy and programme work experience with various UN agencies across the world.

Geci Karuri-Sebina, *Wits School of Governance, University of the Witwatersand*
Prof. Geci Karuri-Sebina is a Johannesburg-based scholar-practitioner who mainly works on city governance issues. She is currently an associate of the South African Cities Network, visiting associate professor with the Wits School of Governance, and a national organiser of the Civic Tech Innovation Network in South Africa. Karuri-Sebina's experience and interests span a range of development foresight, policy, innovation, and practice topics, particularly relating to the intersection between people, place and technological change.

Ann Kingiri, *African Centre for Technology Studies*
Dr Kingiri is an STI policy and development researcher with a focus on inclusive and sustainable development in Africa. She holds a PhD in development studies and has over 20 years of experience working with the public and private sector, and development partners in the area of innovation and development particularly targeting Africa. Currently, she is a senior research fellow and was previously the director of research at the African Centre for Technology Studies (ACTS), a development policy think tank, working to harness applications of STI for sustainable development.

Peter Knorringa, *International Institute of Social Studies, Erasmus University Rotterdam and International Centre for Frugal Innovation*
Peter Knorringa is professor of private sector and development at the International Institute of Social Studies (ISS) at the Erasmus University Rotterdam. A development economist by training, with a PhD from the Free University Amsterdam, he has worked also in the Business School of Tilburg University and has over 25 years of experience

in research and teaching on small- and medium-sized firms, entrepreneurship, local economic development, industrial clusters, the role of trust and networking, global value chains, private governance and sustainability standards, and, more recently, on frugal innovations. He has done longer-term capacity building projects in Vietnam and Indonesia and advisory work and funded research for the World Bank, UNIDO, ESRC and various Dutch development NGOs in Brazil, China, Costa Rica, Ethiopia, India, Kenya, South Africa, Tanzania and Uganda. He is one of the co-founders and the academic director of the International Centre for Frugal Innovation, one of the multidisciplinary research centres of Leiden-Delft-Erasmus Universities.

Erika Kraemer-Mbula, *DSI/NRF/Newton Fund Trilateral Research Chair in Transformative Innovation, the 4th Industrial Revolution and Sustainable Development, University of Johannesburg*
Prof. Kraemer-Mbula specialises in science, technology and innovation policy analysis and innovation systems in connection with equitable and inclusive development. Initially trained as an economist, she holds a master's degree in science and technology policy from the Science and Policy Research Unit at the University of Sussex, and a doctorate in development studies from the University of Oxford. In addition to holding the Research Chair in Transformative Innovation, she is a Visiting Professor at the University College London (UK) and a research associate at the Centre for Law, Technology and Society, University of Ottawa (Canada).

Glenda Kruss, *Centre for Science, Technology and Innovation Indicators (CeSTII), Human Sciences Research Council*
Dr Glenda Kruss is the executive head of the Centre for Science, Technology and Innovation Indicators (CeSTII) at the Human Sciences Research Council (HSRC). She holds a master's degree from the University of Cape Town and obtained a DPhil from the University of Ulster in 1992. Before joining the HSRC in June 2001, she was associate professor in the Education Faculty at the University of the Western Cape. Over the past 20 years, she has worked in the field of innovation studies to understand the role of universities and public research institutes in economic and social development, and the determinants of skills and knowledge flows within sectoral, national and global systems of innovation. Her current research focuses on contextually appropriate datasets, measures and indicators of science, technology and innovation for inclusive and sustainable development in South Africa and sub-Saharan Africa. She has collaborated widely on comparative research projects in Africa, Latin America, Asia and Europe, and has led large-scale projects for national government, building alliances and networks between researchers, policy-makers and practitioners in South Africa and the Global South.

Keun Lee, *Seoul National University (SNU) and University of Johannesburg*
Keun Lee is a distinguished professor of economics at the Seoul National University (SNU), head of the Center for Comparative Economic Studies of SNU, and Visiting Professor at the University of Johannesburg. He is a fellow of the CIFAR (IEP Programme) in Canada, and Chairman of the Board of the Center for Economic

Catch-up. He is the winner of the 2014 Schumpeter Prize, and the 2019 Kapp Prize. He also served as the vice-chair of the National Economic Advisory Council, advising the President of Korea.

Edward Lorenz, *University of Aalborg & University of Johannesburg*
Prof. Edward Lorenz is emeritus professor at the University of Côte d'Azur in France where he held the position of professor of economics from 2004 to 2019. He is also distinguished visiting professor at the University of Johannesburg and adjunct professor at the Aalborg University Business School in Denmark. He is the former vice-president of Globelics, an international network of scholars working on innovation and development, and he is interim president of Eurolics, the European branch of Globelics. He has regularly provided expert advice on innovation policies to the OECD, EUROFOUND and the European Commission, and has contributed to numerous expert committees including the Measurement Working Group of the Directorate for Science, Technology and Industry at the OECD, the OECD Working Party on SMEs and Entrepreneurship, and the expert group invited to discuss the 'Future of Europe's innovation policies' by the DG Enterprise and Industry of the European Commission.

Albert Edgar Manyuchi, *Global Change Institute, University of the Witwatersrand*
Dr Manyuchi is a transdisciplinary scholar whose research focus is on public health, climate change, science and technology and innovation policy. Pandemic preparedness and response research is an important theme in his research area. His research mainly focuses on Africa. Dr Manyuchi works with Anova Health Institute and has research collaborations with the Graduate School of Technology Management of the University of Pretoria and the Global Change Institute of the University of the Witwatersrand.

Nazeem Mustapha, *Centre for Science, Technology and Innovation Indicators (CeSTII), Human Sciences Research Council*
Dr Mustapha holds a PhD in applied mathematics from the University of Cape Town. He currently leads the R&D measurement and analysis programme within the Centre for Science, Technology and Innovation Indicators (CeSTII) of the Human Sciences Research Council (HRSC) in South Africa. Dr Mustapha led the development of research into the measurement of innovation in the informal sector at the Centre, which is his primary research interest currently. In the recent past he has also opened up new areas of measurement and research on intellectual property and technology transfer in publicly funded institutions, and on the innovation capabilities of state-owned enterprises. In addition to participation in conferences on innovation, Dr Mustapha regularly interacts with innovation policy-makers in his work and also has advised provincial and national bodies on innovation measurement in his personal capacity.

Nora Ndege, *Africa Research and Impact Network & African Centre for Technology Studies*
Nora Ndege is a science, technology and innovation (STI) policy and development researcher with a focus on innovation for inclusive and sustainable development in Africa. Her career passion lies in innovative research and policy analysis that links

multilevel policies to local resources and development realities in a manner that creates sustainable development opportunities for the poor. Nora has a keen interest in the role of science and innovation in solving Africa's developmental challenges.

John Ouma-Mugabe, *Department of Engineering and Technology Management, Graduate School of Technology Management (STM), University of Pretoria*
Prof. John Ouma-Mugabe is a professor of science and innovation policy at the Graduate School of Technology Management (GSTM) at the University of Pretoria, and a senior associate fellow at the Science Policy Research Unit (SPRU) at the University of Sussex, UK. He is an associate at the Council on Health Research for Development (COHRED) in Geneva, founding director of the Foundation for Innovation and Technology-Africa (FIT-Africa) in Pretoria and Nairobi; and member of the board of directors/trustees of the Calestous Juma Legacy Foundation (CJLF) in Boston. He is the former executive director of the African Centre for Technology Studies (ACTS) in Nairobi and former director of the Office of Science and Technology of the New Partnership for Africa's Development (NEPAD). He was a programme officer of the International Diffusion of Biotechnology Programme of the International Federation of Institutes of Advanced Study (IFIAS) in the Netherlands. Prof. Mugabe holds a PhD degree in political science (political economy of science, technology and environmental policy) from the University of Amsterdam. He is a fellow of the African Academy of Sciences (AAS) and the World Academy of Art and Science (WAS).

Jacob Park, *University of Johannesburg & Castleton University*
Prof. Jacob Park is a visiting professor at the University of Johannesburg's DSI/NRF/Newton Fund Trilateral Chair and an associate professor at Castleton University's College of Business. He serves as the Chair: Business, Best Practices, Accountability and on the steering committee of IUCN/World Conservation Union's Commission on Environmental, Economic and Social Policy (CEESP). He has served as the coordinating lead author of the *UN Environment Global Environment Outlook (GEO-6) Report*, lead author for the *United Nations Millennium Ecosystem Assessment* initiative, and as an expert reviewer for several Intergovernmental Panels on Climate Change (IPCC) publications including the *Sixth Assessment Report*. He is co-executive editor of *Subsistence Marketplaces*, co-chair of the shareholder consortium of the *Journal of Agriculture, Food Systems, and Community Development*, associate editor of the *Journal of Social Entrepreneurship* and the *Journal of Environmental Studies and Sciences*. He serves on the editorial boards of *Business Strategy and the Environment* and *Emerging Market Case Studies*.

Mark Pelling, *IRDR, University College London*
Prof. Mark Pelling is a professor of risk and disaster reduction at the Institute of Risk and Disaster Reduction, University College London. He has served as a coordinating lead author for the Intergovernmental Panel on Climate Change Sixth Assessment Report and Special Report on Managing the Risks of Extreme Events and Disasters to Advance Climate Change Adaptation (SREX), and as lead author on its Fifth Assessment Report. He is a member of the Scientific Steering Committee of the Stockholm Environment

Institute and the development team for the Future Earth Risk Knowledge Action Network. In recent years he has published on disaster risk reduction, adaptation to climate change, and resilience and transformation.

Il-haam Petersen, *Centre for Science, Technology and Innovation Indicators (CeSTII), Human Sciences Research Council*
Dr Il-haam Petersen is the chief research specialist at the Centre for Science, Technology and Innovation Indicators (CeSTII) at the Human Sciences Research Council (HSRC). She holds a DPhil in sociology from Trinity College Dublin. Il-haam's research focuses on inter-organisational innovation networks, particularly the micro-foundations of innovation, and experimentation with new methodologies for understanding and measuring innovation in informal settings. Her recent research has followed an engaged research approach, including experimentation with novel participatory methods such as photovoice and digital storytelling.

Aimé Sègla, *Université d'Abomey-Calavi, Benin & Max-Planck Institute*
Dr Dafon Aimé Sègla holds a PhD from Université Paris 7, CNRS, France, in logic, epistemology and history of science and technology. Later, he joined the Max-Planck Institute in Berlin, the Martin-Luther University in Halle, and is currently associate professor at Université d'Abomey-Calavi in Benin Republic. His interests include empirical research on African cultural traces of science and technology, concepts and logic in language and cognition by linking Africa past and future (mathematics, biology, traditional food industry, medicine, appropriate technologies, languages and digital resources).

Ogundiran Soumonni, *Wits Business School, University of the Witwatersrand*
Diran Soumonni teaches innovation policy and management at the Wits Business School, University of the Witwatersrand, in South Africa. He also serves as the director of its master's in management in innovation studies programme. His teaching and research interests include comparative innovation systems, energy innovation, innovation for sustainability, nanotechnology innovation and philosophical paradigms in scientific research. Inspired by the work of the Late Burkinabé Prof. Joseph Ki-Zerbo on 'endogenous development', his current research advances a more historically grounded perspective on 'endogenous innovation'.

Krishnie Thaver, *Wits School of Governance, University of the Witwatersrand*
Krishnie Thaver is an accomplished engineer, technical writer and data analyst. She is currently an alumna of both the University of Witwatersrand and UNISA with a BSc Hons in Chemical Engineering and a BCom in Decision Sciences respectively.

Dieunedort Wandji, *Institute of Development Studies*
Dr Dieunedort Wandji is currently a research officer on the multi-sited project Islands of Innovation in Protracted Crises: Building Equitable Resilience from Below, which covers Côte d'Ivoire and the Democratic Republic of the Congo.